Text and Image

Text and image are used together in an increasingly flexible fashion and many disciplines and areas of study are now attempting to understand how these combinations work. This introductory textbook explores and analyses the various approaches to multimodality and offers a broad, interdisciplinary survey of all aspects of the text-image relation. It leads students into detailed discussion concerning a number of approaches that are used. It also brings out their strengths and weaknesses using illustrative example analyses and raises explicit research questions to reinforce learning.

Throughout the book, John Bateman looks at a wide range of perspectives: socio-semiotics, visual communication, psycholinguistic approaches to discourse, rhetorical approaches to advertising and visual persuasion, and cognitive metaphor theory. Applications of the styles of analyses presented are discussed for a variety of materials, including advertisements, picture books, comics and textbooks.

Requiring no prior knowledge of the area, this is an accessible text for all students studying text and image or multimodality within English Language and Linguistics, Media and Communication Studies and Visual and Design Studies.

John A. Bateman is Professor of Appliable English Linguistics at the University of Bremen, Germany and has been teaching courses with significant multimodal components for many years. His publications include *Multimodality and Genre* (2008), and *Multimodal Film Analysis* (with Karl-Heinrich Schmidt, 2012).

Text and Image

A critical introduction to the visual/verbal divide

JOHN A. BATEMAN

Routledge
Taylor & Francis Group

LONDON AND NEW YORK

First published 2014
by Routledge
2 Park Square, Milton Park, Abingdon, Oxon OX14 4RN

and by Routledge
711 Third Avenue, New York, NY 10017

Routledge is an imprint of the Taylor & Francis Group, an informa business

British Library Cataloguing in Publication Data
A catalogue record for this book is available from the British Library

Library of Congress Cataloging in Publication Data
Bateman, John A.
    Text and image : a critical introduction to the visual-verbal divide / John Bateman.
        pages cm
    1. Modality (Linguistics) 2. Visual communication—Psychological aspects.
    3. Discourse analysis—Psychological aspects. 4. Semiotics. 5. Rhetoric.
    6. Psycholinguistics. I. Title.
    P99.4.M6B27 2014
    415'.6—dc23   2013046459

ISBN: 978-0-415-84197-9 (hbk)
ISBN: 978-0-415-84198-6 (pbk)
ISBN: 978-1-315-77397-1 (ebk)

Typeset in Akzidenz Grotesk and Eurostile
by Keystroke, Station Road, Codsall, Wolverhampton

Printed and bound in Great Britain by
TJ International Ltd, Padstow, Cornwall

Contents

Figures

Tables

Acknowledgements

The Author and Publishers would like to thank the following copyright holders for permission to reproduce material:

Table 6.1 Rhetorical figures; from Daniel Chandler, *Semiotics: the basics.* © 2002, p. 136, Table 4.2 "The four master tropes". Reproduced by permission of Routledge.

Table 11.1 Visual-verbal linking from Theo van Leeuwen © 2005, *Introduction to Social Semiotics*, p. 230, Figure 11.4. Reproduced by permission of Routledge.

Figure 1.5 Family tree of 'images' according to W. J. T. Mitchell © 1986, *Iconology: images, text, ideology*, p. 10. Reproduced by permission of the University of Chicago Press.

Figure 1.6 Paul Klee '*Anfang eines Gedichtes*', 1938, 189. Reproduced by permission of the Zentrum Paul Klee, Bern.

Figure 1.8 From COMICS and SEQUENTIAL ART by Will Eisner. Copyright © 1985 by Will Eisner. Copyright © 2008 by Will Eisner Studios, Inc. Used by permission of W. W. Norton & Company, Inc.

Figure 3.4 Recount genres from J. R. Martin and David Rose © 2008, *Genre Relations: mapping culture*, p. 133, Figure 3.6. Reproduced by permission of the authors and Equinox Publishers.

Figure 4.1 Words and images. Maria Nikolajeva and Carole Scott © 2001, *How Picturebooks Work*, p. 12. Reproduced by permission of Routledge.

Figure 5.2 Panel sequence from Neil Cohn © 2010, 'The limits of time and transitions: challenges to theories of sequential image comprehension', *Studies in Comics* 1(1), p. 143. Reproduced by permission of Neil Cohn.

Figure 5.3 Panel sequence from Neil Cohn © 2012, from Cohn, N., Paczynski, M., Jackendoff, R., Holcomb, P. J. and Kuperberg, G. R. (2012), '(Pea)nuts and bolts of visual narrative: structure and meaning in sequential image comprehension', *Cognitive Psychology* 65(1), Figure 18. Reproduced by permission of John Wiley and Sons, the Cognitive Science Society, Inc. and Neil Cohn.

Figure 5.5 From COMICS and SEQUENTIAL ART by Will Eisner. Copyright © 1985 by Will Eisner. Copyright © 2008 by Will Eisner Studios, Inc. Used by permission of W. W. Norton & Company, Inc.

Figure 7.2 E. F. McQuarrie and D. G. Mick, 'Visual rhetoric in advertising: text-interpretive, experimental, and reader-response analyses', *Journal of Consumer Research* 26(1), p. 43, Figure 2. Reproduced by permission of the University of Chicago Press.

Figure 8.2 Page from P. Holden (1996) *Birds of Britain*, Collins. Used by permission as part of the GeM corpus of multimodal documents (cf. Bateman 2008 and www.purl.org/net/gem).

Figure 9.3 Pictorial metaphor in Margot van Mulken, Rob le Pair and Charles Forceville © 2010, 'The impact of perceived complexity, deviation and comprehension on the appreciation of visual metaphor in advertising across three European countries', *Journal of Pragmatics* **42**(12), p. 3420, Table 1. Reproduced by permission of Elsevier.

Figure 10.8 Text-image structures from Kenneth Kong © 2013, 'A corpus-based study in comparing the multimodality of Chinese- and English-language newspapers', *Visual Communication* **12**(2), p. 190; Figure 11. Reproduced by permission of SAGE Publications and Kenneth Kong.

Figure 11.3 Geography textbook analysis from J. R. Martin and David Rose © 2008, *Genre Relations: mapping culture*, p. 179, Figure 4.31. Reproduced by permission of the authors and Equinox Publishers.

Figure 13.2 Eye-tracking results from Jana Holsanova, Henrik Rahm and Kenneth Holmqvist © 2006, 'Entry points and reading paths on newspaper spreads: comparing a semiotic analysis with eye-tracking measurements', *Visual Communication* **5**(1), p. 29. Reproduced by permission of SAGE Publications and the authors.

Figure 13.3 Eye-tracks for contrasting radial and serial designs (© Jens Tarning) from Jana Holsanova and Andreas Nord © 2010. 'Multimedia design: media structures, media principles and users' meaning-making in newspapers and net paper', p. 97. Eye-tracks reproduced by permission of the authors; radial and serial designs reproduced by permission of Jens Tarning.

Figure 13.4 Eye-tracking results from Morten Boeriis and Jana Holsanova © 2012, 'Tracking visual segmentation: connecting semiotic and cognitive perspectives', *Visual Communication* **11**(3), p. 274, Figure 7. Reproduced by permission of SAGE Publications and the authors.

Figure 14.1 Panels from Scott McCloud © 1994, *Understanding Comics*, p. 49. Reproduced by permission of HarperCollins Publishers.

Every effort has been made to contact copyright-holders. Please advise the publisher of any errors or omissions, and these will be corrected in subsequent editions.

PART I

Relating Text and Image

In this first part of the book we begin by considering a little more carefully just what might be meant by 'text' and 'image' – we will see that this is by no means as clear as might have been thought. We also see just why a consideration of how text and image work together is both scientifically interesting and of considerable practical import. Given that text and image now appear together in increasingly flexible ways, the interpretative demands raised for readers and viewers are also growing. Unit 1 gives us our first view of the challenges and defines just what we will be considering as text and image in the rest of the book. Unit 2 then shows more of the diversity of texts, images and text-image combinations that we will need to consider as well as working through some early accounts proposed for explaining how text and image work together. This then establishes some general goals for text-image research and description and sets the scene for the analyses and frameworks to be covered in subsequent parts of the book.

MODULE I

Starting Points

Text-image relations in perspective

In many respects, and in many contexts, combining text and images is seen as the most straightforward, the most natural thing in the world. People have been putting textual information and images together for thousands of years – for just about as long as there have been textual information and images to combine, in fact. For all of this 'naturalness', it is equally common to hear of the 'text-image divide', of how text and image go about their business in very different ways. This is sometimes seen as a beneficial complementarity, at other times as a more competitive struggle for dominance. With such differences of opinion, it is perhaps not so surprising how much uncertainty and debate the practice of 'combining' text and image causes. The issue of 'text-image' relations frequently recurs in both academic and practical discussions. And, currently, it finds itself again at the peak of a wave of interest.

Many of the reasons giving rise to this continuing attention lie in the nature of the 'objects' being related: 'texts' and 'images' are generally addressed by very different groups of disciplines and those disciplines often take very different views both on just what they are describing and how descriptions should be pursued. But in order to relate things, there has to be some ground for comparison. And this can easily come to mean seeing texts more like images or images more like texts just so that comparison can get started. This can be a source of considerable friction: when those working on language are seen as telling those who work on images how their object of enquiry is to be investigated, or those working on images make statements about language and its ability or inability to offer useful views on images, the potential for conflict is considerable.

The purpose of this book is to take a fresh look at the questions and challenges involved in understanding how combinations of texts and images work. The book is divided into several modules, each leading us into different aspects of the text-image question. In this first module, we take our first look at the two domains that we will be concerned with – that is, text and images themselves. The main focus will be on how approaches to these areas construct their respective subject matters. We will bring together several disciplines, methods, frameworks and application areas in order to show text-image relations from several perspectives. The fundamental idea is that it is only with a broad approach of this kind that we can gather sufficient experience for the next round of text-image relation research.

MULTIMODALITY AND 'MEANING MULTIPLICATION'

Text and images are sometimes referred to as different 'modes' of communication. We will refine this idea further as we proceed, particularly for the case of 'images', but this simple description already allows us to situate our task in this book against a particular background of research. We will be relating distinct *modalities* of information presentation. Text-image relations and their study consequently fall within the general area of *multimodality* – the investigation of diverse modes of expression and their combinations.

Combinations of this kind are sometimes considered in terms of *meaning multiplication*, a metaphor promoted by the socio-functional semiotician Jay Lemke (Lemke 1998). The idea is that, under the right conditions, the value of a combination of different modes of meaning can be worth *more* than the information (whatever that might be) that we get from the modes when used alone. In other words, text 'multiplied by' images is more than text simply occurring with or alongside images. In order to explore what kind of results can come out of such a multiplication, we need to have a better idea of just what is being multiplied. Somehow the meanings of one and the meanings of the other resonate so as to produce more than the sum of the parts. But in order for meanings to 'build on' each other in this way, there must be some contact, some internal properties that allow multiplication to take place. This raises some interesting theoretical challenges.

To suggest what is involved here, consider as an example apples and bananas. It is easy to add them – we do this whenever we buy them at the supermarket and put them in a shopping bag. The result is simple: we have an apple and a banana. What then could it mean to *multiply* them, to have more than just a collection of individual pieces of fruit (cf. Figure 1.1)?

There are a number of possibilities, some less far-fetched than others. Perhaps we use them as ingredients in a fruit salad and, somehow, the way their individual tastes work together achieves a certain new quality, different from the fruits when eaten alone – great chefs are probably exploring this new frontier all the time. Alternatively, perhaps we achieve a new hybrid fruit exhibiting interesting features of both by some process of genetic engineering. In each case, contact has been made at some deeper level between the apple and the banana (e.g., in the molecules responsible for their taste, or in their respective genetic codes) in order to create something new. The results in these hypothetical cases are not then simply

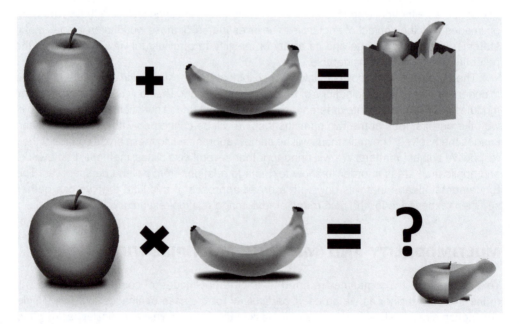

Figure 1.1 Multiplying meanings?

apples and bananas mashed together, but *new structural organisations* recombining and re-contextualising basic properties of the original fruits.

This is exactly what we will need to look for when we attempt to multiply text and images – otherwise we just have text and image in close proximity, without interaction and, therefore, without meaning multiplication. It is certainly possible to have such weak connections of text and image, but these alone would explain neither the long history of using text and image together nor the explosion in such practices that we are experiencing today. After all, if images and texts could do just as well by themselves, they would not need to be used together as often as they evidently are. Getting clear about this from the outset is very important for our current endeavour. Although it is a commonplace to suggest that text and image when used together somehow combine, 'blend', or 'synthesise' to give us new possibilities, we need to know *how and in what ways this works (or does not work)*.

To explore this question well, however, we certainly need to avoid assuming that the two, images and texts, are *more* similar than they actually are – this would be equivalent to assuming that apples are in fact bananas (or *vice versa*) and so there is no problem combining them. Note that when we do this, we do not get anything *new* when we combine them – just more mashed bananas. Similarly, if text and images were more or less the same, then combining them also would not lead to anything substantially new. The most fundamental issue of all, therefore, when addressing text-image relations, is to find points of comparison within text and within image that are well motivated and productive rather than reductive and distorting so that one comes to look more or less like the other.

We must also take care not to go too far in the opposite direction. If text and images were 'completely' different, totally incommensurate, then combining them would not produce anything sensible either. Too many approaches fall foul of these extreme positions. They either claim text and image to have nothing in common – so researchers on images and researchers on texts should not even talk to each other – or assume images and texts are too similar, so there is nothing to learn from each other anyway!

Both strategies are disastrous because they give rise to walls between disciplines and approaches that are anything but helpful. The result is a kind of 'disciplinary myopia' where research questions and solutions develop (or not) in splendid isolation despite, in many cases, the existence of rather parallel concerns in other areas. As we proceed, therefore, we will practise being both more differentiating and more open so as to bring out just how texts and images may be similar (so that we can multiply them together) *and* how they are different (so that multiplication gives us more than addition). To do this, we will compare and contrast a broad range of approaches across disciplines and subdisciplines as we go.

GETTING STARTED: VIVE LA DIFFÉRENCE

The following quotation from the French linguist Émile Benveniste seems in many respects obviously correct and reiterates a position made by many researchers and theoreticians from diverse disciplines over the years:

Semiotic systems are not 'synonymous'; we are not able to say 'the same thing' with spoken words that we can with music, as they are systems with different bases. In other words, two semiotic systems of different types cannot be mutually interchangeable.

(Benveniste 1986: 235)

Different ways of making meanings – which is what we can take 'semiotic systems' to be – indeed appear very different. But this raises our multiplication puzzle: if they are so different, how can they so readily combine?

It may appear obvious how to put some things together, and sometimes it might genuinely *be* obvious, but this cannot always be taken for granted. Will it always work? Are there situations when we need to be more cautious about putting different ways of making meaning together if we want to communicate successfully? And what kinds of theoretical tools and perspectives do we need for being able both to ask and answer these kinds of questions? These are the starting points we need to address before getting underway.

Issues

To refine these concerns and become more concrete, take a look at the map shown in Figure 1.2. We are generally familiar with this kind of representation, and this goes a long way towards helping us read it without too many problems. Although it is rather different from maps that we usually see these days, it is still obviously a map. This means that we can be fairly sure that the visually depicted areas have something to do with land and, between them, what we can see is probably the ocean.

We assume this for a number of reasons. On the one hand, we can assume this because of the rather more 'wave'-like drawing in the ocean, together with something that looks like a whirlpool, some ships, and a sea creature; on the other hand, the white areas might be more or less familiar shapes of things we know as countries as well as sporting a few trees and buildings scattered around – and they also have some text on them, looking perhaps like names of countries, towns, and so on. Thus, because we know the kinds of things that the sea has (or has been thought to have), the kinds of things that we find on land, *and* are familiar with the practice of putting these onto flat pieces of paper, linen, canvas, and so on, we can 'read' what appears without apparent effort – that is, without *apparently* knowing much at all.

That this effortlessness is an illusion, however, is quickly revealed whenever we encounter representations with which we are *not* familiar. Then 'just seeing' is replaced by a more conscious attempt to work out what is going on. For example, if we were not familiar with old maps of this kind and their tendency to combine geographical detail with pictorial depiction, then we might well wonder what strange states of affairs are being reported – huge whirlpools due to global warming, perhaps? Far more likely for us is that other features of the map have

Figure 1.2 A map of what is to come?

already triggered the appropriate assignment of this representation to the category of 'old maps', since this is just not how maps are drawn these days. For example, the boats and (we can probably assume) the sea creature are evidently not intended to be read as being drawn to the same scale as the items shown on land. And neither of these is shown on the same scale as the land and sea themselves.

In fact, more than this, all these distinct representations are not even built within the same *ways* of making meaning – they are pulling in quite different conventionalised directions for using visual depiction and combining them in the service of whatever it is that the map is intended to communicate. They are, to use the more technical term, drawn from rather different (but also related) *semiotic systems*. The overall result is coherent and communicates various messages, but it is put together from several distinct meaning-making systems. And here the more interesting questions start – just what *are* the various ways of making meanings employed here?

A rather naïve and commonsensical glance at the map might lead us to offer as a first guess: 'words' and 'images'. But we have already mentioned that the depiction of the countries and their coastlines follows rather different rules from those of the ships and the dragons depicted in mortal combat in the ocean. Moreover, the words depicted are also clearly visual in that we can see them – the image pattern making up the shape 'HELGALA' is placed in the picture just as the wave tops are – and there are differences among these words that are not attributable to their *linguistic* properties as words at all. They vary in size, for example.

This means that even 'within' the visual information on offer, the particular forms distributed around the map are being used to carry different kinds of meaning and are doing this in different ways. Some of the visual information is being used to depict objects, oceans, coast-lines, and so on, while other visual information is being used to form what we might recognise as words. In addition, similar kinds of visual information are also being employed for different jobs with respect to the map as a whole. Some lines represent coastlines, others suggest shades of light and dark – these are very different kinds of representational relationships.

Even among the words that appear, there are different roles being played. For example, 'HELGALA' is probably going to be assumed to be a *name* of the area of land or island indicated by the boundaries around the land area where it appears: it might therefore be thought of as a 'label' of something. In contrast, the phrase 'Hic est horrenda caribdis' (i.e., 'here are horrible whirlpools') presented in smaller letters upper centre in the image is *not* naming something, it is giving a description and a warning to the potential map user – which is a very different kind of 'speech act' from naming. The ocean in the middle is also *not* being given a name with the phrase 'Here be dragons' – again, this text doesn't label, instead it indicates that there is a part of the ocean where there may well be dangers and unknowns. That is, to be more exact, the general area in the world that corresponds to the area of the map where the words appear is being evaluated with respect to its availability for navigation, the general state of knowledge concerning it and so on.

This then starts us off on our quest for relations between text and images. And we can readily find many more. Consider, for example, the fresco shown in Figure 1.3. Even though this information is not inherently 'given' in some sense by the image, there is not much doubt that the words on the scroll snaking through the middle of the extract are somehow to be attributed to the figure from which the scroll appears to be issuing. This lack of doubt notwithstanding, nowhere does the image 'state' or assert that if one reads the words on the scroll, then these words are to be attributed to the person that is presented visually in close proximity to one end of that scroll. This is our interpretation of the depiction made in order to maximise our understanding of the coherence of what we (take it that we) are seeing.

Figure 1.3 Detail from a fresco at the Camposanto, Pisa (fourteenth century AD)

This relationship is already much more than a simple 'illustration' or 'labelling'. The combination of text on the scroll and the surrounding image in this case corresponds more to a relationship that would be expressed in many natural languages with a quite specific grammatical construction: for example, for the case of English, 'X says that Y'. This relationship is carried here purely visually.

Note also that this has moved a long way from any 'naturalistic' representation: there is little chance that anyone above a certain age and in cultures broadly familiar with pictorial depictions is going to assume that someone opened their mouth and a scroll with words came out. But one still needs to know how to 'read' the visual information being presented in order to avoid such interpretations.

And what of the mixture of text and visual material presented in the representation shown in Figure 1.4 – just which parts of this representation are 'image' and which parts are 'text'?

Figure 1.4 An organic compound: image or text?

Superficially we might take it as a depiction of a molecule because the letters look familiar from chemistry classes. Unless we have also learnt about organic chemistry and its conventions, however, we will not know what the particular lines connecting these labels, their shapes and whether they are single or double, mean. These are also no longer pictorial representations at all in the naïve sense of 'resemblance' – the lines and their connections have very specific conventional meanings that would be impossible to decode without more information about how such molecules are currently assumed to 'work'.

The list of such conventions for this particular case is also not open-ended: it makes little difference how large the diagram is drawn – we cannot deduce from this that some of the atoms are further apart than others. We also cannot just add another link into the six-sided figure to have a seven-sided figure – this would quite literally be 'meaningless' in the system of representation being used here. It would be like writing a 'b' with two curved parts at the bottom rather than one, or writing a note in a musical score with a dashed vertical line instead of a solid one. Such depictions can, of course, be given meanings, but require explicit definition and extension of the conventions in force.

Thus we can see that conventions are historically and socially anchored and can change over time. Text-image relations need to be seen against this background. There may also be relations or organisations of relations that *recur* over time. This may be due either to commonalities in purpose and production contexts or to propensities of the human cognitive system, or complex mixtures of both. Exploring text-image relationships in detail therefore requires an openness to these kinds of influences and appropriate methods for getting at them.

Sometimes we can work out these kinds of relationships on the basis of what is shown; others we must learn. But what is it, precisely, that we are learning or working out? What is the nature of these relations between text and image? Do they have particular properties that we can say something about? Can one make any connections at all or are there natural (or conventional) boundaries? Answering these questions and, probably more important, finding out about how people *have tried to* answer them before, that is, the search for methods, will be our main task throughout the book.

Our goals to come

We are told (and shown) from all sides that our society today has become more 'visual'; this is no doubt true. It is also sometimes claimed that the old rule of the written word has been broken – the image has won out over the word. This is, in contrast, rather overstated: despite the increase in 'visuality', it is rarely the case that the written word disappears. What we instead find all around us is a far richer range of *combinations* of different ways of making meanings. Visual depictions commonly *include* words and so the visual and the verbal are evidently working together. When this is done well, what results is something *more than* either could achieve alone. The purpose of this book is therefore to start us off on a more systematic exploration of how this combination of the visual and the verbal works and what makes it so powerful.

I selected the depiction of the map used above with its rather old style quite deliberately. In it I combined a very small fragment from an existing map, the *Carta Marina* ('map of the sea') from the sixteenth century and attributed to Olaus Magnus (1490–1557), and a warning that may well be relevant for us as we proceed – in the broad area of 'text-image relations', there are certainly many dragons waiting to be put to flight (and more than a few whirlpools). In fact, we know surprisingly little about how such relations work.

This has various very practical consequences. When these relations do not work, we find badly designed textbooks, uninterpretable (and perhaps even dangerous) instructions, advertisements that fail to persuade, documents that say the opposite of what they intend, health information that misleads, and much more besides. We return to some of these more specifically later. The book will address the question of how we can *go about studying these issues.* There are many areas where we need explicit investigation to tease out what is going on – the answers are not all already on the shelf, ready to be taken down and 'taken as directed'.

Word and image combinations nevertheless occur almost everywhere and so have attracted the attention of many different kinds of researchers – from art history to linguistics, from advertising studies to children's literary research, from document design to philosophy, and many more. But no one single discipline has all the keys we need for solving the problem. Indeed, there are many different problems depending on the questions that are asked – and so different disciplines may well be asking different questions. This means that we should look at a broad range of researchers and the kinds of combinations of words and images they have been concerned with, as well as the theoretical and descriptive approaches they are employing, to help us get further.

This diversity of approaches also has a downside. We rarely, if ever, find open acknowledgement of the full breadth of approaches working on the text-image question. Similar insights are often reached anew, repeatedly and separately in their respective traditions. This suggests one last metaphor that we can take from our old map. The entire area of text-image relations is a patch of choppy sea, with many waves obscuring the view – individual approaches are small boats down in the troughs of these waves. There may well be currents and wind directions that push many of the boats in the same directions, but down at sea level we cannot see them.

This means that we need to get some distance on the matter in order to recognise useful comparisons and significant differences. So for this, we will set out some key areas where text-image relations play a central role as well as the most significant frameworks that have been developed to describe and explain them. By getting beneath, or above, the choppy sea of individual accounts couched within separate disciplines, we will be in a better position to bring together the various results that have been achieved to date and to see where some of the currents are going and where the dragons and whirlpools are.

FIRST CLARIFICATIONS

The separation of word and image has a very long history; at least since Plato, words have been seen as something created, artificial, conventional, whereas images are thought to be somehow natural and readily understood – W. J. T. Mitchell, one of the most important figures in the study of visuals of all kinds, suggests that the separation is perhaps *so* basic that it may always have been at least acknowledged if not explicitly theorised (Mitchell 1986: 75).

But what *are* 'texts' and 'images'?

Both terms are used in such a variety of ways that without further restrictions it is almost impossible to say just what they are including and what not. Sometimes this breadth of possible meanings is beneficial, in that it invites connections to be drawn between things that otherwise might seem quite unrelated. But, at other times, the diversity can give rise to problems and confused discussion. Above we skipped happily between 'word', 'image', 'text', 'picture', 'visual', 'verbal', 'depiction' and several other designations – but this will turn out to be rather thin ice for the weight of analyses and frameworks that we will need as we proceed. We must be rather more specific about just what we will be looking at.

This also needs to be a *motivated* restriction: if we leave out phenomena or cases that are actually central to our concerns, then the entire edifice may collapse. A too narrow definition of, for example, 'image', or a too broad definition of, for example, 'text' can quickly lead us into problems. Making some sense of the proliferation of terms and overly flexible usages of 'text' and 'image' is then the first major problem to be addressed.

'Text'

'Text' starts off sounding relatively harmless. You are currently reading a text – you can tell because there are words on the page (or screen) in front of you. As is often the case, however, such straightforwardness quickly disappears when subjected to closer scrutiny. Perhaps someone (or something) is reading this 'text' to you? Then is what you *hear* still 'the' 'text'? Linguists tend to use 'text' as a technical term applying to any extended and contextually situated and functional piece of language behaviour – so we have both written and spoken 'texts'. Here we will only concern ourselves with the former.

This would also continue being relatively harmless, if sometimes not quite matching our everyday senses of the word, were it not for a much more radical extension of the scope of the meaning of the term 'text' that developed during the middle and latter parts of the twentieth century. This extension took place in philosophical and cultural movements that saw language as doing something much more than simply 'describing' the world. Many schools of thought came instead to see language as being *constitutive* for both society and the individual. Language, in this role, gives the members of a culture the basic terms and organisational patterns they need for making sense of their world and of themselves.

This 'linguistic turn' (cf. Rorty 1967), heralded in the work of philosophers such as Martin Heidegger and Ludwig Wittgenstein, came to influence the study of cultural phenomena across the board. Even in areas traditionally quite unconnected with language and storytelling, the notion that humans make sense of the world by constructing stories became a widely held position (cf. Foucault 1969). Under such views, our language abilities constitute the basic engine driving society, the development of individual personalities within society and, in the most extreme cases, 'reality' itself – constituted by various 'discourses' that create and maintain meaning for the societies and individuals using them (cf. Berger and Luckmann 1967).

This development has many points of relevance for general issues of meaning-making, of the nature of texts and images and much else besides. But for current purposes, we focus on a relatively small 'side issue' in the area of terminology. With language being assigned such a foundational role for almost all aspects of social and individual life, it began to seem natural to treat almost everything as a 'text'. A culture can be a text, as can a cathedral, our subconscious, the historical development of a city over time, and much more. With such an explosion of possible applications, one might well doubt that we can talk sensibly of text-image relations at all. We will need to reign in this enthusiasm for just what may be a 'text' in order to be more specific about what we are talking about.

The extension of 'text' to include almost anything was pursued particularly far in the field of **semiotics**. Semiotics is commonly defined as the 'science of signs'. It claims for itself the task of describing how anything can be considered to have 'meaning' – which is certainly a rather broad undertaking. 'Text' is then simply anything that can be analysed using the techniques of semiotics: a text in this sense is simply a sign that we can interpret for its meanings.

And so, again under this view, naturally a 'city' can be a sign because we can interrogate it for perhaps hidden meanings such as differences in social classes, trade routes out of the city along roads and rivers, distribution of industry and so on. This means that 'text' comes to refer more to a *role* that something, some entity or behaviour or pattern, is assigned in semiotic studies rather than referring to some type of entity identifiable on its own terms. 'Text' is then anything that you choose to analyse as a 'text' – which again makes any notion of 'text-image' relations rather vague.

Although such a broad conception of 'text' can lead to considerable insights, it is *not* the path that we will take here because for our purposes it has a rather obvious downside. If it were possible, even plausible, to talk of, for example, paintings as being texts – after all, some do speak of 'reading paintings' when they are to be interpreted – then this would make rather a mockery of our goal of explaining text-image relations! If images are also texts, then we would just be studying text-text relations, which is usually considered a rather different enterprise. This then throws us right back in the middle of the terminological problems. Are we actually examining 'text'-'visual text' relations or, perhaps, 'written text'-'visual text' relations?

Such circumlocutions are worrying on many counts. To mention two: first, they seem to suggest that 'written texts' are not visual, which is odd to say the least; second: they seem already to assume what we wanted to elucidate – that is, they *assert* that everything we are studying is just various forms of texts even before we have done the work of looking. This would be rather premature as an answer to our question. The idea that text (in a more everyday sense) and images are actually, 'deep down', the same goes against both commonsense and the citation that we gave from Benveniste above. If we were to take this path, therefore, we may well be missing something substantial – as many who take their starting point in the *visual* rather than in semiotics or linguistics convincingly argue.

In short, we have to be wary, in the words of Hartmut Stöckl, a prominent German researcher on the text-image question, of the following:

> The danger in contrasting two modes, however, is that we tend to somehow look at one mode in terms of another. So, mostly, due to language's dominance, we seem to be asking which linguistic properties images have. Thus we run the risk of overlooking some important design features of images which are outside of the linguistic perspective.
>
> (Stöckl 2004b: 18)

This is one of the biggest problems that comes with the adoption of the image-as-text strategy and one that we should take considerable pains to avoid.

'Image'

Let us now consider the other side of the text-image relation, the notion of 'image'. A good way into this part of the discussion is offered by Mitchell (1986). Mitchell draws attention to the very different kinds of roles 'images' of various kinds have taken on over time, going into several of the points we are raising here but providing rather more philosophical and historical background. Mitchell develops a kind of 'family tree' of images – reproduced in Figure 1.5 – that provides for five distinct members: graphic, optical, perceptual, mental and verbal (Mitchell 1986: 10). The idea here is that individual family members might be quite distinctive while some familiar (and familial) traits still allow siblings to be seen as belonging to the family as a whole.

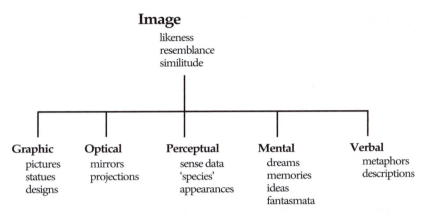

Figure 1.5 Family tree of 'images' according to Mitchell (1986: 10); used by kind permission of the University of Chicago Press

For Mitchell, the members of this family of images all share overall qualities that draw on "likeness, resemblance, similitude", although this may fall out rather differently for the individual family members involved. The notion of 'resemblance' is probably the most crucial one when considering images. Naïvely it would seem to offer an obvious difference between text and image since a picture of a dog 'looks like' a dog while the word 'dog' looks like many other words, but certainly not like a dog. As is often the case, things are not quite so simple – but there does seem to be some germ of truth here that we might be able to build on.

Mitchell distinguishes the individual family members of the family tree further as follows. Examples of graphic images are pictures, statues, designs of various kinds; optical images result from mirrors and projections; perceptual images are the 'sense data' gathered from the world; mental images occur in dreams and other 'internal' processes; and verbal images are created through language by means of visual metaphors or 'graphic' descriptions of situations or states of affairs. There are various motivations for drawing these kinds of distinctions. Mitchell separates them partly on the basis of the disciplines that have concerned themselves with the 'phenomena' thus identified – or created, if we take the view of disciplines at least partly bringing their objects of study into existence. Being explicit about this linking to individual disciplines is important – particularly for our concerns here – because many of these distinct kinds of images then bring with them long traditions of discussion. Both the problems to be considered and the methods and theoretical frameworks developed vary according to discipline.

Our concern here will be with one small slice through these possibilities – we will be considering only those images to which we gain access by direct, physical visual perception. In essence, then, we are examining only Mitchell's *graphic* images plus a particular subset of what he groups under 'projections', since the technological manner in which an image is made accessible to us will not concern us over much. Whether we see our combinations of image and text on paper, on a computer monitor, projected on a screen or scrawled on a wall will not be used to demarcate what we are examining because we want to cast our net of places where 'physically realised' text-image relations occur relatively broadly. This is *not* to say that distinct 'contexts of consumption' (consider TV *vs.* art gallery *vs.* cinema) have no effects – it is well documented that they do. But, for current purposes, we will take 'images' simply as things you can physically see and 'text' as visually realised instances of language use. Now, these still appear to overlap, so we have one more step to take in order to refine 'image' sufficiently to talk of text-image *relations*.

Distinguishing text and image

What, then, if images *are* texts? Can text and image 'overlap'?

Consider the work by the artist Paul Klee from 1938 shown in Figure 1.6: are we dealing with an image or a text here? If we follow the discussion of the possible origins of this work explored by Aichele and Citroen (2007), then the work is very much a text – indeed, a kind of love letter. But it is also very clearly visual: it is made up of colour applied to a supporting surface and deploys the space of the 'canvas' largely independently of most of the constraints typically imposed by 'text' (although individual words do appear, which then rely on the use of space required by text). How do we go about characterising such an artefact according to the distinctions that we need to draw?

To begin, we should try to minimise appeal to notions such as 'borderline' cases, or potential mixtures of text and image. This is often done but has a strong methodological disadvantage – being too quick to admit borderline cases can result in their proliferation. If in the long run (and usually much more quickly), most of the examples analysed turn out to be borderline cases, it is arguable that what has actually happened is that the starting point was wrong. The analysis did not make the divisions and distinctions necessary to make sense of what is being examined, and so one immediately has to cross the boundaries that one (inaccurately) assumed to be relevant. We want to make sure that we avoid this danger as far

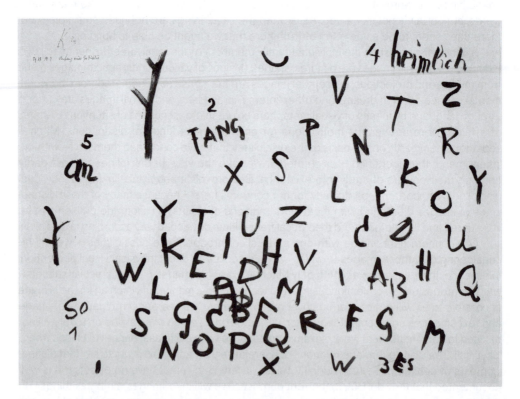

Figure 1.6 Paul Klee 'Beginning of a poem', 1938 (Paul Klee, *Anfang eines Gedichtes*, 1938, 189, Beginning of a poem, coloured paste on paper on cardboard, 48.3 × 62.8 cm, Zentrum Paul Klee, Bern)

as we can. So, one of the things that we will want to avoid is to allow our distinctions to blur and merge together so that, in the end, we cannot say anything much at all.

Of course, this is not to deny that there may well turn out to be genuine borderline cases. It is just better by far to make the strong methodological assumption that there are no such cases so that we are forced *first* to probe more deeply. Imagine trying to measure the lengths of things with a piece of elastic – whether we find differences in the lengths of various objects will depend more on whether we want them to be different or the same, that is, how far we stretch the elastic. Methodologically, this is a very weak position. We need to find some more stable measuring material if the comparisons and distinctions we make are to be able to stand up for themselves.

So, in the present case, what can we be sure of?

First, the work is clearly visual, flat and material – if we turn the light out, the work disappears. Secondly, it also appears to be using various visual instantiations of text. In many respects, then, the painting is clearly both text and image – but in which respects precisely? It needs to fit somewhere in our account but without undoing useful distinctions.

Much confusion can be avoided from the outset by explicitly distinguishing linguistic and non-linguistic influences on visual form and, moreover, recognising that these *can coexist*. For example, there is frequent discussion of the 'visual' aspects of text – typography and layout are one of the most obvious ways in which text has a visual presence, but we can also consider more extreme variations as found in comics where the text might be shaped to show tone of voice, emotion, sounds, even motion and grouping of characters, or artworks, where the quality of the visual representation of 'texts' might take on any of the properties attributed to visual elements in general.

The phrase 'the properties attributed' to visual elements is the key here. When we are dealing with different kinds of ways of making meaning – that is, with different semiotic modes – we usually want to draw attention to and discuss *very different kinds of properties*. Consider the words that appear in the Klee work: we can ask if they are correctly spelled, or we can ask how they fit together into a grammatical sentence and what that sentence (literally) means. These are all linguistic properties. When instead we ask about their colour, their positioning on the canvas, the force of the stroke used to create their lines, then *we are not talking about the same things*. In the former case, we are talking about linguistic entities, defined by the linguistic system; in the latter case, we are talking about visually distinguishable areas within an overall visually perceptible visual frame and these have their *own*, quite different properties.

We cannot mix these up without making a lot of rather incoherent statements or questions. For example, asking what the grammatical subject of a sequence of brush strokes is does not make much sense: we would be applying properties defined for the linguistic system to the wrong kind of entities. This may sound obvious, but we nevertheless still sometimes hear equally anomalous questions concerning the possible grammatical subjects and objects, or the 'morphemes' and 'syntax', of pictures and other visual representations.

This issue is made more difficult, and much more interesting, by the fact that *we do not yet always know* just what properties are relevant for some modes of meaning-making. If, in the Klee work, we stop looking at the individual strokes and instead talk about the composition of the work as a whole, of groupings of marks within the frame, perhaps of combinations of marks looking like letters and those looking like other things, then it is not immediately clear just what sets of properties are going to be the most revealing. We have moved into areas of (visual) composition and aesthetics and these have their own accounts of what properties will need to be paid attention to.

To provide some order here, we will from now on use the term **semiotic mode** to refer to some organised bundle of properties held in common by some material that, when used following agreed conventions, provides some community of users with a distinctive way of making meanings with that material. 'Semiotic mode' will therefore be our technical term for a particular, identifiable way of making meanings, regardless of what materials are used to do this. One can have semiotic modes using any kind of material, from pencil on paper to moving patterns of lights on city buildings, from hand gestures to traffic lights, from arrangements of flowers to airport signage. Crucially, just what semiotic modes there are is always a socio-historical question – that is: we have to look and see.

When we know what semiotic mode is being used, we then also know a lot about the properties that need to be paid attention to in order to make useful statements about the particular case of meaning-making we are looking at. If we did not know, for example, what semiotic mode the red-amber-green glowing patches on a traffic light belong to, we would not have any basis for action. The properties that we can see would not have any meaning; indeed, even more fundamentally, *we would not even know which properties are relevant to look at* (cf. Bateman 2011) – perhaps the height of traffic lights indicates how seriously you should take the red light, for example; or perhaps the really important difference is in the timing between the changes in lights. It is the semiotic mode that tells us what to pay attention to and what to do with that in order to build interpretations.

There are, then, three complications. First, we do not always know what semiotic modes are being used in some artefact or object of analysis. Second, we do not yet know what semiotic modes there are and what properties they determine. And third, any particular material we look at (or feel, or smell, or hear, or touch, or any combination of these) might be being used *for many different semiotic modes at the same time*. This third complication is particularly important for us here. Its consequences reach into every aspect of the text-image question.

For example, in the Klee work, the evident occurrence of letters and words tells us that one of the semiotic modes being used here is linguistic; however, the form of the composition as a whole, with its use of various shapes and patterns spread across the 'canvas', also tells us that there are going to be other semiotic modes at work – but which? While *some* of the visual properties of the artefact are 'claimed' by the requirements of the semiotic mode of language, there are evidently many more at work which are less well understood. The former aspects constitute its 'text' nature; the latter its 'image' nature. Explaining the relation between them is then far from obvious. Indeed, even identifying just which non-linguistic modes are working together with the linguistic modes in the concrete examples of text-image combinations we discuss in the units to follow will be a constant challenge.

THE NEED FOR TEXT-IMAGE RELATIONS RESEARCH

Now that we have raised some questions about what image and text are and how they relate, it should be easier to see why this area is beginning to be studied more broadly. In particular, we need to become much clearer about just what communicative loads text-image combinations take on and whether these combinations are intelligible for those being subjected to them. Whereas for an artwork it is understandable, and perhaps desirable, that the relationships raise challenges and demand investment of effort, this is not always the case. If we are trying to communicate effectively but employ combinations that are not intelligible, we are obviously not going to be very successful. This also raises the issue of just how we go about *learning to interpret* such combinations. Can we improve our abilities to use combinations of text and images by teaching this explicitly? These questions arise in parallel in several distinct domains of application.

Design

Images are everywhere; they are easier to produce than ever and many designers and communicators have realised that unless images are present, their products may seem not to be 'up to date'. This does not always mean that the results are readily intelligible, however. Consider the pair of water dispensers shown in Figure 1.7; these were found next to each other somewhere in Switzerland. Now, we probably agree that the one on the right looks much more modern than the positively old fashioned one on the left – but what is it saying? Try answering this *before* looking at the one on the left!

When we approach this question from the perspective of text-image relations, there are a number of issues that we should automatically pay attention to. Most of these will be described and illustrated in detail in subsequent units. The very first thing we need to do is to consider carefully what components and elements we are being confronted with and how these are related. Some of these elements may be textual, others may be image-like. The panel on the left, for example, does not really contain any images as such, but it does make use of 'image'-like qualities by means of its layout. There are material objects, a light showing that the machine is operating and the buttons to be pressed, and some text labels. In contrast, on the right-hand side, most of the text labels have been replaced by images – not (quite) all of them though.

If we take the words of the left-hand panel *together with* the images of the right-hand panel, then we certainly have few problems understanding what is going on and what, more specifically, the images depict. The upper right-hand button is evidently for cold water and its image shows a glass with ice cubes floating in it; the lower right-hand button is evidently for sparkling water and the image shows bubbles (or probably more accurately water drops) above the 'water' in the 'glass' – note here that without the decoding context we might well be hard pushed to recognise any of these entities.

Figure 1.7 The control panels of two water dispensers that happened to be standing side by side (lower picture)

For some reason (we would have to ask the designer to know why), the left-hand panel has a completely confused 'layout' – it makes sense to call this **layout** in exactly the same sense as layout design in magazines, textbooks and so on because it works in very much the same way. Is 'COLD' labelling the light or the button? Perhaps it is intending to mean both and so cleverly situates the words equidistant from the light (meaning that the machine is operational and can produce cold water) and the button for receiving that water – that is, what the information and graphic designer Edward Tufte refers to as a *multifunctioning graphical element* (Tufte 1983: 139). The one problem with such elements, as Tufte notes, is that when they go wrong they are virtually unintelligible to anyone trying to use them.

This problem is fixed on the right-hand side, which is then definitely an improvement. But what happens with the label for the lower left button? The designer has decided that images should be used. For cold water and sparkling water, there appears to be an 'iconic' solution – we show something that is actually cold (ice) or what makes the water sparkle. Now, how do we depict that nothing at all is done to the water, it just comes out the tap as it is? We can see the solution that was adopted and wonder about its efficacy. It is probably safe to presume that there are cases where the new machine is placed without there happening to be an old machine next to it. In such cases, what is the user of the device to do? I don't think that I would have come up with the reading 'ambient' for a long time, if at all. Perhaps 'A' for 'aqua'?

What I *would* assume, however, is that whatever comes out of the tap when I press this button, it is *not* going to be iced water or sparkling water. So perhaps there are not too many options left given the range of standard ways of serving drinking water. We might imagine a standard dialogue at a restaurant when ordering water:

A: Water please.
B: Sparkling or still?
A: Still, please.
B: With ice?
A: No thanks.

If we want to end up at this point in the dialogue, then we should just press the button marked with the 'A'. This kind of relation between images, text-image relations and communicative *acts*, such as the dialogue acts in the restaurant, will be taken up in Unit 12 as one of the many ways researchers have tried to make sense of text-image relations.

Design is concerned not only with physical artefacts of this kind, of course. To take an example from a completely different area: can people fill in administrative forms? The composition and organisation of such forms is also a design question – in this case, *document design*. And, as the design expert Rob Waller and others have shown in detail, badly designed forms lead to an impressive waste of time and effort, and consequently money. This result extends to a host of other 'public information' documents, even leading to legislation in some countries for 'plain' language. This needs also to include attention to design (Wright and Barnard 1978, R. H. Waller 1979, Frohlich 1986, Jansen and Steehouder 1992, Waller 2012).

Recipients may be able to respond flexibly and strategically when processing 'multimodal' presentations in a manner that supports task-driven explanations: that is, recipients will take from the material on offer what they need to get some interpretative task done. This is mostly what happens when attempting to get a glass of water from the water dispensers pictured above. But it is also known that the particular ways in which information in different 'modes' is brought together in a multimodal communication can have significant effects on the intelligibility of that information – that is: design makes a difference (cf. Schriver 1997). Results from practical document design show clearly, for example, that information in different 'modes' is processed far more effectively when the fact that certain information is to be 'combined' by the recipient is *explicitly signalled* by including appropriate attentional cues (cf. Meyer 1975, Holsanova and Nord 2010). In contrast, with bad design there is little control over whether the intended information is accessed or accessed in the right way, which can lead to surprising consequences – we return to this in Unit 13.

Poorly presented information can also lead to actual incoherence. It is not the case that recipients can always extract intended meanings. Presenting meanings multimodally in an effective manner is a practical challenge in its own right, addressed in the field of *information design* (cf. Wurman 1996, Tufte 1997). Simply placing information 'together' is insufficient to support multimodal coherence. In fact, Pegg (2002) argues that even certain conventional styles of information-presentation where text and image are loosely coordinated place considerable demands on their readers. They are then a prominent source of interpretation errors, which Pegg takes as good grounds for arguing for a far more visual approach to text, making greater use of the spatial possibilities of the page:

> Writers underestimate the opportunities for such errors; attention has to be carefully carried from the linear format to the two-dimensional format and back again. . . . It is so elaborate and prone to error that it does not seem, intuitively at any rate, to conveniently match human cognition. We might look at the system as one that rigorously and determinedly builds so many ties that it essentially admits the need for bridging – acknowledging a deficiency and going to great lengths to do something about it.
>
> (Pegg 2002: 174)

Strongly signalling textual organisation through clear visual organisation is not, however, enough by itself. In fact, if information is placed together in a manner that *appears* to be well designed, this can already be sufficient to cause recipients to overlook incoherent information and *believe* that they have been given coherent information – even when they have not (cf. Glenberg, Wilkinson and Epstein 1982).

Such issues are now being taken up quite explicitly in sophisticated layout and page composition, which itself ranges from more visually prominent paragraphing to diagrammatic text layouts showing argument structure and other connections. All of these have been, and continue to be, studied extensively in document design (cf. Bernhardt 1985, 1986, Waller 1987).

Visual and text-image design is therefore an issue in many, if not all, contexts of use: for appliances, their composition and use of multimodal information should be intelligible; in instructions combining text and images, what should be done needs to be clear and unambiguous; in educational contexts, one should strive for educational materials whose purposes are clearly communicated by typographic and other layout choices and not confused or contradicted by such choices. There are detailed interactions between presentational forms and coherence that need to be explored and interpretation cannot be considered to be solely the job, or responsibility, of the recipient. 'Form' and presentational style are certainly 'meaning bearing' in their own right. In all of these contexts of use, text-image relations remain an area demanding detailed attention.

Literacy

The common notion of 'literacy' in education is one that is solidly conjoined with the under-standing of *text*. Being literate means that one can read written language. Moreover, as argued by many commentators, the past 200 years has seen such a focus on language, particularly written language, that the very notion of intelligence has been strongly linked with *verbal* literacy. Education consequently focuses on extensive training in the use of language. Other forms of expression either are considered specialised arts for those so gifted or are left implicit.

What then happens in today's 'multimodal' climate, where designers are seeking to use combinations of texts and images (and other modalities when the technology available supports it) at every opportunity? The answer is: rather little. Children are still in many cases expected to develop any skills necessary for interpreting and using such combined visuo-textual information on their own, *implicitly*. There are many reasons to doubt whether this is an optimal strategy.

One cause of considerable problems is the assumption that images exhibit 'transparency' with respect both to what they show and, rather more problematic, how they show it. This belief goes back to some basic properties of how visual perception works. As pointed out by many psychologists of visual perception, we do not 'learn' to see in the same way that we must learn to read – the process appears to be far closer to learning to walk. In fact, it is even easier than walking since seeing comes first. There is then a tendency to believe that there is not much to teach. But, clearly, *understanding* what we see is a very different matter. This is the case whether we are dealing with scientific visualisations, even simple ones such as maps, bar charts or pie diagrams, or with artworks carried out in an art tradition that we are not familiar with. There is then evidently very much to learn.

As an explicit reaction against this 'linguocentric' state of affairs, we now see proposals for addressing visual education, sometimes employing labels such as 'picturacy' (Heffernan 2006), 'graphicacy' (Roth, Pozzer-Ardhengi and Han 2005) and the like. The idea underlying these moves is that the interpretation and use of visual materials needs to be taught. So many areas now rely on visual information that expecting the requisite knowledge for interpreting sophisticated combinations of text and image 'just to happen' is in many respects naïve. 'Multimodal literacy', or 'multiliteracies', works against this naïve position and attempts to readjust the educational balance so as to include adequate coverage of non-verbal forms of expression, even in early schooling (Unsworth 2001, 2006, Anstey and Bull 2006). Attention to this issue is often called for when addressing new media, where the occurrence of mixed media information presentations is particularly striking (Mayer 2009), but its scope of appli-cation is actually far broader.

The need to consider visual and text-image education more explicitly does not apply only to those being educated. There may also be misunderstandings concerning the role of visual materials amongst educators. Miller (1998), for example, gives interesting evidence that the role and function of visual materials in scientific articles is completely different from their function in popular sources such as magazines or newspapers. This has consequences both for the design of the visual materials and the way that they are connected to the text they occur with. This can easily be overlooked or not understood by educators unfamiliar with scientific articles and who base their understanding of the workings of visuals on their experiences with popular media. This may be quite inappropriate, however. In addition, even testing materials such as exams have rarely been thematised with respect to their use of relations between images and text and so can also be, as a consequence, vague or misleading. This is a particularly unfair situation for those being tested!

Visual literacy as such is now most commonly seen in terms of adding in mindful and appropriate uses of typography, font selections, colour and so on even when writing traditional texts. This extends to selection of appropriate graphic material, typically as illustrations of points made or as visualising numerical data. In general, design of this kind is seen as a 'rhetorical task', making all elements selected conform to and support the overall purpose of a piece of communication – we return to visual rhetoric in particular in Unit 6. Recommendations and analyses of 'visual design' from the perspective of literacy can be found in technical writing journals (cf. Bernhardt 1986, Kostelnick 1996, Stroupe 2000) and several volumes showing diverse approaches to multimodal literacy have appeared (Kress, Jewitt, Ogborn and Tsatsarelis 2000, Jewitt and Kress 2003). There is also an International Visual Literacy Association (IVLA: www.ivla.org) with corresponding journal, where many definitions of visual or graphic literacy circulate – there are still many unresolved issues, however (cf. Brill, Kim and Branch 2007).

Approaches to theory and practice need to be combined here and there is much to do in order to understand what is involved. A better treatment of text-image relations is again one important component necessary for progress within this general area of concern.

Review

The primary assumption that needs to be defused when dealing with image and text-image understanding is the pre-theoretical one that there is actually little to explain. Under this view, recipients of multimodal messages simply 'make sense' as best they can of what they encounter relying on the general 'problem solving' capabilities of humans. There would then actually be little to pay attention to since putting together the evidence is a matter of common sense.

However, although human problem-solving capabilities are without question very high, the demands made by text-image relations usually appear to be rather more focused. We are less concerned with attempting to find some interpretation willy-nilly, and more concerned with uncovering what it is about text-image combinations that guides their recipients along particular lines of interpretation rather than others. Being aware and practising text-image design or reception is a matter of visual literacy and requires extensive study in its own right.

WHAT WE WILL BE EXAMINING AND WHAT WE WILL *NOT* BE EXAMINING

We sometimes hear that images and texts lie on a spectrum, or continuum, and there are, as Mitchell (1994) provocatively suggests, no essential differences between words and images in any case. One of the main factors contributing to the lack of separation between text and image is, as we suggested above, that the terms employed are themselves anything but clear. We have seen, for example, how traditional semiotics tended to bloat the notion of 'text' to include almost anything that is subjected to semiotic analysis. A rather similar expansion in use has taken place in the case of 'images'. Now, when *both* 'text' and 'image' are expanded in this way, it is unlikely that an account that tries to say something about text-image relationships is going to succeed. Just what is *not* a text or an image becomes more the issue.

This discussion goes back a long way. Similar problems are raised in the first recorded discussions on the topic that have come down through history. For example, one debate that has raged in art history and art studies of the visual for a good two thousand years goes under the label *ut pictoria poesis* – 'as is painting, so is poetry'. The idea here is that the 'sister arts' have similar concerns and say similar things. Proposals in this direction occur in a host of phrases exhibiting a similar classical pedigree. A poem is consequently 'a speaking picture', a picture 'a silent poem', and so forth.

The poet and philosopher Gotthold Ephraim Lessing (1729–1781) argued against such a free-for-all, offering a more rigorous distinction that is still discussed and used today. In his *Laocoon*, Lessing distinguishes between, on the one hand, painting as a spatial and static form and, on the other, poetry as a temporal form (Lessing 1853 [1766], Greenberg 1940). This served him not only as a basis for distinguishing forms, but also as a foundation for motivating aesthetic judgement. Following Lessing, paintings not only have difficulties expressing temporality but, further, they *should not* express temporality because that is not what they are good at.

The influence of this position is still very much with us today. Many make reference to the 'intrinsic' or 'inherent' properties of the two forms of expression. Kress (2003) talks of two distinct 'logics' being involved, one of space and the other of time, and the different challenges these set for learners. Similarly, although in a very different discipline, Schirato and Webb inform us in their introduction to visual studies that:

> Time, in short, cannot be 'told' in visual texts or even in narrative pictures; we can only infer it from the structure of the visual text, and the arrangement of its parts.
>
> (Schirato and Webb 2004: 87)

They give a cross-reference to the discussion in Mitchell (1986: 100–102), who is, interestingly, at that point in his discussion arguing precisely the opposite.

One of the major problems with these kinds of positions is that they are so nearly 'self-evidently true': single static visual images clearly do not move and cannot 'show' movement as, for example, films do. This is an unassailable *ontological* difference in their forms or materials. But what this means for what can be 'told' in visual texts, as Schirato and Web phrase it, is far from clear. It has, after all, long been a subject of discussion in art just how a 'static' medium such as painting *can* suggest movement regardless (cf. Gombrich 1982, Cutting 2002). In a similar vein, Stöckl (2002) sets out from a linguistic perspective some of the conditions that a static image needs to fulfil in order to be 'read narratively', while the comics practitioner and researcher McCloud (1994: 100) states with his usual forthrightness that, "in the world of comics, *time and space* are *one and the same*" (original emphasis). This recurring relationship between static images and movement is certainly not supportive of Lessing's argument; we return to this in more detail in Unit 3.

We need to be even more precise about what we are referring to with 'text' and 'image'. We began this task above stating that we would restrict attention to cases where we are dealing with actual visible and physical traces. We will, then, look at texts only from the perspective of their written (or printed), static manifestations on some surface. With 'image', however, we are still dealing with a very broad category and so it will be helpful to further clarify precisely what kinds of visual entities are going to be considered within our remit and which not.

For this, it is important to separate the aesthetic use of distinct modes of expression and the modes of expression themselves. Discussions sometimes mix these in various ways – which is, at best, confusing and, at worst, contradictory. The distinct forms of argument employed in such discussions need careful attention: it makes little sense, for example, to make aesthetic judgements about some artefacts involving visual material – such as painting, or comics, or illuminated manuscripts – and then to let such judgements extend to 'words' or 'images' as such. We must distinguish these perspectives and separate the materiality of a means of expression from what is *done* with that material. The meanings made with a medium cannot be simply derived from that medium's physical or material properties.

In addition, we want to make sure that we end up with positions that we can employ for analysis – that is a *systematic* probing of how texts and images operate together. This means that our concern will be less with talking about images or texts in their own right, and more with identifying some useful perspectives which can bring out those aspects of each that let them operate together. Returning to our multiplication metaphor from above, if text and images were 'completely' different there is nothing to multiply; and if they are the same, then multiplication is in any case of little benefit.

We finish, then, by setting out some of the many things we will *not* be addressing in this and subsequent units. We need to make sure that our view of the visual is not being squeezed into a shape that might, in the beginning, appear to make our task easier – for example by making the visual more like language – but which then, subsequently, makes the task more difficult than it need be by leaving out just what it is that makes the visual distinctive. Being quite restrictive concerning the kinds of images that we will deal with will help us avoid this potential pitfall.

Visual presence

We described above how we would only be addressing images that are 'physically' present and available to perception. This restriction must be seen first and foremost as a *methodological* decision. By being clear about just what kind of artefacts we are going to examine, we make it explicit that any statements made here have an in-built restriction: any mention of image in this book, unless explicitly stated to the contrary, is referring solely to such physically perceivable images in the world: if we turn the light out, the image will no longer be there and what is left is not what we will be addressing.

Memories of the image, descriptions or questions that we can offer after the fact, mental operations such as 'rotating' the image (think of a cube and spin it on an axis), scenes conjured up mentally by skilful uses of language, critical reflections on some concrete painting, and so on are explicitly excluded. For text-image relations of the kind of concern here, the text and the image need to have been *presented together* as joint contributions to a single, perhaps complex, 'message'. The crucial restriction drawn is then: *intended* co-presence of concrete text-material with concrete image-material.

But, again to emphasise the point: this is a methodological restriction. We need not claim that the text-image relations in any of the more extended cases have no relation to the kinds of text-image relations we will see throughout this book (indeed, this is unlikely); what we *do* claim is that they would need to be studied in their own right – in all likelihood *building on* what we discover here.

Both text and image need moreover to be *visually* co-present. This means that another area we explicitly exclude is when the image may be present but the text is not visually instantiated – as, for example, when an image may be discussed in class by means of spoken verbal language. This will be omitted from our present concerns even though the image and the 'text' (as spoken language) are 'co-present' in a common communicative situation. The principal reason for this decision is that in order to do justice to what is going on in such communicative situations, we would need to introduce far more background on *situated spoken language* than would be reasonable. We would need to address intonational phrasing (issues of placing emphasis and so on) *and* issues of gaze (where the interactants are looking) *and* gesture (what they are pointing at) *and* other properties well known from research on face-to-face interaction (e.g., Martinec 2004, Norris 2004, Fricke 2007, Sowa and Wachsmuth 2009, Müller and Cienki 2009).

Much of this work points to a very tight relationship between the verbal and non-verbal modes of expression, which would be very interesting to consider alongside text-image relations as we define them here. Nevertheless, as a further methodological and practical restriction, we will leave such considerations to the side for the time being.

Dimensionality: 'flatness'

We will be examining the relations between (visually realised instances of) text and images (in the sense we have just begun to define). We then want to find situations of use where images and texts occur in places where they not only *can* be related but where they *are* related by virtue of the organisation of the artefacts themselves. This means that we will explore artefacts which themselves combine text and image in particular, determinate (and intended) ways. In this, we will follow Mitchell and particularly his critique of simply 'comparing' arts and media that may well be incommensurate:

> The best preventive to comparative methods is an insistence on literalness and materiality. That is why, rather than comparing this novel or poem with that painting or statue, I find it more helpful to begin with actual conjunctions or words and images in illustrated texts, or mixed media such as film, television, and theatrical performances. With these media, one encounters a concrete set of empirical givens, an image-text structure responsive to prevailing conventions (or resistance to conventions) governing the relation of visual and verbal experience.
>
> (Mitchell 1994: 90)

This is precisely the restriction that we adopt here.

There are still several ways of bringing text and image together in a way that fits the restrictions we have adopted so far. For example, technological advances are making it increasingly straightforward to combine text and image in *three-dimensional* virtual displays – text and image may also even move with respect to each other. Or, more traditionally, even placing labels and exhibits together in a museum with texts positioned strategically around the exhibits can be seen as a further case of text-image relationships – if we open up the notion of image further.

However, this is another area that we will *not* address. By far the most common case for text-image combinations is still when both the images and the visually instantiated forms of the text are 'flat' – this makes it straightforward for images to be placed together with printed or written text within single artefacts. Indeed, the very fact of their being placed together is most commonly a statement that the two are *intended* to be seen as a unit of some kind. It is then the nature of this unit and its text-image relations that we explore.

This point notwithstanding, it is again very likely that three-dimensional text and image combinations are going to make considerable use of, or overlap with, the kind of text-image relations that occur in two-dimensional, static cases. It is also equally possible that new relationships may be found – but, again, we must leave this for future research.

Typography

Finally, to conclude the long list of things that we will not be doing, another area largely omitted from discussion will be the deliberate use of the visual form of texts as graphical units in their own right – in particular, questions of typography. Even though in some places we will not be able to avoid mentioning such aspects, we will not give them systematic attention. There is a considerable literature on typography and its effects and so we 'bracket' this from our attention for the time being. Important contributions in this area that provide much of the foundation that one would need for addressing the text-image aspect of typography in detail can be found in the work of Sue Walker (Waller 1980, Walker 1982, 2001) and Rob Waller (e.g., Waller 1987). Relations of typography to questions of social structure and power are also discussed in, for example, Koop (2012).

Such considerations will only occasionally be mentioned here, in particular in cases where typographical decisions impinge on the kind of text-image relations being constructed. That is: when the visual typographical qualities contribute to how the text exhibiting those qualities is to be related to some *other* visual material, then we will need to say something about it. This draws a distinction between an 'internal' text-image relationship, where the text 'is' the image in the sense that it is the visual instantiation of the text that is being described, and 'external' relationships where the text (i.e., the visual instantiation of that text on the 'page') relates to other images.

Comics and advertisements make particularly frequent use of both of these possibilities as we shall see in Units 5 and 7 respectively. Consider, for example, the comics panel from Will Eisner, a pioneer of both the theory and practice of comics, shown in Figure 1.8. This is indicative of the complete integration of text, image, visual text properties and text-image relations that we discuss later. The visual instantiation of the text plays just as strong a role in the expressive force of the panel as the facial expression and gestures of the depicted character. This then modifies, or further refines, the simple relationship of 'X says Y' that we saw in the scroll example above considerably!

Figure 1.8 Illustration of the use of extended 'typography' as an internal text-image relationship in comics – taken from Eisner (1992: 12); used by permission

Review: our objects of analysis

We can now state more succinctly just what *will* be studied in this book. In short:

> The text and the image will both need to be *visually instantiated* and *intentionally co-present* within a joint *composition* which is *two-dimensional* and *static*.

An important consequence of this is that the text and the image act as a single unit of composition and can become the subject of attention of more than one person at the same time and in the same way. The text-image combination is then also generally 'directed at' an audience – this is what makes it a communicative act.

In addition, the numerous limitations imposed by our methodological restrictions will be largely balanced by the fact that we will be not be limiting the kinds of static, visual, two-dimensional 'images' that may come to play a role. That is, we will accept as potential objects of analysis *any* visually presented material and not restrict the material images that we examine to be 'pictorial' in any narrow sense. Any kind of artefact employed in order to 'communicate' by means of its visual perception will be considered fair game and so will fall within what we will be examining as 'images'.

Thus, although Mitchell lists the following as potential 'borderline' cases: "abstract, non-representational paintings, ornamental or structural designs, diagrams and graphs" (Mitchell 1986: 11), for us there will be nothing borderline about them. Indeed, since the very issue of what a 'pictorial' representation is raises difficult philosophical questions of its own (Goodman 1969), making a restriction to some notion of naturalistic pictorial representation before we start would in any case be premature.

CONCLUSIONS AND DISCUSSION

There are many further interesting research questions waiting to be addressed or to be brought into productive relationships with the areas we focus on here. The techniques and frameworks needed will probably overlap considerably with aspects of what we discuss in this book as far as the kind of work that the combination of the image and language takes on – and at several points in subsequent units we will make at least some mention of potential connections.

It must always be borne in mind, therefore, that by selecting one small area of phenomena to work on – as we are doing here – we are not making the claim that this area is necessarily *distinct* from all other kinds. On the contrary, and as we have already suggested, some of the distinctions and methods of descriptions that we will meet in this book no doubt apply to other kinds of images and other kinds of language use as well – but this is left for future research and exploration to spell out in detail.

We *do* consider it necessary, however, that any such research builds on what we know about text-image relationships in other domains: it is unlikely that something completely novel is occurring. Thus, although we do not investigate, for example, a statue with a title beneath it, nor exhibits in museums, the text-image relations we discuss are probably going to be relevant there, too. That is: these other situations will need to be studied in their own right, but ideally with knowledge of how text-image relations work 'on the page'.

Our main focus will now be to begin developing methods for approaching visual materials employing text-image combinations openly and empirically, asking what kinds of mechanisms are at work. There are very many open issues, challenging questions and difficult problems. Avoiding wrong turnings is going to be just as important as finding the 'one true path', since it is not at present known just what such a path might look like. This will only become clearer when we start examining concrete cases in particular contexts of use.

Text-image diversity:
characterising the relationships

We set out in the previous unit how the general concerns of this book – text-image relations – should generally be placed against the background of research into *multimodality*. It is then somewhat ironic that most of our current academic disciplines emerged, or went through radical definitional phases of self-discovery and re-shaping, at a time of extreme *monomodality*. Gunther Kress and Theo van Leeuwen, two researchers who have done more to establish 'multimodality' internationally as a field of research than any others, argue that the rise of 'monomodality' is actually a relatively recent phenomenon when considered historically. It reached its peak in the late nineteenth and early twentieth centuries and, as a consequence:

> For some time now, there has been, in Western culture, a distinct preference for monomodality. The most highly valued genres of writing (literary novels, academic treatises, official documents and reports, etc.) came entirely without illustration, and had graphically uniform, dense pages of print. Paintings nearly all used the same support (canvas) and the same medium (oils), whatever their style or subject. In concert performances, all musicians dressed identically and only conductor and soloists were allowed a modicum of bodily expression.
>
> (Kress and van Leeuwen 2001: 1)

This culturally positive evaluation of homogeneity, sameness and monomodality was reflected across all fields of activity and disciplines and even now continues to hold sway by shaping general cultural attitudes towards artefacts operating with broad combinations of modes.

In the arts, the sciences and popular culture, such monomodality could hardly be sustained indefinitely, however – which is itself a further indication of the significant increase in meaning possibilities that such combinations support. The use of visualisations and other mixed combinations of semiotic modes has long been considered necessary for scientific work in any case (cf., e.g., Gross, Harmon and Reidy 2002, Gooding 2004, O'Halloran 2005) and, in several art movements of the early twentieth century, words and images began again to appear together; some artists, such as René Magritte and, as we saw in the introduction, Paul Klee, even adopted this as one of their trademarks. By the 1960s, therefore, the 'received position' that only monomodal artefacts were worth paying attention to had crumbled. Everyday practice had moved on and combinations of modalities showing text-image combinations at work were already commonplace. There was then a growing acceptance of the validity of exploring cultural artefacts and actions that were evidently not striving for some kind of monomodality 'purity'.

As a consequence, it became increasingly evident that the meanings made by combinations of text and images would need to be given attention in their own right. A ground-breaking step in this direction then followed in the work of the French philosopher Roland Barthes

(1915–1980). Barthes' early work still stands as the starting point for all those concerned with text-image relations, regardless of discipline, and so we will begin by setting out his proposals in more detail. We then take this further with respect to both real and constructed examples of text-image relations 'at work'. In each case, the question to be raised is just what is going on. How can we characterise the text-image relations involved and how far does Barthes' description help us? This will also give us an opportunity to sketch some of the early proposals that were made extending Barthes' original ideas, raising many of the questions that will be of concern in subsequent units.

GETTING THE BALL ROLLING: ROLAND BARTHES

As mentioned above, the prevalence of monomodality stretched even to how individual disciplines were defining their subject matters. As Kress and van Leeuwen continue their discussion:

> The specialised theoretical and critical disciplines which developed to speak of these arts became equally monomodal: one language to speak about language (linguistics), another to speak about art (art history), yet another to speak about music (musicology), and so on, each with its own methods, its own assumptions, its own technical vocabulary, its own strengths and its own blind spots.
>
> (Kress and van Leeuwen 2001: 1)

This was equally the case then for linguistics, even though some very general claims were made for the field as a potential general science of signs (Saussure 1959 [1915]). In fact, linguistics was suggested as a potential 'master' pattern for all kinds of semiotic systems, despite the fact that it made virtually no contact with the kind of meaning-making evident in, for example, images.

The subject matter of linguistics as a discipline was instead defined as an abstract 'system' of language centring upon the vocabulary, pronunciation and grammar that must be assumed for each competent native speaker. Other forms of meaning were placed well out of the limelight, and were sometimes even suggested to be like language anyway.

A narrowing of attention of this kind was no doubt necessary and valuable for progress in the discipline at the time. But, as attention turned in the 1960s to the analysis of artefacts in which language occurs with other modalities, the boundaries that had been erected began to show their more negative consequences. On the one hand, there was a growing demand to expand linguistics beyond the boundaries of grammar and the sentence in order to deal with texts and real instances of communication. On the other hand, the meaning contributions of other semiotic systems were becoming increasingly difficult to ignore as the use of visual media in culture exploded. It was quite unclear, however, how linguistics as a discipline could meet this challenge. Something, therefore, needed to change. Both considerations are taken up in the work of Roland Barthes.

Barthes' 'three messages'

Barthes argued that, in order to deal with such everyday artefacts as advertisements, photographs, film, clothes, food and much more, it would be necessary to escape from many of the restrictions inherent in the traditional view of linguistics descended from Saussure. Linguistics made far-reaching claims about how meanings are formed but it was unclear how these proposals might be extended to non-linguistic artefacts and behaviours.

Barthes suggested that it would be necessary to develop "a second linguistics" concerned not with 'words' and 'grammar' but with *discourse*. This was a crucial move prefiguring the subsequent emergence of text linguistics and discourse theory. There was, at the time, little to build on, however. Although some accounts were beginning to emerge for talking of properties of texts (cf. Greimas 1983 [1966]), frameworks were still schematic, exploratory and certainly not oriented towards non-verbal phenomena. Barthes then proposed one of the first, and most influential, frameworks in which the traditional objects of research within linguistics might be related to non-verbal material such as images.

Barthes developed his account on the basis of detailed analyses of advertisements and news photography. What is significant about such artefacts is that text and image not only commonly co-occur but together co-determine the meanings of the whole. This is a classic illustration of 'meaning multiplication' as introduced in the previous unit. Barthes addressed a range of everyday images and asked how it was that we could extract meaning from them at all. Then, and more importantly, he attempted to systematise his conclusions by considering very specifically just *what kinds* of meanings there might be. In this respect, he was particularly driven by the challenge of explaining how a photographic image could both be 'obviously' of some particular subject matter and 'at the same time' have cultural implications concerning how it was to be 'read' that clearly went beyond what was depicted.

One of the earliest examples Barthes discusses was an advertisement for a company selling Italian food in France made up of a photograph of a shopping bag, some vegetables, packets of cheese and spaghetti. Barthes proposed that such an artefact necessarily contained three quite distinct 'messages': a linguistic message, a *coded iconic* message, and an *uncoded iconic* message. These different messages, all present in an image at the same time, draw on different kinds of knowledge in order to be recovered.

The first kind of message is relatively straightforward: the linguistic message is simply any words or other linguistic material that might appear. Here any description developed in linguistics or related fields might be applied. In his example advertisement, the textual elements were limited to the brand name of the packaged products and a simple advertising slogan.

The third kind of message, the *uncoded iconic* message, then takes up the task of describing or accounting for what the image 'actually shows' – that is, the particular physical objects and their physical properties as shown in certain spatial arrangements. Barthes considered this to be a 'quasi-tautological' type of sign. In the field of semiotics that Barthes was contributing to, it is common to talk of *signifiers*, the marks, actions or other material that are carrying meaning, and *signifieds*, which is what the signifiers mean. This usage goes back to Saussure (1959 [1915]), who argued that, for language, the linkage between signifier and signified was **arbitrary**. That is, that the word for dog in English is 'dog' and in French 'chien' is just an arbitrary convention of the languages concerned. It could have turned out differently and in other languages obviously has.

Much of Saussure's framework and the approaches to linguistic description and theory that developed from this over the course of the twentieth century rely crucially on this notion. Indeed, the entire enterprise of 'structuralism' was erected on this foundation: structuralism approached meanings in terms of systems of contrasts between features that are, in themselves, meaningless and arbitrary. It is only *patterns of contrast* that give rise to meaning. Barthes, following many who begin with the study of the visual rather than with language, saw the relationship between a photograph and what it means as being completely different. The photograph 'looks like' what it is showing, it is not drawing on arbitrary patterns of contrast and does not rely on a 'conventional' connection to what is shown:

> we have here a loss of the equivalence characteristic of true sign systems and a statement of quasi-identity. In other words, the sign of this message is not drawn from an institutional stock, is not coded, and we are brought up against the paradox . . . of a *message without a code*.
>
> (Barthes 1977 [1964]: 36)

Consideration of the extent to which any image may be uncoded leads to a substantial minefield of philosophical debate. Over the years many have joined the fray, arguing one way or the other. Goodman (1969), for example, develops a sustained attack on the view that pictures gain their meaning by any natural 'resemblance' to what they depict, drawing on arguments concerning the conventionality rather than naturalness of drawing and painting in 'perspective'. 'Naturalness' assumptions seem to require the prior existence of 'neutral' observers but, as Gombrich (1959) argues, the problem is then that there *is no such thing as an innocent eye*. A concise and very readable review of some of these arguments, particular those of Goodman, can be found in Lopes (1996: 58–68). Barthes' own evaluations of this position also changed over his career.

For present purposes we can distinguish the level of interpretation Barthes was concerned with by identifying the kinds of knowledge that this kind of message draws on. Barthes relates the 'uncoded' message with perception plus some basic 'anthropological' knowledge – that is, the knowledge that almost any child would have: here are some vegetables in a shopping bag with some pasta. Barthes calls this kind of message the *literal* message, or **denotation** of the image. It is 'just' what is shown in the image, and is by itself

> a sufficient message, since it has at least one meaning at the level of the identification of the scene represented; the letter of the image corresponds in short to the first degree of intelligibility (below which the reader would perceive only lines, forms, and colours) . . .
>
> (Barthes 1977 [1964]: 42)

This message is, however, strictly 'virtual' – an analytic abstraction required by logic. Any real image is going to be immediately and necessarily 'impregnated' with further meanings beyond the 'mere anthropological'.

These further meanings Barthes defines as **connotations**. These are also read off of the advertisement but are by no means so direct. Barthes picks out, for example, the obvious 'Italianicity' of the depiction – the colours of the vegetables, packing and pasta echoing the colours of the Italian flag – as well as the coding of 'freshness' from the condition of the vegetables and the connotation of 'cooking and shopping oneself' by virtue of the produce shown partly spilling from an open shopping bag. Barthes considered these additional meanings to be just as obviously intended as the bare literal depiction, contributing equally to the communicative force and effectiveness of the visual image overall.

These non-literal kinds of meanings Barthes considered to be obviously 'coded' because they draw on arbitrary sets of distinctions and contrasts in a manner similar to the arbitrary patterns of contrast assumed for language by Saussure. This in turn opened up the door to a treatment of visual materials applying just those techniques of extended analysis adopted for the evidently 'coded' form of language. Barthes and others subsequently extended this approach, applying it to many other domains – such as fashion and food as remarked above.

Barthes eventually stopped pursuing this direction of research because he considered there to be inherent limits in considering all cultural artefacts to be 'coded' in this simple fashion. Part of this problem, however, was the very undeveloped notion of 'coding' available at that time. On the one hand, many researchers were becoming aware that there would need to be some *dynamic* process of active meaning-construction but, on the other, no frameworks were available within which dynamic phenomena could be satisfactorily modelled. We will skirt this issue for the time being, returning to it below when we consider the theoretical status of text-image relations as such.

For now, more important for us is Barthes' concurrent proposals for teasing apart the different functions that the texts and the images appeared to be taking on with respect to each other in the artefacts he examined. This will give us our first classification of text-image relations and the starting point for almost all studies of text-image combinations since.

Barthes on the respective meanings of texts and images

One basic property of images that was widely assumed at that time was that the meanings that images carry are inherently vague or less determinate that those carried in linguistic messages. This is discussed from many different perspectives and for very different reasons. Barthes accordingly began by claiming that all images "are polysemous: they imply, underlying their signifiers, a 'floating chain' of signifieds, the reader able to choose some and ignore others" (Barthes 1977 [1964]: 39). This can be observed quite literally in some older conventional uses of images. In the field of art history, for example, Meyer Schapiro pointed out in the early 1960s that

> correspondence of word and picture is often problematic and may be surprisingly vague. In old printed Bibles the same woodcut was used sometimes to illustrate different subjects. These, however, were episodes with a common general meaning. The picture of Jacob's birth was repeated for the birth of Joseph and other scriptural figures, and a battle scene was serviceable for illustrating several such encounters. It is the place of the woodcut in the book, at a certain point in the text, that permits us to grasp the more specific meaning.
> (Schapiro 2006: 11–12)

Barthes' response to this was to suggest that societies develop ways of 'fixing' the 'floating chain of signifieds' so as to make their images interpretable. Considering the images together with texts is then one important way in which this can be achieved.

When text plays this role of fixing interpretation, Barthes talks of **anchorage**. Anchorage is a text-image relationship in which a particular denotation is selected out of the interpretations possible for an image. In Barthes' words: "The text replies – in a more or less direct, more or less partial manner – to the question: *what is it?*" (Barthes 1977 [1964]: 39). Typical examples of anchorage are to be found in newspaper captions, where the function of the caption-text is precisely to inform the reader of what they are looking at in the picture. Without an appropriate caption, the meaning of what is being shown would often be, at best, unclear.

Much discussion of meaning, of semiotics, of cultural systems and so on at the time Barthes was writing was couched in terms of struggle and dominance. Barthes thus saw anchorage as a relationship of *control*: the text serves as the "creator's (and hence society's) right of control over the image" (Barthes 1977 [1964]: 40). In this case, therefore, the relation between text and image exhibited in anchorage is far from an equal one. The 'freedom' of the image is 'subjugated' to the order of the text.

There are also situations of text and image occurring together where their inter-relationship is balanced more equally. Barthes contrasted these situations with anchorage by considering text and image then to stand together as necessarily separate but inter-dependent parts of a single whole. The type of relationship holding between text and image in such cases Barthes referred to as **relay**. Here, the meanings created in the combination stand as complementary elements of a "more general syntagm" (Barthes 1977 [1964]: 41), in which the meaning of the whole combination is located. 'Syntagm' is a term derived from linguistics referring to some demarcated unit of analysis. By using this term, Barthes suggests that certain combinations of text and image are themselves legitimate units of analysis – that is, they need to be seen together as parts of a single whole.

On the basis of his experience at the time, Barthes suggests that 'relay' is rare in static presentations, but important for comic strips and films (Barthes 1977 [1964]: 41). He thus saw the relation between dialogue and action in film, or relations in comic strips, as typical examples of relay in action, where both may contribute equally to the overall meaning. This imbalance between the use of relay and of anchorage certainly seems to have undergone substantial change. Nowadays, the 'sharing' of meaning across distinct modalities required in the definition of relay appears common in quite diverse types of document and not at all only in comics.

Finally, Barthes argued that the kind of relationship found in anchorage, where the text 'supports' the image, making the intended interpretation of the image clear, is actually the reverse of what he takes to be the more traditional role of images – that of providing **illustration**:

> in the traditional modes of illustration the image functioned as an episodic return to denotation from a principal message (the text) which was experienced as connoted since, precisely, it needed an illustration; in the relationship that now holds, it is not the image which comes to elucidate or 'realize' the text, but the latter which comes to sublimate, patheticize or rationalize the image.
>
> (Barthes 1977 [1964]: 25)

In the case of illustration, then, the image 'supports' the text, providing more details about a message which is essentially textual.

This leaves us with a three-way classification of text-image relations that continues to structure many discussions of the text-image question to this day. The classification is shown with its internal organisation in Figure 2.1, represented graphically as a **systemic classification network**. We will often use this form of graphical representation as we proceed; it was originally developed for grammatical description but actually offers a general formalism for capturing

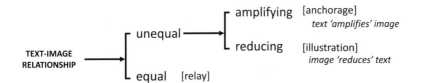

Figure 2.1 Barthes' classification of text-image relations represented graphically as a systemic network

structured collections of alternatives. Although the current example is a simple taxonomy, we will see some more complex classification possibilities in later units.

WORDS AND IMAGES TOGETHER: MORE EXAMPLES AND SOME PUZZLES

We have already considered a range of examples where text and images occur together. Further examples can be gathered more or less without limit. Some of the ways in which the text and image combine and function together in these examples have been mentioned on a case-by-case basis. Barthes' characterisation then began to consider the range of such inter-relationships more systematically. The categories proposed by Barthes accordingly offer us a first suggestion of how a more systematic account might proceed. We can then consider how any of our (and other) examples fit within his scheme.

This offers a first sketch of a *method* for pursuing research in text-image relations. A classification scheme can be proposed that is intended to cover all the cases of text-image combinations that are to be examined. The individual cases of combinations are then classified according to the classification scheme. For this, the scheme needs to be sufficiently well defined that classification can proceed in a reliable fashion – in particular, a valuable goal is to strive here for **inter-coder reliability**. This means that different people carrying out the classification independently of one another should come to the same decisions concerning where each case fits. To the extent that cases cannot be straightforwardly categorised, the classification may need to be changed or its definitions refined. This encourages a test-and-refine cycle by which more robust classifications can be progressively developed.

As an example, we could ask where the 'speaking scrolls' that we saw in Figure 1.3 in the previous unit would fit in Barthes' three-way classification. The information provided seems most clearly to be a case of 'relay' because there is a single syntagm to which the text and the image contribute equally – the syntagm made up of someone speaking and the scroll of 'floating' text. These are separate but inter-dependent: if either one is removed the meaning of the 'syntagm' collapses. This also fits with Barthes' suggestion that comics commonly exhibit relay as their means of combining text and image since, to a certain extent, the form of expression in the fresco is suggestive of a speech balloon.

Applying the classification scheme to a completely different area and still being able to come up with a reasonable assignment in this way can be taken as providing supporting evidence for the scheme. There is then the further question to consider of whether we can offer more fine-grained distinctions. If the cases that are grouped together under a particular class – here, relay, for example – appear too heterogeneous, we should consider looking for possible subcategories to group these into classes.

Barthes' approach did, therefore, appear to help with the characterisation of text-image relations, showing them to be subject to particular organisational schemes with differing meanings. Consequently, by the late 1970s and early 1980s, his scheme had been taken up in earnest and several researchers in various countries had begun to explore whether the account was sufficient or required extension or refinement. In part, this went together with an early boom in text linguistics and the goal of extending linguistic treatments of text to include artefacts exhibiting text-image combinations, such as advertisements, comics and other complex cultural artefacts. French and German researchers were particularly active in this regard (cf. Oomen 1975, Bardin 1975, Kloepfer 1977, Moles 1978, Spillner 1980).

As one example of this work, Spillner (1982) was already at this time setting out preconditions for progress beyond the more explorative discussions offered hitherto. He saw it necessary both to pursue a 'typology' of the possible relationships holding between visual information and textual information and to carry out empirical investigations of how the recipients of such 'semiotically complex' texts actually went about finding the relationships. It is remarkable in many ways that these preconditions are still to be met – as we shall see in many of the units following, proposals for typologies of such text-image relationships abound, but systematic studies showing how they are actually perceived and understood by their recipients are still very much a rarity. This situation will need to change substantially for further progress in the field as we discuss further in Units 12 and 13.

Spillner's text-image relations

Bernd Spillner's early work formed part of the then newly emerging tradition of German text linguistics. Spillner made several contributions concerned with extending linguistic attention beyond the traditional linguistic concerns of sentences, phonology, morphology and grammar so as to address an increasingly broad range of natural 'contexts' in which language use could be studied. As we will hear more of with respect to the text-image approaches of Hartmut Stöckl and Manfred Muckenhaupt in Unit 12, German text linguistics has long been concerned with identifying the contrasting properties of various kinds of texts in order to be able to relate texts and their properties to their situations of use (cf. Sandig 1972). A central question raised at that time and still with us today is the degree to which it is possible to systematise this relationship – this is the broad area of **register**, or **text type**, theory that has been addressed from the perspectives of several linguistic 'schools' (cf. Hasan 1973, Gregory and Carrol 1978, Biber and Finegan 1993, Lee 2001).

Spillner (1982) starts by setting out some of the text-image relations that he finds necessary for characterising how the two modalities work together. He then goes on to report on an informal experiment on their reception; we return to this below. Spillner already takes it for granted that combinations of texts and images can function together as single, semiotically complex, 'textual' units that should be analysed as such. Within such complexes, particular constituents of the unit as a whole can be occupied freely by textual and visual material. Within the context of such single functioning communicative artefacts, then, the goal must be to explain how verbal and non-verbal material can mutually complement and 'co-determine' each other.

Spillner sees the simplest form of relationship between text and image as one of 'priority' with respect to the message as a whole. This is a logical extension of Barthes' position – whereas Barthes only considers a variation of priority within the anchorage-illustration contrast, Spillner opens up the possibility that priority might be a more general distinction. This means that it would always be possible for one semiotic mode employed to *determine* the meaning communicated by another.

Spillner offers several compelling examples. One of these – drawn from advertisements, a particularly challenging source of text-image relations – contains the phrase (originally in German): "fewer people are driving in the rain with the wrong tyres". This taken by itself seems a simple statement, most likely interpreted along the lines that more people are buying suitable tyres for driving in the rain. However, in the advertisement it is presented as part of an image showing skidmarks on a wet road and a broken fence. The image in this case therefore refocuses the intended interpretation of the text in a dramatic turnaround, indicating that the number of such drivers is growing less because they skid off the road with fatal consequences.

As Spillner notes, the image then *anchors the polysemous nature of the text.* Such reattributions of textual meaning by their accompanying visuals appear quite common in advertisements; we will see more cases in Unit 7. In asymmetric situations of this kind, then, one semiotic modality will be primary and the other secondary and both text and image are capable of taking on the primary role (Spillner 1982: 92).

It is also possible for symmetric relationships to apply, where the semiotic modes are deployed more equally, each taking responsibility for some part of the message. Here as well Spillner refines further the different possibilities that text and image respectively make available. Texts he takes to be supportive of a considerably broader range of visualisation possibilities, while images are inherently less uniquely determined and so can receive a variety of interpretations depending on the texts accompanying them.

Spillner also discusses cases where one semiotic system – that is, either texts or images – takes on functions of the other. Text, for example, can attempt to communicate properties such as conservatism, dynamism and so on by virtue of typography; or may be 'shaped' or deformed to bring out or emphasise aspects of the meanings communicated – one example he offers of the latter is an advertisement where the word for 'exhaustion' is presented with its final letters leaning at progressively steeper angles, visually suggesting imminent collapse. This means that the text itself visually 'illustrates' or 'enacts' its own meaning. This is a further example of the internal text-image relations related to typography introduced in Unit 1 ('Typography', p. 27). Converse cases are when, for example, an idiom or proverb is depicted literally as an image. These usages stretch the categorisations provided by Barthes considerably and so raise the question of precisely which other relationships are going to prove necessary.

Moreover, in considering the relations between text and image in such contexts, one is quickly led to the need to address the *inferential* processes of interpretation that readers and viewers perform during reception. This leads to Spillner's second precondition for progress in analysing text-image relations: recipient studies.

Text-image relations and the reception process

To explore the process of reception in action, Spillner took an advertisement for margarine, re-created and slightly adapted here in English as shown in Figure 2.2, and asked groups of 'experimental participants' to answer some simple questions on their experience of attempting to understand the advertisement.

As can be seen from the figure, the advertisement consists of a large textual message and an image of an open margarine tub. The text is prominent and presented as the top part of the advertisement. There is also textual information prominent on the margarine tub itself – on the lid the name of the margarine and two textual messages: "50% less fat" and "50% fewer calories" can clearly be read. Each message is shown so that the '50' is prominent in comparison with the rest of the text present, which sets up a further resonance 'within' the separate textual components – 'halb' means half in German and so the visually prominent '50–50' 'restates' this implicit message. This means that we have relations across text and layout and at several levels of design, including the level of the advertisement itself and of the depicted product's packaging.

The main point of interest of this example for Spillner lies in the problem that, although both the text and image appear clear and unambiguous in terms of what they say or depict,

**From 1st May
the outdoor pools
are open again**

Figure 2.2 Re-created version of a diet margarine from 1972
discussed by Spillner (1982)

they have nothing to do with each other. Nevertheless, they seem to combine to produce a positive effect in favour of the advertised product. They are presented together, appear as a single syntagm, and so might be considered a case of Barthes' relay but, as with the skidding in the rain example discussed above, they also co-determine each other's interpretation to such an extent that aspects of anchorage appear difficult to rule out. This point is also clearly made by Stöckl (1997: 123), who suggests that some aspect of 'anchorage' may always be present, but this then feeds into a dynamic process of meaning-construction rather than being simply fixed. And Barthes himself suggests that these functions may 'co-exist' (Barthes 1977 [1964]: 41).

Spillner investigated the nature of this process of interpretation more closely by asking students to describe what the advertisement meant (Spillner 1982: 102). A rather short list of common 'themes' offering potential solutions for the puzzle emerged. These ranged from rather imaginative suggestions – such as: because one doesn't have time in summer to spend time spreading butter on sandwiches, it is a good idea to use margarine – to considerations of health and fitness – such as: margarine is as healthy as sport, or one needs to look good in summer because of having to put on swimwear at the pool, so margarine will help achieve a good figure.

Eighty per cent of Spillner's 56 participants in the experiment selected these latter kinds of themes, showing that despite the disparate nature of the information given textually and visually, the intended positive effect of the advertisement was achieved. There were also interesting differences of other kinds: for example, while 31 per cent of male participants selected the looking good in swimwear option, 68 per cent of female participants suggested this interpretation. Most saw the need to engage with the advertisement as a puzzle to solve as leading to a more positive evaluation of the product and of the advertisement – a result that we will see discussed in more detail in Unit 7.

With this informal experiment Spillner moved into an area still far too often neglected: do the accounts of text-image relationships that are proposed have anything to do with what readers and viewers actually do when confronted with the material analysed? It is common to read of claims about how readers/viewers might interpret what is presented, but such claims are rarely backed up with evidence that this is actually the case rather than an assumption of what appears 'obvious' or self-evident for the analyst. This is insufficient and so work in the future will need to pay far closer attention to substantiating such claims. Spillner shows well that this can be approached even with rather modest means and methods.

Constraining the search for text-image relations

Although it is possible to push this margarine example into the framework suggested by Barthes, the result is in many respects less than satisfying. When we have interpreted the image, we might say that we have a case of Barthes' *anchorage* because the text has constrained the picture of the margarine from a product in general to a particular solution to the problem of dieting. But this is a *post hoc* analysis – that is, we can only suggest it once we already know the answer. The text-image relationship as a consequence seems to start out as relay, with separate but inter-dependent contributions to a single syntagm (the text and image considered together), but then those contributions begin to co-determine one another, anchoring image or text or both. Analyses like this do little to help us see how an interpretation comes about, which is actually what needs to be the main concern.

This point is also made forcibly in an early discussion of text-image relations by Kloepfer (1977). Kloepfer begins his discussion with a similar brief characterisation of the kinds of relations that hold between text and image, briefly described as follows. First, Kloepfer extends his account beyond the characterisation offered by Barthes by filling in some logical gaps in the 'paradigm' – that is, the range of possibilities theoretically possible. Whereas Barthes only explicitly considers cases where text and image pull in the same direction, Kloepfer adds in the option of text and image being 'divergent'. And in the cases where text and image do work together ('convergent'), this is further subdivided according to whether text and image are dependent ('additive') or operate in parallel, each making their own contribution. Finally, the additive relationship is itself subdivided according to whether that relationship is, following Kloepfer's terminology, 'raising to a higher power' or 'amplifying' (*potenzierend*) or 'modifying' (*modifizierend*). The former takes something and makes it stronger; the second changes the original in some way.

The classification is summarised graphically, again in the form of a systemic classification network, in Figure 2.3. Depicting different approaches in a similar graphical form like this allows readier comparisons and contrasts to be drawn. Often we shall see that rather similar distinctions are made, even though their internal organisation may differ. This explicitly raises the question of just *why* the internal organisation is different and whether improvements can be proposed.

What this representation does *not* help us with, however, is the fact that the meanings of the terms used in various frameworks might not always be obvious. Whereas accounts of this

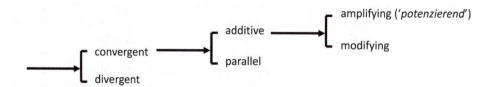

Figure 2.3 Classification of text-image relations from Kloepfer (1977: 129) expressed as a systemic network

nature may seem internally consistent, it is often by no means clear how they are to be aligned with other accounts. For example, it might be that Kloepfer's *potenzierend* corresponds in intention to what we have termed meaning-multiplication above, or it may be a form of Barthes' 'relay' or, as we shall see particularly in Unit 10, one of the kinds of logico-semantic relationships for combining information – in particular, *enhancement*, although this might also be what is intended by 'modification'. Similarly, 'parallel' may correspond to 'relay' in that separate contributions are made by text and image.

Let us consider as an example the straightforward caption 'Summer 1968' for a picture or photograph. According to Barthes, the caption fixes (anchors) the meaning of the image: the picture may have been any summery scene, now it is tied down to one summer. According to Kloepfer's classification, we are clearly in the convergent area, but deciding whether we are dealing with a parallel relationship (since the year is not in the picture) or an amplification (since we do not change the fact that the picture is in summer) or a modification (since we change the information to include a particular year) requires further commitments concerning just how the relations are to be applied. Moreover, these commitments *must then be maintained for all applications of the framework*, otherwise mutually inconsistent classifications will result.

Making comparisons and suggestions for how different terms relate *across* frameworks is an especially fraught business – it is often far better to pursue such exploration *with respect to examples* and particular cases, attempting to classify the same cases with respect to the variously suggested classification schemes. If it is not clear how some examples are to be classified within some scheme or within some particular area of a scheme as a whole, then those distinctions should be put to one side until a more specific definition has been provided. As we shall see when we have introduced several more of the frameworks on offer, it is possible that a more refined proposal for the troublesome area can be drawn from other accounts.

After having introduced his classification scheme, however, Kloepfer (1977: 129) goes further and emphasises that this is in any case not enough. Kloepfer considers the meaning-making process to be dynamic and polyfunctional, even *changing* the 'codes' in use; he presents several examples of this drawn from advertisements and comics. The classification scheme offered is then just a way of getting this processing started and issues of the interpretation are actually central.

This process of interpretation can be followed in more detail with respect to text-image relationships in Spillner's margarine example. When confronted with the advertisement, Spillner found that most viewers quickly put two and two together and draw the line of inference relating (1) being at the swimming pool, (2) wearing swimming gear, (3) probably therefore disclosing more of their bodies than usual, and (4) hence facing the social pressure to make those bodies conform to certain stereotypes. This is what then finally involves the need to get 'into shape' with the help of a suitable diet, which the low fat margarine might well be part of. When spelled out like this, the reasoning chain appears quite long and contorted. It is then really quite a challenge to explain just how it is that the vast majority of recipients of such an advertisement come so smoothly to the evidently intended interpretation.

Identifying particular *schemes* of inference might make this process more likely to succeed and also suggest reasons why the interpretations recipients make are so consistent. What is needed, therefore, are *systematic* ways of exploring such complex 'semiotic' artefacts. For example, it seems unconvincing if each new advertisement, or other artefact, has to be addressed as a completely new, one-off phenomenon raising unique problems to be solved: certainly in our consumption-oriented societies advertisements are one of the most frequently

Figure 2.4 Two constructed advertisements for diet margarine

occurring communicative artefacts of all and we do not (usually) stand before each poster or magazine advertisement in bewilderment as to how to proceed. Even if we do not instantly 'get' what is meant, we still know that we are dealing with an advertisement and that there is something *to* get. We then are more likely to proceed with the advertisement as with the one in Spillner's example, as a problem to be solved, looking for the ways to put the pieces together so that sense is revealed. If we could characterise the overall space of possibilities for putting text and image together, we would be in a better position to understand how such artefacts operate.

Whereas the margarine advertisement seems to provide relatively little guidance as to what kind of text-image relationship might obtain, many artefacts are more specific in guiding their recipients in particular directions of interpretations rather than others. Consider the two contrasting constructed 'advertisements' in Figure 2.4, for example.

In both cases there is far less interpretative work to do than in Spillner's example. In the first, there appears to be simply some kind of anonymous but specific positive evaluation of the margarine with respect to its taste; in the second, the explicit indication of a quotation pushes interpretation in the direction of reporting on someone's experience of eating the margarine. The visual and textual properties in both cases help constrain the likely inter-pretations – which is then far from a free-wheeling searching for potential narratives to embed the material on offer. It will therefore be beneficial to search for *sources of constraint* in the

Figure 2.5 A further constructed advertisement for a diet margarine

ways in which text and image are presented such as this so that we do not assume that interpretations of text-image relations are more free than is actually the case.

This interpretative guidance can be made even more specific – consider the constructed example in Figure 2.5. Here the visual conventions that have been applied – those of comics and speech bubbles that we will discuss in more detail in Unit 5 – make a clear *visual assertion* of what is being communicated. And this holds even though the result is barely sensible: is the margarine tub talking? This shows that the force of the visual representation itself can be very strong and that, again, we cannot leave the process of working out text-image relations purely to commonsense and the free exploration of narrative contextualisations.

Further text-image relations: system or open-ended list?

Such considerations combine to motivate the task of looking both for repertoires of text-image relations and solid evidence concerning just which relations might apply in particular cases. Barthes' early proposal of a three-way distinction starts us off on this search, but we need to take it further with respect to a far broader range of materials in order to begin characterising just which possibilities arise, where they arise, and how we can tell.

This empirical search can be complemented by appropriate theoretical considerations – Barthes was also, for example, considering philosophically just what kinds of relationships might be possible. Spillner's and Kloepfer's considerations follow this course in part as well, attempting to fill in the 'space' of logical alternatives. This is a very useful way to proceed at the outset since over-simplifications can readily give rise to problematic 'borderline' cases that have more to do with weaknesses in the model proposed than with genuine problems. If, for example, Barthes had suggested only relay and illustration, debate about which of these two categories should be adopted in cases of anchorage would have been wasted effort: it would have been the classification that was at fault.

We will see in several of the units below how various sources of argumentation are taken up in order to motivate distinct repertoires of relationships in this way. However, when a classification has been proposed on whatever logical or philosophical grounds adopted, the necessary next step is to see if it is *empirically adequate*. This means testing it with respect to data, classifying cases of text-image relationships and seeing if any predictions made concerning the effects of those relationships can actually be supported. This drives research forward, raising hypotheses that need to be checked back with respect to empirical data – a process we discuss further in Unit 13.

Drawing on other earlier work in French in this direction by, for example, Bardin (1975) and Moles (1978), as well as the discussions of Spillner (1982) and others, Nöth (1995: 454) sets out an extended repertoire of text-image relations already going considerably beyond the proposals made by Barthes. The suggested relations here are:

- illustration, where the picture is 'semiotically subordinate' to the text, as in book illustrations,
- pictorial exemplification, where the picture provides additional new information with respect to the text that is intended to provide an example of what the text describes – Nöth takes this as a subtype of Barthes' relay,
- labelling, where a textual element identifies a picture – Nöth points out that it is possible for such labels both to be cases of relay, when the label is the identifying name under a photographic portrait of someone otherwise unknown, and to be cases of anchorage, as in titles of works of art,

- mutual determination, which seems to combine relay and anchorage, as in some of the cases discussed by Spillner above (Spillner 1982: 90),
- contradiction, which Nöth describes as rare – although, as we shall see, something like a contradiction appears often in text-image combinations in advertisements and picture-books for children.

While this list certainly extends the possibilities, it is unclear both whether there are other possibilities that are not yet included – Nöth suggests that there will be – and to what extent the categories here are mutually exclusive, overlapping, consistent or even reliably recognisable.

While clear cases can be found, it is usually only when we attempt to *apply* a framework to real examples that the problems and difficulties show themselves. Consider the case 'labelling', for example. It appears suspicious that in some cases the label can be anchorage and in others its 'opposite', relay. The designation 'label' therefore seems to be operating at a different level of abstraction. One might presumably provide a label for a picture or for some pictorial information in several ways and so 'labelling' might be referring instead to what someone is *doing* with a text in relation to an image rather than addressing the text-image relation itself. This shows that any classification suggested needs to adopt *homogeneous* criteria for its distinctions and operate within clearly defined levels of abstraction. Mixing levels of abstraction and classification criteria is certain to make use of any resulting framework difficult.

Similarly: can perhaps an 'exemplification' also perform the function of an 'illustration'? Here again, it seems important to consider what roles the picture and texts are *intended* to play and which levels of abstraction are being described. In this case the terms used appear to lead more in the direction of 'rhetoric' and communicative acts that we will also hear more of in subsequent units. This in turn raises questions such as: are there limits on what relations can be 'intended' between image and text? And how can we know how to find appropriate interpretations rather than others? The need for considerably more systematisation is evident.

WHAT *ARE* TEXT-IMAGE RELATIONSHIPS?

Regardless of whether we have an account such as Barthes', proposing that one of a small set of relationships is possible between text and image, or one of the more refined lists that we have just seen containing several more relationships, the question remains as to just what the *nature* of these relationships is. What are the catalogues of text-image relations catalogues of?

The answer to this question is crucial in several respects. First, different answers lead to different assumptions concerning both the motivational evidence that can be drawn on when providing a classification and the mechanisms that might be involved in determining text-image relations. And second, different answers set different criteria for classification. When different aspects are being attended to, it can be no surprise that different modelling decisions result – comparing classifications that take different starting points is more likely to lead to confusion than anything else.

Some descriptions, as we shall see, simply assert that there are relationships holding between text and image and describe them as if they are there to be 'discovered' in the material on offer. This seems rather unlikely – particularly in the light of the margarine example discussed by Spillner, where readers and viewers of the advertisement had considerable work to do even to *find* possible relationships. The sense in which text-image relations are evident 'in' the material or data analysed therefore needs to be considered rather carefully. How this particular issue plays out makes a considerable difference both for the kinds of evidence that can be drawn upon and the predictions that can be made.

So: are we 'discovering' relationships between texts and images that are somehow 'there' in the artefacts explored? Or are we *constructing* relationships that somehow contribute to our understanding of what an artefact is communicating? Is that construction part of an abstract *description* of what we take an artefact to mean or is it a proposal for actual cognitive or psychological mechanisms that we can experimentally investigate? Any account needs to take positions on these questions.

Certainly *some* of the relations may be more directly attributable to text and image and the artefacts they appear in. Pegg (2002), for example, compiles another set of text-image relations drawing on a historical consideration of text-image combinations over time. Pegg argues that the invention and use of print contributed to both a very stable and a very restricted set of text-image relations *at the level of form*. Citing examples from the sixteenth century onwards, he demonstrates that the following four relationships occur again and again:

- images can be *ancillary* where they are placed in a position near to the parts of the text they relate to, leaving the work of relating text to image to the reader;
- images can be *correlative* or *integrative*, where images are overlaid with labels, call-outs and the like to indicate specific points of contact between the text and the image – a common variant here is a combination with an ancillary relation mediated by captions;
- images can be *substantive* where the image and the text are combined within single compositional forms – this can itself vary in that the text may be distributed around a visual/spatial form, or the text itself, in its composition and layout, may reflect significant meaning differences.

Each of these relationships is largely determined by the physical layout and composition of the artefacts. This then provides information on text-image relations of a rather different kind to those considered above. The nature of the communicative *functions* of these relationships is factored out as an additional, logically separate question.

A rather different orientation again can be found in much of the multimodal work from the late 1990s and early 2000s that began by extending broadly linguistic descriptions into other areas. Two of the more established proposals of this kind are those developed by Gunther Kress and Theo van Leeuwen (Kress and van Leeuwen 2006 [1996]) and Michael O'Toole (O'Toole 2011 [1994]). Both Kress and van Leeuwen and O'Toole draw on the form of descriptions developed in the social semiotic theory of **systemic-functional linguistics**, which now arguably represents the most widespread general approach to multimodal description and theory worldwide.

Researchers in this tradition accept as a basic tenet that language is critically shaped by the demands made of it by the social contexts in which it operates. This means that *even the internal organisation of language* is seen as a functional response to the socio-cultural 'work' that language performs in constructing and maintaining social configurations. Then, since *all* communicative behaviour takes place in social contexts and for social purposes, it is a relatively small step to consider other forms of expression to be equally subject to constraints of this kind and similarly to have their internal organisation shaped by those demands. This predicts that language and images will share general organisational features since they are both socially constructed meaning-making resources. In other words, there should be certain very general communicatively motivated distinctions that recur in both language and in images.

Approaches of this kind commonly go on to assume that many traditionally defined aspects of **visual composition** can be used to establish *visually motivated* units that support 'functional' interpretations comparable, although different, to interpretations made of language. Notions of 'form', 'masses', 'weight', 'balance', 'movement', and so on from art criticism and the psychology of vision (cf., e.g., Arnheim 1974) are used to suggest that when viewers encounter a visual representation, their visual system will already 'segment' it in certain ways. This provides a basis for comparison across text and image since the communicative functions at work are assumed to be broadly similar across the verbal and visual modes. We will see this technique applied in several of the frameworks we describe in later units and a simple example of 'functional interpretation' is given in Figure 3.2 below.

Nevertheless, adequate attention must still be paid to the very *different* properties of texts and images. In particular, whereas we know, by and large, what parts and relationships can be pulled out of a linguistic analysis of a text, a corresponding procedure for visual materials is problematic. The significance of this difference is often under-estimated in more recent linguistically influenced work on text-image relations. In these accounts detailed bases for comparison between texts and images are formed by characterising visual distinctions of colour, typography, text formatting and so on in a manner very similar to a kind of simplified 'grammar'.

Although this makes it possible to compare what language is doing with what the visuals are doing, the potential range of variation in each area considered is enormous. There are, in addition, entire disciplines dedicated to them – such as art criticism, typography, information design and many more – and so it quickly becomes unclear just what some simplified listing of, for example, the possibilities of lines and curves, of colours and shadings of black and white, of a few font sizes or inter-line spacing, and so on that a linguist might come up with can contribute.

This raises some serious doubts about any simple application of linguistic abstractions to pictorial material in two respects. First, because such descriptions tend to be simplified, they may help to direct attention during analysis but can hardly lay claims to completeness or, from the perspective of professionals in those areas, even accuracy. Second, because they tend to be decontextualised, it is unclear whether *in any specific case* they are going to reveal useful distinctions.

As a simple example of this, consider Figure 2.6. This presents a generic 'icon' of a face – actually it is not very iconic in the original sense of the term provided by the semiotician Charles Sanders Peirce (pronounced 'purse'), but usage varies and we will for current purposes just adopt a fairly everyday – albeit philosophically problematic (cf. Goodman 1969) – sense

Figure 2.6 "This is not a face"

of 'resemblance'. Now, Lim (2004) argues with respect to a very similar face that we can identify the meaningful choices made in the forms of expression selected here – that is, the black line, the two small black circles, the larger circle – in a similar way to the selection of units during linguistic analysis:

> Should any of the choices be altered at the rank of the Expression plane, for example, should the eyes become green, or the thin black line becomes a red brush stroke, the meaning of the picture would change.
>
> (Lim 2004: 227)

This suggests that we can set out the distinctions 'on offer' in a manner entirely similar to the listing and organisation of phonemes, morphemes and other basic 'parts' of linguistic representations.

But the problem is that this is simply not true for pictorial depictions. Unless we know what the image is being used for, we can say very little about what can be changed and what not. The line standing for the mouth might become a little longer or a little shorter, the shape of the outer circle might change and so on. We can see this to be the case because this is not, in fact, an exact copy of Lim's figure; it is just a 'similar' face made without consulting the original. Nevertheless, it is unlikely that this face will be seen to have a different 'meaning' despite all kinds of differences being present if we did an exact comparison.

The situation is actually far 'worse' than this for 'grammar-like' descriptions of this kind – and, from the perspective of the possibilities for visual communication, also far *better*. This fundamental property of the visual opens up an enormous flexibility for meaning creation. This is brought out well in the following recount of his first discovery of the power of *re-contextualisation* in visual art by Ernst Gombrich, one of the seminal figures of visual analysis in the twentieth century:

> I well remember that the power and magic of image making was first revealed to me . . . by a simple drawing game I found in my primer. A little rhyme explained how you could first draw a circle to represent a loaf of bread (for loaves were round in my native Vienna); a curve added on top would turn the loaf into a shopping bag; two little squiggles on its handle would make it shrink into a purse; and now by adding a tail, here was a cat.
>
> (Gombrich 1959: 6)

One can also, as Gombrich notes, switch interpretations by changing captions, by placing more background in the image (natural habitat) and by putting an image into a sequence of images (Gombrich 1959: 235). It is precisely this flexibility which contributes substantially to both the increase in power that one obtains when combining text and images and the difficulty in coming to terms with this process in an appropriate way.

This opens up a further crucial area of concern. We must not only address the challenge of text-image relationships as a taxonomic exercise, setting out catalogues of possible connections, but also consider closely what these relationships are intended *to do*. In other words, what are the *consequences* of some relationship holding? Nöth (1995: 453) already summarises the issue succinctly here:

> both addition and duplication are unduly simplified characterizations of the text-image relation. Instead, the juxtaposition of picture and word usually results in a new holistic interpretation of the scripto-pictorial or the audiovisual message.

That is, we need to consider what the meaning-making process does with any text, image and text-image relationship in order to make any resulting meanings. This process may itself even feed back and influence how the contributions of the texts and images being combined are to be considered or described; indeed, Stöckl (2004a: 250) goes so far as to doubt the independent existence of contributions in any case – text and image are in his account always to be seen as parts of an indivisible whole and it is this that determines the contributions that are being made.

Notions related to this kind of 're-contextualisation', or mutual interpretative complementarity, are increasingly appealed to in discussions of multimodality, Lim being no exception. This dynamic aspect of the dynamic process of interpretation has a long history in discussions of text-image relationships as we saw above (e.g., Spillner 1982, Kloepfer 1977, O'Halloran 1999, Nöth 2004, Iedema 2007). It constitutes a fundamental property of text-image relationships that we will need to return to again and again in subsequent units. We will need approaches and analysis methods that accept this aspect of visuality at their core.

This has important consequences for text-image relationship analyses. Any actual instance of a text-image relation posited in an artefact will always need to be seen as a *hypothesis* concerning interpretation. This hypothesis will be made on the basis of evidence both in the texts and images themselves and drawn from the context of use of the text-image combination. Such hypotheses may go wrong – they are, to use the technical term again defined by the semiotician Peirce, *abductive*. An abductive hypothesis is a hypothesis that appears best to explain the data on the basis of the *currently available evidence*. With more evidence, that hypothesis may require revision. This will also often apply to the 'contents' of our descriptions of text and image themselves; co-contextualisation can thus also lead to re-contextualisation.

Accounting for text-image relations by constructing repertoires of possible relations, no matter how organised, is then of necessity a way of setting out the kinds of abductive hypotheses that can be made. Rather than allowing *any* kind of hypothesis, we seek to delimit just those hypotheses that are available to producers and interpreters of text-image combinations for making sense of what is presented.

All of the accounts described in subsequent units must actually be seen in this light, even when they do not themselves make this aspect of their status explicit. Sometimes they even work against this status by claiming their account to be 'grammatical' or due to some other kind of evidence. But the cases where there is anything like a genuine 'grammatical', that is, structural, relationship holding are, as we shall see, few and far between.

CONCLUSIONS AND DISCUSSION

In this unit we saw that the scientific investigation of just what kinds of meanings text-image combinations achieve largely began with the work of Roland Barthes. Since then many researchers and research traditions have turned to the text-image question. These have attempted progressively to achieve more systematic and exhaustive repertoires of text-image relations so as to be able to explain how recipients make sense of the different kinds of materials being combined.

Since the late 1990s, the awareness of multimodality as a research issue has grown considerably. The role of multimodal artefacts – both as objects of analysis and as the preferred form of communication in an ever broadening range of applications – is now well established. In modern times, the prevalence of artefacts that include both pictures and texts, ranging from newspapers to children's picture books to technical manuals and science texts, has prompted renewed scientific discussion and consideration of the relationship between visually and verbally presented information within many, quite diverse disciplines.

This has been due not only to the ease of access to visual material now made possible by electronic media, but also to the changing status of the visual as such in contemporary society. A variety of claims concerning visual and pictorial cultural 'turns' have been made (cf. Mitchell 1994), placing studies of visual communication high on several research agendas (Mirzoeff 1999, Müller 2007). There can be little doubt that most culturally significant artefacts now make substantial appeal to the visual and to overlook this would threaten their integrity as objects of study.

Significant challenges remain to be faced. It is unquestionably far more fashionable nowadays to deal with visual material – for example to offer more attractive-sounding study programmes – and informal analysis of 'images' and their possible connections to the 'texts' they appear with may, to the beginning student or multimodal novice, seem both easier and more interesting than a detailed linguistic analysis.

But here lurks a considerable danger. The analysis of image-text combinations is *more* difficult than linguistic analysis alone for the simple reason that there is 'more' to do!

Instead of the analysis of one (already extremely complex) semiotic mode, the would be analyst is faced instead with the task of accounting not only for *several* (already quite complex) semiotic modes but also for their *combinations*. This involves a range of uncharted territories whose complexities we are just beginning to discover. As a consequence, and despite growing interest, our understanding of multimodality is still under-developed and there is a considerable need for further research. Accounting for text-image relationships can also be seen as offering a finely focused point of entry into this more general area of concern.

PART II

Visual Contexts

In this part of the book, we focus on some contexts where both text and images coexist and – our main interest – combine to provide new meaning-possibilities. For each of the contexts that we examine we will introduce the main approaches and disciplines that are involved. Three basic functions for discourse traditionally proposed from a linguistic perspective are *informing*, *narrating*, and *persuading*. We will focus here on the latter two, taking in approaches to text-image relations in these two broad environments of use.

Each context considered has explicitly raised the relationship between text and image as in some way constitutive for its concerns. Often we find discussions where the coexistence of image and text in a symbiotic relationship is singled out as an 'essential', sometimes even 'unique', property of the media addressed – even though *all* of the different approaches we address are of this kind.

Thus, one of the main motivations for looking at a *range* of contexts here and not simply diving into one of them, or even not differentiating at all and taking examples from everywhere at once, is that we will see that the different contexts bring about rather different practices for combining texts and images. Far too often there is talk of 'text-image relationships' as if this is already known to be a consistent single area of investigation. Looking more closely at different contexts shows us more of the diversity of relationships to be considered.

Another motivation is that we will see how different disciplines approach the text-image question in their own domains of interest. In fact, many of the individual areas addressed have extensive literatures of their own. We will introduce the principal research in each area, providing pointers for how to take study of the respective areas further. Disciplines bring with them particular ways of framing their questions and defining what constitutes a good answer. We thus find issues raised by text-image relationships highlighted with respect to a variety of methods.

This is an important benefit of making sure that we see how the text-image relationship has been addressed from a wide range of perspectives. Many points of overlap in approaches will become evident – sometimes these points of overlap have been noted, sometimes not, because disciplinary boundaries tend to act as institutional mountain ranges or rivers preventing communication. When working within one research tradition, even a new one, there is often enough to be done just keeping up with that tradition rather than going on trading (or raiding) expeditions to others.

But this can also be problematic of course. None of the disciplines involved have all the answers. One of the goals pursued here will therefore be to show that there are places of contact, of overlap, where it would be beneficial, sometimes even essential, to open up the channel of communication further. Doing this raises many exciting challenges – there is an immense range of possibilities to follow. Achieving such connections is a large part of the challenge facing text-image relation research to come.

MODULE II

Visual Narratives

A brief introduction to narrative

Visual narrative is alive and well – in fact, it is booming. And this is the case for static media just as much as it is for dynamic media such as film. This sets an interesting challenge. One of the most prominent fields of application of text-image relations is in the service of performing visual narratives. But telling stories is something which is often taken as *inherently requiring* temporal development. As one prominent narrative theorist would have it: "narratives, in the most simple sense, are stories that take place in time" (Berger 1997: 6).

On this basis, the very existence of 'visual narratives' can already be seen as evidence against any notion such as Lessing's set out in Unit 1 ('What we will be examining and what we will *not* be examining', p. 23) that visuals can (or should) be restricted to expressing meanings that are narrowly spatial and 'atemporal'. This makes it even more important to consider how this comes about: what is it about static visuals, text and narrative that allows them to function together and, evidently, function together so well – despite the intrinsic staticness of the medium? How do these kinds of static entities 'tell stories' at all?

Before starting, though, we can note that there are some ways of bringing visual depictions and stories together that we will *not* be considering. For example, because our focus is on the role of text-image relationships, we will not be particularly concerned with visual narrative that works by 'suggestion' alone since this violates our self-imposed restriction at the outset to *co-present* text and images working together. After all, if we see a picture of someone falling off a horse, then it is no wonder that a whole host of further ideas be entertained: why was the person on the horse, where did they come from, what happened next, where was the accident, was it an accident? – and so on and so forth. All of these efforts can be seen in terms of attempting to come up with a *narrative* to make the objects and events fit. This kind of narrative construction work is not essentially concerned with text-image relations, however.

Some visual artefacts are even constructed precisely to *encourage* such work – for example, by placing various otherwise unmotivated 'clues' in an image that something more is going on than a simple depiction. Classical illustrations of religious or mythological themes often function in this way as well, placing sufficiently clear 'references' to known stories in an image that viewers can fill in a host of missing information and thereby relate the image to the story even without an explicit indication given by a title (which *would*, of course, fall into our area of concern since the title and the image would then be co-present).

We do not consider such interpretative work here for two principal reasons. First, semiotically and visually, this is a relatively simple kind of interpretative process requiring only the prerequisite background knowledge. That knowledge might itself have demanded considerable skill and experience to collect, but that is a separate issue. Second, this kind of interpretation is often achieved without the support of text-image combinations – it therefore falls outside our main focus in any case.

There is another, very common way of suggesting that a narrative interpretation is relevant, however, that *will* be of central concern to us. This is where some image under analysis occurs in a context that (a) demands narrative interpretation and (b) is *itself materially co-present* with the image being interpreted. The most obvious example here is a *sequence* of static images arranged to 'tell a story'. This kind of artefact is, it will turn out, completely different from the case of suggesting a story with a single image. This difference is often underestimated and the study of, for example, the moving image is then considered to be a natural extension and similar affair to the study of single images. Although there are overlaps in how the two modes operate, there are also radical differences in their 'semiotic potential'. As we shall see in more detail in the following two units, sequences of *static* images then stand some way between these two extremes and give rise to a host of sophisticated uses of text-image combinations for visual storytelling that we will need to address.

So much for setting the scene – which, as we will see, is also one of the usual components of narrative. In this and the following two units we explore several issues raised by the phenomenon of visual narrative – that is, the use of visual materials in 'storytelling' – and its particular consequences for shaping and using text-image combinations.

NARRATIVE AS SUCH AND VISUAL NARRATIVE IN PARTICULAR

Nowadays, narrative constitutes a research area that is attracting considerable attention. Diverse research directions have adopted 'narrative' as their main organising theme and employ it for a broad range of research concerns ranging from the study of myth through to forms of explanations for science and cultural studies. This growth of awareness of narrative is sometimes referred to as the 'narrative turn'; we will hear more of this below. In general the narrative turn involves a broad-ranging reassessment of the role of narrative in a variety of cultural projects. Following the narrative turn, it has become increasingly commonplace to use narrative as a metaphor for understanding how both social practices and individual 'sense-making' operate. Alongside this development, there has also of course been the explosive growth in the acceptance of the role played by *visual* depictions in any case. We are concerned with precisely this explosion in this book all along. These two facets then come together in the exploration of *visual narrative* as a relatively recent, but already flourishing, new research 'tradition'.

Within this 'tradition' there is room for a perhaps surprising diversity of approaches. In fact, there are already signs of 'disciplinary' boundaries emerging between approaches and their particular areas of concern. As always, such boundaries serve to direct attention along certain channels of communication rather than others. To work against this tendency, therefore, in this unit we will briefly consider narrative in general before going on in the following two units to consider two such newly emerging 'traditions' of narrative visual research – first, children's picturebooks, and second, comics, or 'sequential art'. Although both of these areas of research are centrally concerned with visual narrative, they have, until very recently, hardly interacted with each another at all, despite many apparent similarities.

There are several useful sources of frameworks that can be drawn on to address the specifically narratival nature of visual narratives. These naturally come from 'beyond' approaches to the visual – studies of single visual artefacts, such as paintings and other single artworks, are still relevant but do not provide very much information on just what makes something a *narrative*. This is important because when we know what a medium is trying to do – that is, what it is being used for – we can start uncovering more of the relevant distinctions that are being made, both visually, textually and in combination. Moreover, knowing what the medium is being used for allows us to motivate such distinctions in terms of their functions in that medium. Thus, if we consider text and images to be working together in the service of narrative, it will be beneficial to have a good working knowledge of what narrative as such entails.

Two complementary frameworks addressing narrative will be described here. The first is drawn primarily from literary studies – particularly approaches taken in *narratology*; the second is drawn from linguistics – particularly text linguistics and *genre* research. Both have paid considerable attention to questions of just what a narrative is, what it does, and how it can be described. We then bring these together for the purpose of exploring visual narratives and their workings in the following two units. Both kinds of framework provide important insights for when we extend our attention from 'traditional' narrative – typically seen as, and occurring in the form of, text – and move on to multimodal combinations of text and images.

We begin, though, with some further basic observations on the nature of visual material and its interpretation as a foundation for 'narrative' uses of that material, picking up again the observation made in Unit 1 about taking seriously the ability of static media to express temporal relationships.

STATIC MEDIUM *VS*. DYNAMIC INTERPRETATION

We have already seen in our discussion of Lessing in Unit 1, and his proposals for a 'proper' division of labour for the arts, that there are problems in equating material properties of a medium and just what can be done with that medium. Traditionally, this was discussed with reference to poetry and painting as archetypal examples of the textual and visual modes respectively. Under such a view, the very term 'visual narrative' would seem contradictory. Understanding both just *why* this is not the case and *how* visual narrative works then takes on an important role in our broader task of exploring text-image relationships.

After all, painting, for example, is really and truly a *static* medium: paintings just don't move – it is as simple as that! But this physical material property of the artefacts themselves actually says surprisingly little about just what one can *do with* paintings. The desire to express stories visually in painting and similar artefacts is probably as old as images themselves – that is, at least as old as 30,000 years in the case of cave paintings, although exact dating is still a difficult issue. The meaning of such paintings is also much debated, although some kind of symbolic, religious or magical use is generally assumed.

However, whenever such images contain depictions compatible with actions and movement, it is difficult to believe that they would not be interpreted by some, if not all, of their originally intended recipients as being embedded within some stories of action – either explicitly by being used as visual material during actual events of storytelling (perhaps embedded within other rituals but stories nonetheless) or implicitly, by seeing and understanding what is depicted in terms of sequences of activities known from real-life experience (or other stories).

By the time we reach more recent times, visual artefacts with strong narrative components are easy to find – one example is the well-known Bayeux Tapestry, where we have entered an explicitly narrative visual realm. The tapestry, thought to have been created sometime in the 1070s, shows the story of the decisive battle between Normans and Saxons at Hastings in 1066. Figure 3.1 shows an excerpt depicting the death of Harold, Earl of Wessex. We have

Figure 3.1   Bayeux Tapestry: Scene 57, Harold's Death

here visual depictions and textual additions that are mutually related by being placed in close proximity. The texts are placed above or near the actions they appear to describe or evaluate.

This artefact is obviously a narrative, but is also clearly visual, static and contains text. Some have even gone so far as to claim this as one of the first 'comics', which raises some tricky issues of definition that we return to below – is something a comic just because it combines text and images to tell a story? Probably not – especially as we shall see some rather different kinds of text-image combinations employed in the service of storytelling as we proceed. But the question of just *how* one should go about defining and delimiting forms of expression that combine different 'modalities', such as texts and images, is a worthwhile one to take further and discuss. The questions that need to be asked here lead directly to many fundamental issues (cf. Meskin 2007).

The Bayeux Tapestry also lets us raise important issues for visual narrative in general that we need to address, at least briefly, before getting started both on the nature of narrative and the particular kinds of visual narrative we will explore. For example: in what sense, precisely, is the tapestry 'static'? Although it is clearly static at the level of material form, our interaction and reception of the tapestry introduces a whole host of distinct but related *dynamic* phenomena. Let us list some of these explicitly.

Dynamic depiction in static materials

To begin, the events being depicted in the tapestry are clearly not static: we do not have pictures of people standing around, of sitting on horses, views of the sea and hills, and so on. We have instead highly dynamic events – even, in the present case, an arrow reaching its target and people riding horses and hitting each other with large heavy objects. The manipulation of visual *vectors* in an image is a standard way of giving rise to such dynamic interpretations. Visual vectors result whenever there are explicit or implicit 'lines' created by the visual forms in an image; such lines may be made up of rows of similar objects, the direction of limbs or other prominent edges or linear objects, or be implied by depicted movement, gaze and so on.

Many researchers have described the range of interpretations that can be made of images containing vectors. For example, the framework for visual description and its functional interpretation developed by the socio-semioticians Gunther Kress and Theo van Leeuwen (Kress and van Leeuwen 2006 [1996]) that we mentioned in Unit 2 ('What *are* text-image relationships?', p. 44) uses such vectors to distinguish different classes of visually expressed 'events'. They even term visual representations containing movement vectors *narrative* visual processes because of their potential contribution to narrative-like constructions. Abstract visual representations of events of this kind – or as we see them called in later units, 'visual transitivity frames' or 'visual process configurations' – are seen as Gestalt units that impose particular ways of seeing on a visual depiction as a whole. They thus ascribe particular 'functional' roles to the 'masses' and 'forms' visually present in the image.

We can see this illustrated in Figure 3.2, which shows a sketch of one of the images at the beginning of Maurice Sendak's *Where the Wild Things Are* (1963), a very well-known

Figure 3.2 Sketch of an image from Maurice Sendak's *Where the Wild Things Are* (1963) showing the presence of an action (motion) and participants (Actor and Goal). The circumstances or *setting* is given by the background with respect to which the motion occurs

children's picturebook from which we will take several examples in the units following. For such an image we can note first that it exhibits a clear visual dynamism of its own, despite being static. We show this in the figure with the help of the explicit vector visualising the direction of flight of the main character, who is called Max. Max's movement is carried by the orientation of his limbs, his overall orientation, and the fact that he is in the air (an inherently 'unstable' position: at least for small boys).

The presence of a vector means that Kress and van Leeuwen's 'narrative' visual process applies. This classification in turn requires an 'actor' and a 'process', which are clearly given in this case by the source of the vector, Max, and the motion vector of his movement itself. Kress and van Leeuwen's classification also allows for an optional visual 'goal' – in the present case such a goal is arguably present in the form of the dog, which is both the object of the motion and of Max's gaze. Max is then 'actor' and the dog 'goal' as suggested in the figure. Several further classes of visual events are described by Kress and van Leeuwen, all based on the presence or absence of particular types of visual vectors.

More generally concerning such visual depictions, we can cite the words of the prominent visual theorist Rudolf Arnheim, who writes:

> *Visual experience is dynamic . . .* What a person or animal perceives is not only an arrangement of objects, of colours and shapes, or movements and sizes. It is, perhaps first of all, an interplay of directed tensions. These tensions are not something the observer adds, for reasons of his [*sic*] own, to static images. Rather, these tensions are as inherent in any precept as size, shape, location, or colour.
>
> (Arnheim 1974: 11)

Static visuals are therefore quite capable of suggesting movement (cf. Gombrich 1982, Cutting 2002).

Dynamic perception of static visuals

Returning to the tapestry, it is not static in a second way as well: even the process of its perception is far from static. It is sometimes stated in descriptions of the visual and its differences from text that text has to be read in sequence while pictures one takes in 'all at once', 'as a whole', or 'simultaneously'. The Bayeux Tapestry shows how unlikely such a model is: the tapestry is, after all, over 70 metres long! It is therefore necessary to consider rather more carefully the interaction between a recipient and the visual material that that recipient is responding to.

The tapestry does appear to be divided into 'scene'-like units where particular events significant for the story are depicted, but even these are not going to be seen 'all at once' because this is not how human visual perception works. Whereas some aspects of the composition and distribution of forms and masses in the visual field are perceived in a Gestalt fashion (cf. Arnheim 1982), details need to be selected sequentially by moving the very small area of fine focus of the eye to collect information for interpretation. This is not a conscious process and is usually not subject to control; we return to this important issue and the use of *eye-tracking* methodologies for studying text-image relations in Unit 13 later. As most more careful discussions of pictures and images of all kinds note, human attention is highly selective and moves rapidly over the material in the visual field, switching from one thing to the next *even in the process of perceiving* what we are seeing.

There is then a need to be far more cautious about any statements of the form that static pictorial depictions are available and processed 'all at once': they clearly are not. This is an important result for all areas of visual research and not just narrative. Here, however, we use it to make a further point: the temporal order of points where the eyes are looking in an image *has nothing to do with the temporal information conveyed pictorially.* That is, just because we look at one part of a picture and then another part of the picture, this says nothing about our assumption of the order in which the depicted elements occur. Again, considering the Bayeux Tapestry extract should make this clear: where do people look first and what relation could that have to the events being portrayed?

Generally research on visual perception has established that particular areas of contrast, corners and similar visually distinctive areas will attract attention (that is, the eyes will place these areas in the area of the retina with maximum resolution and 'fixate', gathering information). Also, and for fairly obvious evolutionary reasons, people are 'hardwired' to recognise human faces and to examine them for information about their intentions, state of mind, where *they* are looking (perhaps they have just seen an approaching sabre-tooth tiger) and so on: human figures and particularly faces therefore attract attention even before one is at all 'aware' consciously of what is being seen.

This has important consequences. Researchers in various fields, visual narrative among them, have in the past been tempted to make suggestions that visual comprehension can be tracked by considering the 'reading path' that a viewer or reader of some material follows. The reading path is the course that someone's gaze will follow while interpreting that visual material. There are some broad and relatively robust results of this nature – for example, it is known that there is a reliable correlation between the general direction of a reading path and the direction of writing in some cultures. Thus readers (or rather, writers) of English will tend to visually track images from left to right, while writers of Arabic will visually track images from right to left.

Fuhrman and Boroditsky (2010), for example, compare English and Hebrew speakers and conclude: "Written languages appear to organise their readers' attention in a vector from where text usually begins to where it usually ends" *even in entirely nonlinguistic contexts*. Subsequently, for English writers, 'earlier' timepoints are expected on the left and 'later' timepoints on the right; for Hebrew writers, the expectation is reversed. There is therefore an association between temporal order and language writing direction: the written word organises visual behaviour and such correlations can have narrative consequences.

Narrative consequences

Events seen on the left by a left-to-right reader may well be assumed to be temporally prior to events shown on the right. But it is important to separate out this kind of more abstract interpretation from the simple fact of a reading path placing an order on where the eyes happen to look. If there is a large colourful object on the right of an image, then the eyes will probably be drawn to it first; there may then be a much smaller, less prominent figure on the left of the image that will be attended to afterwards. But, regardless of this 'gaze path', the assumption may still be made that the order of temporal succession is from left to right.

This is illustrated well in another example from Sendak. In Figure 3.3, we see two consecutive doublepage spreads from *Where the Wild Things Are* in which Max encounters his first Wild Thing. Interesting here is the design of the entire spread *and* its relation to the previous page. Within the previous spread the centre of attention can be seen clearly to be

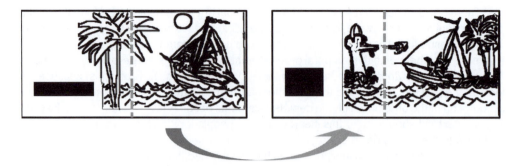

Figure 3.3 Sketched version of two consecutive doublepage spreads from Maurice Sendak's (1963) *Where the Wild Things Are* showing relative positions of Max and a visually prominent monster; the pages also show the central fold and the position of textblocks

on Max. Moreover, as the page is turned Max is found again at the same spot – then, when the page turn is complete, the viewer/reader is confronted with a far more visually prominent monster over on the left-hand side. This can be expected to cause some surprise – only *after* the page-turn does the reader encounter the monster on the left. Nevertheless, when the page turn is complete, the usual conventions of temporal relationships may apply.

We have to be careful, therefore, in considering notions of reading paths and their consequences for interpretation. An event on the left may be interpreted as occurring before an event on the right, but this is not 'because' we first look at the event on the left. The relationship is more subtle and relates to considerations of visual convention. Moreover, if the visual material is not being interpreted narratively in any case, then *there may just be no interpretations of temporal sequence at all.* The eyes gather evidence for particular interpretations in the context of particular interpretative goals (see Unit 13, section 'Eye-tracking methods', p. 243). The lesson then is to be very cautious when making impressionistic claims of what readers/viewers 'do'. And, moreover, never to build theories of interpretation on such impressionistic claims. In short: if ever a phrase such as 'we would normally look at X first because it is on the left' is encountered, beware!

Visually present information will generally be extracted in an order dependent on visual salience and attention goals. It is then only *on the basis of* such information that we begin to weave together events, placing these in order, determining who is doing what to whom and so on – that is, building a story from the available material.

SO WHAT'S A STORY?

Let us now turn from these rather 'low'-level concerns – that is, what the eyes are doing – to the more abstract notion of what is being done with the visual material. We have talked of narratives and stories: what are these? And, most importantly for this unit, how have they been approached theoretically and descriptively? What do we need to know before considering specifically *visual* narrative? We address this first from the tradition of narratology and then turn to linguistic genre research.

Narratives and narratology

The study of stories as an area of research in its own right has several origins. Since storytelling seems to be a universal activity across human cultures, the role and value of such storytelling for those cultures has been much debated. Stories are used for inculcating values, for preserving a sense of history and cultural identity, for creating and maintaining myths of all kinds, and sometimes even for entertainment!

Around the beginning of the twentieth century, just as in several other areas, interest grew in exploring the notion of the story in a more systematic fashion. Certain scientific methods seemed to offer powerful new tools for gaining understanding of their objects of study. One such was the demonstrated success of botany as increasingly fine classifications of complex plants began to reveal underlying regularities, formalised in the now well-known classes of species and their varied subtypes. Subdividing objects under study into parts and wondering how the parts were inter-related in a functioning whole also seemed to offer a promising line of investigation in other fields. This was even attempted for stories in the work of Vladimir Propp. Propp was one of the Russian formalists, a school of thought on aesthetics and form that emerged in the early years of the twentieth century. Russian formalism subsequently had a significant impact on many areas of analysis where narrative concerns were raised.

Propp's best-known result was his characterisation of the 'morphology' of the folktale (cf. Propp 1968, first published in Russian in 1928). Perhaps surprisingly, the sense of 'morphology' appealed to here involves botany as just suggested and not its now rather common use in linguistics. Folktales had long been considered of interest for comparative cultural and historical studies. Examining them more formally was therefore considered a promising avenue of research for revealing deeper commonalities across cultures as manifestations of human nature. In his study, Propp succeeded in identifying recurring patterns of units and functions that appeared to occur in all the folktales that he analysed.

We won't examine his proposals in detail since what is important for us here is not the framework itself but the significance his work had for later research. The very fact that it appeared possible to apply a kind of formal, structural analysis to abstract cultural artefacts, such as folktales, had an immense influence on the emergence of structuralist approaches to culture, to literature, to ethnography, to linguistics, to writing filmscripts and much more – particularly in the 1950s and 1960s when translations of Propp's study became more generally accessible and well known. The seminal work of Roland Barthes introduced in Unit 2 ('Getting the ball rolling: Roland Barthes', p. 31) can also be seen as an outgrowth of this tradition.

As far as storytelling, or narrative, is concerned, Propp's analysis of parts and structures enabled a systematic distinction to be drawn between *what* story was being told and *how* that story was being presented. And both facets of the whole could be examined for regularly occurring properties and organisations. For example, considering the story being told, Propp argued that a recurring property of the folktale was a trajectory, or development, whereby a principal protagonist encounters some difficulty or problem, has to face a series of setbacks or adversaries, but finally overcomes these and manages to reimpose a state of equilibrium.

This overall structure provides for a number of roles, or 'narrative functions', that need to be filled when pursuing a narrative. These include the main proponent him or herself (the hero or heroine), enemies that attempt to hold up progress, helpers or teachers who intervene when the main character is about to give up, and so on. As set out and illustrated in its most popular form by Vogler (1998), this structure forms the mainstay of a considerable majority (some would suggest all!) of mainstream Hollywood films and is almost treated as a key to commercial success. Nowadays, to talk of a film or TV series 'story arc' has become common-place when talking about narratives of this kind, showing just how far early academic and theoretical studies have now worked their way through into everyday life.

The availability of Propp's work and the spread in the 1960s of structuralist accounts developing from it also supported a steady increase in its applications to verbal art in literary analysis. Many subsequently tried to define what a story, or narrative, is by appealing to the necessary properties of narrative trajectories. If there is no character that undergoes a challenge and then, after difficulties, resolves it, then we do not really have a story in the sense intended. After all, if someone relates a sequence of utterances such as "I went to the super-market. I bought some milk. I went home again", probably the only likely response is "And? So what?" – a sequence of events has been recounted, but it is unclear what purpose the recount is to serve. If on the other hand, we hear:

> I went to the supermarket to buy some milk. A huge truck was parked in front of the store, I couldn't get in. I argued with the truck driver for ages and finally managed to get the truck moved. I could then buy the milk and go home.

while not being in danger of a nomination for a Nobel prize for literature, we *have* heard a story with a point and are more likely to express sympathy or at least a token nod of interest, rather than wondering why we have just been told what we have. This means that we clearly need something more than just a sequence of events if we are going to accept that we have heard a story.

Just what the nature of this 'more' is has led to a substantial body of research, mostly characterised nowadays as constituting the field of **narratology**. Narratology attempts to unravel just what the necessary conditions for being a narrative are as well as exploring in detail how narratives are constructed, how they function, and how they have the effects that they do on their audiences.

Several distinctions are considered basic. For example, the novelist E. M. Forster distinguished early on between 'story' and 'plot' in a style owing much to Russian formalists such as Propp. His definition and examples are now often cited when considering what goes into a narrative:

> Let us define a plot. We have defined a story as a narrative of events arranged in their time-sequence. A plot is also a narrative of events, the emphasis falling on causality. 'The king died, and then the queen died.' is a story. 'The king died, and then the queen died of grief' is a plot. The time-sequence is preserved, but the sense of causality overshadows it. Or again: 'The queen died, no one knew why, until it was discovered that it was through grief at the death of the king.' This is a plot with a mystery in it, a form capable of high development. It suspends the time-sequence, it moves us as far away from the story as its limitations will allow.

(Forster 2005 [1927]: 87)

Terms and their definitions constitute a difficult issue within narratology. Variations and terminological debates abound. What Forster is calling 'story' in this quotation, for example, we also termed 'recount' above. And, in fact, 'story' is now rarely used in the neutral sense that Forster assumes for it here: a child who asks to be told a story and then receives our first milk-buying episode above is probably not going to be very happy; with the second version, perhaps more so. We will not consider such debates here, however – the relevant lesson lies in the basic distinctions drawn, which are usually sufficiently clear for our present needs. So, instead, we will emphasise just those areas of concern that will enable us to follow the discussion into visual territory.

The main focus points we take on below from narrative and its study are already present in Forster's suggestions, at least in embryonic form. We address the nature of the relations between events in a narrative (causation), the distinct kinds of time that narratives build on (double-time structuring), and given or withheld access to information and states of knowledge and the attributed *sources* of such information (focalisation and perspective). The main point of departure for most discussions of narrative and narratology today is that of the French literary researcher, Gérard Genette (Genette 1980, 1988), Seymour Chatman (Chatman 1978) and Gerald Prince (Prince 1982). General introductions to narratology can be found in, for example, Herman (2009), Fludernik (2009) and Bal (2009 [1985]).

Causation

We can see in Forster's description above that he puts the emphasis strongly on some kind of entailed 'causality' that holds between the events described, rather than simply a temporal sequence. The kind of causality at issue here is itself interesting since it is certainly not the causality of physics. This has also been discussed at length in narratology, aesthetics and philosophy. What we appear to have is a kind of 'contingent' causality: when two events are related temporally in a narrative, the first may not have literally caused the second, but we still have a sense that the second may not have occurred unless the first had occurred, that the two events have some kind of connection that is far stronger than simply occurring one after the other 'by chance'.

This strong sense of connection is one of the reasons why the model of narrative now finds application in several non-fictional areas as a *mode of explanation*. Narratives appear to impose order and sense on events, a sense that is usually strongly connected with goals and purposes. There are therefore models of narrative explanation in history, sociology, the news media and even geography and climate change (cf., e.g., Czarniawska 2004, Johnson-Cartee 2005, Coffin 2006).

This is a result of the so-called **narrative turn** that we mentioned above and which has been taken up in several disciplines traditionally quite unrelated to 'storytelling' (Fisher 1987). Human beings are so well versed in understanding narratives that explanations couched in narrative terms can seem revealing and useful. The question of whether such 'explanations' are *really* explanations (if there can even be talk of 'really' in such contexts) – that is, of whether they pick out genuine properties of the phenomena being described – is a separate one, one which we will not pursue here although, as acts of persuasion, such narratives can certainly appear visually as well as verbally and so can be subjected to the same kinds of analysis that we describe here.

Time

Another aspect that Forster mentions is nowadays considered definitional for narratives proper: that is the fact that the temporal order of the events as related and the temporal order of the events themselves can diverge. When we learn first the queen died and only later that it was as a response to the prior death of the king, the order of events in the 'story world' has been reversed in the telling. Many narratologists take this 'double time structure' as *the* defining property of the objects and performances that they study. If one can only recount elements in the order that they occurred, then clearly the possibilities for adding interest into the recount are severely limited. This interacts closely with the next area we discuss, the access to knowledge or information that a narrative provides.

Allowing recounted time and event time to diverge opens up the door for a host of important narrative techniques, such as, using the now common terminology of film for convenience, flashforwards, flashbacks and so on. It is also possible to vary the 'speed', or duration, of the two time tracks independently of one another. For example, whereas the events in the world of the story might take several years, the narration might jump over them in a phrase – "Several years later, I needed milk again". Or, conversely, the events in the story might be of rather short duration, while their depiction in text may take considerably more time due to every last detail of the action being picked out for description, plus perhaps aspects of the situation, the way the sun was shining, the angle of the rain, the reflections in the supermarket window, and so on. This potential allows the storyteller to speed up narration for dramatic effect, slow it down, establish various rhythms, delay development for suspense, and so on.

The existence of two temporal orders is described with a range of terms but is not itself controversial. In addition to Forster's 'story' and 'plot', largely equivalent to the Russian formalist terms 'fabula' and 'szujet', we have 'story' (*histoire*) and 'discourse' (*discours*) and finer, sometimes contested characterisations. The basic idea should, however, be clear: just because A happens after B does not mean (as illustrated here) that we have to mention A after B. Language allows us to change the order of presentation for other purposes – and the purposes of concern here are those of storytelling. Double-time structuring should actually be seen as a property of (at least) *language in general* rather than being specific to narrative: a scientific report may, for example, present the results of experiments first and only later describe what led up to the experiments and then their performance. In the context of scientific reports, however, we do not talk of a flashforward (although it might become so if turned into a film about a scientific discovery). But for current purposes we keep our focus on narrative concerns.

Focalisation and perspective

Where we have two levels unfolding with different temporalities, this organisational feature can be put to substantially more work. For example, whereas events may exist in some kind of abstract space of equality, a God's-eye view where all are accessible, their presentation within a narrative with a specific temporal unfolding is quite different. Only certain information is made accessible at any time. Moreover, the question of who has access to the information in order that it can be related gives rise to yet further variation and potential for narrative effects.

For example, a story can be related from the God's-eye view perspective, where the narrator can see everything and go inside characters' heads as required to say what they are thinking or desiring, or the story can subject itself to limitations, of *not* knowing (or at least as presenting itself as not knowing) just what some character thinks or is up to with the actions they are performing. All of these variations fall under the central narratological area of **focalisation**, often described in terms of distinctions such as 'who sees' *vs.* 'who tells'. A narrator, for example, as the one who is telling the story, may well narrate events from the internal perspective of one of his or her characters.

Several 'degrees of focalisation' are introduced by Genette in order to describe these differing possibilities and their narrative effects. *Zero focalisation* is the description of the author who potentially knows everything about the details of their story – what characters can see and feel as well as what they cannot. *Internal focalisation* shows the internal workings of one of the characters and the view, perception, construction that that character has of the storyworld. *External focalisation*, in contrast, is *in* the storyworld but *external* to any of the characters – as Jahn (2005: 174) usefully characterises it, a presentation "restricted to behaviourist report and outside views, basically reporting what would be visible to a camera". Thus, an author (zero focalisation) cannot actually see what is in the world he or she describes ("who tells?"); in contrast, the characters in that story can well see (and hear, smell, feel, etc.) that world. Chatman introduces here the useful terms *slant* for authorial shaping of the depiction and *filtering* for shaping brought about by the views of particular characters.

The area of focalisation is one of the most hotly contested in narratology exhibiting considerable variation in the definition of terms. One basic choice is whether to adopt the view of Genette or the revision of this offered by Bal (2009 [1985]): the description by Jahn (2005) sets out the terms of the debate clearly, but the matter itself remains somewhat complex. Bal's account is held to be perhaps more discriminating for actual cases of literary analysis, but opinions differ. We will leave it there for now.

There are also variations possible on the basis of just who gets to speak. A story might be narrated by an external narrator – someone who just tells the story; the story might however also be narrated by (or be presented as if narrated by) one of the characters in the story. The latter case corresponds to so-called 'first person' narratives. More complex variations are possible. For example, a character in the story might tell a further embedded story and in that story either the same character might occur (again either as just one of the characters or as the one telling the story) or some completely different set of characters – and so on, *ad infinitum*. The potential of such 'framing' narratives has been used in literature through the ages and in many cultures. Various technical terms are introduced for these possibilities as well, and these in turn have led to considerable discussion.

The distinctions build on the old notion taken over from Ancient Greek writings and rhetoric of *diegesis*. Traditionally diegesis (telling a story) contrasts with mimesis (showing a story). Some arts, such as literature, naturally correspond to diegesis, while others, theatre or film, may have more aspects of mimesis. Regardless of whether these distinctions can be made watertight, however, we get the following labels: a first-person narration is termed *homodiegetic*, a third-person narration is termed in contrast *heterodiegetic*. If the narrator is immersed in the world of the action, then we have *intradiegetic* narration; if not, then we have *extradiegetic* narration.

The main purpose of this profusion of terminology is to offer terms that allow distinct literary styles and techniques to be identified, described and discriminated from one another for the purposes of aesthetic analysis of authors, of historical periods, of changes in literary conventions and so on. Thus the utility of individual variants of narratological theory should, as is usually the case, be seen both with respect to how well they get the job of literary analysis done and with respect to specific research questions. Since that is not our purpose here, we will not need to follow the lines of argument and debate further at this point. The characterisations we have seen so far recur in almost all narratological accounts, albeit with slight rearrangements and perhaps varying terms. The *phenomena* at issue should now at least be relatively clear.

One last consequence of the separation of the story and how it is presented is critical to our present concerns, however: the selection of medium of expression for telling a story is considered free. That is, a story can be presented in very different media. Although narratology was traditionally, and to a significant extent still is, focused on literary works and 'storytelling', there has been increasing interest in recent years in considering narratology 'across media' (cf. Ryan 2004). The fundamental premise for this move was already present in Barthes:

> The narratives of the world are numberless. Narrative is first and foremost a prodigious variety of genres, themselves distributed amongst different substances. . . . Able to be carried by articulated language, spoken or written, fixed or moving images, gestures and the ordered mixture of all these substances; narrative is present in myth, legend, fable, tale, novella, epic, history, tragedy, drama, comedy, mime, painting . . . stained glass windows, cinema, comics, news item, conversation.
>
> (Barthes 1977 [1966]: 79)

Thus narratives are seen as a certain kind of social behaviour that can be characterised in terms of certain patterns of organisation and social functions – but how those narratives are expressed, whether in language, in visuals, or a mixture is unspecified. This is then where the obvious connection to visuality and to text-image combinations comes in.

NARRATIVES AS A LINGUISTIC GENRE

Stories are not only analysed in literary discussion and talked about in everyday life, they are of course also *told* in everyday life – this means that storytelling is a cultural practice typically involving language, which makes it fair game for study as a *linguistic* phenomenon. Seminal research on the structure of stories from this perspective was carried out by the sociolinguist William Labov and colleagues in the 1960s and 1970s. Labov and Waletzky (1978), for example, analysed the kinds of stories told by members of various subcultures in North American inner cities, particularly New York. One of the results of this research was a refined abstract model of narratives that also made predictions concerning the linguistic forms that occur and their placement within a narrative as a whole.

Even informally produced stories of the kind Labov and Waletzky studied were found to exhibit regular properties. The patterns discovered were reminiscent of some of Propp's descriptions and consisted of optional stages setting the scene, the raising of problems to be resolved, resolutions to those problems, and optional codas wrapping things up, restoring the equilibrium. This model has served as the basis for many subsequent linguistic research efforts that have progressively tried to provide more precise and accurate models of naturally occurring stories. Such research looks at stories by relating them to the intended purpose of the 'narrative' and establishing the distinct kinds of linguistic expressions that can be found across the various stages of a narrative.

One of the most developed accounts of this kind is that pursued in the framework of **genre research** in systemic-functional linguistics by Jim Martin and colleagues (e.g., Martin and Plum 1997, Martin 1992, Martin and Rose 2008). Very broadly, genre is one way of describing how particular styles of 'design' – be that linguistic or other forms of communicative behaviour – go together with particular communicative functions. In the case of linguistic texts, the styles of design are linguistic choices made from within the linguistic system.

More technically, standard accounts of genre define genre in terms of two facets: (1) collections of "typified rhetorical actions based in recurrent situations" (Miller 1984) and (2) ordered elements exhibiting consistent formal features of expressions (Swales 1990, Martin

1992); a brief overview of many of the approaches to genre can be found in Bateman (2008). In short:

> A genre in a linguistic sense is a socially recognised class of texts (either spoken or written) that is used for a specific social purpose and which has a regularly occurring structural organisation recognisable by virtue of distinctive patterns of linguistic phenomena.

Different kinds of communicative purposes play out differently and have varied 'stages' that can also be identified and described by virtue of the linguistic options taken up. In a sense, this is a modern version of the original Beginning, Middle and End literary structure going back to Aristotle. It also places narrative against the background of a much broader range of genres, asking to what extent they relate to one another and whether particular 'subtypes' or subgenres can be identified on the basis of differing linguistic patterns.

Tying the recognition of genres more closely to linguistic forms as a linguistic approach requires is beneficial for several reasons. Most importantly, perhaps, it allows us to move beyond impressionistic classifications. Applying detailed analyses of the linguistic properties of the artefacts explored offers not only a sharper view of how narratives (and other genres) are organised but also shows how narratives relate to other kinds of genres by virtue of similarities and differences in the patterns of linguistic features that can be found. This allows genre analysis to probe deeper, mapping out entire *families* of related genres that differ with respect to the fine-grained linguistic options and staging that they support.

The repertoire of genres available in a culture is now considered by many to go some way towards defining that culture (Martin 1992, Kress 1993). This gives an important path of connection to some of the rather broader uses of 'discourse' that one finds in areas such as cultural studies – for further discussion, see, for example, Spitzmüller and Warnke (2011).

Some examples of related genres are suggested in the diagram in Figure 3.4 from Martin and Rose (2008). Each of the 'bubbles' in the figure denotes a particular grouping of texts that share recognisable features and so which may be treated as belonging to a single 'genre'.

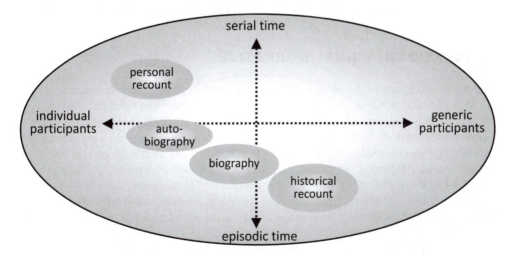

Figure 3.4 A map of more or less closely related genres from the area of *recount genres* from Martin and Rose (2008: 133, Figure 3.6)

Bubbles that are close to each other share more of their linguistic features than bubbles that are further apart: for this reason, Martin and Rose refer to this as a *topological* perspective on genre.

The underlying idea of topological descriptions is that instances of language use are classified along several dimensions simultaneously – just two are shown in the figure, the preference for serial time *vs.* episodic time and between individual, personalised participants and generic participants; in general very many more dimensions would be considered. The diagram shows how 'far apart' instances of language use are from each other on each of the dimensions modelled. It is perfectly possible for instances to be very close to each other on some dimensions and far apart on others. Genres are defined as conventional *labels* for particular populated regions in the overall space.

The topological view makes it far easier to deal with the perennial banes of genre studies: hybridisation and change. Seeing genres in an overall 'space' of genre possibilities provides a better metaphor for approaching genre growth and development than models based on strict classifications of types and subtypes (cf. Bateman 2008). Genre regions may naturally change over time as genres develop, merge, split and die.

Genre, in this more technical sense, is of considerable relevance when we move to visual narration and visual communication more generally. Genres in linguistic texts play out sequentially: these are the genre's stages. In visual media, however, these stages may be both co-present *and* expressed in different modalities. Van Leeuwen (2005b: 127–131), for example, suggests that genre itself may be a 'multimodal' entity, with various modalities being used in the different stages. The assumed relative homogeneity of choices made within a genre stage might then well be expected to apply when those choices involve forms of visual expressions as well. We will see this again applied to analysis in Unit 11. This also suggests a further function of text-image relations as one way of explaining how combined uses of different genres and differently expressed stages may co-operate.

In short, genre provides another part of our growing toolkit for approaching actual uses of text and images together – without being aware of the potential influence of genre, we would be in a far weaker position for finding similarities and identifying differences. Again, it is very useful to know as precisely as possible what some communicative artefact is trying to do and the conventions that have developed to support this *before* engaging in concrete analysis.

CONCLUSIONS: VISUAL NARRATIVE

All of the kinds of constructs we have shown in this unit for exploring and describing narrative can also be considered from the perspective of visual communication and visual narratives.

The kinds of distinctions of perspective, the assertion of contingent causality, variations in choice of narrator and expressions of time that we have seen, all stand as basic strategies available for telling stories. It is then relevant to ask how these strategies can be played out when we have more than just language at our disposal. Can we vary the perspective from which a story is told visually? Can we show different degrees of focalisation and arrange how time flows differently? And what happens to basic narratological distinctions between 'who tells?' and 'who sees?' when we are in a visual medium? Can anyone be said to 'tell' at all? Are there visual narrators?

Similarly, the attention given to the precise linguistic features required for particular stages in a linguistic genre can be extended to ask whether we can find particular *visual* properties that help do similar work. Do we find specific patterns of visual depiction when we look at different stages? Can we relate distinct stages with different patterns of focalisation, causation and so on from the narratological perspective?

All of these questions raise open issues that are currently actively debated in the research literature. Note, for example, that we cannot simply put all of the participants involved in the production and reception of a visual narrative together as 'seeing' since the role of someone viewing the narrative is quite different from that of someone forming the narrative – and this is partly what the 'who tells?' *vs.* 'who sees?' distinction is already capturing. Thus it may be useful to consider replacing 'who tells?' by 'who presents?' in order to maintain contact with the body of narratological research while still moving into non-linguistic areas.

Visual narrative: Picturebooks

The term 'picturebooks', that is, written as a single word, has emerged to refer to a family of printed artefacts that crucially rely on texts and images. Although not necessarily the case, picturebooks are generally intended for young children and adolescents. Many workers in the field suggest that picturebooks represent one of the most important sites both for socialisation and for the development of a broad range of reading skills and other kinds of literacy. Picturebooks can, however, equally be directed at an adult readership and even at both audiences simultaneously.

Researchers working on picturebooks generally distinguish picturebooks from other artefacts by virtue of their particular reliance on visual information. In one of the most detailed introductions to the field currently available, Nikolajeva and Scott define picturebooks as follows:

> The unique character of picturebooks as an art form is based on the combination of two levels of communication, the visual and the verbal. Making use of semiotic terminology, we can say that picturebooks communicate by means of two separate sign systems, the iconic and the conventional.

> (Nikolajeva and Scott 2001: 1)

Now, given that this book is concerned with all forms of this particular combination of sign-systems – the relation between text and images – we should certainly address picturebooks as well. But since we are also examining a broad range of *other* cases of text-image relations, it is less clear precisely what Nikolajeva and Scott might mean here with 'unique character'. In just what way might this be 'unique'? Or is this yet another example of the disciplinary myopia that we raised as a general problem in this and many other areas in Unit 1 ('Multimodality and "meaning multiplication"', p. 5)?

We will try to refine this issue as we proceed. However, no matter how it falls out, we can certainly expect investigations of picturebooks to engage with many of the issues of central concern to us here since their reliance on texts and images is undeniable. There is hardly a writer on the subject of picturebooks, in fact, who does not propose some kind of classification of the relations that are exhibited between text and image in picturebooks. One of the more detailed and also earliest catalogues is the following from Schwarcz (1982). Texts and images in picturebooks may be related by:

- congruency
- elaboration
- specification
- amplification
- extension
- complementation
- alternation
- deviation
- counterpoint

Many of these should already look familiar from previous units, and will become even more so as we proceed – as usual, there is a certain similarity and repetition in the kinds of relationships that are proposed here and elsewhere.

It is in fact striking just how often similar lists are suggested in different areas without, apparently, very much interaction across the distinct inquiries. One might then even go as far as to suspect that perhaps only certain kinds of relationships are possible, since it is precisely these that keep on recurring. We will explore this avenue as we proceed and also think about why this might be the case and how there might be exceptions.

Even though Schwarcz's proposal appears quite detailed, Nikolajeva and Scott nevertheless claim that: "we still lack tools for decoding the specific 'text' of picturebooks, the text created by the interaction of verbal and visual information" (2001: 4). What exactly they find to be missing is, on the one hand, a lack of specificity and reliability in proposals – for example, how do we know precisely whether we have a 'deviation' or a 'counterpoint' – and, on the other, an account of just *what consequences follow from* one or the other relationship holding – for example, if we have an 'extension', what does this do for the combined picturebook 'text' and its uptake?

Our focus here, therefore, will be on approaches which have tried to say more on this issue. In short: we want to know what kinds of relationships there are, how we can reliably identify them and tell them apart, and what they then do for the interpretation of the entire text-image combination – all considered from the specific perspective of empirical and theoretical investigations of picturebooks.

FIXING OUR PERSPECTIVE ON PICTUREBOOKS

Picturebooks are currently studied from several standpoints. Because of their primary target audience of younger readers, the most prevalent perspective has probably been the role played by picturebooks in education and early socialisation. Issues of literacy, of language acquisition, of aesthetic appreciation, of cognitive development and of acculturation and raising awareness of social issues are consequently never far from a picturebook researcher's agenda.

Another perspective, however, is that of art history – many picturebooks contain visual depictions of very high quality, inviting connections with art historical traditions as well as aesthetic evaluations drawing on their relation with other visual forms. There are also historical studies, examining how picturebooks have developed over time, and literary treatments, considering picturebooks as just one additional genre within the broader category of children's literature. For all of these areas Nikolajeva and Scott (2001) provide extensive references.

Among these, the literary tradition is one that is particularly strong in its shaping of the methodology and research questions of researchers working in the picturebook field. Methods commonly adopted include those of narratology, which we saw in the previous unit, and some particular models of literary interpretation, such as the reader-response theory of Iser (1978). Nikolajeva and Scott accordingly consider the storytelling aspect of picturebooks building on notions such as characterisation, narrative perspective, time, representations of reality or fantasy and other literary forms. Our selection of treatments for discussion is again of necessity rather narrow compared to the diverse range of literature available on picturebook research in general – as elsewhere in this book, we will focus specifically on the text-image issue.

Such a focus is possible without distorting the object of enquiry because the question of how text and images relate in picturebooks is, in one sense, largely 'orthogonal' to the other areas of concern raised. That is, from within each such perspective – be that educational, narratological, art-historical and so on – one can sensibly *also* focus on the text-image relationship. We can, for example, ask how the nature of the text-image relationship in picturebooks has changed over time. Equally, we can ask what kind of cognitive capabilities and developments are necessary in the child in order that the picturebooks be understood. There are even, as we saw in Unit 1, classical precedents in art for combining words and images for narrative effect, and so we could ask how the combination of words and images in picturebooks fits into these traditions and histories of art forms.

All such endeavours presuppose that we are able to say something useful about the text-image relationship. This is not independent of such endeavours, as each might provide useful information about the use, or processing, or aesthetics of such relationships, but the enquiry itself is logically distinct.

DEMARCATING PICTUREBOOKS FROM OTHER VISUAL NARRATIVES

The first characterisations of text-image relationships to be found when considering picture-books are entailed by the definition adopted for the notion of the picturebook itself. Some authors suggest that that definition should state that in a picturebook, pictures are *the most important elements*, while others emphasise more the *working together* of text and image elements. So we can see that we will need to say something about text-image relationships even to circumscribe what is going to be included as a picturebook and what not.

Nikolajeva and Scott employ a broad characterisation of text-image relationships as their way into categorising different kinds of picturebook. This move from talking about text-image relationships to talking about types of picturebooks is not immediately obvious and we will return to it below. However, for various reasons, it is pervasive in the picturebook literature. Entire picturebooks come to be characterised according to the text-image relationships they appear to employ. This is suggested in a diagram by Nikolajeva and Scott (2001: 12) that sets out a useful 'map' of the entire territory ranging between word and image; we repeat this here for ease of reference in Figure 4.1.

The left-hand side of the figure shows narrative artefacts, the right-hand side non-narrative artefacts. These are all arranged on a continuum between words at the top of the diagram and images at the bottom. Examples of picturebooks that are not stories are given as alphabet books and so on, where images may be associated with each letter of the alphabet – clearly for educational purposes and quite young readers. It would also be relevant to extend the discussion into this area and explicitly consider the non-narrative use of text and picture combinations for school textbooks, 'serious' comics explaining scientific and cultural theories of various kinds and so on; the literature in this area is currently undergoing very rapid growth. For the vast majority of picturebooks, fiction or non-fiction, however, the question of their relation to narrative remains an important and revealing one and so we will keep this as our focus here.

The central region of the diagram in particular marks out the abstract logical possibilities for forming relations between text and images considered relevant for picturebooks. This corresponds more or less to the list of text-image relations given by Schwarcz and reiterates some of the early lists of text-image relations proposed by Kloepfer, Nöth, Pegg and others that we saw in Unit 2. Much of the overlap between this and other frameworks comes from the basic possibilities that exist when relating two states of affairs, actions or objects in any case: that is, we can distinguish between cases of 'sameness', similarity or compatibility,

WORD

narrative text	nonnarrative text
narrative text with occasional illustrations	plate book (ABC book, illustrated poetry, nonfiction illustrated book)
narrative text with at least one picture on every spread (not dependent on image)	

symmetrical picturebook
(two mutually redundant narratives)

complementary picturebook
(words and pictures filling each other's gaps)

"expanding" or "enhancing" picturebook
(visual narrative supports verbal narrative,
verbal narrative depends on visual narrative)

"counterpointing" picturebook
(two mutually dependent narratives)

"sylleptic" picturebook (with or without words)
(two or more narratives independent of each other)

picture narrative with words (sequential)	exhibit book with words (nonnarrative, nonsequential)
picture narrative without words (sequential)	exhibit book (nonnarrative, nonsequential)
wordless picturebook	

IMAGE

Figure 4.1 A space of possibilities for relating words and images (Nikolajeva and Scott, 2001: 12)

between cases of difference or contrast, between cases of contradiction, and between cases of mutual irrelevance or non-connection.

Given this, we can then ask what possibilities for narrative expression does the medium of picturebooks provide? Should we demarcate picturebooks from other visual forms of narrative? And if so, how?

Picturebooks and comics

First, there are several points of similarity to other forms of expression, also usually mentioned in the picturebook literature. The boundaries might not always be absolutely watertight but it is still useful to make the distinctions. Most obvious, perhaps, is the possibility of a connection with comics. Both involve sequences of images, both are discussed in terms of being a combination of words and images, and both are widely described as being 'visual narrative'.

We discuss comics in their own right in Unit 5. Here, we focus specifically on some of the ways in which picturebook researchers have approached the division – even though, as Hatfield and Svonkin (2012) note in their introduction to a recent symposium on the issue, the question of demarcation between comics and picturebooks has mostly been skirted rather than addressed. This avoidance is interesting in its own right. Given that comics and picturebooks appear so unquestionably to be artefacts strongly combining text and images into integrated wholes – as in *imagetexts* in the terms of Mitchell (1994) or Sirapik (2009), or *iconotexts* as defined by Hallberg (1982) – it cannot be that the two areas have nothing to say, or teach, one another.

In both comics and picturebooks, then, the information portrayed can be distributed over the individual media employed (text, image) and so can be shared out across text and image in various ways. Interesting questions are whether this 'sharing out' can be characterised in ways that distinguish different kinds of 'imagetexts' – that is, do comics and picturebooks distribute their meanings in distinctively different, even 'unique', ways? If not, then there would be few grounds for keeping their study as separate as it has been up until now and there would be much to learn from parallel accounts. We shall see that there are both interesting similarities *and* differences between the two forms – but we will need rather more detailed analysis to characterise the overlaps and to move beyond the basic kinds of text-image relationships usually presented.

Some researchers attempt to characterise both picturebooks and comics in terms of *genre*, suggesting that comicbooks and picturebooks may be different genres within an overall space of possibilities. The genre question in our current context then asks whether comics and picturebooks are perhaps differing but related genres. We introduced the linguistic notion of genre briefly in the previous unit (Unit 3, 'Narratives as a linguistic genre', p. 68) and set out one illustrative 'space' of genres graphically in Figure 3.4, p. 69. Unfortunately, this does not appear to lead to a useful characterisation in the present case since one can use picture-books and comics for very diverse social purposes and in a variety of situations – it would appear difficult, therefore, to say anything much about them in terms of genre. Issues of genre and of the picturebook *vs.* comics distinction appear largely orthogonal.

Although it may well be the case that within any particular historical period the range of genres taken up by picturebooks and those taken up by comics are distinct, this does not seem to be grounds for demarcation. Taking, for example, the didactic genre as *definitional* for picturebooks probably limits them far too much, just as limiting comics to 'fiction' or 'narrative' would, as we will see more in Unit 5, impose similarly questionable boundaries.

Opinions continue to differ here and there is no fully accepted solution at this time. One suggestion from op de Beeck (2012: 468), for example, is that "picture books are graphic narratives that operate in a medium known as *comics* (plural form), even though a picture book is not always *a comic* (singular)" (original emphasis). This explicitly introduces another level of description into the account, that of 'medium' – picturebooks then, appear to be one use of a specific medium. This has the advantage of avoiding a difficult to maintain genre distinction, but only at the cost of bringing in 'medium' as another far from straightforward term needing explication in its own right (cf., e.g., Elleström 2010, Bateman 2014).

One of the founding fathers of serious picturebook research, Perry Nodelman, also sees both comics and picturebooks as cases of visual narrative – as we are doing throughout this and the following unit – but focuses in addition on the different 'meaning-making strategies' that the two forms demand. These appear to be different because *competence in one does not appear to automatically provide competence in the other.* As he acknowledges:

> Approaching comics with the meaning-making strategies I have derived from my experience of picture books is something like lacking gills; I find myself confused about how to fit together the various kinds of verbal and visual information comics typically provide in order to grasp the stories they are trying to tell.
>
> (Nodelman 2012: 436)

This, although interesting, does not yet tell us too much about the difference, because both different media and different genres may require different meaning-making strategies – if we are not familiar with the conventions of either, then understanding will be problematic.

Nodelman accordingly goes on to consider some *formal* distinctions that might explain his difficulty. One of these is that picturebooks are generally far more constrained in their deployment of texts and images than comics: the texts and the images, although *intended* to be joined in interpretation – and hence meet our definition of intendedly 'co-present' from Unit 1 – are by and large presented *separately* on the page. This is a clear sign of their evolutionary heritage in another kind of artefact, that of illustrated books. Similar distinctions and considerations arise in Nel's discussion of the difference from the same symposium. Whereas comicbooks are commonly seen to rely on, citing McCloud's (1994: 9) work on comics which we will hear more of in Unit 5, "pictorial and other images in deliberate sequence", picturebooks "more commonly rely on juxtapositions between text and image" (Nel 2012: 445).

We can illustrate the notion of 'juxtaposition' as it is meant here by taking another doublepage spread from Maurice Sendak's *Where the Wild Things Are* (1963). Superficially, this appears like text and image working together, but a closer look shows a very specific kind of co-operation in play. The main features relevant for our current discussion are reproduced in the sketch version of the spread rendered in Figure 4.2. In particular, we need for the moment only to consider the following three facets: (1) the story characters and events

Wild things ask Max to stay but Max says no **A**	Wild things are upset but Max sails away **B**
	Image of Max sailing away is far left
note: not the original text	*note: not the original text*

Figure 4.2 Sketch of a doublepage spread from Maurice Sendak's *Where the Wild Things Are* (1963): Max leaving the Wild Things

as depicted graphically or as represented or participating in the verbal component, (2) the positioning of the text and pictorial content, and (3) the *relative positioning* of that content.

We need now to start being rather more precise about the particular elements that we are going to talk about during our analysis. Establishing criteria for the reliable identification and demarcation of units is an essential precondition to doing any kind of detailed analysis and there are a broad range of schemes available (cf., e.g., Saint-Martin 1990, Trifonas 1998, Zettl 2005, Kress and van Leeuwen 2006 [1996]). For present purposes, the elements that are relevant can be obtained by *visually* inspecting the overall composition of the page, bearing in mind its, possibly medium-specific, 'layout'. So here the question is: what elements appear visually to 'belong together' on the page and which appear visually as separate. Fortunately, this is fairly straightforward in the present case – but it must still be addressed explicitly in order to avoid errors or misrepresentations of what is being shown.

First, then, we have a single picture spanning the two pages of the spread: the unity of this visual element as a single image is clear. Second, we have the textual portion below this. However, this 'textual portion' *is itself clearly separated into two elements*, one on each page. This begins to show why we need to be precise. If we just talked of the 'text' and the 'image' in this case and then related them, we would miss details important for the analysis. Thus, in summary: there are three distinct elements on the page all together. There is the single picture and the two text blocks, annotated in the figure as A and B.

Within each of the verbal and pictorial elements we might then draw on further smaller elements for analysis: for the verbal portion we can employ typography and grammar; for the pictorial portion, elements of design and composition. We will see several frameworks for such descriptions as the book proceeds. Here we can content ourselves with some more informal remarks on connections because, even with this minimal kind of explicit decom-position of the page, we can nevertheless start noticing intriguing *differences* to how visual narration works in comics. Again, for the moment, we rely on our intuitive understanding and experience – that is, just think of how a comic page looks and compare it with what is going on here. In Unit 5 we return to more technical descriptions of comics and so will complete the picture from the other 'side'.

When we consider this kind of analysis, we can then see that, first, the text and the visual are related but *only at the level of the entire episode* presented in the spread. That is: on the one hand, the picture shows Max waving goodbye and the Wild Things in various states of disappointment. On the other hand, the text elements break up the leaving into two com-ponents: (1) Max being asked to stay and saying no in text block A, and (2) the Wild Things roaring and carrying on as Max sails away in text block B. Only the second of these episodes is actually depicted in the visual material, however. As some authors have suggested, therefore, the picturebook will tend to pick out of the stream of the narrative particular highpoints or key moments for which a visual rendition can be productively given. The first text element in this spread, text block A, is thus a kind of narrative setting or preparatory stage for the events shown and is not actually related closely to the image at all.

Next let us consider the image and the text together. Here there is a spatial connection (that is, on the page) between the Wild Things roaring (text block B) and the visual depiction of this – these are quite near one another in the layout and so conforms nicely to proposals for effective multimodal design such as those set out by Mayer (2001). But, in stark contrast to this, Max sailing away is *maximally far* from its verbal description – on the extreme left of the doublepage spread rather than on the right where the corresponding sentence is. To match the text it would clearly have been easier to use a mirror image of the visual so that 'first', that is, in the order congruent with reading the text, the Wild Things are encountered and then, on the extreme right, Max sails away. However, as Nodelman observes, this would have completely undermined the overall spatial organisation employed throughout the story where Max sails 'out' to the right and 'back' to the left, and so would not have been a good choice more 'globally' for the visual narrative. This design decision then naturally also conforms well to the conventionalised use of left-right discussed in Unit 3.

This then is juxtaposition at work. The doublepage spread illustrates exactly the separate lives led by text and visuals in picturebooks despite their co-presence on the 'page'. They are only loosely coordinated, often at the level of entire episodes. There may also be finer-grained resonances across parts of the text, for example, words and phrases, and the visual material that may be intended to be picked up during reading, but not necessarily. When this does occur, the effect is like a caption – more information is provided anchoring the visual information; however, unlike a caption, the text is not signalled particularly by its layout position as being a caption – the relationship is *created dynamically during reading*.

> The text and the image are therefore offered independently for the reader to relate and it is very much up to the reader to make that connection. The spatial layout of the information on the page does not prejudge the issue of what kinds of relations are going to be found or even what *parts* of the text and image should be brought together.

There are, of course, exceptions to this relative independence of text and image, but only of a limited kind. For example, a piece of text in a picturebook may be placed somewhere in the image, but only as long as it is reasonably unobtrusive and can be extracted as a whole. Thus relatively 'empty' places in the image, areas of a single colour or shade, and so on, are also natural candidates for housing text. The text is not thereby integrated into the image, more overlaid 'on top of' the image. The precise positioning of the text within the image generally does not, in such cases, carry narrative weight of its own – although there are no doubt exceptions that employ such positioning to effect the rhythm of information disclosure or other temporal effects, which turns out to be the rule within comicbooks rather than the exception. For example, it is also possible in picturebooks for the space taken up by a piece of text to be used constructively to indicate a path of motion or a connection between visual elements – this is probably the tightest form of integration achieved and appears quite rare.

Another form of limited exception is when picturebooks employ multiple images on a single page. This is usually restricted to repetitions of relatively simple visual themes or presentations of one or two elements, perhaps combined visually. Conversely, comics may also employ single images taking up an entire page or doublepage spread as is the norm in picturebooks. But this design decision acts *in the comics context* as a narratively significant and perceptually salient exception influencing the entire rhythm of reception at that point. The more common proliferation of individual images in comics then moves them closer to film, whereas the lack of proliferation in picturebooks moves them closer to illustrated books and painting. Each of these patterns brings with it differing possibilities for meaning-making and associated conventions of interpretation.

Some of these differences have direct consequences for the text-image relationships that are employed. For example, the fact that comics have a large number of generally smaller images brings text and pictorial material together on a much finer scale. Even perceptually, it is usual that a reader/viewer is looking continually at both pictorial and textual material, following the speech and thought balloons associated with individual characters, taking in setting information in any captions and ambient 'noise' information as well ('Pow!', 'Bang', etc.). These are some of the text-image relationships we turn to with respect to comics in Unit 5.

The closer relationship between narrative events and fine-grained imagery in comics also supports another property often discussed for comics: the tendency to use space for time – that is, moving around the space of the comics page, often both within and across images, is also considered to be moving in storytime. Nel (2012) suggests that this is rather rare for picturebooks because the temporal gaps between images are usually much larger. Cases where space is explicitly used as time within single images in picturebooks draw on an old artistic tradition of depiction in which a single image includes individual figures shown at different places, thus indicating that different times are shown.

Images of this kind are called 'simultaneous pictures' (from the German *Simultanbild*). Typically such images, in traditional art and in picturebooks, will make it clear by visual means that a character is being shown repeatedly and the actions with which the character is involved help demarcate the temporal relationships intended. Nikolajeva and Scott (2001) discuss cases of this technique from Sven Nordkvist's *Festus and Mercury* picturebooks – an example that has also been studied using eye-tracking techniques as we will see in Unit 13.

Finally, the very fact that in picturebooks the general rule is to separate out the text and the images over a much larger spatial extent – in many cases, for example, having text on one side of a doublepage spread and the pictorial content on the another, encourages maintaining them as two voices that dialogue with one another rather than supporting tighter 'integration'. Sipe (1998) then goes as far as to suggest an explicit oscillation from the text to image (or from image to text) and back again, each time changing and adapting the information placed in relation to the other. Sipe and others suggest that this might even be taken to mirror the thought processes involved in and during interpretation, showing what is going on 'in the head' as we bounce from interpretation to revised interpretation – ascertaining whether this is really the case, however, would require rather more detailed psychological experimentation than it has been traditional to employ in picturebook theorising up to now. Some of the work employing eye-tracking on picturebook materials could be enlightening here.

Distinguishing modes of visual narrative

Given these differences in the usage, possibilities and conventions holding between text and images in even closely related forms of visual narrative such as picturebooks and comics, we evidently need to be careful. Merging comics and picturebooks together would make it more difficult to characterise the text-image relations that occur in each. And this is one of our recurring motifs: in general, appropriate *separations* of kinds of multimodal artefact will help us see *both* the differences and the similarities in how text and image work together more clearly.

In our demarcation of picturebook here, therefore, we will rather err on the side of caution and be quite restrictive. In this we follow Nodelman (2012). Although there are picturebooks that employ the resources of comics – most obviously seen in the adoption of speech balloons and similar – the fact that it is generally so easy to identify them as 'visitors' to the picturebook form speaks in favour of recognising their rather different origins. We will therefore consider such visitors as marking an 'adoption' or 'import' of the style of visual meaning-making that has developed within comics rather than as being 'native' to picturebooks themselves. The text-image relationships involved with such borrowing will consequently be dealt with 'at source': that is, when we consider comics in their own right.

There are also strong semiotic motivations for adopting this strategy of separation. Again as Nodelman suggests, the kinds of meanings that can be made with these imports from comicbooks are rather different to the meanings usually discussed in picturebooks. Much of the discussion of text-image relations in picturebooks highlights precisely the flexibility and contingent interdependence of the interpretations of text and image. We will see this in more detail below. But this is precisely *not* what is done with, for example, a speech bubble. The speech bubble is a strongly conventionalised visual expression of someone (the person or object that the tail of the speech bubble points to) saying something (the material shown verbally within the speech bubble). There is little room for any other relationship between the text and the image in such cases – and this is completely unlike the normal kinds of under-specified relations found in picturebooks proper.

This rather deeper semiotic difference is probably the real reason why communication between and across the two forms of comicbooks and picturebooks and their respective communities has been limited. Despite superficial similarities and (possibly growing) points of overlap, they work in different ways.

This is not to say that such borrowings and changes in media over time are infrequent. They may even come to change the definitions that one must adopt. As Salisbury and Styles note:

> the boundaries . . . have become blurred: the use of multiple framed images and speech bubbles for four- to seven-year-olds is increasingly commonplace.
>
> (Salisbury and Styles 2012: 98)

This is also no doubt due to the growing acceptance of graphic novels and 'comic'-like forms in society – their use for children and explicitly 'educational' purposes is no longer stigmatised. Nevertheless, it is still beneficial to maintain a distinction between the different developments of the expressive resources with respect to the 'originating' media and to track them carefully as they come together and influence one another – and *not* simply to lump them all together to begin with.

Picturebooks defined (for now)

For present purposes, therefore, we can take the following three inter-connected properties as 'definitional' for picturebooks. These also appear to cover and generalise the suggestions made in the picturebook literature:

- First, picturebooks necessarily rely on text and image: this means that we rule out artefacts consisting *only* of pictures (this may be controversial as there are some arguable candidates) as well as books consisting *only* of text (this is not controversial).
- Second, picturebooks are a page-based medium: this means that they consist of a sequence of physically framed units within which images and texts can be arranged to produce composite, juxtaposed layouts.
- And third, the images and texts are only loosely coordinated: this means that the messages of the texts and the messages of the images are not tightly integrated by virtue of their compositional layout and conventional interpretation.

The first and second criteria serve to distinguish picturebooks from static image sequences and films; films in particular we have omitted to keep the discussion more focused, even though there is much to be said here. The third criterion distinguishes picturebooks from comics – as the discussion above of speech bubbles and other formal differences should have clarified.

The third criterion is also intended to distinguish picturebooks from illustrated books. In illustrated books, the text tells the story and at some points in that text, there may be a picture providing a visual expression of the story events or settings at those points – this was Barthes' notion of 'reducing' the text that we saw in Unit 2 (cf. Figure 2.1, p. 35). The text is then clearly dominant. This cannot be the case with picturebooks, where the story is "twice-told" but "interdependent" in the words of Agosto (1999). Picturebooks are, in other words, "insistently dual" (Nodelman 2012: 443) in their weaving together of image and text contributions.

HOW TO ANALYSE PICTUREBOOKS

With this definition of picturebooks behind us, we can explore more closely the text-image distinctions pursued in the analysis of picturebooks by considering the approach of Nikolajeva and Scott (2001). As noted above, this is one of the most developed treatments of picture-books within the picturebook field and so provides a good illustration of how this research is undertaken and with what aims.

Nikolajeva and Scott's approach is broadly compatible with its origins in literary research, but they also take important steps towards providing analytic tools for further picturebook studies. For our present concerns, we need to consider these in the light of how they might support tighter accounts of text-image relations.

Reader-response theory and picturebooks

One of the theories informing Nikolajeva and Scott's approach is the literary account of reader-response primarily associated with the work of Iser (1978). This framework was proposed in order to overcome some clear deficiencies noted with respect to earlier models of the role of the reader in literary interpretation and aesthetic response.

If one, for example, were to assume that the meaning of a text is largely 'within' that text and so one merely needs to **decode** its message, then a broad range of phenomena become very difficult to account for. In such a model, the reader can have very little influence on interpretation – and this seems widely at odds with the breadth and richness of alternative or complementary meanings that any work of literary art appears to bring to life. If the reader is simply decoding a pre-given, fixed message, then it would be equally difficult to explain why literature should be at all interesting and there would be few grounds for explaining deeper involvement with a text's story and the kind of deep aesthetic experiences that literature can give rise to.

But, on the other hand, clearly a reader of a text is not completely free concerning their interpretations. After all, it makes some difference whether one reads this book or that book – the choice is not immaterial for what the reader then does: there is *some* relationship between what a text actually says and the kinds of responses that readers have, the question is which.

Iser's alternative to the simple decoding model builds on a realisation that was beginning to take root in several disciplines concerned with text in the early 1970s: that is, that inter-pretation needs to be seen as a *dynamic* process actively involving the reader. A text is then not seen as 'having' a meaning that the reader simply has to derive, but rather as setting out a structured web of 'instructions', 'hints' or 'guides' for a reader to follow when producing interpretations. In this account, a text becomes a structured context that 'implies' a particular reader and reader's activity. The instructions given can never be complete – indeed it is unclear just what 'complete instructions' for interpretation could be. They do, however, serve to open up certain horizons of interpretation rather than others; a definition of the meaning of text closely related both to discussions in semiotics (cf., e.g., Posner 1969, Eco 1990) and to the early work on text-image relations that we discussed in Unit 2. During this process of interpretation, readers draw on their knowledge of the world, previous experiences, knowledge of the text, knowledge of literary genres and so on. The reader is then an *active co-constructor* of any interpretation that the text then receives.

Iser characterises the structure of the instructions brought about by any text in terms of *gaps* or *blanks*. These are 'places of indeterminacy' created by the use of particular textual strategies in the creation of a text. The active role of the reader then resides in filling in the gaps created structurally by the text at hand. For example, and quite trivially, the use of the pronoun 'she' in a text creates a gap that needs to be actively filled by the reader: who is being referred to? The text cannot fill this in itself; this is something only the reader can do. The text can only indicate to a reader that there is such a gap to be resolved. Conventions of various kinds concerning just how pronouns may be successfully deployed in text provide methods for following the instruction to fill in the gap. Gaps can also be significantly more subtle and complex, driven by literary techniques and textual patterns of many kinds – an example at the level of an entire story or novel could be the classic 'who dunnit?'-gap created by the genre conventions of crime or detective stories and followed through as the text unfolds in the fine-grained details of information delivery, focalisation and so on.

Aesthetic enjoyment of, and involvement in, a text can then be explained in terms of the active role that the reader plays. Cognitive engagement with some task – here filling the gaps – is well known to have a deeper effect on the acting subject. Iser offers several suggestive analyses, drawing connections between filling in gaps and other basic perceptual phenomena known from psychology. The account becomes rather descriptive and exploratory at this point, however, and still needs considerably more explicit characterisation.

Returning now to picturebooks, the suggestion followed by Nikolajeva and Scott is that a similar process of active reader engagement holds but that, in contrast to a traditional literary text, structural gaps for completion can not only be created both textually and visually but also can be *filled* both textually and visually. In particular, the text can create structural gaps that can be filled by the visuals and the visuals can create structural gaps that can be filled by the text.

This is an appealingly simple way of explaining some operations basic to picturebook interpretation. Again, building on our textual example, if the text in a picturebook uses the pronoun 'he' then the pictorial component accompanying that piece of text may well provide good candidates for filling in further information about just who or what that 'he' is. A more interesting example is where Sendak's *Where the Wild Things Are* picturebook begins by informing the reader/viewer that Max is involved in various kinds of 'mischief' – but it is left to the visuals to fill in the 'gap' as to just what kinds of mischief those are. Any implicit questions created in the text or visuals might be filled in this way. With respect to Nikolajeva and Scott's overall map of the territory shown in Figure 4.1 above, therefore, the central area suggests a range of potential relationships between the verbal and pictorial components of picturebooks that each involve distinct kinds of gaps.

We can then start characterising more finely what kinds of gaps may be involved in order to strengthen our descriptions. One way to do this is to ask just what functions images *can* take on with respect to the words, and *vice versa*. With functions identified we could proceed to the next question and ask how the information gained by filling in any of these respective gaps can be combined with the information from other sources, including the visual and verbal material.

Picturebook text-image relations

A first overview of such functions can be derived from the understanding of narratives in general, as achieved in narratology and introduced in the previous unit. Thus, as Fang (1996) sets out, a useful preliminary catalogue of the work that pictures take on in picturebooks includes: *establishing setting*, *defining and developing characters*, *extending or developing plot*, *providing different viewpoints* (relative to the text), *contributing to textual coherence* (by providing referents for pronouns and so on), and *reinforcing the text* (by restating visually what is said in the text).

These categories can be further organised with respect to the specific kinds of work they describe. Setting, character development and different viewpoints relate to narratological narrative functions; extending/developing and reinforcing relate to how more or different information can be added to what is expressed in the text; and coherence relates most centrally to the technical details of how the text-image combination is functioning as a combined unit of interpretation. The list therefore provides a useful but preliminary way of characterising how the images and texts are related in any specific case. It is preliminary in two respects: first, it has not yet been established that we can reliably recognise the functions that hold in all cases; and second, it has not yet been established if this list is all there is, or whether we will need further relationships.

Each of the distinct kinds of relationships constrains what kinds of gaps are seen or created for completion by the text-image combination. If the gap filling proceeds straightforwardly in the sense of simply providing information that was missing, then we have Nikolajeva and Scott's 'complementary picturebooks': that is, each mode fills in the other's gaps. But, as we saw in the figure, there are several rather more complex relationships, ranging from full redundancy (both images and texts tell the same story) through complementarity to opposition and independence.

This partly overlaps with the notion of alternative viewpoints but is actually at a different level of abstraction. 'Different viewpoints' is a *narrative construction* that may be *based on* the fact that different information is being given – as such, it is an *interpretation* that is made of the material on offer. This relates again to our discussion of the status of text-image relations as discourse hypotheses in Unit 2 ('What *are* text-image relationships?', p. 44). It is useful to separate out such distinct levels of description to make the analysis more robust by reducing the amount of interpretation required in earlier stages of analysis. By employing categories that are more firmly anchored in the objects being analysed the reliability of the analysis overall can be increased substantially.

To take an example: filling in pronoun referents and similar relations between text and image is fairly basic. We can therefore take text referents (such as 'he', 'Max', 'the Wild Things') as establishing *recognition* goals to be applied to the accompanying visual material. The text in this case gives good reasons both for segmenting the visual material in particular ways rather than others and for labelling what is depicted. It is possible for this to function in the opposite direction as well, as we saw in discussions of Barthes' polysemy in Unit 2, although there the greater variety of potential interpretations for any image needs to be borne in mind. Filling in setting and character information follows similarly. Once a connection has been achieved between text characters, events, places and so on, matching information can be imported from the visual material and 'attached' to the relevant entities in the text. Just how such attachment operates will not concern us for the moment, although there appears to be clear psychological evidence for such processes as we will see in Unit 13. We can also describe this in terms of the text and image themselves as set out according to the framework of *cohesion* that we will see in Unit 8.

Extending/developing and reinforcing information are rather different as well. They refer more to abstract logical relationships between the information that is given in the text and that given in the images. This is another, further area where the relations between text and image have received detailed study – we will have more to say about this in Units 10 and 11. For now we can note that this needs to be placed at a different level of description because any image provided with a text can be said to 'increase' the information given. If the text says that someone went to school, and the image provides a sunny day, with country hills, nearby woods and so on, we might analyse the text-image relationship narratively as providing 'setting' but that setting is certainly *also* 'extending' the information that was given in the text. This means that the notion of whether 'more' information is being given or not itself requires closer examination. As we proceed in this and subsequent units, we will consider a number of ways in which we might make these kinds of distinctions more precise.

There is also the possibility that the information provided does not really 'add' information but rather *conflicts* with what is presented elsewhere. Categories in this area are addressed in the similar classification offered by Agosto (1999). Agosto considers picturebooks as a whole to be examples of 'interdependent storytelling' as we have seen above and so distinguishes explicitly between two main categories: *augmentation* and *contradiction.*

In Agosto's case, however, the focus is very much on storytelling strategies rather than text-image relations *per se*: thus the categories under augmentation include: irony, humour, intimation (where typically the visual adds clues for complete interpretation of an otherwise comprehensible but incomplete text), fantastic representation (where the text may be realistic and the visuals represent imagination) and transformation (where the combination of visuals and text drastically transforms the impact of one or other); while those under contradiction are irony (again), humour (again), and disclosure (where the reader knows something that the protagonists do not know – a case of differential knowledge handled by focalisation and point-of-view in narratological terms). Agosto gives examples of books falling under each of these and notes that more than one strategy may be realised at once – that is, the categories are not *mutually exclusive.* She then goes on to suggest that a large part of the value of such dual storytelling is the challenge it presents for learning readers and the boost that reconciling the different storytelling strands can offer for cognitive development.

Nikolajeva and Scott also express some doubt, however, that the text-image relationships in picturebooks represent some distinct phenomenon of their own:

> Many picturebook critics dwell upon the interrelationship of text and image as though there is something radically different involved. . . . While all of these are useful metaphors for understanding the relationship between two kinds of communicative technique, in fact the degree of friction or harmony involved can simply be considered an extension of narrative techniques involved in telling any story. A storyteller adds visual and aural dimensions to a narrative through voice and gesture and can offer harmonic or ironic cues to aid the understanding of the audience. The techniques employed in verbal narrative can also work with or in contradiction to each other. Words spoken, words

describing action, and characters' emotions expressed in inner monologues can all support a single interpretation or can produce a complex interrelationship of meaning that simulates the complexity of life. . . . Within this context, the iconic-verbal communication that the picturebook conveys is different in degree rather than in essence.

(Nikolajeva and Scott 2001: 82)

The extent to which this is true depends entirely on the levels of abstractions considered. At the most abstract level of 'storytelling' as a social behaviour that can be realised in many different ways with equally varied materials – as more recent concerns with transmedial narratology argue – then there may well appear to be little of *essential* difference between pictures and texts. Nikolajeva and Scott make references to what pictures and texts respectively 'do best' but subordinate these to more generic strategies of storytelling.

But the claim of no essential differences is then circular: storytelling is defined independently of the particular media and so, by definition, anything undertaken in any medium for storytelling will fall within this. Similar accounts can be given for any medium – and receive similar critique: is film, just another kind of storytelling for example, or are there essential differences between film and, for example, novels? Since we know that there *are* differences, something here appears to have been missed.

The danger accompanying the 'all is storytelling'-view is that descriptions hide the differences that are due to the distinct materialities and semiotic modes that are mobilised – that is, they fail to address the crucial issue of **medium specificity**. One aim must then be to explore *beforehand* whether there are differences supported by the different material forms. Until this has been approached on a broader empirical basis, it is difficult to say what the answer will be. It is rather obvious, almost tautological, that a variety of general storytelling techniques will be found when examining any story – be that story a picturebook, film or novel – the challenge, however, is to turn that around and ask more what the individual media are doing which may *not* already have been conceptualised from the perspective of storytelling in other media.

There is evidently still considerable work to be done ascertaining what is happening in picturebooks as a form in their own right and this may well feed back and change or expand our view of just what 'storytelling' is.

CONCLUSIONS AND DISCUSSION

Given the above discussion we can now summarise quite succinctly the respective role of text and image in picturebooks.

We can begin with the characterisation of illustrated books (and their converse, picture books with captions and small text fragments) shown graphically in Figure 4.3. This diagram is to be read as follows. The basic units of an illustrated book (shown on the left of the figure) are made up of the unfolding text, distributed over pages. For any episodes, characters or settings that are introduced in that text, there may be, but do not need to be, illustrations. Importantly, the functions of the text with respect to the images are restricted. They appear to 'add' additional detail to the text *only in limited ways*.

We mentioned above that there are various frameworks for describing in more detail the different ways in which information can be 'added'. As one useful and very general characterisation of the kinds of 'adding' relations possible, we can draw on the notion of logicosemantic *expansion* developed within systemic-functional linguistics – we will see this distinction in

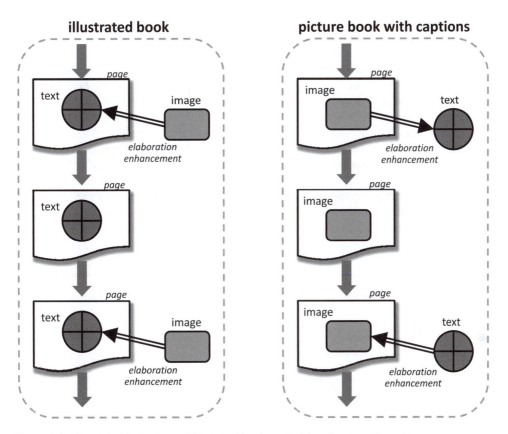

Figure 4.3 The abstract structure of illustrated books and picture books with captions

several guises in subsequent units when we discuss specific frameworks for describing text-image relations.

Expansion comes in three flavours, each picking out a logically different way in which information can be added to other information. Illustrations as used in illustrated books are generally restricted to just two of these categories: *elaboration* and *enhancement.* Additions of these kinds provide extra details about *what has already been presented* in the text. This may include information such as spatial configurations, clothing, appearance and so on, or may 'anchor' what has been presented with additional information such as where something is occurring, when, how, and so on. The former kind of addition is elaboration; the latter enhancement.

It is also possible to consider the converse situation where the narrative is carried by the *visual* elements with occasional text additions. This is shown on the right-hand side of Figure 4.3. The relations possible between image and text in this case are generally of an even simpler variety, such as labelling the pictures or repeating the main narrative point to be carried forward in the pictures following.

Since both text and image are visually separate, each offers a potential 'access point' or 'entry point' into the activity of reading/viewing their containing artefacts. We can refer to these as **tracks** serving to carry the narrative. As we can see in both the case of illustrated books and picture books with captions, only one of the tracks, which we can call the primary track, is presented completely; the secondary track is, in contrast, more or less fragmented. This incompleteness of the secondary track undermines its ability to function as a main carrier of the narrative. In the case of illustrated books, since not every episode needs to be illustrated, there may be significant gaps. It is the text that then fills those gaps and so the work that can be done visually is restricted. The converse holds for picture books with captions.

When we move to picturebooks proper, this situation changes. For picturebooks, the unit that advances the narrative is not an image or a text, but the imagetext combination. This combination is itself structured, however, in that now one or more of *all three* expansion relationships might hold and they may hold in either direction. The third expansion relation is that of *extension*. Extension goes further than elaboration and enhancement in that it allows the narrative really to be moved on – rather than staying 'in place', extension drives the text forwards, providing new episodes, alternatives, commentaries and so on (cf. Unit 10, 'Logicosemantic relations', p. 195). With this logical organisation, therefore, *both* text and image can play a role in advancing the story. The corresponding abstract structure of artefacts of this kind is shown in Figure 4.4.

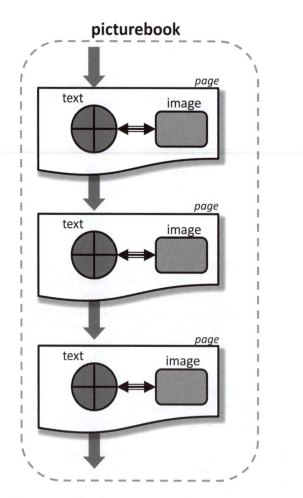

Figure 4.4 The abstract structure of picturebooks

This means that the image may provide extra details for the text or the text may provide extra details for the image. The addition of the third kind of expansion also allows the image and the text to diverge, to present *alternatives* to one another: this is only possible with the extension relationship. Moreover, the two tracks are now presented as equal, providing for different possibilities for access and *dual readerships*. It may then be that that an adult reads the text aloud while a child follows the image sequence – each consequently having a rather different (but inter-related) reading/viewing experience.

This position re-constructs theoretically the characterisation of picturebooks in terms of 'double orientation' proposed by Lewis (2001). For Lewis, picturebooks are always able to 'look in two directions' at once, and this opens up a space for changing or playing with generic expectations in often interesting and engaging ways – in the case of the more so-called 'postmodern' picturebooks, for example, even drawing explicit attention to the existence of those generic expectations in the first place. As Lewis suggests:

> I think that this inherent double orientation is probably what Schwarcz, Golden, Agosto and Nikolajeva and Scott are trying to grapple with when they attempt to distinguish between symmetry, enhancement, counterpoint, deviation, augmentation, contradiction and so on ... But I believe that they mistakenly identify as characteristic of particular picturebooks something immanent in all picturebooks. They mistake potentiality for a circumscribed actuality.
>
> (Lewis 2001: 68)

That is to say, as soon as one has pictures and texts being presented together in the same artefact as intended components, or facets, of the same 'message', their co-presence will insist that they be interpreted in terms of each other. Moreover, the different properties inherent to text and image respectively will *necessarily* create a doubled-up perspective. Even in the case of the simplest illustration – seen traditionally as 'just' showing episodes from the text – the fact that the visual material and the text necessarily provide different information will bring a double orientation into existence – as our beginning quotation from Benveniste in Unit 1 claimed: different semiotic systems do different things.

Lewis also cites Nodelman here, referring to Nodelman's suggestion that text and image always stand in an 'ironical' relationship (Nodelman 1988: 221). But the simple pictorial illustration cannot in any reasonable sense be said to be 'ironic' – the meaning of irony is too specific. Lewis suggests that Nodelman is correct to assert that there is *always* a close relationship of playing text and image off against each other in picturebooks, but the precise nature of that relationship, what Lewis describes as 'double orientation', is something rather more general and abstract, a name for the small family of potential inter-relationships that individual authors have identified. Thus:

> Picturebooks always open at least two windows upon the [picturebook] text so that we might see it in more than one light. . . . [T]he words on their own are always partial, incomplete, unfinished, awaiting the flesh of the pictures. Similarly the pictures are perpetually pregnant with potential narrative meaning, indeterminate, unfinished, awaiting the closure provided by the words.
>
> (Lewis 2001: 74)

This point is also made strongly in the semiotic approach of Sipe (1998).

Finally, our characterisation of picturebooks in terms of the abstract structures given above also reveals a fascinating 'semiotic gap' in the potential of picturebooks as a whole.

As we shall see in detail in Unit 10, the notion of *expansion* that we have employed here is itself actually just one of two possible general forms of 'adding' information: the other is *projection*, which generally holds between an event of 'saying', 'thinking', and so on and what is said, thought, and so on. We have already seen several examples of text-image relations of this kind in previous units (cf., e.g., Figure 1.3, p. 10).

Now, it seems that relationships of projection are not used between the separate elements of text and visuals in the case of picturebooks. The closest that they come is to have a quoted text (e.g., on one page) and a picture of someone obviously talking (e.g., on another page). This is quite different to projection proper, however, as it relies on a loose coordination of compatible text and image and leaves the reader/viewer to fill the narrative gap. In stark contrast to this, projection turns out in comics to be one of the major organisational resources employed, playing a crucial role for binding diverse elements together. This then suggests a further clear semiotic distinction between comics as a medium and picturebooks. We follow this up in more detail in the next unit.

Visual narrative: Comics and sequential art

Views on the value of 'comics' have varied considerably over the years and depending on who is doing the evaluation – "Of all the lively arts the Comic Strip is the most despised, and with the exception of the movies it is the most popular" observed Gilbert Seldes in 1924 (Seldes 1924: 213). Even in France, where visual narrative forms are generally held in considerable esteem, we find as late as 1964 academics taking up arms: "[Our goal is to] carry through a difficult struggle against a type of literature that is loathsome by any measure" (Bron 1964: ii, cited and translated by Willems 2008: 1).

One of the grounds offered for this tirade is striking for our current concerns. Alongside suggestions that the themes handled in comicbooks were potentially of an immoral nature, which we will say nothing about, their unsuitability was equally considered to reside in the very adoption of pictorial information as a narrative resource. Again citing Willems (2008: 1) citing the above report's review of positions taken in France in the late 1950s:

> Reading a modern youth magazine no longer involves any intellectual activity; the image takes over, and this type of 'reading' consists in a passive abandon to sensory stimuli that exert violent impressions on the child's mind and bypass any critical process. Moreover, the concrete representation of the scenes depicted rules out the use of the reader's imagination.
>
> (Dubois and Dubois 1964: 24; translation by Willems)

The similarity of this style of argumentation with traditional rejections of the visual going back to Plato (and probably beyond) and continuing right up until the present day should give us pause for thought.

We return to a similar avoidance of visual strategies evident in studies of rhetoric in Unit 6. And the blatantly divergent positive evaluations of, on the one hand, picturebooks as a force for cognitive and social development in the child (Unit 4) and, on the other hand, comics as a tool of the devil are also, to say the least, intriguing. There is little doubt that this is largely grounded in the very different cultural contexts, communicative goals and conditions of production that comics have 'enjoyed' over the past 100 years or so, but reading such debates makes it easier to understand Barthes' discussions of society's 'fear' of the visual and its consequent need to 'repress', 'sublimate' and 'control' the image (Unit 2).

We will be more concerned here with a closer consideration of how comicbooks function and the role that text-image relations play in this. To demote reception practices to 'a passive abandon to sensory stimuli' is to miss the point: sensory perception is rarely passive and the organisation and structure of comicbooks meshes with active perception in powerful ways. Comicbooks may well 'bypass' critical processes – but, when they do, this is an *achievement* of the organisation of the medium and not a necessary result of putting things in pictures.

Strong images can have strong effects, but with comicbooks we are looking at something more than images, regardless of how strong (or not) images may be individually. Effect is known to be linked closely with *involvement* and the depth of involvement that a tightly woven narrative can create for its viewers/readers is considerable and long-lasting. It is also potentially far more *complex*, in that a narrative arc provides a scaffold within which an almost endless array of cultural values and preconceptions can be set up, questioned, reinforced or negotiated.

It is largely for these latter reasons that comics research is now in a stronger position than ever before. New studies of the cultural role of comics and their power to reflect or shape opinions and social norms are appearing with increasing regularity (cf. Bongco 2000, Magnussen and Christiansen 2000, McAllister, Sewell, Jr. and Gordon 2001, Klock 2002, Duncan and Smith 2009, Berninger, Ecke and Haberkorn 2010, Goggin and Hassler-Forest 2010, Dittmer 2012). General introductory texts on the medium of comics, its basic organ-isational forms and features, are becoming common and there are already many to choose from with more on the way (e.g., Schüwer 2002, Wolk 2007, Ditschke, Kroucheva and Stein 2009, Stein and Thon 2013, Miodrag 2013, Cohn 2014). In addition, several historical discussions of the medium are already classics in the field (e.g., Kunzle 1973, Bader 1976, Harvey 1996) and attention from aesthetics and philosophy is growing as well (e.g., Carrier 2000, Meskin 2007, Meskin and Cook 2012). There is, therefore, no shortage of places to look when beginning to consider comics as a field of research. As with picturebooks, there is now a wide and rapidly growing body of literature on comics from all perspectives – taking in their production, reception, role in society, ideological implications, graphic art traditions, use of language, historical development as a medium, and much more.

Discussion and proposals for analytic methods for comics start off in very much the same tone as do those for picturebooks. Much is made of their combination of the modalities of language and images, again often described as a 'unique' feature of the medium. However, as we noted in Unit 4 during our discussion of the distinguishing features of comics and pic-turebooks, the respective research communities concerned with comics and with picturebooks have actually had strikingly little interaction. We suggested that there may be some good semiotic reasons for this separation and argued at the end of Unit 4 that there are some significant differences between just how text and image work together that distinguish the two forms. We now take this further, beginning with a more detailed account of the properties of comicbooks and their treatment within the comicbook field.

Most general introductions focus on the rather more superficial or evident nature of the expressive resources evident in comics – speech balloons, pictures, captions and the like. Although important for talking about comics, we will also need to push this a bit further. For this we will draw on some of the more sophisticated analytic models for comics now emerging – particularly those from Neil Cohn and Thierry Groensteen – in order to attempt to characterise the nature of text-image relations in comics in a more general and revealing fashion. This can then feed back into analyses of other aspects of comics, be that their social interpretation or narrative form or whatever.

The best-known introduction to comics is probably still that of Scott McCloud (McCloud 1994) so we will begin with this and some of the points that McCloud raises as our way into the topic. As we proceed, we will see some rather different image-text relations being proposed from those we have seen up until now. We will also need to address the question of *units of analysis* somewhat more carefully for comics than we did with picturebooks. When considering comics, there are interesting challenges to be faced even prior to identifying what is to count as 'text' and 'image' at all.

BASIC RESOURCES OF THE COMICBOOK

McCloud's account of comics is particularly striking because it is itself written as a comic. McCloud uses this selection of medium to prove 'by demonstration' that it is perfectly possible to employ comics for serious purposes that go well beyond juvenile entertainment; the growing use of comics both for non-fiction, for example concerning science, and for serious literary works, supports this further. McCloud sets out his proposed analytic framework in a tight interweave of visual and verbal form; we will, for various reasons, be restricted more to the verbal component of his account here and so it is more than worthwhile returning to the original to see how the ideas are developed.

Defining comics

McCloud's 'working definition' of comics draws largely on another classic of comics research, that of Eisner (1992), and is echoed in most general introductions:

> Juxtaposed pictorial and other images in deliberate sequence, intended to convey information and/or to produce an aesthetic response in the viewer.
>
> (McCloud 1994: 9)

But, as McCloud himself notes, this definition still appears to include many artefacts that one might not want to consider as comics – picturebooks, for example!

Just as was the case with our discussion of picturebooks, the question of just what is and what is not a comic is not straightforward. Some are happy to mark the beginning of comics with the works and writings of Rudolphe Töpffer (1799–1846) on stories expressed in sequences of graphically represented scenes; others are prepared to be less restrictive. McCloud, for example, finds a broader application of the term perfectly acceptable, and willingly embraces the consequences – similarities with the Bayeux Tapestry, with which we began our discussion in Unit 3 (cf. Figure 3.1), for example, make it difficult to avoid calling the tapestry a comic if we follow McCloud's definition.

Whether or not an author wants to argue that the Bayeux Tapestry is a 'comic' often depends more on the general argumentative – or even, as Meskin (2007) suggests – 'polemical' point being pursued. If one wants to show that comics have a long and artistically rich tradition, including the Bayeux Tapestry (and many other historical exemplars both before and after) among your forbears may well turn out to be a sound strategic move. But in many other respects, this view is not entirely convincing. For Meskin (2007), arguing from within media studies, aesthetics and the philosophy of art, considering the Bayeux Tapestry as a comic goes too far. Meskin takes jazz as a demonstration, arguing that if a piece of music from the seventeenth century were discovered to exhibit features we nowadays commonly associate with jazz, this by no means turns the piece of music into a piece of jazz. Indeed:

> Nothing could have counted as jazz in the seventeenth century, and any theory that implied that there was an instance of jazz 350 years ago or more would be anachronistic. Think of how the incorporation of the Bayeux Tapestry into the category of comics would reshape our appreciation of it. 'Where are the speech-balloons?' we might be led to ask. 'How radical to embroider a comic!' I take it that these would be distortions.
>
> (Meskin 2007: 374)

The historical tradition and social embedding of an artwork is then equally important for its inclusion or not within some category.

Some more 'work-internal' distinctions may be able to take us further. At the end of the previous unit, we drew several distinctions between various combinations of text and image that appeared to be pulling books constituted by pictures with captions, by text with illustrations and picturebooks proper in different directions. The main distinction there was the different kinds of relationships, or different ways of 'sharing' the communicative work, across 'text' and 'image'. We now consider these issues again but from the comics side of the fence.

Wartenberg (2012), for example, attempts a philosophical argument for distinguishing comics from other kinds of imagetexts. His main argument is that the line of demarcation to draw lies between comics and 'illustrated' books in general, arguing in addition that picture-books as children's literature belong to illustrated books rather than comics. For Wartenberg such artefacts always presuppose an ontological priority for their texts: the images then provide additional information licensed by the text.

Wartenberg holds this to be the case even for artefacts that exhibit what he defines as a *canonical* relationship between text and image. This is when the images accompanying a text become so strongly associated with the text that the 'work' in question can no longer be considered separately from the pictures. Examples he offers here are Lewis Carroll's (and John Tenniel's) *Alice in Wonderland* (1865) and A. A. Milne's (and E. H. Shephard's) *Winnie-the-Pooh* (1926–1928) – and indeed, in all these cases it is difficult to consider the works in question as consisting only of the text. The images then *define* what is considered as the work while still, Wartenberg argues, being illustrative.

While picturebook researchers might agree with such considerations in the case of illustrated books, they would not at all agree that this accurately characterises the situation with picturebooks. As we saw in many of the positions reported in Unit 4, it is absolutely axiomatic for picturebook research that text and image are *equal* partners; any description that grants priority to the text is then seen as just not having understood how picturebooks work.

There is certainly much to be said for this position. Picturebooks may have 'evolved' from illustrated books, but the many examples that can now be offered of independence of text and image as contributing equally to a combined narrative demonstrate that assigning precedence to the text is going to be at best a shaky affair, reminiscent of Barthes' observations concerning the 'rarity' of relay in Unit 2 ('Barthes on the respective meanings of texts and images', p. 34). In picturebooks 'proper', if either the text or the images are removed, the *intended* narrative crumbles. This is also the case with comics of course, and so the question then is whether definitions such as Wartenberg's in fact *erase* important differences between comics and picturebooks (rather than managing to define only comics as he claims). This would then be equally unwanted by both those who study comics and those who research picturebooks!

It would seem that we need to be more careful in our account of the *communicative load* being carried by images and texts respectively. To state that a text is 'prior' may be a self-fulfilling prophecy when the bare bones of the narrative might be recoverable from the text alone. This should not be considered an adequate argument for stating that the images are then 'optional' or less important. In the Sendak picturebook that we have used as examples at various points in previous units, we come quite close to an illustrated book. Wartenberg could well argue here that the text is prior – if there is no text, then we have not been introduced to Max, do not know that he has been called a Wild Thing, do not know that he is being sent to bed without any supper, and so on. The pictures illustrate these circumstances. They are therefore constrained to show what has been given in the text.

There is also, however, clearly a sense that not only do the pictures go about showing *much more* than is given in the text – which is not so remarkable because any illustration may do this too – but also that *what* they introduce is far from simply illustrative. In other words, the images take on a considerable narrative role of their own. This is then one line that needs to be drawn between illustrated books and picturebooks: the more narrative load carried by the pictorial material, the more we are dealing with picturebooks rather than illustrated books. When the narrative proceeds in episodes that are all more or less equally shared between text and image, then we are definitely in the realm of picturebooks rather than illustrated books. These are the distinctions that were suggested graphically in Figures 4.2 and 4.3 in Unit 4.

Moving on to comics, we can make further distinctions building on this. Whereas picturebooks provide text and image combinations that relate to entire episodes, a distinctive feature of comics appears precisely to be that they engage in *microscale* visual narrative. That is, in a comic each and every moment of the narrative is carried verbo-visually. Thus, whereas the picturebook might describe a few turns of a dialogue between child and grandmother or grandfather in a single text element presented alongside, that is, 'juxtaposed' with, a pictorial representation of a 'conversation' between child and adult, the comicbook version would break the dialogue down into individual utterances, perhaps individual words and sentences *within* utterances, *each being shown both visually and verbally* – it is in this sense that we noted in the previous unit in passing that comics come far closer to film than to picturebooks.

This difference is illustrated in Figure 5.1, where we construct a simple comics-style version of the single doublepage spread from Sendak's *Where the Wild Things Are* that we discussed in Unit 4 ('Picturebooks and comics', p. 75) and showed in Figure 4.1.

Figure 5.1   Example episode of 'Max leaving' from Sendak's *Where the Wild Things Are* (1963) redrawn as a rough comic

Microscale visual narrative of this kind demands possibilities for expression that are beyond the usual capabilities of picturebooks and which provide a veritable playground for exploring the deployment of space on the page. For example, issues of framing and of providing spatial arrangements of panels play a major role in adding detail and nuanced positioning of the reader/viewer with respect to what is being shown on a, often literally depending on the genre of comic, blow-by-blow basis.

The most general statement of this, as we shall return to in more detail below, is that of Groensteen. Groensteen provides the most sophisticated semiotic account of comics to date, describing them as an orchestrated use of 'space' – that is, the space on the page. The first and foremost question concerns what uses will be made of that space, how it will be divided up, how it will be connected, and what narrative and other functions will any of those divisions and connections be asked to carry. Out of this we can 'grow' notions of panels, frames, speech balloons, motion lines and much more besides.

These linguistic, graphical and pictorial resources are now rather well known. In short: comics are made up of *pages* or *doublepage spreads* which are divided into collections of more or less strongly framed **panels**. Within panels we find more or less stylised pictorial depictions, while the empty space *between* panels is known as the **gutter**. There are also a variety of textual elements that may appear both within and across panels, such as **captions**, **speech balloons** and **thought bubbles**, as well as free-floating *sound effects* ('Warrrooooom!'). There is also a veritable menagerie of 'non-iconic' graphical elements that may also appear both within and across panels, such as motion lines, visual sound and other sensory effects, and so on – Kennedy (1982) calls these **visual runes** and discusses their motivation in some detail; runes are also taken up and applied further to comics in Forceville (2011). Crucially, however:

> These resources have evolved in the ways they have because of the expressive uses made of them – they are not 'pre-given' by the medium.

For our present purposes, therefore, we will adopt the notion of microscale verbo-visual narrative expressed two-dimensionally on a framed 'display canvas' (page, spread, screen, etc.) as our working definition for comics. This definition stands as a starting point for characterising comics from the perspective of a *semiotic mode* rather than as a product or type of artefact or art form. The commitment to 'narrative' will be revised from a broader linguistic perspective at the end of this unit, but will serve for the time being. The majority of the organisational features that one finds deployed in the comics medium derive from the possibilities for meaning-making that the semiotic mode supports. These certainly include those aspects that studies of comics have attended to whenever talking of relations in comics between individual combinations of words and pictorial elements occurring in 'sequence'.

Frames, panels and gutters

Before focusing on the text-image relations in comics themselves, we need first to address in slightly more detail the contexts in which those relations occur: that is, series of panels and collections of frames. These two characterisations in fact correspond to two broad orientations towards comics and their analysis.

McCloud and many others focus on the one-dimensional *sequentiality* inherent in Eisner's naming of the medium: **sequential art** (Eisner 1992). Groensteen, as just mentioned, focuses equally on the *two-dimensional* nature of comics as a page-based medium. These two perspectives are by no means in conflict – both are necessary in order to understand the workings of comics. Indeed, one interesting challenge is to explore just how it is that readers/viewers of comics move between them so well, turning two-dimensional layouts into 'one-dimensional' reading paths (cf. Cohn 2013b).

When traversing any selected reading path, there is automatically the question of what occurs *between* panels, that is, in the 'gutter'. McCloud proposes seeing the gutter as the place where the reader has to actively work with the material presented in order to turn a sequence of separate and distinct images into a coherent 'story'. Comics artists work with this possibility by showing more or less of what the reader needs to know – in effect controlling how much the reader/viewer has to provide on their own. In the terms of reader-response theory that we introduced in Unit 4 ('Reader-response theory and picturebooks', p. 82), this corresponds to constructing various kinds of 'gaps' that the reader/viewer has to resolve. McCloud draws here on the psychological and Gestalt-theory notion of *closure*, suggesting that reader/viewers attempt to bring the material in the images and assumptions about their inter-relationships into a coherent 'whole', thus exhibiting (local) closure with minimal loose ends; this is then a different sense of 'closure' than that of *narrative closure* long studied in literature (cf. Carroll 2007).

McCloud explores this further by cataloguing the distinct kinds of *inter-panel relations* that seem to have evolved as expressive resources for constructing comics. The precise number, nature and even existence of relations between panels in a comic is still a matter of open research. McCloud suggests the following six distinct kinds: *moment-to-moment, action-to-action, subject-to-subject, scene-to-scene, aspect-to-aspect* and *non-sequitur* (McCloud 1994: 74). Scene-to-scene corresponds to a larger break in the narrative and, were we to apply this scheme to picturebooks, is probably the most common relation found there. It is also analogous to a break between scenes in film. The other relations vary from minor transitions or changes of viewpoints within episodes to the largest break where no connection can be found at all.

McCloud uses this classification to perform a brief cross-cultural comparison of comics styles. He suggests that the dominant strategy in mainstream American comics (65% of the relations in McCloud's analysis of comics by Jack Kirby) is action-to-action, where suc-cessive panels show two successive narrative actions immediately following on one another. The second most common relation (20% in the sample) is subject-to-subject, in which successive panels show differing viewpoint within a scene without any necessary advance in time. An example he gives is one panel showing a sportsman running a race and breaking the tape at the finishing line followed by another panel showing someone clicking a stopwatch – both presumably happen at the same moment but show different 'subjects' within the episode.

In contrast, in a sample of comics from the Japanese comics designer Osamu Tezuka, McCloud finds a very different balance. Action-to-action is still the dominant relation but there are almost as many cases of subject-to-subject relations. Moreover, there are also cases of moment-to-moment and aspect-to-aspect as well. Moment-to-moment panels show what resemble single frames in a piece of film, with a minimum of change to show time is moving – visual cues in the panels typically indicate that we have a single event broken down into individual moments. Aspect-to-aspect is a similar construction, but without the necessary advance in time. McCloud gives as an example a view in one panel of a country house followed by a panel showing a window, then another panel showing another part of the house, and so on. McCloud suggests that such transitions "establish a *mood* or a *sense of peace*, time seems to *stand still* in these quiet, contemplative combinations" (McCloud 1994: 79).

These results naturally raise many interesting questions concerning different individual, national and other styles and the ways in which these may change over time. Many would suggest that Japanese-style comics now exert an enormous influence on Western comics also, and so the patterns found by McCloud may already look rather different.

As always, however, performing such analyses relies on the categories being reliably applicable. For this, we need to be able to distinguish them in all cases that we encounter. Whereas many of McCloud's transitions seem relatively easy to see, when applied to comics in general there are sufficient 'difficult cases' as to raise doubts about the effectiveness of the classification as it stands. Several further sources of information need to be drawn upon to maintain the distinctions given.

For example, how precisely do we distinguish subject-to-subject from aspect-to-aspect? Both present different aspects of a single scene or episode without any necessary advance in time. But the main difference appears to be the status that the panels have for the narrative. Subject-to-subject relations pick out different but related activities occurring together at a point in the narrative; aspect-to-aspect relations instead pick out different states or situations holding at some point – in the terms of verbal expression, they are far more like *descriptions*. This means that 'nothing happens' in the panels related as aspect-to-aspect transitions; we simply see different static depictions of states of affairs that obtain. A distinction of this kind cannot be 'read off' of the image alone but requires a hypothesis about how the depicted material is being worked into the story being told. In other words, the question faced is: are we being shown a state or action significant for the narrative in its own right or are we being shown something that is simply typical of a broader state of affairs?

Thus, since providing a classification depends in part on a particular model of how the narrative is being told, there may be places where different analysts may come to different conclusions. This is always a situation that we should pay attention to when performing analysis. Sometimes such differences reflect genuine differences in possible interpretations; sometimes they reflect instead problems in the categories used for analysis. If the categories are not 'tight' enough, then they only offer a loose fit for the material examined and we have to treat any counts of the relations that apply with caution.

McCloud presents many other aspects of how comics function but, again, we will focus for present purposes on text-image relations. Here again McCloud suggests a possible classification (McCloud 1994: 153–154); his categories are summarised in Table 5.1 together

Table 5.1 McCloud's (1994: 153–155) classification of word-image relations in comics

Type	Description
Word-specific	the images 'illustrate' the text without adding anything particularly new of their own
Picture-specific	the words do "little more than add a soundtrack to a visually told sequence"
Duo-specific	"both words and pictures send essentially the *same message*"
Additive	words "*amplify* or *elaborate* on an image or vice versa"
Parallel	word and pictures follow different courses without interacting
Montage	words are treated *as integral graphical parts of* the picture
Inter-dependent	the pictures and words "go hand in hand to convey an idea that neither could convey alone"

with his brief descriptions. Here, too, it may not always be possible to clearly distinguish between cases and further organisation might be beneficial. The contrasts made, for example, between duo-specific and inter-dependent seem to be a matter of degree, while both word-specific and picture-specific need to be judged carefully according to the information relevant for the narrative since, as we have emphasised at many points in the preceding discussions, strictly speaking word and image will *always* present something new with respect to the other simply by virtue of their differing expressive capabilities.

It is interesting to compare classifications such as these with the kinds of text-image relations suggested for picturebooks and, indeed, as we shall see in other units, with other proposals for text-image relations at large, regardless of the material they have been developed for. As usual, there are some patterns which continue to recur – for example, the distinctions drawn here between parallel and interdependent, as well as the very notion of 'interdependence' as such, have direct correlates in the discussion of picturebooks above. There are also other schemes that have been developed specifically for comics. Abbott (1986), for example, makes the classic three-way filmic distinction between narration, dialogue and sound effect and considers the panel as the smallest unit where such relationships between text and the rest of the comic can play out.

There are also more or less substantial differences both in the content or scope of individual relations and in the organisation of the categorisations even within McCloud's list. Montage, for example, is the only relation that explicitly refers to specifics of the *compositional layout* adopted for text and image; the others all assume that the text and the image are 'separate', although, unlike the common case with picturebooks, still necessarily *parts* of single images. As Abbott indicates, however, there are many ways in which a text can be *part of* an image and these possibilities have been pushed particularly far in comics. This means that they actually require detailed descriptions in their own right and offer a particularly rich area for further theory building. Forceville (2010), for example, provides an interesting analysis of the diverse *forms* that the balloons in comics can take for narrative effect, while Cohn (2013a) goes still further and sets out a general framework for text-image relations in comics as such. We return particularly to Cohn's account below, after introducing the general framework within which he is working.

There are also typographic conventions within the texts displayed that must be considered, such as highlighting the most important words or concepts. This is the dominant style of textual presentation in comics and also the reason why many of the quotations we have drawn from McCloud above include so many emphasised words! In general, this presentation of textual material builds on comics' awareness that *all* material that it uses has a visual component, which is then available for manipulation for narrative and aesthetic effect. Often the use of boldface typography in comics does not correspond, for example, to stress in spoken language as emphasis in written text usually does – it would be interesting, therefore, to follow this up more closely to see just when it *is* employed. And different typographical choices can reflect different 'voices' or character traits or states of mind – as we illustrated with the example from Will Eisner in Unit 1 in Figure 1.8.

It will be worthwhile at this point, therefore, to expand the view of comics beyond that offered by McCloud. We focus on two developments, both of which are concerned with visual narrative but take very different starting points. The first is the linguistically inspired characterisation of visual narrative in comics developed in several important publications by Cohn (Cohn 2010, 2013c, 2014). The second is the most sophisticated approach to comics that has been developed applying notions from semiotics, that of Groensteen (2007 [1999]).

These two positions themselves 'speak' very different languages – the former that of cognitive neuroscience and empirical investigation, the latter that of semiotics and close 'textual' description. Discussion between them is as a consequence not straightforward as there can be basic disagreements in methods and goals. The position taken here will be simply to place them side-by-side as potential sources of insight into how the medium of comics works, rather than as being in any way 'competitors'. Unless we are careful, arguments pushing for one type of approach *instead* of the other may close off profitable avenues of future research.

COMICS AND VISUAL NARRATIVE: NEIL COHN

The comics practitioner and theorist Neil Cohn has recently produced a considerable number of important research papers exploring the nature of comics as a medium for visual narrative. Cohn's starting point is the rather traditional sounding suggestion that the use of images in sequences may be similar to the use of words in sentences in spoken languages – and hence may constitute a 'visual language'. Cohn means this, however, in a very different and far more precise sense than either the multitude of rather loose metaphorical analogies drawn between languages and other media over the years or the rather more well founded, but often equally tendentious, claims of traditional semiotics.

In fact, this entire area of debate is one that demands a discussion far more detailed than is possible here. There are still those who use 'comics as language' as if this were self-evidently true, just as there are those who consider proposals of any close relationship between 'comics' and 'language' to be self-evidently absurd. Positions in both camps generally suffer from some of those reoccurring problems identified right at the beginning of this book in Unit 1 ('Multimodality and "meaning multiplication"', p. 5). Talking of comics-as-language in a naïve sense, just as some form of communication, is often relatively empty of content because language proper has some rather specific properties – semiotically, cognitively and socially – which need to be addressed in detail when relating any form of communication back to verbal language if the metaphor is to do any work. But, *denying* any relation between comics and language must then do this as well, otherwise it is unclear what is being said.

Unfortunately in both cases we find discussions that appear as if they are engaging with the 'other' side but which actually exhibit significant deficiencies. Most blatant are gaps concerning current states of knowledge in linguistics – thereby distorting what is said about language to the extent that it becomes unrecognisable for those working in the field – and, equally, discussions showing at best sketchy knowledge of recent developments in semiotics – which has also moved far beyond structuralist models of arbitrary associations between signifiers and signifieds. Arguments can then trot out old chestnuts such as the 'arbitrariness' of the sign, the continuous nature of images, and many more to secure their own positions. One needs, therefore, to be very wary when reading such texts. Many of the arguments that circulate cannot be taken at face value and even otherwise quite sophisticated discussions can be vitiated by weak foundations in the respective states of the art in areas being criticised.

Turning back to Cohn, then, it is important to understand the ways in which his linguistically informed characterisation of comics actually represents a radical break with former traditions of drawing loose language-based analogies. Building instead on the full breadth of what is currently known about the neurocognitive processing of language, Cohn is engaged in conducting detailed empirical and experimental investigations of how the readers/viewers of comics respond to finely controlled variations in comics form, organisation and contents. These experiments are in turn informed by a sophisticated model of what is involved in understanding comics, which is then progressively refined by the experimental results. By these means, Cohn opens up new and intriguing possibilities for probing how comics are understood – in important respects, going far beyond what can be done by 'textual' analysis alone.

In making this strong comparison between (verbal) language and any visual language that might be operating, Cohn is careful to consider only quite abstract properties of the linguistic system and the mechanisms presumed to support those properties during brain processing. It is this that places the connection he draws between 'language' and visual narrative on a new footing. There are, for example, robust empirical results concerning what happens in the brain while processing linguistic syntactic structure. It is then rather natural to ask whether any similarities can be found during the processing of other structured materials, such as visual narratives. To the extent that similarities can be found, there is then evidence that the brain may be responding to verbal organisation and sequential visual organisation in similar ways.

This sidesteps any unrealistic pronouncements about visual 'syntax' or other more super-ficial comparisons between language and visual organisation, positive or negative. The notion that some kind of structural relationships may be operating with respect to both visual and linguistic material is far more general. As Cohn and colleagues explain:

> We emphasise again that the narrative structure used to comprehend sequential images is quite different from syntactic structure used to comprehend single sentences. As the saying goes, 'a picture is worth a thousand words': by and large, images can convey at least as much meaning as entire sentences, and we therefore conceive of the narrative structure of sequential images as more analogous to narrative structure at the discourse level of language. Nonetheless, there are several structural commonalities shared by narrative structure and syntax. . . . It is therefore possible that computing structure across sequential images recruits processing mechanisms that are shared with language.
>
> (Cohn et al. 2012: 33–34)

The connection made here to discourse is broadly similar to the point we made in Unit 2 ('What are text-image relationships?', p. 44) concerning the status of text-image relations. Cohn goes much further, however, in his consideration of the availability of syntax-like mechanisms for the sequential processing of visual materials.

A good starting point for understanding Cohn's position is to consider problems that he raises with respect to McCloud's proposals for relations between panels that we introduced above. Connecting sequences of panels together in this way suggests one method for understanding how reader/viewers of comics might be making sense of the one-dimensional sequence of panels as they move along the sequence. But, just as with verbal language, understanding a sequence of words in an utterance does not stop there. The words in sequence are used as evidence for building structure – in the case of language, syntactic structure – in order to uncover dependency and hierarchical relationships holding among the elements perceived. Thus, although the sequence of words heard or read may be one-dimensional, the structures built on top of those words and which lead to meaning certainly are not.

Psycholinguistic experiments have been probing these structures for decades and it is now uncontroversial that a variety of relationships are constructed during processing (cf., e.g., Altmann 1997). We can see these at work even in very simple cases of linguistic syntactic ambiguity. Consider the following standard example as might be used in an introduction to linguistics:

(1) The farmer watched the birds with the binoculars.

If we were perverse (or linguists), we could ask why it was that the birds had binoculars. More importantly, we can 'measure' empirically by means of a whole battery of different kinds of tests that someone hearing or reading this sentence has more 'work' to do when they encounter the 'with' because they have to decide *which syntactic structure to build*: specifically they must decide whether they construct a sentence where 'with the binoculars' is attached to the verb 'watched' or they construct a noun phrase where 'the binoculars' is attached to the 'birds' – that is, 'the birds with the binoculars'. Both structural organisations are possible in theory – and there are many cases where the latter attachment would be the one preferred, as in:

(2) The farmer watched the birds with the long beaks.

Structurally, therefore, the brain has some work to do to sort out the preferred inter-relationships, to select one alternative rather than others, and to throw away any that it does not want. Cohn argues that this must be the case for comics as well, since when interpreting a sequence of panels reader/viewers do much more than simply connect things one after the other.

Our pre-theoretical perception of the experience of reading comics certainly supports this – we are constantly putting more organisation on to what we encounter than can be captured as a flat string of transitions between panels. Cohn (2010) shows this further by discussing the contrasting panel sequences in Figure 5.2. Cohn argues that panels have a variety of properties that can be used in combination with their sequencing in order to motivate structures that hold over, and thereby group, collections of panels into larger units. Such structures bring with them constraints – and this is what turns loose organisation where, in principle, anything goes into a resource for deriving meanings. In McCloud's account, for example, no statement can be made about which kinds of inter-panel relations might hold and when; they are simply applied to panels as found as best one can. No constraints on possible sequencing arise and so the description remains just that, a description.

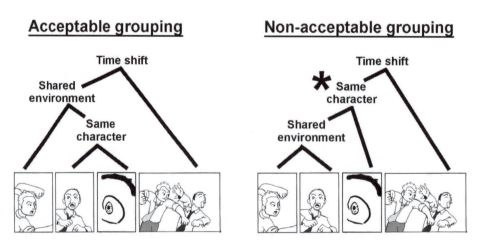

Figure 5.2   A proposal for an ungrammatical panel sequence from Neil Cohn (Cohn 2010: 143). Used by kind permission of the author

Cohn, in contrast, establishes structural organisations that bring constraints on just what kinds of sequences and hierarchical organisations are going to be produced. It is these constraints that support processing and attributing meaning to panel sequences. Just as in language, structures are there in order to make sense of what is being interpreted. In the panel sequence shown on the left of Figure 5.2, then, we see four panels decomposing an exchange of blows between two people in a typical microscale fashion. As in film, we have cuts between viewpoints and even, in the third panel, an extreme close-up.

Cohn argues that this sequence is straightforwardly intelligible and, moreover, that the extreme close-up in the third panel *will be semantically associated* with the person shown in the second panel. Since there are two people involved in the story up to that point, this interpretation needs to be explained. To do this, Cohn employs the notion of structure shown in the figure. Certain *structural configurations* within which panels may be located are defined. Thus, there are configurations where time is not moving on but which show aspects of a single situation – Cohn calls this *shared environment*, analogous to McCloud's aspect-to-aspect. There are also configurations which may focus in and present details, Cohn has here *same character*. And there are configurations where time moves on, Cohn's *time shift*. These are then used to specify preferences for grouping panels – essentially, shifts in time group at the highest level, followed by shifts among characters at the same time, followed at the lowest level by maintenance of the *same* character and time (Cohn 2010: 142).

Now, whereas it is perfectly possible to build a shared environment from more complex elements, Cohn suggests that it is not possible to take a shared environment and attach more specific elements – such as 'same character' – because it is unclear to which internal elements of the environment the more specific element can refer. This is the situation depicted on the right of the figure. The structure here attempts to impose a different grouping on the panel sequence, one which leaves the meaning seriously in doubt. And yet, the one on the right would correspond to the kind of 'linear' unfolding that a series of panel transitions would suggest – each panel simply gets added onto the 'structure so far'.

This begins to demonstrate that there is far more to 'reading' the panels than a simple linear addition. The second and third panels need to be grouped 'before' they can be used *together with* the first panel to make a composite unit that is then capable of participating in a time shift to the next moment in the depicted event sequence. This kind of description is not possible when we only have transitions between panels. It also makes interesting predictions concerning how sequences of panels may or may not be interpreted, including cases of potential ambiguity closely analogous to the linguistic examples we used above in (1) and (2). The ability to make predictions that can then be tested in empirical investigation is the crucial feature that begins to allow progress beyond impressionistic description.

The additional organisational properties that we can see operating here also bring the account more closely into contact with the description of narrative that we introduced in Unit 3. The panels as presented do not slavishly follow the temporal unfolding of depicted events; they break up that time flow into phases of relative movement and stasis, thereby influencing narrative rhythm and allowing a potentially far more involving construction of narrative for the reader/viewer. This is directly related to the reader/viewer's reception processes:

> this need for grouping panels to connect to later parts shows that panel progressions do not always mimic the iconic movement of experienced events, because some sort of mental activity beyond knowledge of event states must connect non-temporal rela- tionships.

(Cohn 2010: 140)

This knowledge beyond events Cohn describes in terms of narrative organisation and the structural configurations that support it. This is then information that is really inherent to the medium and to storytelling, thereby demanding its own detailed study.

The line of argumentation that distinct kinds of panels can be defined, and patterns of use identified, allows Cohn to go further, drawing on some basic principles of linguistic organisation. Reoccurring patterns of use, or *distributional properties*, motivate seeing panels as playing a similar function in their respective semiotic system as words do in the system of language. This is a daring move and must be understood, not in the superficial sense of claiming that a 'picture' (the panel) is like a 'word' in terms of its 'content', but rather as a result of applying the well-established methodology for defining units developed over long years of theory development in linguistics. Specifically, words are a minimal unit in syntax because these are the elements that the rules of syntax combine into larger, meaning-bearing structures – *not* because they may refer to the world or identify or label objects. Thus:

> this ... approach to panels as syntactic units acknowledges that they are subject to dis-
> tributional regularities within a syntagmatic sequence in the same way that words are. That
> is, panels are not the visual equivalent of words (and neither are elements of an individual
> image). Rather, both words and panels play similar structural roles within the confines of
> their own systems of grammar.
>
> (Cohn 2007: 37)

As Cohn notes, this is also rather different to those who pursue relationships between narrative elements as a question of discourse, for example as in socio-semiotic accounts. There is clearly much left to explore here concerning this renewed connection of structural organisation and narrative.

Finding distributional regularities among comics panels is a methodologically more well grounded and theoretically interesting way of uncovering structural relationships holding over groups of panels than that suggested by McCloud's one-dimensional sequences of transitions. On the basis of his investigations, Cohn makes detailed proposals for a 'syntax' of sequences of panels, intended to act in ways similar to the syntactic organisation in language, with similarly measurable consequences for processing – both when a sequence obeys the principles Cohn sets out and when a sequence deviates.

An illustration of this structure for description is shown in Figure 5.3. The labels for the elements of such structures can be seen in terms of microscale narrative functions taken up when depicting story events. Thus, for example, each component is made up of a 'peak' of action, optionally preceded by an immediately preparatory unit called 'initial'. The peak can also be followed by a 'release' of the action. This structure is then additionally taken to be **recursive**, just as is the case with language structures. Therefore elements can be internally structured, showing on smaller scales precisely the same kind of organisation that can be found on the larger scales. In the case in the figure, for example, the higher-level Peak element is itself broken up into a small scale unit which itself contains an Initial, Peak, and so on.

Cohn *et al.* (2012) presents several experimental results gained from brain imaging studies and reaction time tests for panel sequences that obey, and do not obey, the rules Cohn sets out. Exploring how readers actually process comics materials therefore constitutes an important new direction for comics research. It allows Cohn to raise a host of interesting questions and also invites the application of some novel research methods for probing the working of comics more deeply.

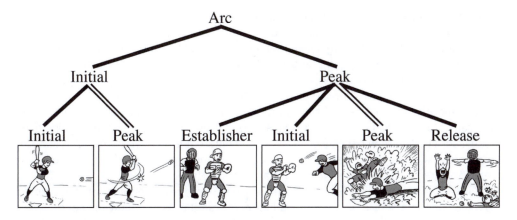

Figure 5.3 Example panel sequence structure proposed by Neil Cohn (Cohn *et al.* 2012: Figure 18). Used by kind permission of the author

GROENSTEEN AND THE SEMIOTICS OF COMICS

A rather different way into the analysis of comics is presented by Thierry Groensteen (Groensteen 2007 [1999], 2013 [2011]). Whereas most introductions to comics concentrate on the basic elements of panels such as frames, speech balloons and so on, including combinations of such visual devices, visual styles and language within panels, Groensteen approaches the entire issue of comics from a rather more fundamental, semiotic perspective asking how it is that meaning-carrying distinctions can be formed from the material available in the comics medium at all.

A straightforward point of contrast with, for example, the approach of Cohn is that Groensteen starts from the 'page' or doublepage spread as a basic unit of analysis rather than from sequences of panels. Cohn's view is then more like language, seeing similarities in how meanings and structures are built up across a linear sequence, where Groensteen's view is inherently spatial. Although Cohn also explores issues related to spatial organisation – particularly how complex page layouts are *turned into* sequences during reading (e.g., Cohn 2013b), the point of access is always related back to cognition. Groensteen's starting point attempts to highlight more properties attributable to the medium as such.

Groensteen consequently relates the basic decisions, made in both comics production and analysis, to a consideration of just how the space presented in the visual field is deployed. Groensteen then defines pages in comics as *multiframes*, that is, some kind of division into framed subspaces, and within this, "successive images do not just make up a string, they comprise, from the outset, a totality. Readers approach the page both as a fraction of a story and as a visual unit" (Groensteen 2013 [2011]: 135–136). Groensteen sees this multiframe as "an instrument for converting space into time, into duration" (Groensteen 2013 [2011]: 138) and so describes the effects of varying two-dimensional layouts in terms of rhythm, beats and duration. This emphasis on spatiality and its use by the medium is then more thoroughly rooted in the visual and its *differences* to language.

In short, Groensteen sees a comicbook as an arrangement of spaces distributed over a comicbook's pages and constructed to 'work together' for the author's (or authors') purposes. This may include words and images, but then again, may not. When text and image are present, they are as particular uses of the space as a whole and need to be seen in this respect when considering their meaning contributions and interactions. Clearly, most comics *do* contain text and images – but this is the beginning of an enquiry rather than an end: what *else* do they contain? And what kinds of images and what kinds of text, playing what kind of functions, in what kind of spatial organisation?

For example, anything that takes up space has a shape and so panels are no different; there is therefore the issue of *framing*, precisely what shape a panel is given – this can be meaning-bearing in its own right and so shows that simply talking of 'panel' is going to be insufficient. A tall narrow panel is going to have a different effect (when placed in context) than a broad wide panel; an irregular panel with spikes and angles has a different effect from a round and regular panel, or even lack of frames altogether.

Groensteen also takes this a step further since to talk of panels is already to have moved from the page to a smaller unit – there is therefore also the issue of how the set of panels placed on a page are *themselves* spatially interrelated. This is the issue of layout, which takes on a very specific and additional constellation of meaning possibilities when we move into the medium of comics. This is important for us here as well – since we have been talking about images most generally, in principle including diagrammatic and abstract images, then *the layout of comics falls within our scope also*. This is also an aspect of the 'image' that can form components of text-image relations, as we shall see below.

Groensteen describes the entire area of comics layout and the intentional use of com-posed panels into superordinate wholes in terms of what he calls **spatiotopia**. Panels are then defined according to their shape, size and what Groensteen calls their *sites* – that is, where they occur within the page, within smaller or larger groups of panels that Groensteen terms *multipanels*, or within the work as a whole. The framing that gives rise to panels itself takes on a variety of functions – Groensteen offers six: closure, separative, rhythmic, structural, expressive and the readerly, that is, the contract entered into between comic-maker and reader that something worthwhile and deliberate is being singled out for expression. Groensteen gives extensive examples and discussion. Meanings building on these functions can be created by panels and by combinations of panels that are themselves visually salient in some way. This means that there may be meaningful structural combinations of panels of any size, both continuous and discontinuous as panels and layout from different parts of a comic are brought into relation (cf. Groensteen 2007 [1999]: 99–100).

The areas used meaningfully within comics then stretch upwards, beyond the panel; they also stretch inward, within the panel. Here we find such familiar notions as speech balloons and thought bubbles, captions and so on – all are uses of space and are therefore subject in addition to any other constraints that may hold to the overriding 'spatial logic' of presenting a composed communicative artefact. This is echoed in Cohn's (2013a) recent discussion of text-image relations, which is quite compatible with a semiotic viewpoint, as we shall see below.

A second area distinguished by Groensteen is **arthrology**. This comes in two variants, one a specific form of the other. These are often discussed separately and the more general form is sometimes not discussed at all. The more specific variant is close to simple sequence: a strip of panels is used to 'break-down' the action of the narrative (*if* it is a narrative comic – this is not an essential feature of comics as several researchers, including Groensteen, Eisner, McCloud and others emphasise) into 'readerly' verbo-visual 'utterances'. The sequentiality shows itself in various technical features of the information depicted in the panels.

However, in general, connections need not be made simply to the panels immediately surrounding any given panel: connections can be made to anywhere in the comic – Groensteen distinguishes here two cases as well: what he terms 'synchronic' connections that are connections on the same page and which, therefore, can be perceived by the reader/viewer 'at the same time' (hence 'synchronic') *in situ*; the other Groensteen terms 'diachronic' connections – these are connections with panels on *other* pages. These are not then co-present and need to be reconstructed by the reader/viewer. In both cases, however, there is a more or less complicated notion of constructing bridges between particular elements deployed.

The basic mechanism supporting this is termed *braiding*, which Groensteen defines thus:

> Braiding is precisely the operation that, from the point of creation, programs and carries out this sort of bridging. It consists of an additional and remarkable structuration that, taking account of the breakdown and the page layout, defines a *series* within a sequential framework.
>
> (Groensteen 2007 [1999]: 146; original emphasis)

Here Groensteen makes use of a difference between 'sequences' that are seen as following some 'narrative project' – that is, telling a story – and 'series' which are more connections of form relying on technical features of what is depicted. This is then also analogous to the linguistic notion of *cohesion* that we will see applied multimodally in Unit 8. Cohesion is also a relationship essentially of form that operates across structural boundaries. The notions of cohesive texture and braiding are then quite comparable.

This more extensive view of what constitutes comics and the means available to the medium for making meanings opens up a range of further text-image questions that have, to date, barely been asked let alone answered. The organisation of spatiotopia has some relationships to discussions of diagrams, but is also quite distinct in that the meanings for which these particular kinds of diagrams are used are far removed from those to which diagrams are employed in more technical domains. And yet, there are nevertheless similarities because of the formal aspects involved: the notion of spatiotopia is concerned with a meaningful division of space, just as in the case with diagrams. What precisely those meanings are, however, is another issue and one should not jump too quickly to the assumption that the 'same' meanings are operational in both areas. More empirical studies are required.

TEXT-IMAGE RELATIONS IN COMICS

The most thorough and detailed review of the various possibilities for bringing text and image together in the context of comics is that given by Cohn (2013a). In this article, Cohn takes up the issue of how comics (and some other related media) employ text and image together as his main focus. He proposes a broad four-way set of alternatives consisting of **inherent**, where any text that appears is actually part of the image material; **emergent**, which includes speech balloons and thought bubbles; **adjoined**, where text and image are related only indirectly via captions or spatial proximity; and **independent**, where text and image are 'fully separate' and relations are only signalled by in-text references of the form 'see Figure 3', 'Plate 12 shows' and so on – a use of language investigated by Paraboni and van Deemter (2002) as **document deixis** and typical of the **text flow** semiotic mode introduced in Bateman (2008: 175).

Since this latter category explicitly takes text and image as *not* being structurally related, we will not consider it further here. Cohn does note, however, that the lack of explicit inter-connection found under cases of independence can create problems of interpretation and suggests that more visually aware 'textual' practices may offer a solution. This is then similar to the points made by Pegg (2002) that we saw in our discussion of design in Unit 1 ('Design', p. 19).

For the other categories, Cohn usefully introduces the notion of 'interfacing' between modalities. Text and image may be integrated in various ways but a particularly relevant development in comics is the evolution of formal resources that allow text and image to participate equally in genuinely composite messages. These formal resources – of which speech balloons are just one specific type – are constituted by structural locations that support the structural interfacing of the involved modalities. Interfacing is a particularly close kind of relationship and is most finely articulated in Emergent text-image relations. We will return to Emergent text-image relations after briefly discussing the two remaining, much simpler text-image relation types first.

Inherent text-image relations

Inherent text-image relations are when the two modalities are both present within a depiction as contributing components at a single level of semiotic abstraction. The simplest case is when, for example, some visual depiction of the world also includes objects that might also realistically involve textual information, such as when names of shops or signs of various kinds might appear in a drawing of a street, and so on. In McCloud's scheme of text-image relations this is *montage* (cf. Table 5.1)

More abstract cases occur when a representation, which can be either pictorial or textual, includes components drawn from the respective other modality. This includes the *rebus*, in which a picture of an item can replace the word for that item in a sentence (cf. Unit 12, Figure 12.1). McCloud also offers an illustration of the converse, where textual elements may replace parts of an image – as in his drawing of a face in which the eyes have been replaced by two instances of the written word 'EYE' (McCloud 1994: 28, 207). Cohn calls this *substitutive inherency*.

Adjoining text-image relations

Adjoining text-image relations occur when the textual and image information are presented separately, usually in their own visual 'frames'. This means that text and image are not directly connected to one another, although they are visually integrated. The interface between the two modalities is in this case relatively distinct – the text may be explicitly framed or simply placed in visual proximity to the images that it relates to. If we consider the entire page or doublepage spread of a picturebook as offering a structural unit, then adjoining would also describe most cases of picturebook text-image relationships as we saw in the previous unit.

Adjoined text-image combinations include framed caption of all kinds. Cohn offers examples of adjoined captions both within panels, which he terms *bundled*, and 'across' panels, which are then 'unbundled'. Sequences of unbundled captions can serve a variety of functions, such as maintaining continuity across panel transitions or providing a parallel 'reading track' alongside the visual sequence. This is again reminiscent of the 'double orientation' that we saw claimed for picturebooks at the end of the previous unit, although typically in the case of comics the verbal information present in such units reflects the microscale development of comics as a whole and so contrasts with the more extensive textual narrative development typical of the picturebook.

Emergent text-image relations as interfaced modalities

Emergent text-image relations are the most interesting case discussed by Cohn by far. Cohn argues that emergent relations operate within an abstractly structured text-image interface that anchors image and text together in a particularly powerful way. The standard cases of speech balloons and thought bubbles are then just concrete instances or, to use linguistic terminology, 'realisations' of this abstract general structure.

The interface consists of an abstract configuration relating three elements that are always logically present, even though they do not always need to be visually depicted. The configuration is made up of a carrier, which is the space that serves functionally to hold some material (which is usually text but can also be images), a root, which is the visually depicted entity associated with the information presented in the carrier, and the tail, which connects root and carrier, typically by linking them visually.

This interface can be illustrated most easily in the form of a speech balloon – but it is crucial to keep in mind that the carrier–tail–root configuration characterises an *abstract semiotic resource* for interfacing verbally expressed information (typically in the carrier) and pictorially expressed information (the root). Each of the logical components of the interface may occur in a rich variety of visual forms. For example, the carrier might have an explicit shape – for example, an oval or cloud or more complex varieties still (cf. Forceville 2010) – or be implicit; the tail might be reduced to a simple line, be indicated by the shape of the text (*compositional enclosed*), or be replaced by spatial proximity altogether and so not be explicitly depicted by some connecting vector at all; and the root might be more or less specific in what is designated, not be visible at all due to its being entailed but 'out of frame' or even, another example Cohn presents, because of the lights in the storyworld being turned off, so all that we can read in the comics are the speech balloons with their tails without seeing who is 'talking'.

Cohn gives many illustrations of these and other alternatives, running through the individual cases that his more abstract characterisation both covers and suggests. The systematic presentation of possibilities leads to a far more exhaustive overview of just what is possible in this area. The framework as a whole also allows him to draw similarities between distinct kinds of text-image relations that are more often described separately. For example, he includes textual material representing sound effects – such as 'Bang!', 'Pow!' and so on – as also falling within the scope of the emergent interface structure. In these cases, it is usual for the tail to be expressed only by spatial proximity and for there to be no (visually) explicit carrier. Apart from this, however, Cohn sees this as falling within his general scheme.

Cohn also presents a representation derived from Abbott (1986: 156) as a more generic way of showing the structural components of the emergent interface. This involves separating out comics according to two planes: the **representational plane**, which contains the pictorial representation of the storyworld, and the **framing plane**, which contains all verbal material, such as spoken language, sound effects, thoughts, text directed at the reader and so on. The carrier is then a spatial region in the framing plane; the root is an entity depicted within the representational plane; and the tail is the link between the planes – the tail then serves what Cohn describes as an **indexical** function, *pointing out* which entity in the representational plane the information delimited in the framing plane is to be associated with. This is suggested graphically in Figure 5.4, which pulls apart our earlier reworking of the Sendak episode in comic form in the style suggested by Cohn. One might also consider more levels, as typically the case in film and its potentially unbounded number of 'diegetic', or story, levels – Cohn offers several examples of such extensions and self-reflexive designs for comics.

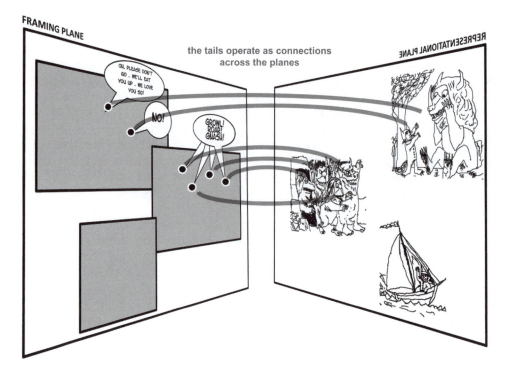

Figure 5.4 The framing (left) and representational (right) planes of comics illustrated with respect to our constructed Sendak episode

Cohn then distinguishes particular uses of the emergent interface in terms of what he terms *functional primitives*. Two are proposed: **root awareness** and **adjacent awareness**. These describe whether or not the root is aware of the content carried by the carrier (±RA) and whether or not others in the panel are aware of that content (±AA) respectively. A normal speech balloon is therefore {+RA,+AA}, since both the root and those around would, in the depicted storyworld, be aware of what is said; a thought bubble is {+RA,−AA} because thoughts are 'private' to the root; captions are {−RA, −AA} because they are generally *non-diegetic* (to use the relevant term from narratology and film theory: cf. Unit 3) and so not accessible to the storyworld; and sound effects are {−RA,+AA} because all in the panel can generally hear them but the cause of the sound – e.g., a door slamming – is not aware of anything since it is not animate or conscious. This then fills out the entire *paradigm* of four distinct types of uses of the interface.

Cohn's description contains many other details that need to be carefully worked through, although space precludes our doing this here. There are also places where further issues are raised which may in turn lead to opportunities for extension or more detailed exploration. Cohn suggests, for example, that uses of the emergent interface can also apply to *diagrammatic representations* – in particular, he sees cases of {−RA, −AA}, which Cohn terms **satellites**, as covering text labels and *call-outs* of the kind typically occurring in diagrams. A 'call-out' is the standard design term when visually depicted elements receive additional information via textboxes that are connected in some way.

Cohn considers these to be further examples of his emergent text-image relation. In uses of this kind, the carrier may then be implicit or a simple box, while the tail typically takes the form of a simple line or an arrow. Although this posits an interesting point of overlap across the semiotic modes of comics and diagrams, it is not clear that the two can really be assimilated in this manner. Both of the distinctions Cohn takes to underlie satellites – that is, root aware-ness and audience awareness – are generally irrelevant in the case of diagrams and so do not constitute genuine 'choices'. They may then conform to some other 'interfacing' scheme that brings text and images together in diagrams but whether or not this is a similar organisa-tional resource to that found in comics needs closer attention.

Cohn could pursue this further from the cognitive perspective in order to ascertain whether any differences can be isolated during processing – however, even if the same mechanisms are found to be at work, it may nevertheless be the case that the required *semiotic* descrip-tions are different. One sign that there is a broader range of differences to consider is the fact that the satellite constructs a different *directionality* for the tail than the other three emergent situations do. In all cases apart from satellites, the directionality is from root to carrier; but for satellites, the direction is suggested to be from carrier to root.

This may indicate a conflation of different functionalities. The indexicality of the tail in comics is no doubt as Cohn describes it: it serves to point out a particular functional role in the configuration defined by the emergent interface. This functional role is that of a semiotic source of the contents given in the carrier. This conforms to treatments of speech and thought in terms of *projection* – that is, the semiotic configuration of speaking and thinking, and of sounds and their sources (cf., e.g., Unit 4, 'Conclusions and discussion', p. 86). There are then two quite distinct functions involved: a textual function of pointing and a content function of the role of 'producing' some content.

In diagrams, the latter function is not applicable and it may be this that makes the direc-tionality behave differently in satellites. If the tail is, for example, realised by an *arrow* – as often found in diagrammatic representations – then it is the carrier that is visually the 'source' in the sense that it says something about something else. But in cases where a simple line is used, the issue of directionality is by no means so clear. The visual connection may be indicating a labelling relationship or some other kind of nondirectional identification. Discussion of this issue has also been pursued from a very different starting point in discourse-based treatments of visual layout, as we will see in Unit 11 ('Multiple simultaneous discourse relations', p. 219).

There may then be a different kind of text-image interface operating in the semiotic modes employed in diagrams with their own possibilities of expression. Arrows certainly work very differently (and more strongly: Galfano *et al.* 2012) than any other kinds of connectors and so, from the perspective of comics, may better be seen as an 'import' from the world of diagrams. To take this further, contact needs to be made with the extensive literature existing on diagrams and their processing as well (cf., e.g., Tversky, Zacks, Lee and Heiser 2000).

Another interesting area for further consideration that Cohn raises overlaps and refines considerations *of the use of space* as prioritised by Groensteen. As Cohn explains: "Carriers can be seen as micro-sized panels, similar to Inset panels that are set within another 'dominant' panel" (Cohn 2013a), which means also that carriers can 'grow' and take on more of the prop-erties of complete panels. This flexible use of the 'space on the page' is increasingly required when dealing with more contemporary and experimental comics.

However, despite the emergent interface being commonly used for text-image combina-tions, it is equally possible, as Cohn illustrates, to use it for relating *image-image* combinations in similar ways. From our perspective, this could be argued to constitute a more abstract case of text-image relationships. The emergent interface itself is a conventionalised semiotic resource that has properties *both* of the visual – since it uses space – *and* text – since it is far from continuously variable in its basic organisational structure, as Cohn effectively demonstrates.

Following Cohn's proposals for closer connections between verbal language and visual language, therefore, the emergent interface as such might be shown to have parallels with more structural configurations in grammar. There may then also be further connections to be drawn with other accounts that bring text and image together within the structural bounds of 'grammar-like' configurations, such as those we will see developed in cohesion-based models in Unit 8 and subsequent units.

Relations between text and multiframes and multipanels

Finally, we can briefly consider one further class of text-image relations in comics that draws more on directions set out in Groensteen's account – in particular on Groensteen's emphasis on larger, visually driven groupings of combinations of frames, both within pages and across more distant units via braiding. Text may play a role in structuring larger units spanning several panels, may help create braids by linking different image and text elements on or across pages, or may highlight particular spatial configurations that otherwise might go unnoticed. Groensteen's discussion of the "Fearful symmetry" chapter from Alan Moore, Dave Gibbons and Richards Watts' *Watchmen* constitutes a telling example of the latter (Groensteen 2007 [1999]: 99–100).

When text is added into this view, we can consider in more detail further functions of what Cohn would describe as unbundled satellites, or captions. Cohn's account suggests that they can add a separate 'reading track' and, of course, this entire track can then operate in interesting ways *together with* the visual track.

Almost ironically considering earlier positions taken against time in static media (cf. Unit 3), this tightly interfaced connection to language brings back into the medium a very close relationship with time and temporal unfolding. McCloud and others for example, have discussed how the simple fact that a text is read, and so unfolds in time, can be used to impose temporal relationships back onto accompanying visuals: this can be seen in any use of speech balloons in single panels where the contents of the balloons represent turns in a dialogue. Cohn talks of this in terms of the events that are being depicted – when events that have particular temporal dependences are shown, then the interpretation of the corresponding visuals will conform to the temporal relations present. Thus, even though visually two people with speech balloons are both simultaneously present, their acts of speaking will be read as ordered.

This then also applies in 'larger-scale' cases, where the rhythm and temporal unfolding is controlled over sequences of panels. An example from Will Eisner is shown in Figure 5.5. Here rhythm is achieved largely by the presence or non-presence of dialogue contributions.

The second panel here is not then a situation where 'no one' is speaking, it is a *marked non-occurrence of speaking* – what researchers in the field of Conversation Analysis call a 'noticeable absence'. For example, if someone asks a question and there is no answer, this is not the same situation as silence – the question creates a structural slot in interaction that is expecting to be filled; if it is not filled, then specific consequences of interpretation follow from this (cf. Heritage and Atkinson 1984, Gardner 2008). This is very similar in the example from Eisner here – a statement contingently expects some kind of follow up, when this does not come, we have a specific interpretation of what is being shown.

The text-image relation at issue here is then one of *synchronisation* and *timing of delivery* and may serve to group entire collections of panels on the page. This could also be related more to issues of performance and delivery as is occasionally mentioned with respect to picturebooks when they are being read aloud to children. Within comics, making sense of the

Figure 5.5 Use of text for temporal spacing of narrative in comics in an example from Eisner (1992: 124); used by permission

speech balloons as contributions to ongoing dialogue is one of the standard ways of imposing temporal coherence on sequences of static images in the storyworld.

A structurally similar usage with rather different effects for reception is the corresponding non-temporal version of the same technical resources. As with carriers in general, unbundled captions can themselves be expanded in size and used as a *spatial* structuring device for more complex panel configurations. In this case, the text employed within extended captions might take on larger-scale organisational functions, grouping events together into larger episodes and so on. Here the text interacts more with the layout as a whole in the service of adding semantics to spatial configurations of panels. And here again, an explicit *contrastive* analysis of the function and reception of such spatial organisations in comics and other media where layout is actively used for guiding readers would be very valuable.

CONCLUSIONS AND DISCUSSION

We have now arrived at a rather general characterisation of just what a 'comic' might be, seeing it as a particular configuration of ways of making meanings verbo-visually exhibiting its own rather distinctive flavour. We can usefully contrast the organisation involved here to the descriptions of picturebooks and illustrated books given at the end of the previous unit.

Any description in terms of a combination of text and images has been shown to be rather too simplistic to characterise how comics are operating. We have now seen that unless we talk about the words and the separate functions they perform – including at least the four of captioning, speech and thought, sound effects and 'diegetic' presence – *and* the pictorial renditions of event and states of affairs offered *and* the visual, non-iconic indications of motion and emotion *and* the compositional make up as expressed in the panel layout of episodes, slices of action, descriptions and their mutual interactions and inter-relations, then we are not really talking about comics.

Naturally one has to understand texts to be able to follow a comic (if it contains words); and equally, one has to have a certain pictorial literacy as well (if it contains pictures) – but these separate competences are not then to be exercised in isolation and then combined to see what comes out – the combination necessary occurs much earlier, and involves *its own* additional sets of skills. Cohn describes this fine-grained joint operation of text and images, particularly within the emergent interface, as giving rise to **composite signals**. This means that both the text and the image components are so tightly combined that they are really taken up as a single source of information during cognitive processing.

Their interaction is then far closer than the kind of double orientation discussed with picturebooks. There need be no double orientation in comics, the orientation is typically *single* and *composite*. Moreover the active deployment of layout of panels and groups of panels and their spatial relationships serves actively to guide reader/viewers' attention over these tightly integrated composites. Cohn refers here explicitly to **attention units** as a basic unit of comics' design and reception.

To allow more direct comparison with the picturebooks and other artefacts described in the previous unit, therefore, we set out in Figure 5.6 a diagram similar in form to those of the previous unit but showing the very different internal organisation at work in comics. The individual elements within pages connected by arrows can be taken as covering both multi-panels in the sense of Groensteen and particular cases of attention units functioning as composite signals as discussed by Cohn. The 'text-image interface' shown includes the relationship of 'projection' that we introduced in the previous unit; this offers a close point of contact with Cohn's consideration of carrier–tail–root as an abstract semiotic resource as we suggested above.

When examining the text-image relations in these kinds of artefacts, it is then crucial to see both the 'text' and the 'image' contributions as internally diversified and to follow where the combined contributions are seeking to take the reader/viewer. This involves, as in all the cases of analysis that we discuss, paying close attention to any artefact that is being analysed rather than assuming, for example, that it is simply a story being illustrated or a sequence of

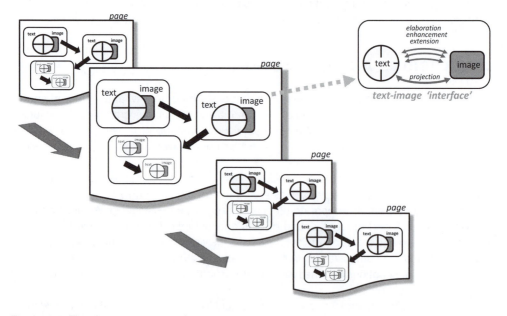

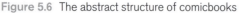

Figure 5.6 The abstract structure of comicbooks

pictures with verbal annotations. The kind of 'unity' that such artefacts achieve is very much their own.

There are various ways of taking this further. For example, once one has this rich resource for making meanings, there is no reason why it should be restricted or even driven by narrative. The complex units made available as the building blocks of comics allow a whole range of uses. Eisner (1992) includes sections on various uses of 'sequential art' including technical instruction comics, giving technical information about how to use various devices, and 'attitudinal instruction' comics. And McCloud's (1994) entire introduction is a *tour de force* in the non-narrative comicbook form. Other modern comicbook artists – such as, quite prominently, Chris Ware – are also producing work that challenges the boundaries of 'narrative' as such, just as is done in other art forms. It is then not so much that the 'story' allows us to work out what the diverse words and images mean, but rather that the complex combination of semiotic resources currently available in the medium of comics can be used to make artefacts belonging to a broad range of genres.

In any case, with this degree of inherent complexity and power to guide the attention of reader/viewers through narrative and other communicative forms, we can end as we started and give the last word back to Seldes:

With those who hold a comic strip cannot be a work of art I shall not traffic.

(Seldes 1924: 231)

MODULE III

Visual Persuasion

Visual rhetoric

Rhetoric considers how the effectiveness – or at least the force – of a message can be influenced by how that message is expressed. Differences in phrasing are well known to have different effects and so rhetoric attempts to map out just which variations lead to effective uses of language under which circumstances. 'Effectiveness' in the sense of rhetoric traditionally meant the power to persuade or convince some audience of the truth of some suggested propositions or of the necessity of carrying out some particular course of action rather than others. As a consequence, rhetoric has for much of its existence been considered part of the domains of language, literature, public speaking, politics and argument.

Rhetoric of this kind goes back a long way. Classical rhetoric originated in the Greek and Roman traditions of oratory (particularly with Aristotle and Cicero). There the variation of messages in the service of persuasive effectiveness given particular circumstances of use was subjected to extensive study. Rhetoric came then to be defined as the investigation of patterns of language usage that are considered, first, to stand out in some way – that is, to be memorable or noticeable due to some distinctive turn of phrase, form or style – and, second, to be usable for exerting particular effects on hearers or readers. By means of employing **rhetorical devices** a speaker would aim to convince his or her audience more compellingly, be able to commit more complex and elaborated messages to memory, *and* show that they 'knew the rules' of appropriate speaking.

All three capabilities and effects were obviously very important for public speaking of all kinds. The use of rhetorical devices for memorising complex messages was, for example, especially important prior to technical solutions such as teleprompters. Stylistic devices that would help a speaker memorise a message could be expected to work on the audience as well – they, too, might then remember the message for longer and so the effect of the message would be longer-lasting, continuing to work on members of the audience over time.

Many guidelines for composition originate from traditional catalogues of rhetorical devices. Even very basic compositional rules of thumb – such as using three items (not two or four) in a list to emphasise a point or to be memorable ('sex, drugs and rock-'n'-roll', 'blood, sweat and tears', 'Friends, Romans, countrymen', '*Liberté, Égalité, Fraternité*', and so on), or employing alliteration so that the first sound of words is repeated, or in combinations (e.g., '*veni, vidi, vici*') – can be traced back to the extensive lists of variations in style that classical rhetoric compiled.

Naturally – and this is the point of our considering this brief bit of history here – the wish to convince, persuade and be memorable is by no means something that is restricted to *verbal* messages. So there have been suggestions over the years that the ideas worked out in rhetorical studies may have wider application. In particular, as the awareness of the importance of visual material for effective communication has grown, there have been several moves to apply the notions of effectiveness worked out in the study of rhetoric to other kinds of messages – including, most importantly for us here, both visual messages and messages made of combinations of text and image.

Since images have long been known to have a particularly strong force of attraction, to be able to interest or shock their viewers and to remain ingrained in the mind for a long time after exposure, it might seem rather obvious to consider them from the perspective of rhetoric. It is then probably surprising to see just how late this was in fact attempted. Due to a mixture of, on the one hand, a narrow focus on language on the part of those studying rhetoric (cf., for example, the brief discussion of the expansion of studies of rhetoric to the visual given in Foss 2005) and, on the other, an equally long tradition (often said to go back to Plato) of regarding visual means of persuasion almost as 'unfair' – as bypassing the proper bounds of reason and rational argument – rhetorical studies of images are a rather recent invention.

Such qualms about whether or not it is reasonable to consider pictures as tools of rhetoric need not detain us here. Indeed, in Barthes' seminal article that we began with in Unit 2 ('Getting the ball rolling: Roland Barthes', p. 31), rhetoric even takes pride of place in the title: *The Rhetoric of the Image* (Barthes 1977 [1964]). There Barthes predicted that "some of the figures formerly identified by the Ancients and the Classics" might also find application for other semiotic systems than the verbal. Our concern in this unit will be exactly this – to examine this proposal further and to see how it has been followed up.

This area as a whole is now known as **visual rhetoric**. However, visual rhetoric, just as rhetoric itself, is not the property of any one tradition or school and so there are quite a few distinct takes on how one can apply rhetorical notions to the visual. There is no one 'received view' of what visual rhetoric is or should be, nor of how one can go about studying it. As is often the case, we consequently find different slants being taken on rhetoric in different areas of application and in the different disciplines that are asking the questions. We will therefore have to make a selection – and, as usual, we will focus more on those accounts either where text-image relations have played a strong role or where important foundations for the rhetoric of text-image combinations have been laid.

EARLY MOVES TOWARDS 'VISUAL RHETORIC'

The main motivation for some group of researchers to turn to the tradition of rhetoric for insight and sources of explanatory models for visual communication is mostly the same, regardless of any other differences that might hold. Rhetoric is concerned with *effective communication as such* and so, whenever the issue of a message's effects on an audience is at the centre of attention, rhetoric may well be considered a source of insight. Within these overall boundaries, however, variation in the use made of rhetoric is considerable.

Some researchers attempt to apply the 'full package' of classical rhetoric, which deals with far more than isolated variations in forms of expression. Here, the process of construction of effective oratory – all the way from coming up with what is to be used as an argument through to its final delivery – receives detailed study. Approaches building on this take the entire model of effective communication developed classically for verbal language and apply each stage and aspect of the model to forms of modern communication involving visual materials. In contrast, there are also researchers who take little more than the term 'rhetoric' in its everyday, non-technical sense of being persuasive. And numerous researchers can be placed in the middle of this range, focusing on single particular aspects of rhetoric as seems useful for their concerns.

Towards the more minimal adoption of the framework, we have, for example, Kostelnick and Hassett (2003), who address an extensive range of visual designs involving all kinds of bar charts, graphs, illustrations, diagrams, logos and other forms of visual presentation. These are all argued to fall within traditional concerns of rhetoric primarily because of the need to combine *convention* and *invention* in order to be effective. An essential component of this practice is then imitation – tried-and-tested models are varied and combined with novel elements. As Kostelnick and Hassett suggest:

> Whatever motivated designers to imitate, however, that impulse fits squarely within the realm of rhetoric, which has traditionally inculcated discrete sets of practices, the mastery of which required artful imitation. . . . Rhetors were trained to win arguments by imitating methods of stylistic devices and patterns of arrangement . . . . Although not always explicitly argumentative, and obviously different in the ways their forms are produced and interpreted, visual conventions extend this long-standing rhetorical tradition because they are similarly shaped by the communities that imitate them.
>
> (Kostelnick and Hassett 2003: 73–74)

Being able to pick apart conventions and traditions, and to see these in their historical context, offers much for teaching and analysing visual representations (cf. Kostelnick 1989).

Other rather minimal applications of rhetoric follow Barthes in suggesting a few broad classes of relationships that may hold between text and image for effective communication, only loosely relating these classes to the classical rhetorical devices we will see more of below. The application of very general rhetorical considerations pursued in the field of document design by Karen Schriver (Schriver 1997) offers an example of this kind. Here general rhetorical considerations are used to shape and inform design practice.

Schriver argues that the document design field as a whole suffered in the past from traditions where analytical and, above all, *teachable* approaches to document evaluation had not been a priority. Two such traditions are the 'craft tradition', which focuses on 'how-to' skills, and the 'romantic tradition', in which creativity plays the central role. Schriver points out that both bring problems for analysis: craft is, almost by definition, only to be learnt by doing, by repeated practice, whereas creativity is, almost equally by definition, something which seeks to avoid being placed in learnable boxes. Schriver's proposal for a way forward is to draw on the broad application of rhetoric developed primarily within composition studies in the twentieth century (cf. Freedman and Medway 1994, Bernhardt 1996). Here there is a strong emphasis on evaluation and improvement and an explicit analytic stance is placed very much in the foreground. This can then provide a basis for document *evaluation* where designers closely scrutinise the effect that their design choices have on the intended consumers of their documents and use rhetorical arguments to motivate or critique the designs selected (Schriver 1997: 80–90).

This approach is now in fact increasingly common within discussions of document design. A good document should be one whose purpose, structure and argumentation is clear. This means that the functions of the parts of a document should be readily recognisable in terms of *the entire meaning offered by the document.* We return to Schriver's position and the kinds of text-image relations that she proposes below.

More complete adoptions of classical rhetorical notions were suggested early on for visual and mixed visual-verbal messages in the approaches of Bonsiepe (2008 [1965]), Gaede (1981), Kennedy (1982) and Durand (1987). Many of these early approaches took their examples from advertisements where the persuasive function is obvious. Kennedy, in particular, argued that the traditional categories long developed in the study of literature should stand as a useful tool for exploring the use of visual representations and depictions. He consequently searches out and characterises visual examples for many of the traditional rhetorical categories that we introduce below. Other approaches, such as those of Durand and Gaede, also considered rhetorical techniques as ways for exploring design concepts. Rhetorical figures then offer a creative space of visualisation techniques within which designers could let their imaginations run free while still maintaining an expectation that the results will not only be attractive, but effective as well.

Although we will not focus on the classical system of rhetoric underlying such approaches here, we still need to introduce some of the basics in order to see how they were applied when accounts addressing images and text-image combinations began to emerge. We therefore turn to this task briefly next.

TRADITIONAL RHETORIC AND ITS CATEGORIES

The idea behind traditional rhetoric is that it is possible to identify particular *rhetorical devices* by which the most effective form of presentation of a message might be chosen. In order to achieve this challenging goal, scholars attempted to classify in ever finer detail just what distinct kinds of 'rhetorical devices' there were and to present these as guidelines for effective expression.

This was naturally a difficult exercise because the delimitation of just what is a rhetorical device and what not is essentially a functional one. This means that it is not possible to say in advance and purely on the basis of 'form' just what rhetorical devices there are. The definitions adopted essentially boil down to 'stylistic deviation that works'. Somewhat more technically, then, a rhetorical device is "an artful deviation" (cf. Corbett and Connors 1998) that in some way 'bends' or shapes a message so that attention is drawn to the message beneficially for its persuasive force or memorability.

Traditionally rhetoric concerned itself with compiling extensive catalogues of all the 'artful deviations' it could find. This led in turn to the criticism most commonly made of classical rhetoric – that is, that its cataloguing of forms appears to take on a life of its own. The Wikipedia entry for rhetorical figures of speech, for example, contains around 200 rhetorical devices ranging from the everyday (e.g., 'humour' as the provocation of amusement) to the positively arcane (e.g., 'hypocatastasis' as an "implication or declaration of resemblance that does not directly name both terms"; cf. http://en.wikipedia.org/wiki/Figure_of_speech). Rhetoric gradually came to be presented more as prescriptive rules of correct expression. It was then not so much the effectiveness of the argument that played the primary role as showing that one knew and could employ complex rhetorical forms.

The consequence of this progression was that, after several centuries of enjoying considerable prestige, by the beginning of the nineteenth century traditional rhetoric had begun to fall out of favour. As in all areas of language, today's prescriptive rules of correctness tend to form tomorrow's outdated fashions; what might be praised as appropriately plain and direct language at one time can well be seen as inordinately flowery and ornate at another. And so any body of knowledge proclaiming on formal ground to define effective speech will, sooner or later, face problems.

It was only in the mid-twentieth century that the need to find more effective methods for teaching communication and composition on a large scale led to rhetoric being taken up again. It was also possible to undertake a more revealing theoretical reappraisal of rhetoric at that time. Whereas at the beginning of the nineteenth century, the understanding of language and language behaviour available from linguistic, psychological, sociological and philosophical perspectives was, in most respects, rudimentary, by the 1950s and 1960s many areas of investigation had established themselves that directly overlapped with rhetoric's traditional concerns. Active research in communication studies, linguistic pragmatics and discourse analysis was available and this offered foundations for a more beneficial and less prescriptive approach to the traditional questions of rhetoric.

The use of 'deviation' as a starting point has, for example, received substantial criticism in many areas of aesthetics and literature (cf. Halliday 1971, McQuarrie and Mick 1996, Stöckl 1997: 42). In contrast, several linguistic theories and theories of communication now assign critical roles not to deviations but to *expectations*. Both the theory of *Speech Acts*, introduced by the philosopher John Austin (Austin 1962), and *Relevance Theory* (cf. Sperber and Wilson 1995 [1986]), for example, suggest that when a hearer or reader notices something contrary to expectation they will search for 'additional' meanings being made over and above the bare minimum of information communicated. These additional meanings combine with a hearer's satisfaction in 'solving the puzzle' so as to offer an at least partial explanation of the workings of rhetorical devices. Whenever a 'receiver' of a message has to do some interpretative 'work' to engage with the message, involvement is increased, which may then give rise to effects of persuasiveness and memorability.

Variations of effects of these kinds can be brought about by introducing 'additional' interpretative work at various levels of linguistic abstraction, that is, at the different 'strata' of the linguistic system known from linguistics. Here are several examples, operating at the linguistic level of form – particularly involving sounds, words and phrases – taken from the work of McQuarrie and Mick (1996) on advertisements. McQuarrie and Mick have been working on applying rhetorical features to visual and text-image combinations for a considerable time and we will see several of their research results in the unit following.

(1) a. KitchenAid. For the way it's made ['rhyme': repeated sound]
    b. Early treatment. Early cure. ['anaphora': repeated word]
    c. You never had it so easy. Your tires never had it so good. ['parison': repeated syntactic structure or phrase]
    d. Stops static before static stops you ['antimetabole': reversal of syntactic structure]

Rhetorical figures of this kind require little understanding of *what* is being said – the patterns foregrounded by perception are already present in the linguistic material itself. This is what makes them common in nursery rhymes and other language forms used by and with young children as well. We will see in Unit 8 that many of these kinds of patterns also overlap with what is known as **cohesion** in linguistics, since this is also partially concerned with issues of form repetition and variation.

Cases of rhetorical figures operating at the linguistic stratum of *meaning* tend to be more complex and varied. These range across both semantic differences and, what McQuarrie and Mick term, 'destablisations' in meaning. A few examples, again compiled from McQuarrie and Mick (1996), are:

(2) **Substitution**
    a. Experience colour so rich you can feel it. ['hyperbole': exaggeration]
    b. Don't you have something better to do? ['rhetorical question': change in assertive force]

    c. The imports are getting nervous. ['metonym': using a portion or associated element to represent the whole]

(3) **Similarity**
    a. Say hello to your child's new bodyguards ['metaphor': referring to band-aids]
    b. Today's Slims at a very slim price ['antanaclasis': repeating a word in two different senses]
    c. Built to handle the years as well as the groceries ['syllepsis': verb meaning changes as text proceeds]

(4) **Opposition**
    a. This picture was taken by someone who didn't bring a camera ['paradox']

In each of these cases it would be possible to imagine a more direct, plain and conventional version of the 'same' message. The instances of *similarity* shown under example (3) might, for example, have been expressed instead as 'Say hello to your child's new band-aids', 'Today's Slims at a very low price', or 'Built to handle the years as well as to take a lot of groceries' respectively.

    These non-rhetorical versions are direct and also somewhat dull – they are unlikely to draw attention to themselves and are certainly not memorable. The rhetorical 'deviations', on the other hand, indicate that more interpretative work is to be invested and thus have a very different 'feel' to them. This difference is then precisely what rhetoric tries to account for in order to be able to apply it productively for communicative effect.

A FIRST CLASSIFICATION OF RHETORICAL FIGURES: McQUARRIE AND MICK

As alluded to above, in classical rhetoric proper there are many distinct kinds of named classes of rhetorical devices. Although it may seem plausible that a conceptual dissonance or resonance brought about by 'artful deviation' will raise some level of attention when noticed by a recipient, this is hardly enough to build a reliable tool for effective communication. Simply listing different devices does not yet say very much about what those devices may do and what they can best be used for. As a consequence, different kinds of organisation have been proposed over the years to provide some order. The goal is then to be able to say just what *effects* the choice of one device rather than another might have for the communication of a message.

    To illustrate how this goal can be approached, we can examine some of the classification systems that have been proposed for organising rhetorical devices according to their likely effects. To begin, one distinction drawn already in classical rhetoric is that between *schemes* and *tropes*. Schemes are related to variations in form, while tropes are concerned with more conceptual or semantic variation. This is clearly related to the different levels of abstraction now commonly assumed in linguistic studies as well. Schemes, for example, include both repetition and reversal where the change at issue varies the form of the message; tropes generally involve uses of semantic relatedness or incongruence. As a consequence of the different levels of abstraction invoked, it is generally assumed that schemes are more straight-forward to process – they can be recognised 'directly'. Tropes, in contrast, are considered more challenging because they always require some degree of understanding of the situations or states of affairs described.

As verbal illustrations, we can take alliteration as an obvious instance of a scheme. For example, we do not need to know what the words mean to recognise the motif of sound repetition in *veni, vidi, vici*; in contrast, 'synecdoche' (a subtype of metonymy related specifically to part-whole relations: that is, a part stands for the whole), as found in 'hey, my wheels have been stolen' – where 'wheels' denotes 'car' or other form of transport – or 'Washington refuses to comment' – where 'Washington' refers to an entire country or its government – clearly requires background cultural knowledge of the kind that vehicles may have wheels and that Washington is a seat of government. These are not facts that can simply be 'read off' of the text.

Schemes and tropes are also sometimes contrasted in terms of the degree of regularity they express – schemes, due to the explicit traces they leave in form, are said to have an 'excess' of regularity; tropes, due to their semantic basis, show more a lack of regularity, or even an irregularity. Irregularity is also symptomatic of incongruity at a semantic level of processing, which again would motivate its different treatment by recipients during interpretation.

Several finer classificatory frameworks have been suggested. The one that is probably best established with respect to classical rhetorical distinctions is a further refinement and motivation of tropes into three categories: metaphor, metonymy and irony. There are, however, still variations in how these traditional rhetorical terms are defined and some experts single out synecdoche as a particular category in its own right. Chandler (2002: 136–138) offers further discussion and summarises the distinctions in a form popularised by Burke (1945). Examples are shown in Table 6.1.

Among these categories, metonymy and synecdoche are relations of 'contiguity' – that is, the entities standing in a metonymic or synecdochal relation are actually *connected in some way* – for example, managers may actually wear suits; customers are actually members of the general public. Metaphor is distinct from these in that its related entities are generally drawn from different domains and so are not 'of themselves' connected – it is the use of the metaphor that brings them together. Working hard is in no way *inherently* required to be at a coal face, for example. Irony is then a rather different kind of opposition again, based on the logical relationship of negation. Applying these kinds of rules of thumb allows most rhetorical figures to be placed at least approximately within a single coherent overall framework.

A further proposed classification of verbal rhetorical figures is developed by McQuarrie and Mick. This builds on the classical rhetorical traditions of schemes and tropes and was also

Table 6.1 Table of distinct types of rhetorical figure; from Chandler (2002: 136, Table 4.2 "The four master tropes")

Trope	Basis	Linguistic example	Intended meaning
Metaphor	similarity despite difference (explicit in the case of simile)	I work at the coal face	I do all the hard work around here
Metonymy	relatedness through direct association	I'm one of the suits	I'm one of the managers
Synecdoche	relatedness through categorial hierarchy	I deal with the general public	I deal with the customers
Irony	inexplicit direct opposite (more explicit in sarcasm)	I love working here	I hate working here

used subsequently for exploring visual rhetoric. The purpose of an improved classification from McQuarrie and Mick's perspective is a particular specialisation of the general concern of rhetoric – they wish to provide more systematic organisations of the possible rhetorical devices so that they *may be related more directly to audience effects*. As well as matching exactly the long-stated goals of rhetoric, this is clearly a central concern in consumer research, McQuarrie and Mick's target community. Knowing what effect an advertisement is going to have and whether it is going to sell the product or not is always going to be an important concern when researching artefacts that are meant to persuade.

McQuarrie and Mick find the scheme-trope distinction particularly promising because of the different levels of 'difficulty' that follow from each category. Predictions can be made concerning how an audience encountering an artefact, such as an advertisement, will respond. Rhetorical figures belonging to different sides of the scheme-trope distinction should then be processed differently by their recipients – we will see the results of experimental studies of this issue in the next unit.

McQuarrie and Mick group the individual types of rhetorical devices traditionally listed together according to the scheme-trope division, organising them further under broad categories of repetition, reversal, substitution and destabilisation as suggested in the examples above. This takes the original notion of 'artful deviation' and treats it instead in terms of basic *operations of change* that may be applied to any message to generate the various rhetorical figures observable in practice. Change is imposed at various levels – such as the level of form, giving rise to schemes, and at the level of semantics, giving rise to tropes.

These notions together give a quite general classification scheme. Simplifying McQuarrie and Mick's account somewhat, and again re-expressing it as a systemic classification network

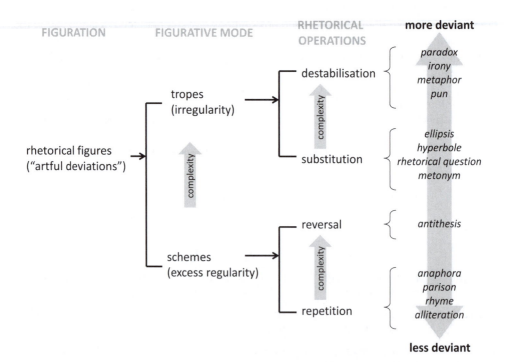

Figure 6.1   Types of rhetorical figures based on McQuarrie and Mick's (1996: 426) figuration taxonomy

to improve comparability with other approaches, their classification is as suggested in Figure 6.1. Increasing complexity for the receiver of rhetorical figures is expressed graphically in the figure by moving upwards on the page.

We will see some of these particular classes of rhetorical devices below when we consider them from the perspective of their relevance for text-image combinations. More detail on the many classes as they have been worked out for verbal language can be found in the extensive literature of rhetoric and rhetorical theories (e.g., Corbett and Connors 1998).

FROM VERBAL TO VISUAL RHETORIC

McQuarrie and Mick's proposal is a useful systematisation of the entire range of rhetorical figures but was actually only intended for verbal discourse. Visual rhetoric begins with the observation that both purely visual representations and combinations of text and visuals working together seem to allow variations reminiscent of classical rhetorical devices. Researchers thus began considering whether existing catalogues of rhetorical devices could be applied when the contributing material has a visual component. Classifications of rhetorical strategies might then provide appropriate descriptions of why some visual and verbo-pictorial artefacts have the effects they do. Under this view, co-occurring text and image receive coherent interpretations by virtue of *their joint participation in 'rhetorical figures'*.

Early proposals tended to echo traditional rhetoric by setting out (rather long) lists of potential rhetorical devices, classifying 'figures of depiction' that are, arguably, visual versions of classical verbal figures. One such classification is proposed by Durand, who organises his framework along two dimensions (Durand 1987: 296). Along one dimension rhetorical figures are classified according to the type of relation they entail – such as identity, similarity, difference and opposition; along the other dimension kinds of rhetorical 'operations' are given. Operations are again the kind of change required for the rhetorical figure to come into existence that we saw in McQuarrie and Mick's account of verbal rhetoric and, again, hold at two levels: that of form and that of content.

In Durand's system, however, the operations considered allow material to be *added*, *suppressed*, *substituted* or *moved* with respect to other elements within either level. Thus one might have a *similarity* of *content* involving a *substitution* – this corresponds to, or defines, the rhetorical figure of metaphor. In contrast a similarity of form involving substitution gives an 'allusion'. Identity with suppression is 'ellipsis', while identity with addition is 'repetition', and so on. Durand places 30 distinct rhetorical figures in his classification system in this way.

Durand then takes an important step further and considers issues of rhetorical device *recognition*. Durand's suggestion is that analysis should proceed by identifying more specifically the elements presented and how they are being presented in any advertisement being analysed. Although it would be important to extend this for all areas addressed, Durand focuses for the purposes of his article on the area of 'similarity'. If a similarity rhetorical figure is to hold, then there must be at least two elements which are being promoted as similar. Durand draws these elements from his dimensions of form and content, dividing content into 'people depicted' and the 'product'. For each possibility he considers when a similarity or a difference is being drawn. This gives a kind of decision tree that leads from the details of any specific advertisement to the particular rhetorical figure that is taken to apply. The tree is shown graphically in Figure 6.2.

Another framework is proposed by Gaede (1981). Gaede also builds a library of relations holding between the visual and verbal contributions to documents – particularly advertisements,

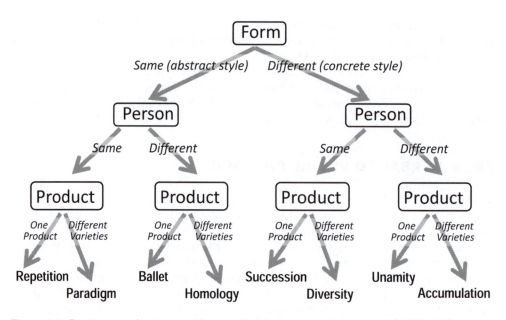

Figure 6.2 Decision tree for rhetorical figures of similarity derived from Durand (1987: 299)

front pages, and similar 'one-page' pieces of visual communication – that draws directly on traditional rhetorical categories (cf. Table 6.2). These categories then provide verbo-visual *visualisation methods* available for making expression more effective.

Each of his main categories of visualisation is defined to have collections of 'sub-methods' that identify the nature of the relationship more closely. For example, the type 'visual gradation' includes the sub-methods: amplification through increase-in-size, amplification through visual prominence and amplification through repetition. Similarly, the type 'visual analogy' has the sub-methods 'similarity of methods' and 'similarity of form'. For each of these types and sub-methods, Gaede offers a broad selection of examples.

Gaede considers these visual methods as particular means for achieving or strengthening five basic visual communicative functions: (1) comprehensibility, (2) acceptance, (3) attractiveness, (4) control of interpretation, and (5) dramaticality. For example, for increasing the *attractiveness* of a visual presentation, he suggests *visual analogy* with sub-methods such as 'surprising form similarity', 'surprising association', 'repetition of form that deviates from some norm' and so on. Clearly this scheme is only to be used in combination with intelligent choice on the part of a designer, but Gaede's explicit aim is to set out a range of possibilities that

Table 6.2 Visualisation methods compiled and translated from Gaede (Gaede 1981: 260–261)

Visual analogy	Visual argumentation	Visual association
Visual connection	Visual norm-violation	Visual repetition
Visual gradation	Visual addition	Visual symbolisation
Visual synecdoche (part-for-whole)	Visual causal/instrumental relations	Visual determination/restriction of meaning

designers can consider in order to help them explore systematically a larger space of possible design solutions.

More about this will be picked up the discussion of the framework developed by Hartmut Stöckl (Stöckl 1997) in Unit 12; Stöckl includes a substantial rhetorical component in his account drawing on Gaede, but also extending well beyond this as we shall see.

EXPANDING THE CATEGORIES WHILE STILL RECOGNISING THEM

Durand's attempt to provide a systematic flowchart for recognising visual and verbo-visual rhetorical figures of similarity invites the question of whether one can find similarly specific definitions for other rhetorical figures to aid in their identification. The study of Marsh and White (2003) is one example of how this has been attempted.

Marsh and White draw on broad rhetorical principles in order to explicitly address text-image relations in a variety of forms of information presentation, including both traditional printed and new media. The basis of their classification is a combination of proposals from publications on text-image relations in education, children's literature, semiotics, journalism, library science and information design as well as an examination of a broad range of examples. The resulting classification, containing no fewer than 46 distinct relations that may possibly hold between image and text, is shown reworked as a systemic classification network in Figure 6.3.

The classification is relatively 'flat': at the top level three broad categories of text-image relations are distinguished according to whether the text and image stand in 'no identifiable' relationship, that is, text and image appear to have little relation to one another; close relationships, such as repeating or explaining; or extending relationships, where the image appears to go significantly 'beyond' the information in the text by providing alternatives, documenting information, or contrasting. These broad categories relate to other approaches to organising relations between text and images found in the research literature and have further subcategories as shown.

As discussed in Unit 2 ('Words and images together: more examples and some puzzles', p. 36), suggesting a classification is only half the job (at most). It is also advisable to evaluate any proposed classification to see if it is adequate, complete, consistent, well-defined and so on. Marsh and White consequently attempt to evaluate their framework by applying the classification scheme to a random sample of websites. This leads them to the interesting conclusion that their framework is already 'largely complete'. As we shall see in other units, similar claims are made for other taxonomies as well – even though these barely overlap with Marsh and White's proposals. Stricter criteria for such claims of 'completeness' would evidently also be useful so that more revealing comparisons can be made.

Nevertheless, whereas most approaches we have seen so far start their analyses from the more general classes offered, Marsh and White do offer considerably more detail at the other end of the scale – that is, at the 'leaves' of the classification tree. This is important for improving the reliability of application of the categories proposed. For each rhetorical figure, Marsh and White provide what they term 'scope notes'. Scope notes are intended to give questions that an analyst can raise in order to identify the class of text-image relationship being examined and delimit it from other possible relations. Examples of the scope notes given for a few of the text-image relations are set out in Table 6.3.

Let us look at an example of Marsh and White's analysis. Although having its own particular set of categories to apply, it resembles many other types of such analysis that we have

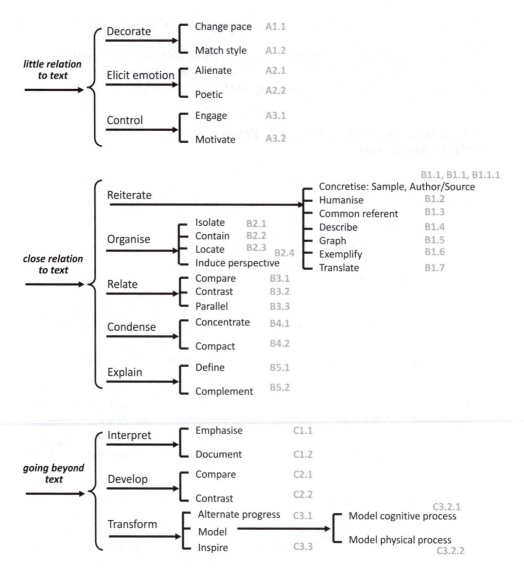

Figure 6.3 Taxonomy of relations between image and text proposed by Marsh and White (2003: 653) reworked as a systemic classification network

seen and lessons learnt with respect to one approach will generally also be applicable to others.

Figure 6.4 shows an example of a NASA educational diagram concerning radio waves. It contains a variety of graphical, pictorial and textual sources of information. Marsh and White characterise these as follows. First, they bring the diagram into relation with the text that accompanies it in the source material: this is repeated here as Marsh and White present it:

> The frequency of each of these waves is what determines whether or not it is absorbed or able to pass through the atmosphere. Low-frequency waves do not travel very far through the atmosphere and are absorbed rather quickly. Higher frequency waves are able

Table 6.3 Some selected 'scope notes' from Marsh and White (2003)

ID	Relation	Scope note
A1	Decorate	make the text more attractive without aiming to produce any real effects on the reader's understanding or memory. Note: can be applied even if other functions are used.
A2.2	Express poetically	suggest the spiritual qualities or effects of the object depicted.
A3.2	Motivate	encourage some response from reader. Note: if desired response is emotional in nature, then use A2 (elicit emotion).
B1.6	Exemplify	present a paragon that captures the essential meaning of a concept. Note: this code is applied to an image-text pair when it is used by the advertiser to present a given product line.
C1.2	Document	provide factual or substantial support.
C3.1	Alternate progress	the text and illustrations 'take turns' in progressing the story.
C3.3	Inspire	using the text as a starting point, the illustration veers away to introduce new content that adheres to the spirit of the original story.

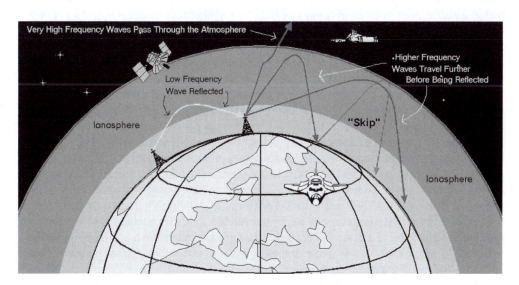

Figure 6.4 National Aeronautics and Space Agency (NASA): Radio Waves (2003)

to pass through the ionosphere and escape into space while the low frequency waves reflect off the ionosphere and essentially 'skip' around the earth. The diagram below will help illustrate this.

(U.S. National Aeronautics and Space Agency, 'Radio Waves (grades 8–12),
Live from the Aurora, Educators' Guide 2003, p. 33)

Marsh and White's general method of analysis takes the text and image combinations – including both the main body of text and the image it occurs with as well as textual elements 'within' the image – and considers, *for each pair of elements identified*, what relations from the classification can be motivated on the basis of the scope notes.

Here, then, Marsh and White begin by arguing that the graphic puts the three types of radio waves described "into perspective, focusing on their physical properties but relating them to more concrete, familiar objects in space, e.g., the satellite . . . and the earth itself" (Marsh and White 2003: 655). They then state that much of the image stands in a close relationship to the text and so makes use of the B-categories of their system. They ascertain this by informally examining the image to see what it depicts and matching this against what is explicitly presented in the text.

Many of the relations used Marsh and White then take to be inter-modal 'translations', that is, replacing a text version by a corresponding visual version: these fall under category B1.7 in the classification network. They also suggest that the diagram "allows the reader to see the waves in their true relations and thus induces perspective", which is category B2.4 (Marsh and White 2003: 656). The diagram makes comparisons between the waves as well, showing how they behave in similar but different ways with respect to the atmosphere according to their respective wavelengths; this Marsh and White categorise as B3.1 (compare). This is suggested to make the text more intelligible – we will see several rather similar text-image connections in later units. Finally, Marsh and White see a relationship expressed in the diagram that is not in the text, and so infer a further C-category – the waves' path and relationships to other physical components, such as radio antennas, expresses a 'physical process' and so constitutes an instance of category C3.2.2 'model physical process'. Thus, to summarise, the primary relations selected here are: B1.7 (translate), B2.4 (induce perspective), B3.1 (compare) and C3.2.2 (physical process).

Questions concerning the reproducibility of the rhetorical analyses shown within this framework remain, however – to what extent different analysts are bound to produce the same results, and to what extent those results can be considered exhaustive, or definitive, for the text, appear to be open issues. While by and large intuitively appealing, just how to select the elements to be related in the text and the diagram is left to the intuitions of the reader/viewer. This may be appropriate if the diagrams and texts are relatively simple, as here, but in more complex cases may equally add a degree of indeterminism and uncertainty concerning both the categories that are taken to apply and what precisely they are applying to. It is also not yet clear to what extent the categories can be reliably distinguished from one another and, sometimes, they may even co-occur: as Marsh and White say, for example, of their relation 'decorate', it is quite possible for this relation to hold in addition to other relations. And it is uncertain why all of the relations proposed appear to place the *text* in a key definitional role: their function is defined in terms of their relation to text rather than also allowing relationships that run in the opposite direction.

We will see a further development building on parts of Marsh and White's account in Unit 10 from Kong (2006). Kong argues that Marsh and White's listing of relations does not yet succeed adequately in distinguishing overlapping and closely related terms and so is less than adequate for constructing a more robust analytic account. The reliance on broadly 'rhetorical' notions does not lend itself to precise descriptions and relies on an interpretation that is always to a greater or lesser degree subjective.

This means that there is still a considerable way to go before such analysis can become both *detailed* and *analytically reliable*; achieving a re-usable and well-defined framework is very difficult to achieve in practice.

CHARACTERISING RHETORICAL FIGURES ON THE BASIS OF THEIR FORM

One way of working towards more reliability is to construct deeper, that is, more hierarchical, classification schemes where differences in 'identity conditions' and 'recognition criteria' at each level of classification are made as explicit as possible. As we have seen, most of the approaches discussed so far have concerned themselves with abstract statements of communicative functions, which can raise difficult issues of interpretation.

Nevertheless, we did see in Durand's decision tree above in Figure 6.2 the beginning of an attempt to draw in more evidence based on *the form* of the artefacts being analysed. This can be taken further. Another scheme of this type working directly from the visual information available rather than applying more abstract categories from verbal rhetoric is that of the Belgian school of semiotic research, Groupe Mu (Groupe μ 1992). These researchers divide their description along two 'strata' of organisation – a *plastic* level for the basic forms, colours, composition, texture and so on, and an *iconic* level where elements appear that can then be interpreted.

Within this framework, rhetorical considerations are situated directly within the iconic level. Some forms of expression are then considered to be directly congruent to interpretations, and hence non-rhetorical, while others deviate from this 'degree zero' and so express rhetorical figures.

These potential deviations are classified along two dimensions, giving four categories. The first dimension responds to the fact that visuals, in contrast to verbal language, allow simultaneous expressions – that is, information of different kinds can be presented all at once rather than being delivered successively as in speech or writing. Such elements are seen as either being combined (**conjoint**) or separated (**disjoint**). The second dimension is defined according to the presence or absence (also partial absence) of one of the elements being brought into a rhetorical relation. The resulting categories are summarized in Table 6.4. We will see further cases of application or adaptation of this framework in subsequent units.

ADDING MORE STRUCTURE

A reoccurring concern with all of the approaches we have seen so far remains the *nature of the elements being related*: how do we find those elements between which text-image

Table 6.4 The Groupe Mu categorisation of rhetorical devices (Groupe μ, 1992: 270–283) – translations adopted from van Mulken (2003)

	Conjoint	Disjoint
In Praesentia	rhetorical devices showing two entities together in the same figure with partial substitution	rhetorical devices showing two entities in different places
In Absentia	rhetorical devices combining two entities so that one of the entities is completely replaced and so does not explicitly appear	rhetorical devices where only one entity is shown and the other has to be deduced from what is shown

relations are meant to hold? While it appears straightforward to talk of 'text' and 'image', as we saw in the Marsh and White example it is often far less clear just which parts of a complex artefact should be picked out for consideration and why.

This relates to the general problem of identifying the *units* of analysis. It is essential to consider this issue in a systematic fashion so as to avoid picking out just those elements about which we have something to say and ignoring (or not noticing) the others. As we have already mentioned at various points in the discussion and will see further below, this requires that we are much more explicit concerning *layout* – this is an important aspect of visual organ-isation in its own right and its inter-relationship and influence on text is considerable. This therefore constitutes another component of text-image relations that is far too often ignored.

The issues of unit identification become more important the more we are concerned with practical analysis rather than abstract proposals for what might happen between text and images. One scheme for practical document analysis and design critique that is motivated by an appropriate consideration of structural units created by layout is that of Schriver (1997). Schriver proposes the concept of **rhetorical clusters** to take layout more effectively into consideration. A rhetorical cluster is a more or less standardised combination of visual and textual material displayed in a recognisable visual form. A selection from Schriver's catalogue of established clusters is shown in Figure 6.5; a similar notion is suggested by Baldry and Thibault (2006) as part of their proposed methodology for analysing page layouts. When one knows the kind of cluster that is at hand, then one also knows a lot about the units that are present and how they are to be interpreted.

Schriver locates the overall functioning and unity of multimodal documents within a new functional rhetoric as follows:

We can think of a document as a field of interacting rhetorical clusters. If the document is well designed, the clusters orchestrate a web of converging meanings, which enable

Illustrations with annotations and explanations

- illustrations
- leader lines and callouts (i.e., labels that identify elements)
- figure numbers, captions and credits

Procedural instructions with visual elements

- scenario (overview / goal of procedure)
- procedures (enumerated step-by-step)
- visual example of machine/device responses
- captions for examples

Body text with footnotes

- body text (including paragraph styling)
- footnote text
- headings and subheadings
- itemised lists
- indented quotes

Front matter of a feature article

- headline (main point)
- byline (author, division)
- tagline, exploded quote, or attention-grabbing lead
- photograph (medium to large)
- caption (under photo if needed)

Figure 6.5 Examples of rhetorical clusters proposed by Schriver (1997: 343)

readers to form a coherent and consistent idea of the content. When documents are not well designed, the rhetorical clusters may seem unrelated. They may compete for attention, contradict one another, or have so many gaps between them that readers find it hard to form a coherent and consistent interpretation of the content. Rhetorical clusters operate dynamically – on single pages, on spreads, or over screens.

(Schriver 1997: 344; emphasis in original)

According to this perspective, document designers then need to be "practicing rhetoricians" (Schriver 1997: 332) and, as such, need to utilise all the tools of their trade to orchestrate information on the page so as to allow readers to rediscover the intended relationships.

Schriver (1997: 412–428) also draws out of her account a further classification for potential text-image relations. This proposal combines previous approaches with some new additions to give five essential relationships. The relation between elements in a document differing in mode – that is, here, either textual/verbal or graphical/diagrammatic/pictorial – can be:

- *redundant,* where the same or largely overlapping information is expressed in two modalities – this is related to notions of dual-coding;
- *complementary,* where the information offered in the two modes is considered of equal importance but differs, each one providing information that complements the information in the other;
- *supplementary,* where one mode is clearly dominant and the other provides subsidiary information;
- *juxtapositional,* where "the main idea is created by a clash, an unexpected synthesis, or a tension between what is represented in each mode" (Schriver 1997: 422);
- *stage-setting,* where "one mode provides a context for the other mode by forecasting its content or soon-to-be-presented themes" (Schriver 1997: 424).

Schriver offers this scheme as a straightforward tool for practical reflexion on the part of designers when considering how to put visual and verbal material together on the page. Being more explicitly aware of the possibilities is taken as an important component of critique and a support for conscious design improvement.

The influence of Barthes in this scheme is readily apparent. Moreover, there are further overlaps and alignments that we can consider between this catalogue and others. Schriver's 'juxtapositional', for example, may overlap with McCloud's 'parallel' (Unit 5, 'Frames, panels and gutters', p. 96). However, Schriver suggests that the combination creates a new 'distinct' meaning in a manner suggestive of the *montage of attractions* from film theory (cf. Eisenstein 1977), while McCloud remains more neutral on this. McCloud in fact uses the term 'montage' himself, but draws more on its traditional compositional sense.

As we can see, naming conventions in this entire area remain erratic, to say the least – there is a lot of 'clearing up' to be done!

CONCLUSION

In this unit we have seen the development of a range of ideas beginning in classical rhetoric and working towards progressive systematisations that can be applied to visual materials and text-image combinations. We can consider their use in any area of text-image combinations where an argumentative or, more generally conceived, 'rhetorical' component is at work. It remains to be seen, however, just how effective such proposals are when taken further.

There are, as usual, a diverse range of positions taken on this issue and we have seen in this unit only a selection. Moreover, the diverse approaches that have emerged employing notions from rhetoric to the visual may or may not make their relationships to other such approaches explicit. We always need, therefore, to be on the look out for similarities and comparisons ourselves – different approaches or communities may each offer useful perspectives for getting a hold on the issues raised. Recurring problems surfacing across different approaches will also be of interest, since these may point to more general or broader theoretical or practical concerns. These should be noted and used when drawing generalisations about the kinds of distinctions necessary for characterising visual-verbal, and text-image, relations at large.

There is clearly much more to investigate. Particularly the areas of *reliability*, *identification* and *effect* within rhetorically based accounts of text-image combinations are in need of considerably more research.

Visual persuasion and advertisements

As noted in the previous unit, advertisements have long been considered good hunting ground for researchers looking for complex examples of multimodal communication. The choice of some version of rhetoric for that study is then a relatively obvious one. Advertisements have the socially established and accepted role of persuading their audience to do something, usually to buy some product, although almost any kind of change in behaviour can be included – as in public information posters or 'anti-advertisements' in health promotion campaigns. It is then natural that rhetoric, as the study of how to persuade, should suggest itself. It is no accident that one of the first treatments of text-image combinations of all – that of Barthes' 'Rhetoric of the image' from the early 1960s that we discussed in Unit 2 – also features discussion of an advertisement.

The connection between advertisements and rhetoric has also been made strongly from the practical side and so should not be considered just as an opportunity to find examples to discuss. Indeed, one proponent of rhetoric research, Stephen McKenna, considers advertising the "largest, most pervasive, and most successful rhetorical enterprise on the planet" (McKenna 1999: 103). He argues further that advertisements therefore need to be given serious professional rhetorical attention.

Similarly, but from the side of advertising, Scott (1994) argues that rhetoric needs to play a more important role even in consumer research and advertising theory. She suggests that previous approaches in consumer research actually failed to make contact with the sheer extravagance of visual meaning creation in advertising. In a paragraph that itself shows off many of the classical features of rhetoric described by rhetoricians over the years and introduced in the previous unit, Scott sets out the actual state of affairs thus:

> The world of advertisements is peopled by fantastic images. A multitude of imaginary characters dance through situations ranging from sensual to playful, from threatening to mundane. The messages are reversed, boldfaced and italicized—set in typefaces with names like Baby Teeth, Jiminy Cricket, and Park Avenue. Products kaleidoscope past our eyes in heroized visual styles borrowed from the Dutch masters—or the Masters of the Universe. Pictures pun, photographs fantasize, illustrations illuminate. In rich colors and textures, a panoply of visual images entice, exhort and explain.
>
> (Scott 1994: 252)

Scott criticises consumer research for adopting a methodological assumption concerning what images do in advertisements that is completely counter to the facts – that is, that images do little more than 'copy' objects in the real world.

Treating images as more or less simple 'copies' of what they are depicting was already in 1994 an unlikely model. Nowadays few would probably even think of such an idea when looking at advertisements. But this just makes the problem and question that Scott raises even more relevant that it was then: just what *are* images doing in advertisements and how do they manage this?

The use of rhetoric in the study of advertisements has grown considerably since these early suggestions for its adoption. There is now a sizeable body of literature – we will look at some more recent studies below. We will not to go into studies of advertising *per se*, however – for further references see book-length studies such as those of Dyer (1982), Messaris (1997) and Cook (2001). Our concern will be restricted to our main focus of attention, relating text and image and the approaches that have been explored with respect to text-image relationships in advertising – particularly, for current purposes, those building on some notion of visual rhetoric.

THE ROLE OF VISUALS IN ADVERTISING

Consumer research's unreflective treatment of images as 'copies' of reality rested on simple views of the nature of photography that we return to in a moment. There is still, of course, extensive *use* of photography and depictions of real-world objects and events in most advertisements. This visuality contributes significantly to advertisements' immediate appeal and their ability to grab attention. What is *done* with these 'real' images is, however, often a very long way indeed from any pretence of simply representing 'the world'. In contrast, Scott's suggestion is that much of the imagery in advertisements must be *worked at* – that is, their audiences have to decode the messages offered in order to see what is intended. Any unreflective 'natural' perception performing automatically then constitutes only a small part of what needs to be addressed.

Moreover, the decoding that is necessary has a serious motivation – after all, the primary purpose of advertising is to persuade and convince. Advertisements have a well-established cultural function and we do not encounter them as abstract puzzles. Thus we are confronted with a classic case of highly designed communicative artefacts, constructed for the purpose of achieving particular effects on their audience, and this is precisely the area of concern addressed by rhetoric.

Scott discusses several examples to argue this point and show the importance of adopting a rhetorically informed perspective. A recreation of one of these is shown in Figure 7.1; the figure is intended to show the basic advertising strategy employed rather than reproduce any details of the original's production values, branding and so on. The original, an advertisement for cosmetics from the company Clinique, depicts a collection of cosmetic articles in a cocktail glass, ready for 'consumption'.

Now, on one level this is a realistic, **indexical** (in the sense of the semiotician Peirce) photograph showing a clear resemblance to what, presumably, was in front of the camera. 'Indexical' means that there is a direct causal link between the representation (the photograph) and what was photographed – this entails that what is shown was actually something real in front of the camera when the photograph was taken. Simply addressing the advertisement at this level, which is what Scott critiques former consumer research for doing, clearly misses the point – this can hardly be what the image is 'about' when employed for the purposes of the advertisement. The particular objects depicted and their inter-relationships are intended to give rise to further levels of interpretation. And, to reach those levels, there must be additional work done by the recipient. If this work is *not* done, or is not done successfully, then the advertisement is not going to make much sense for the potential consumer and so, presumably,

Figure 7.1 Refreshing lipstick?

is not going to be particularly successful as an advertisement for the products depicted either.

Scott suggests that what is occurring here involves a kind of hybrid image, where the cosmetic articles are made to take on some of the qualities that would normally be associated with ingredients for a refreshing drink. Whether or not this is particularly successful as an advertisement is a separate issue – more important here is that both the effect and its manner of achievement cannot be seen as accidents. This, Scott suggests, is a clear indication of visual rhetoric in action:

> Shall we conclude then that Clinique, marketed by one of the most successful manufacturers of cosmetics in America, has simply committed a huge gaffe by running this ad? Not likely.
>
> (Scott 1994: 254)

Answering the questions raised by such use of visual materials is the role Scott suggests for rhetoric.

Using some of the traditional descriptions of effective communication developed in rhetoric, Scott breaks down the design of an advertisement along the dimensions of *invention*, *arrangement* and *delivery*. Invention concerns the selection of the basic idea adopted for expression and arrangement refers to the forms employed. Thus, in the present case, the invention is the idea that the products should be presented as refreshing, and the arrangement is then the design decision to merge them with a refreshing drink. The original rhetorical sense of delivery has more to do with performance and presentation, but this aspect is not so prominent in a modern mass medium such as advertising. Delivery is then suggested here to be the use of visual style to express evaluations, such as a 'heroic' product (or user), a 'romantic' setting (or use), and so on. In the present case, the production values of the original advertisement are accordingly intended to 'connotate' – in the sense of Barthes introduced in Unit 2 ('Getting the ball rolling: Roland Barthes', p. 31) – sophistication and quality.

Combining input from these perspectives represents, Scott argues, a far more appropriate starting point for studying advertisement design and effect than any focus or assumption of resemblance and depiction of the 'world'.

> Advertising clearly demands close attention to be paid to its visual qualities not only as representations but also, if not more, as rhetorical devices employed for deliberate effect.

It is simply not possible to examine advertisements sensibly if one ignores this visual contribution. This is then also the challenge for those who study advertisements, regardless of whether they come from the consumer and advertising studies side or the text-image and multimodality research side. Both need to move beyond the habits and viewpoints of verbally centred research traditions. And this applies equally to any approaches drawing on rhetoric.

VISUAL RHETORIC IN ADVERTISEMENT RESEARCH

We will now explore in more detail how visual extensions of rhetorical accounts have been taken up to address visual and verbo-visual materials in advertising research. In particular, we will target accounts where rhetorical forms and frameworks are employed to relate text and image. To show this in action, we will run through a series of papers and research results applying accounts derived from rhetorical theory to practical research on advertisements combining text and image.

Early approaches – including several that we saw in the previous unit – were often criticised for simply presenting examples with associated rhetorical labels. Such proposals were often difficult to operationalise and only addressed small portions of the overall range of rhetorical possibilities. The classification of rhetorical figures proposed by McQuarrie and Mick (1996), which we also discussed in Unit 6, attempted to move beyond this. Ways were sought for making the attribution of one rhetorical figure rather than another clearer and more reliable. This also led directly to a number of interesting hypotheses and experimental questions. For example, linking *schemes* and *tropes* to complexity in processing (cf. Unit 6, Figure 6.1) makes corresponding predictions about how difficult an audience will find particular advertisements (and other artefacts) using them. Is, for example, an advertisement employing a trope more difficult to understand than one employing a scheme? And, building on this further, following the premise that people are likely to enjoy the challenge of 'solving' a trope, does this also mean that people will rate advertisements containing tropes more positively than other kinds of advertisements? These are questions which can be directly investigated in empirical studies.

McQuarrie and Mick's original classification scheme was only intended for the treatment of *verbal* rhetorical figures. However, as we have noted, treating advertisements *without* making statements about the visual is difficult. It is not then too surprising that McQuarrie and Mick could not avoid at least some comments on visually expressed rhetorical figures. For example, one of the rhetorical devices they place under destabilisation and semantic similarity is *resonance*, which was defined to hold when "a phrase is given a different meaning by its juxtaposition with a picture" (p. 431). This is already inherently a text-image relation. In fact, in earlier work, McQuarrie (1989) had already given a host of further examples of visual representations 'echoing', 'copying' or 'punning' on verbal representations.

One of these examples, also carried over into McQuarrie and Mick (1996), is the verbal message "Will bite when cornered" appearing in a car-tyre advertisement showing (i.e., visually) water splashing as a car makes a sharp turn. This takes us back directly to the kind of verbo-pictorial cases discussed by Scott above and is also reminiscent of the examples discussed by Spillner that we saw in Unit 2 ('Spillner's text-image relations', p. 37). The text interpretation is 'anchored' by the visual material to pull out particular readings of both *bite* and *corner* that would normally not be salient with this phrase.

Additional meanings of this kind can be seen in terms of the rhetorical 'shaping' of the combined text-image message. The role of rhetoric in providing an account of such combined messages is explained by Phillips and McQuarrie as follows. It appears that:

> advertisers select pictorial elements from a palette; that specific pictorial elements can be linked to particular consumer responses; and, most importantly, that the palette of available pictorial elements has an internal structure such that the location of a pictorial element within this structure indicates the kind of impact that the pictorial element can be expected to have.
>
> (Phillips and McQuarrie 2004: 114)

Phillips and McQuarrie consider this 'internal structure' to be made up of combinations of visual and verbal rhetorical figures which, following the earlier work of McQuarrie and Mick (1996), 'adhere to an identifiable template'. Advertisements' audiences will then generally be able to decode rhetorically coded messages because they 'know the game'. They will understand advertisements by following the 'instructions' given by established rhetorical templates – once they have recognised which ones apply. It is then important to show just what properties such template have and how we can identify them. And this is a major challenge: *can* we find out what kinds of template might apply clearly enough to help us with interpretation – either in analysis or during actual reception by an audience in a real context of exposure to the advertisement?

The need not to exclude visual and verbo-pictorial phenomena in their rhetorical framework led McQuarrie and Mick at first to simply apply their classification scheme to all the material occurring in an advertisement, be that visual, verbal or some mixture. Using this scheme, they began a series of experimental studies addressing the various questions we have just introduced. Before proceeding to the studies themselves, however, we need briefly to consider the kinds of methods that such studies generally employ. This is a very different research area to that on narratives that we saw in Units 3–5.

Experimental methods

In consumer research on advertisements as well as psychologically oriented work that now also addresses rhetoric in advertisements, it is important to show reliable effects so that one can be reasonably sure that particular design decisions have the desired consequences (or, equally important, not have undesired consequences). For this reason, the studies are usually *empirical*, *experimental* and *quantitative*.

This means that experiments are designed in order to explicitly test certain research hypotheses. Considerable care is taken with all aspects of the design of these experiments, both because they are very work-intensive to perform and because, if this is not done, it is unlikely that results will be obtained that are sufficiently clear to stand up to statistical tests of significance. Without such tests, there is no guarantee that effects have genuinely been shown – in other words, what occurred in an experiment may have happened by chance, which is not a strong basis for building further theories or for changing or maintaining particular design decisions concerning the features of any advertisements investigated. Experimenters therefore try to balance the range of participants appropriately according to age ranges, gender and nationalities, to levels of expertise concerning the subject of the experiment, and so on for any potentially relevant source of variation.

Experiments also work with bodies of materials that are either specially collected or prepared specifically for the experiment to be run in order to maximise the likelihood that usable results will be obtained. These experimental materials are typically classified according to some reliable scheme into different classes. The responses of the experimental participants are then analysed statistically using a variety of techniques in order to see if there is any correlation with the classes proposed. For example, one might have one class of materials where there are no rhetorical figures (or other kind of text-image relationship) and another class where there are. Then one might run an experiment to see if this makes a difference for their readers/viewers.

Differences might be measured in many ways – from reaction time tests that measure how long experimental participants take to make some decision related (or not) to the materials presented, to more complex problem-solving activities or questions. Certain hypotheses may also be made concerning how material organised according to some classes relates to material in other classes: the responses of experimental participants are then also tested statistically to see if the hypotheses are supported by what the experimental participants actually do or not.

The usual kinds of statistical tests that need to be done when performing such experiments are to verify whether the results for two classes are really significantly different from each other or to see if there is good evidence for the separation of results into distinct groups.

The former means evaluating the probability that the variation observed could have happened by chance. When one can work out that the probability of a result happening by chance is sufficiently low, then one can be confident that there is really an effect coming from the material and the participants. The likelihood of something occurring by chance is typically tested with the **Chi-squared statistical test** or more sophisticated variants.

The latter is generally tested with statistical procedures such as **ANOVA (Analysis of Variance)** which look at the 'mean', or average, values within classes together with the observed variations within the class with respect to the mean. This allows experimenters to be confident that differences in the material or in the participants are really leading to systematically different behaviours or responses. If the variations around averages observed were so large that the groups all run into each other, then it is unlikely that the grouping being tested is valid.

In addition, a range of standard experimental designs are generally employed to ensure that artificial effects are not introduced – for example, the order of presentation of materials may need to be randomised so that effects of training or of expectations arising from particular sequences of presentation rather than what was intended to be studied can be prevented.

Papers discussing these kinds of results, which include most of those we report on in this unit, are presented as psychological experiments and are consequently expected to provide considerable detail concerning not only their precise experimental design, but also the exact statistical procedures employed to validate their results. We will omit this level of detail here in our discussion and instead pick out the main consequences for the consideration of text-image relations. A recent and very readable introduction to statistical methods for linguistics can, however, be found in Lowie and Seton (2013) – methods of this kind can also be straight-forwardly extended to the study of mixed mode artefacts as well.

McQuarrie and Mick's 'text-interpretative' model

In McQuarrie and Mick (1999), the authors take their original forays into the visual aspects of advertisements further, setting out what they call a **text-interpretative** model of rhetorical organisations in advertisements. This empirical paper first attempts to show experimentally that distinctions made by their verbally based classification of rhetorical figures also apply to visual material.

This is a standard empirical approach: before spending considerable time researching some phenomenon, it is wise to check whether any kind of effect can be measured for the phenomenon at all. If it proved impossible to measure any difference in experimental participants concerning whether a rhetorical figure was present or not, then more complex experiments building on this 'phenomenon' (which may then have turned out not to be a phenomenon at all!) might be unwise.

As we have discussed, the most basic distinction drawn in McQuarrie and Mick's classification was between tropes and schemes. This suggested a series of experiments in which experimental participants were presented with advertisements classifiable as either schemes or tropes *visually* in order to see if differences in responses could be measured. To establish this, McQuarrie and Mick accordingly analysed a set of advertisements and selected cases that appeared to visually exhibit rhyme, antithesis (i.e., reversal, opposite or contrast), metaphor and punning.

This choice of rhetorical figures was motivated by the fact that rhyme and antithesis are classified as schemes, while metaphor and puns are considered tropes. Performing experiments on a range of rhetorical figures in this way, rather than focusing on just one, then allowed them to explore whether different rhetorical devices were having different kinds of effects as predicted. As mentioned above and in the previous unit, one predicted difference suggested by the scheme/trope distinction is that more 'deviant' (i.e., more complex) figures would have increasingly greater impact on consumers "up to some point of diminishing returns" (p. 39).

McQuarrie and Mick then also drew on techniques from more traditional reader-response studies to see if their classification correlated with differences in responses on the part of the experimental participants. In reader-response terms, they predicted that the complexity gradient in their classification would have consequences for both 'reader pleasure' and what they term the degree of 'elaboration' – that is, how much effort a reader puts into drawing more information from the advertisement being decoded, integrating what they are understanding with already established knowledge structures and memories. Clearly, from the consumer research perspective, knowing how an advertisement is going to be received along these dimensions would be very beneficial. It might be expected, for example, that increased 'pleasure in the text' would correlate with a more positive attitude towards the product – although this still remained to be verified. Concretely for McQuarrie and Mick's experiments, then, schemes and tropes were both hypothesised to produce a greater impact, with tropes outperforming schemes as long as they do not become too complex or deviant and block interpretation.

To perform the experiments, McQuarrie and Mick took advertisements from their selection and specially prepared pairs of constructed and original advertisements to act as experimental 'stimuli'. The pairs all contrasted according to whether the original rhetorical figure was present or not. An example of such a pair is shown in Figure 7.2, which is one of McQuarrie and Mick's test materials probing the trope of metaphor. In the control case, shown on the right, the product and the safety-belt are simply shown lying side by side on a car seat – this could be a natural, undoctored (i.e., indexical) photograph and does not require any particular rhetorical processing to understand it. In the rhetorically manipulated version, however, the product is *visually integrated* into the safety-belt taking on the role of the buckle.

The intended rhetorical effect is then that the product, medicine against car-sickness, actually acts like a safety-belt, protecting the consumer/passenger or driver. In terms of metaphor theory, which we explain in detail in Unit 9, certain properties of the safety belt – for example, making you safe while driving – are to be 'transferred' to the medication. The experiment was then run with 72 undergraduate students. Again, because of the need to achieve statistically validated results, experiments typically need to involve a sufficiently high number of experimental participants to overcome random individual variation so as to reveal generally valid trends or relationships.

The results obtained in the experiment showed, as would be expected, that the advertisements with some kind of rhetorical manipulation were judged to be "more artful and clever". The prediction made beforehand that tropes would lead to a greater degree of 'elaboration' than schemes was also borne out, although not as strongly as might have been hoped. Such are the trials and tribulations of empirical research – before evaluating the results, it is

MOTION SICKNESS?   MOTION SICKNESS?

TAKE PRAMNOL ON YOUR   TAKE PRAMNOL ON YOUR

NEXT CAR TRIP   NEXT CAR TRIP

Figure 7.2 McQuarrie and Mick: test material for visual metaphor – taken from McQuarrie and Mick (1999: 43, Figure 2); used by permission

impossible to predict with absolute certainty what is going to be shown, if anything. This also underscores the importance of good experimental design.

McQuarrie and Mick then investigated whether greater elaboration could be associated with an increased positive attitude towards the product. As is usually the case with empirical studies of this kind, experimenters need to be extremely careful to avoid building biases or 'confounds' into their experimental design that might lead to significant results being hidden or a lack of discrimination in what might be causing what. McQuarrie and Mick therefore carried out a second study that controlled for the potential influence of an experimental participant happening to *actually use* one of the illustrated products (for example, a gender check was included for an advertisement for women's mascara) as well as for nationality and for 'visual awareness' in general.

The results of this second study showed that for American students (the culture for which the advertisements were designed), advertisements with visual tropes had a more positive impact relative to their controls (i.e., the advertisements without manipulation) than the advertisements with visual schemes had relative to their controls. Interestingly, foreign students participating in the study showed themselves to be "particularly unappreciative" of the advertisements with visual tropes. This is not a result that one would expect and again shows the value, and importance, of conducting empirical research: new insights moving us beyond what might have been assumed by intuitions can always result.

Finally, in a third study McQuarrie and Mick asked participants in the experiment to describe what meanings the individual advertisements had suggested, thus providing reader-response information to correlate with the two quantitative studies. This supported the impression of the previous studies and showed that much of the lack of appreciation of tropes from the foreign students could be traced back to their failing to understand the metaphors and puns being made. McQuarrie and Mick therefore conclude:

> Visual figures, like the more familiar verbal figures . . . , would appear to deserve a place among the executional devices available to advertisers that have a consistent and reliable impact on consumer response. This study provides additional empirical support for the theoretical taxonomy developed by McQuarrie and Mick (1996) [cf. Figure 6.1 in the previous unit] and underscores its generality, inasmuch as we found the distinctions they proposed for verbal language to also hold true when embodied in visual form.
>
> (McQuarrie and Mick 1999: 51)

The combination of empirical response studies and rhetorical 'text' analysis, where McQuarrie and Mick already emphasise that "visual and verbal elements [are treated] as equally capable of conveying crucial meanings and as equally worthy of differentiation and analysis" (McQuarrie and Mick 1999: 38), represented an important new line of research. And, as we briefly mentioned in Unit 2, empirical investigations of more abstract, functional, 'semiotic' or rhetorical descriptions of this kind are still far too rare, even today.

A follow-up study reported in McQuarrie and Mick (2003) then supported these results further. In this experiment, participants were not 'forced' to examine particular advertisements by virtue of the experimental design but instead browsed a cluttered magazine in which various specially altered advertisements had been placed by the experimenters. Even without directing the attention of the readers, the positive results concerning increased impact according to tropes were generally found to hold. This latter study also directly compared verbal and visual rhetorical figures, finding that the visual figures had a greater effect than the verbal, especially when their reading was set up experimentally as 'incidental' rather than forced.

Although supportive of their original classification, McQuarrie and Mick's experiments still left open questions.

In particular, the 'upper limits' of trope acceptability remained quite high: it was only in cases of non-understanding that experimental participants reported decreased appreciation of the manipulated advertisements. McQuarrie and Mick also make the point that there would also need to be some boundary conditions of an aesthetic nature: if a trope were executed in a crude or unconvincing fashion, then this would be unlikely to raise appreciation of the associated product. Just how this might be explored raises many issues of its own.

The experiments were also not very discriminating with respect to the kinds of rhetorical figures investigated. McQuarrie and Mick note that, although they manage to show results for the broad difference between schemes and tropes, there was still too little material to draw reliable conclusions for discriminations lower in their classification taxonomy. It was not yet possible, therefore, to make any strong statements concerning the relative effects of differing rhetorical figures within the broader classes.

Van Mulken's reliability studies

As a step towards analyses capable of discriminating in a more fine-grained fashion between rhetorical figures, van Mulken (2003) raised the question of the reliability of McQuarrie and Mick's scheme of classification. Clearly, if it is not possible to apply the taxonomy reliably, it cannot provide a good basis for more detailed studies. As van Mulken states the problem:

> The number of rhetorical devices, however, is very large. Do all rhetorical devices contribute to the appreciation of ads in the same way? In order to answer this kind of questions we need a framework to describe and classify the different rhetorical devices applied in ads. The literature on figurative speech proposes many different taxonomies that have but one aspect in common: they have been developed for verbal rhetoric. . . . Magazine ads, however, only rarely consist of text alone.
>
> (van Mulken 2003: 115–116)

Few approaches have attempted to apply the full range of rhetorical devices to visual materials. As we have seen, typically some less detailed classification scheme is adopted that may or may not be drawn from traditional rhetorical distinctions. McQuarrie and Mick's classification is similar in that it begins with distinctions motivated by the tradition but only provides three levels of classification.

It was worthwhile considering, therefore, whether further, or different, classifications might be beneficial for carrying out more refined analyses and for generating tighter experimental hypotheses. Van Mulken explores this possibility by evaluating McQuarrie and Mick's classification scheme more stringently. She does this both by drawing on a much larger sample of advertisements than reported in McQuarrie and Mick's studies, where typically only a few examples are tested, and by explicitly *contrasting* classifications made according to McQuarrie and Mick's classification with another possibility, that of Groupe Mu.

We presented the four Groupe Mu categories relevant to the current discussion in Table 6.4 in Unit 6. Taking the examples we have used in this unit as illustrations, we would classify the Clinique example above as belonging to the category *In Praesentia/Conjoint*, and the motion sickness safety-belt example as *In Absentia/Conjoint*. The reliance of Groupe Mu's categories on actual properties of the 'image' material suggests that it might be more generally and reliably applicable than approaches relying on more impressionistic classifications of rhetorical figures. This would make them a good potential contender for more reliable experimental designs.

If form criteria can be identified, then one is in a far better position to recognise when the abstract choices have been made or not. This avoids allowing potentially diverse interpretations to play a role because one can generally hope that at least visual perceptions will be shared across coders and so might be applied to broader samples of data. Moreover, similarly to the McQuarrie and Mick taxonomy, the Groupe Mu classification also makes claims about relative 'complexity'. This suggested how the two approaches might be indirectly compared.

Van Mulken's study took a relatively large sample of almost 1000 advertisements (in French and Dutch) and had three independent 'coders' allocate each advertisement to the Groupe Mu categories and to the McQuarrie and Mick categories. A measure of cross-coder consistency was then calculated using the **kappa statistic**, a standard method for assessing the degree of agreement between coders when employing an agreed coding scheme for some set of data (Carletta 1996).

The results then showed that *neither* classification scheme could be applied with a reasonable degree of accuracy, although the scores for Groupe Mu were slightly higher. Interestingly, when comparing different codings after performing the analysis, coders would typically agree about the plausibility of the others' selections. This suggests that it is not so much that the codings were wrong or that the classifications were inappropriate, but rather that they are insufficiently constrained to lead to determinate results in specific cases. In advertisements where there was more than one rhetorical figure operative, for example, opinions could differ concerning which might be considered 'dominant' or 'central'.

Other problems identified in van Mulken's study were that many examples did not appear to fit in any of the Groupe Mu categories and so could not be coded, and that the classifications were in any case insensitive to the rather common case that more than one rhetorical figure appeared in a single advertisement. In other cases, particularly in the McQuarrie and Mick classification, it was simply inherently difficult to decide between alternative readings: for example, when an incongruent element is fused into some visual, is that an instance of 'replacement' or of the absence of some occluded element? Leaving such decisions open is certain to lead to many cases of uncertain judgement on the part of would-be analysts. These results should therefore be seen as worrying for subsequent experimentation. It is evident that rather more accurate and reliable means of classifying such data will be needed if visual rhetorical explorations are to make progress.

Visual criteria for classification

Building further on the idea that categories related to form, such as the Groupe Mu classification, might provide for more robust analyses, van Mulken, le Pair and Forceville (2010) performed a further study where they relate visual presentation options to measures of complexity and degrees of understanding. For this they relied on three distinct classes of presentation, analogous to the distinctions drawn by Groupe Mu and worked out specifically for metaphor by Forceville (cf. Unit 9): (1) *similes*, where the two elements being related in a rhetorical figure are both visually present, (2) *hybrids*, where the two elements are fused together visually and (3) what they term *contextual* metaphors, where one of the elements is absent; an example showing these contrasting cases can be seen in Figure 9.3 in Unit 9 later.

Van Mulken *et al.*'s study was then able to address a further issue left implicit in the studies we have seen so far. McQuarrie and Mick showed in their experiments that there appeared to be differences in processing complexity across the distinct types of rhetorical figure suggested in their taxonomy. But they did not explicitly address whether these results also correlated with recipients' own *judgements* of complexity, that is, how difficult recipients perceived the advertisements to be. This was then also related to appreciation, in another attempt to refine the boundaries within which increased complexity increased the appeal of the product. The study also, by continuing to look at different cultures (three European countries in this case: France, Spain and the Netherlands), addressed whether this appreciation would show contrasts depending on nationality.

The results on 'perceived deviance' from expectation are interesting in that they reverse some of the preconceptions from earlier studies based on ideas motivated on the basis of rhetorical divergence alone. First, the ordering of the three distinct kinds of visual rhetorical figures was that similes were judged more deviant than contextual metaphor. In a taxonomy such as McQuarrie and Mick's, similes may have been assumed to be the simplest (and so less deviant) of all because all the information necessary to decode the message is explicitly present in a distinct form; the contextual category, on the other hand, would be assumed more complex because the recipient has to 'create' the unpictured element themselves. This was not reflected in the experimental results.

In addition, the hybrid representation was found to be the most divergent of all. Again, since the information necessary is visually present, this would in many other approaches have been predicted to be less deviant. The judgement of deviance then did not align perfectly with judgement of complexity: in this latter case, the results tallied more with previous predictions – contextual metaphors were judged to be the most complex, whereas with respect to similes and hybrid depictions there was a difference between the French and Dutch participants, who did not judge there to be a difference, and the Spanish participants, who did. These results on cultural differences were however quite weak and did not match classifications of the differences between cultures suggested on other grounds; more study would be needed here.

Particularly interesting, however, was the result that fully understood contextual metaphors were *not* preferred to fully understood similes and hybrids, despite being judged to be more complex, and similes were liked as much as hybrids when understood. This means that:

> Understanding relatively difficult visual metaphors does not lead to an enhanced appre-
> ciation of the advertisement. It might be the case that, even if fully understood, consumers
> think of complex metaphors as far-fetched, or contrived. Perhaps the cognitive pleasure
> – the pleasure of having solved a riddle – that is assumed to play a role in the appreciation
> of tropes, is overestimated in the advertising context. We conclude that audiences, perhaps
> unlike academic analysts, do not want to waste time and energy going beyond a certain
> level of interpretative complexity . . .
>
> (van Mulken *et al.* 2010: 3427)

RHETORICAL FIGURES COMBINING VISUAL AND VERBAL COMPONENTS

The advertisements considered so far in the studies described were primarily *either* verbal *or* visual figures. We then need to follow up on the early proposals of Bonsiepe (2008 [1965]),

Gaede (1981) and Durand (1987) mentioned before to see what happens when both visual *and* verbal resources are deployed in the service of creating rhetorical figures in advertisements. This constitutes a natural extension of the experimental procedures reported above to the verbo-visual, multimodal case.

Considering rhetorical figures that combine distinct modalities raises further problems of its own, however, when considering experimental investigations. Several more dimensions of possible variation need to be controlled to make sure that 'noise' is not introduced, making reliable results difficult to achieve. For example, just *where* does the text component occur with respect to the visual component? – that is, does layout make a difference? Does colour and typography, or size? And so on. Thus, although there are some indications that particular rhetorical effects may be correlated with identifiable linguistic patterns, how this might be extended to include visual material in a reliable way is difficult.

Van Enschot *et al.* (2008) report on a study very similar to several of those reported above but explicitly taking on the challenge of 'multimodal' rhetorical figures and schemes and tropes. Data are again selected from advertisements, this time focusing on cases where the rhetorical figure appears to be spread across the verbal and the pictorial. As a working definition, van Enschot *et al.* follow Forceville's characterisations of multimodal metaphor (Unit 9) and take a verbo-pictorial rhetorical figure to be present only when removing either the verbal or pictorial component would destroy the effect. This then shows that both components are necessary.

An example used for a multimodal scheme is an advertisement for a lipstick that is marketed as imparting a high gloss to the lips: the advertisement contains the word 'gloss' but the 'O' of the word is realised by a woman's lips making the shape of an 'O'. This combination is purely visual and does not need to be decoded conceptually; removing either the rest of the text or the pictorially present lips would destroy the figure and so the example is a genuine case of a multimodal rhetorical figure. In contrast, an example of a multimodal trope can be found in the diet example of Spillner's that we saw in Unit 2 ('Spillner's text-image relations', p. 37): removing either the text or the picture of the tub of margarine would have left no message to be decoded – both need to be present even though there is no perceptual combination or association to be found.

The experiment then took four advertisements within each category (no rhetorical figure, multimodal scheme and multimodal trope) and presented these in a randomised sequence to 92 experimental participants balanced for gender (i.e., 50% male; 50% female). The allocation of advertisements to categories was performed in a separate classification task involving 24 students who had been taught how to recognise the categories. Ads that were not agreed on by two-thirds of the coders were not used in the subsequent experiment. This is a good way of achieving an appropriately high degree of confidence that the initial grouping of advertisements does reflect genuine differences in their design.

Experimental participants were then asked to judge the complexity and assess their attitudes to each advertisement by filling in a questionnaire. Participants had to place their answers to questions such as "I think that the advertising message is very obvious", "I think that the advertising message is hidden in the advertisement", "I think the advertisement is attractive", "I think the advertisement is unattractive", "I think that the advertisement is surprising", and so on along 7-point scales. Scales of this kind, called **Likert scales**, are a standard technique for measuring the strength of agreement to questions in psychological experiments – respondents are asked to express their degree of agreement with a collection of statements probing the area under investigation. Participants were also asked whether they had tried to interpret the text in combination with the picture and whether they had been successful, as

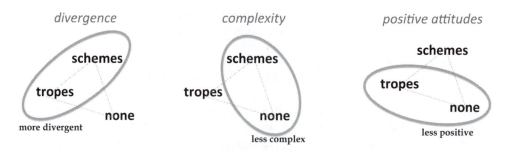

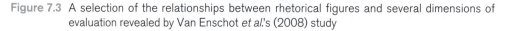

Figure 7.3 A selection of the relationships between rhetorical figures and several dimensions of evaluation revealed by Van Enschot *et al.*'s (2008) study

well as what kind of attitude they had to the product being advertised (in order to separate out potential differences between attitudes to the advertisement and attitudes to the product being advertised).

The results showed some interesting and, again, not intuitively obvious connections. A selection of these is summarised graphically in Figure 7.3. Spelled out in more detail these results revealed that:

■ advertisements with verbo-pictorial rhetorical tropes and schemes were considered more divergent than advertisements without rhetorical figures but tropes and schemes were not differentiated with respect to divergence;
■ advertisements with a verbo-pictorial trope were considered more complex than advertisements with a verbo-pictorial scheme and with no rhetorical figure, but schemes and no figures were not differentiated with respect to complexity;
■ the most positive attitudes towards advertisements were shown for verbo-pictorial schemes, while no difference between advertisements with a trope and advertisements with no rhetorical figure with respect to attitude was found.

This then confirms the scepticism voiced above concerning the degree to which complexity leads to positive attitudes. The tropes were clearly classified as being more complex, but did not receive the highest attitude scores, *even when understood*.

Phillips and McQuarrie's classification of visual rhetorical figures

Following their earlier studies, Phillips and McQuarrie (2004) presented a new classification of visual rhetorical figures in advertising intended to improve on their previous models. One of the motivations they make for the new model is that McQuarrie and Mick's (1996) classification was too closely bound to verbal rhetorical figures and that for visually expressed rhetorical figures different properties need to be considered. The new classification thus built in some specifically visual distinguishing features.

This classification is consequently organised around two dimensions, each taking on one of three values so as to define a 3 × 3 typological matrix for identifying the kinds of visual rhetorical figures present in any advertisement. The first dimension is the one adding in visual qualities of the visual presentation and is similar to the Groupe Mu distinctions discussed above. The other dimension folds in the distinctions drawn from previous classifications of tropes. The resulting matrix is shown in Table 7.1.

Phillips and McQuarrie relate the first dimension of visual structure to complexity and the second dimension of rhetorical 'operations' on meaning to what they term 'richness'. This refers to the openness of the representation for further inferences: the richer a representation, the more the viewer is invited to participate in further meaning making and follow up leads that the visual representation suggests. Thus, in summary, they argue that: "the taxonomy asserts that there are nine, fundamentally distinct, kinds of visual rhetorical figures" (Phillips and McQuarrie 2004: 116). Any advertisement considered should be locatable within some cell of the matrix and, following from this decision, predictions concerning its processing and take-up by an audience follow from the degree of complexity and richness that that cell brings along.

In a move rather different to earlier descriptions, Phillips and McQuarrie argue that rhetorical schemes should *not* now be included since in verbal rhetoric these are relations of form. Visual depictions, however, and as we discussed in Unit 2 ('Constraining the search for text-image relations', p. 40), lack levels of form analogous to verbal expressions and so are excluded. This seems to be going too far, however, since regardless of their individual 'identifiability', reoccurring and contrasting *patterns* are recognisable visually just as well as they are verbally. In other words, there are evidently effects that can be achieved by, for example, visual similarity or repetition. It is then unclear why this category should be removed from the classification.

Another potential limitation of the account that we will be in a better position to appreciate after some of the more refined frameworks for text-image relations derived from linguistic models have been introduced in Units 10 and 11 later is that the relations selected for capturing meaning operations – connection, similarity and opposition – are actually a very small selection from a far broader range of possibilities. If we see these operations as *discourse* operations, as we will suggest below, then it is possible to draw on several far more detailed categorisation schemes. For the present, then, we will leave it as an open question whether these other kinds of relations – such as temporality, causality and so on – might serve to motivate different kinds of visual rhetorical figures more effectively.

Table 7.1 The Phillips and McQuarrie (2004) typology of rhetorical devices: any advertisement should, in theory, be allocatable to one of the cells in the table

	Meaning Operation		
		Comparison	
Visual structure	*Connection*	*Similarity*	*Opposition*
Juxtaposition	–?–	–?–	–?–
Fusion	–?–	–?–	–?–
Replacement	–?–	–?–	–?–

OVERVIEW, PROBLEMS AND ISSUES

A good overview of these and other approaches is offered by Maes and Schilperoord (2007), who then also draw some general lessons for this kind of research and the requirements that now need to be met. Their starting point is to consider the communicative structure of advertisements as establishing relations between two entities, one the product that forms the point of an advertisement, and the other some further entity, person, quality or action. A simple case would be just to say that the product is good: this brings together two entities – the product and the quality, 'good' – but is not particularly rhetorical in its organisation. The purpose of expressing the relationship is to have the effect on viewers that they are more likely to buy the product or to otherwise conform with what the ad is promoting.

The question then central is whether the relationship being drawn employs rhetorical strategies. Maes and Schilperoord take this as the first basic decision to be made: is there a rhetorical relationship at work or not? Only when this decision has been made positively does it make sense to start applying the various machineries for analysing verbal rhetorical figures. This is then built into a set of evaluation criteria for assessing the various proposals that have been made for classifying visual rhetorical figures.

Maes and Schilperoord (2007: 228–229) recommend that a 'sound and useful' taxonomy should meet the following four criteria:

Criterion 1 "to decide whether an ad is rhetorical or not",
Criterion 2 "to analyze the meaning operations that are involved",
Criterion 3 "to analyze the design templates or characteristics that are employed in rhetorical ads",
Criterion 4 "to ground hypotheses concerning viewer's responses to the various conceptual and structural configurations".

They then suggest three levels of abstraction from which it makes sense to consider accounts – the structural, conceptual and pragmatic levels – and apply their criteria to proposals made by Groupe Mu, Charles Forceville and Phillips and McQuarrie. The Groupe Mu and Phillips and McQuarrie taxonomies we saw above; that of Forceville we return to in Unit 9 later.

Maes and Schilperoord's conclusions are then as follows. Only Forceville's account contains explicit guidance for making a decision concerning whether or not a rhetorical figure is present (although Forceville only actually considers metaphor); all three give indications of the visual details that need to hold to identify the elements that a rhetorical figure is being defined over; Forceville and Phillips and McQuarrie identify some of the semantic relationships that are available for relating the identified elements; and only Phillips and McQuarrie explicitly aim at identifying some of the effects and responses that the different rhetorical figures will have on their viewers/readers. Thus no one account meets all of the criteria that they set, although all provide some part of the puzzle.

To provide more guidance, Maes and Schilperoord set out a 'flowchart' for making the necessary decisions when performing an analysis, drawing on their critical discussion. This flowchart is reorganised in graphical form in Figure 7.4.

The first decision point asks the basic question of whether there is a rhetorical figure to be found in the advertisement or not. Here Maes and Schilperoord are rather more strict in their use of 'rhetoric' than some – for example, simply showing a product in a pleasant environment or being used by positively (for some group of potential consumers) evaluated people is *not* considered by Maes and Schilperoord to be a case of a rhetorical figure. Thus

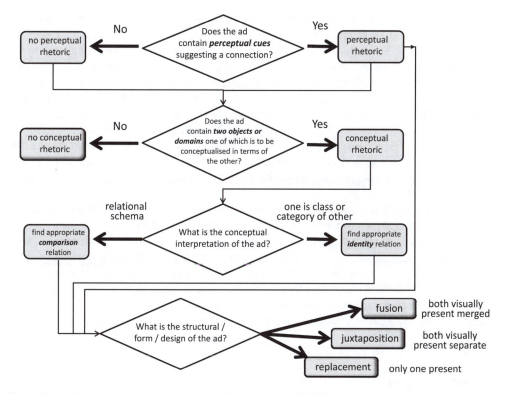

Figure 7.4 Adapted flowchart from Maes and Schilperoord (2007) for determining whether an advertisement using a rhetorical figure is on hand: questions refer to two possible elements or domains selected from the advertisement for testing

they do not consider all means of persuasion in their account as rhetorical – they require a clearly expressed meaning 'deviation' or non-motivated 'addition' or 'replacement' to what might naturally be depicted in order to warrant application of the rhetorical flowchart and analytic machinery.

The presence of a rhetorical figure can then be indicated (contra Phillips and McQuarrie: see above) purely visually by prominent perceptual cues or conceptually, where two domains are brought together for a form of 'co-conceptualisation'. In this latter case, there is usually no natural relationship between the domains, the advertisement itself brings the domains together against common expectations. Two general types of relationships are foreseen at this level: the conceptual relation may be established by means of a **schematic interpretation** or by a **categorial interpretation**.

A *schematic interpretation* relies on a commonsense domain or context that gives rise to a collection of objects, actions and relations that normally occur together: then, in a corresponding rhetorical usage, one of these participating objects, actions and relations might be replaced by the product in order to 'co-conceptualise' that product. One example Maes and Schilperoord offer for this is an advertisement used by Forceville (1996) for motor oil, in which the oil container is shown suspended upside down like a bottle for some intravenously applied solution in a medical situation. The advertisement includes only the text "intensive care". The result is that the schema of intensive medical care is taken over and used to conceptualise caring for a car. Different kinds of comparison relationships can be applied between the product and the object defined by the applied schema; these include similarity, contrast, causal and simple association. Such advertisements are very widespread.

A *categorial interpretation* is when the co-conceptualisation is achieved by relating the elements in the rhetorical figure by means of a type-subtype or class-member relationship. Maes and Schilperoord offer as an example an advertisement for packaged orange juice that shows an orange juicer with a squashed orange juice carton on top of it in place of the usually to be expected fresh orange. The idea here is that the carton of orange juice 'is' a (type of) fresh orange or is a 'member of' the class of things that it makes sense to squeeze fresh juice out of. Maes and Schilperoord admit that there may be schema-based interpretations that might be applied here as well, but argue that the singular role of a fresh orange in the depicted situation justifies the categorial interpretation more: the connection is more than just similarity, it is one of *identity*.

The last part of the flowchart then considers how the rhetorical figure is expressed in the design of the advertisement. Here Maes and Schilperoord adopt the three-way characterisation similar to that used by van Mulken and others, echoing the Groupe Mu classification we saw above. Juxtaposition is then where both elements are visually and separately present; fusion is where both are present but are visually merged; and replacement is simply where one element occurs instead of the other. This use of terms again needs to be compared with others we have discussed – for example, the use of juxtaposition here is rather different to Schriver's strong sense of a 'clash' in meaning that we saw in Unit 6 ('Adding more structure', p. 133), and so on.

CONCLUSION

In several areas concerned with communicative artefacts as acts of *persuasion*, it has been natural to turn to traditional notions of rhetoric, as the art of persuasion, in order to see the extent to which such ideas can be applied to both texts and images. The essential ideas here are that traditional rhetorical figures, such as rhythm, metonyms, metaphors and so on, may also be recognisable both in purely visual depictions and in text-image combinations. An increasing number of authors are exploring this avenue, suggesting ways in which reworked catalogues of rhetorical figures may be relevant for characterising rhetorical figures expressed visually or in text-image combinations.

This unit has introduced the tenets of a rhetorical approach to text-image relationships in advertisements, showing where and why it has been applied. This kind of rhetorical analysis has also served as the basis for some psychological and audience-based studies, exploring whether different rhetorical figures have different effects on their audience.

There are areas of application beyond advertisements, however. Other areas are discussed, for example, in the collection of Hill and Helmers (2004) and in earlier work, such as the classification of visual rhetorical schema by Foss (1994). Wright (2011) also provides many good examples of the use of text-image and visual rhetoric for analysing press and documentary photography, a further area where issues of persuasion are important. There are many overlaps and connections to be drawn out with the accounts that we have used as illustrations here.

Research continues on advertisements and is unlikely to stop any time soon. There are many issues left to explore and to refine. In addition, further methods are being employed as well as there being a broader investigation of how text and images work together. A recent study by Lagerwerf, van Hooijdonk and Korenberg (2012), for example, uses new methods, including eye-tracking (cf. Unit 13), in order to investigate whether different rhetorical figures have an influence on 'anchoring' the visual information in Barthes' sense. Such studies continue to increase our understanding of the interaction of different discourse organisations and the text-image divide.

PART III

Frameworks

In this part of the book, we address some more specific frameworks that have been developed for capturing the text-image relationship. We have seen some of the proposals made in particular disciplines, generally related to particular types of visual contexts, in the previous part. Certain systematic problems tend to reoccur in those accounts, although each offers benefits for some of the research questions asked. Here we change direction and explore how general and how reliable we can make an account.

The frameworks described draw on a variety of different sources for their organisational principles.

Several draw on accounts of the linguistic system, including proposals for grammatical, discoursal and rhetorical organisation (Units 8–11); others take inspiration from communicative actions more generally or from cognitive models and pragmatics (Units 12–13). In each case, we will see some of the same patterns of relationships and questions arising, as well as distinctive contributions.

Frameworks Drawing on the Linguistic System

Multimodal cohesion and text-image relations

Many approaches to text-image relations treat the 'text' and the 'image' as unanalysed wholes. The descriptions given of the inter-relationships may make reference to what is discussed in the text or shown in the picture, but do not concern themselves with the more fine-grained inter-relationships that such a discussion presupposes. But it is rarely the 'entire' text and the 'entire' image that stand in relation to one another: there are usually particular components of each that bring a structured connection between text and image into being.

Probably the most common way of describing relations between text and images when looking 'inside' the text or the image is simply to pick occasions where the text and the image appear to be 'saying the same thing' or 'referring to the same object'. Thus, if a text says 'Max' and there is a picture of a small boy, in many cases it may be unproblematically assumed that these have something to do with one another. This is the informal basis of several of the kinds of descriptions that we have seen so far. There is an overlapping area of *linguistic* description that works in a similar way. This goes under the name of *cohesion*.

'Cohesion' as a technical term was introduced in the work of Halliday and Hasan (1976). The popularity and ready applicability of cohesion as a method of description in the context of text-image relations builds on one of its basic features: cohesion is defined as a *non-structural* linguistic resource — that is, cohesion is a way of relating linguistic entities across all kinds of syntactic and other structural boundaries. This then suits very well the situation where grammatical structures might not even be relevant or existent — as is usually the case in relations between text and images.

In this unit we give the basic definition of cohesion — or more specifically the parts of cohesion that have been most commonly adopted for talking about text and images — and then proceed to the most developed text-image approach of this kind, that proposed by Terry Royce (Royce 1998, 2007) and its further development by Liu and O'Halloran (2009). Cohesion can also be seen as a way of grouping a rather diverse collection of researchers together since, as we shall see, the idea itself is fairly intuitive and often occurs without the particular theoretical foundation assumed by Royce and others.

ORIGINS

The idea of 'cohesion' is taken from linguistic models which have concerned themselves with the nature of *text* — here used in the traditional linguistic sense of any piece of spoken or written language — and the difference between text and isolated sentences. Clearly, if we just put random sentences together, the resulting collection would not necessarily be a text even if all the sentences individually were perfectly grammatical. So various schools of text linguistics have focused on the question of what makes the difference. What properties must a collection of sentences have over and above being grammatical (or at least acceptable) in order to 'work' as a text?

One traditional answer to this question is that a text should satisfy two conditions: not only should it make sense (logically enough), but it should also *show* that it 'hangs together' as a text by drawing more or less explicit connections across its parts. The first condition is often labelled text *coherence*, while the second is called text *cohesion*. Cohesion then studies the ways in which a text can show such connections. The connections present in a text are said to constitute that text's *texture* (cf. Hasan 1985).

As mentioned above, one framework in which the linguistic notion of cohesion has been developed in considerable detail is that set out in Halliday and Hasan (1976). Although somewhat similar mechanisms of text construction have been proposed in several text linguistic traditions, it is Halliday and Hasan's which has had the broadest impact. Cohesion, in contrast to coherence, is specifically oriented towards the concrete linguistic details of individual texts, or instances of language use. It seeks to show the contribution of patterns of *lexicogrammatical* selections to being able to see texts as functioning 'wholes' in their own right.

The guiding definition for cohesion is then that an element in a text functions as *cohesive* when it is necessary to find *some other element* in the text for the former element's interpretation. The most obvious examples of elements functioning in this way, that is, cohesively, are pronouns when used in sequences of sentences such as:

(1) Take the apples. Core *them*. Then place *them* in a saucepan.
(2) The sun rose. *It* was a dull orange.
(3) "Many people visit us here. *They* are always very interested in what we have to say."

The condition that the other element looked for be found *in the same text* is crucial for the definition of cohesion. Thus, the pronouns 'we' and 'us' in example (3) above are *not* considered cohesive – at least not if the sentences were said by someone in a conversation or dialogue as suggested. This is because we do not need to look anywhere else in the text to work out who they are referring to: this information is given in the context, by the person speaking, rather than anything elsewhere in the text.

This is actually the most important constraint that applies: if interpretation requires finding another element in the text, no matter (with one exception that we return to in a moment) what or where that element is, then it is cohesive. If the element is interpreted by looking outside of the text into the context of use, then it is not. Some authors do not make this sharp distinction, adopting cohesion more broadly – it is useful, however, in order to separate out the distinct sources of evidence and knowledge deployed in text production and interpretation.

This then helps us with some more tricky cases. Another form of cohesion occurs with definite articles, like 'the', as in a sentence sequence such as:

(4) You will need a large frying pan and six eggs. *The* frying pan should be well greased. Beat *the* eggs with a whisk.

Both the elements 'the frying pan' and 'the eggs' function cohesively because, in both cases, you have to look back in the text to find just what frying pan and which eggs are meant. In contrast, the element 'the sun' in example (2) is again *not* cohesive because we do not need to look in the text to find which sun is meant – unless, of course, we are in a science fiction or astronomy text, where it could be used in a quite different way. The technical terms for this distinction are *endophoric* and *exophoric*: the former are pointers (which is what 'phoric' means) inside (*endo*) the text, the latter are pointers outside (*exo*) of the text. There are several other categories distinguished in the theory; Halliday and Hasan (1976) provide details.

Now, whenever two elements are related cohesively, they are said to be connected by a *cohesive tie*. Cohesive ties can then be linked together to create *cohesive chains*. In sentence sequence (1), for example, we have a small cohesive chain made up of three elements linked by cohesive ties: 'the apples', 'them' and 'them'. It is also reasonably safe to assume in this case that 'the apples' is also functioning cohesively with respect to an earlier part of the recipe, for example at least to the list of ingredients.

It is precisely this collective operation of the various cohesive chains that can be found in a text that is intended to give a concrete and operationalisable sense of its *texture*. As we have already seen, cohesive ties can hold between any elements used in a text regardless of their structural position or relationships – and this is the second constraint just mentioned: cohesion is generally held *not* to apply when the elements considered occur in a syntactic structural relationship. So cohesion is looking somewhere else in the same text *outside* of any determining grammatical or syntactic structure. This will not bother us too much, however, since with text and image combinations we are not generally looking at syntactic structure at all.

The chains formed from cohesive ties can then grow to be of any length. They can even combine and separate as a text develops, as shown in example (5):

(5) The two children set off at once. Mary took the high road. John took the low road.

Here the single element 'the two children' (again presumably cohesive with their intro-duction earlier in the text) splits into two, 'Mary' and 'John', which each might then be developed further with their own cohesive chains built with 'she' and 'he' respectively.

There are also other types of cohesion relevant for text description and the creation of texture. Halliday and Hasan identify six distinct kinds and describe each of these in consid-erable detail with many examples. The type of cohesion we have discussed so far builds on *reference*: references constituting a cohesive reference chain are made up of the individual cohesive ties that link phrases sharing a common referent. Reference is a semantic relation-ship, it is concerned with what the elements involved mean. In this case, then, a cohesive chain can be considered a *realisation*, or form of expression, of a sustained (discourse semantic) strategy operating *within* a text for making sure that that text picks out some single referent 'outside' of the text for as long as it needs to.

In contrast, some types of cohesion build more on the *form* of the elements in the text. For example, repeating a word is also held to have a cohesive effect: a text's texture is certainly affected when a word is reused rather than selecting a different word. This is a case of *lexical* cohesion, depending only on the form – it is concerned with whether a particular lexical choice, normally a word, reoccurs or not. Another form of lexical connection that adds texture is known as *collocation*. Collocation is when two lexical choices have a higher than usual probability of occurring together – common examples are 'pepper and salt', 'right and wrong', and so on. These are then also said to form cohesive ties.

Finally, for current purposes, there is a type of cohesion that builds not on specific semantic references but on semantic connections in general. These are called *lexical semantic rela-tions* or *sense relations*. They are identified in most schools of linguistics that concern themselves with lexical semantics in any way (cf. Lyons 1977: 270–335, Chapter 9). The usual lexical semantic relations defined include: hyponymy (type-subtype relations: e.g., 'animal'–'dog', 'furniture'–'chair'), antonymy (opposites: e.g., 'hot'–'cold'), meronymy (part–whole relations: e.g., 'car'–'door', 'house'–'chimney') and synonymy ('same' or very similar meaning: e.g.,'big'–'large').

Putting all of these definitions together means that it is quite possible for different types of cohesion to combine in single linguistic elements or phrases. In (4), for example, we have not only reference operating – by virtue of the use of 'the' – but also repetition, since 'frying pan' and 'eggs' both recur. We still need to separate out these distinct types of cohesion, however, because they can occur independently of one another:

(6) You will need a large frying pan. Put the thing on the stove.

In this case, we still have reference, but no repetition. We need to pull the two forms of cohesive tie apart, therefore, so that we can follow each potential contribution to texture as and when it occurs.

Performing a cohesive analysis of a text then works by finding all the cohesive ties that can be motivated by applying the definitions. Whenever a text-internal, non-structural reliance on other elements in the text is found, a cohesive tie is constructed. The resulting collection of ties is then intended to be indicative of the text's texture, showing how lines of cohesion are woven together in distinctive patterns, where gaps in cohesive connections can be found, as well as areas which are particularly dense in their cohesive commitments, areas where particular types of cohesion operate rather than others, and so on.

An example of a text fragment annotated with the kinds of cohesive ties we have discussed so far is given in Figure 8.1. We will use this analysis further below when we place it back in its original multimodal context. The text indicates some of the elements operating cohesively by placing them in bold or italic font and, on the right-hand side of the figure, some of the more prominent cohesive chains are set out explicitly.

| **Birds** of the open ocean, **Gannets** *breed* on small islands of the NW coast of Europe. **They** move away from land after *nesting* to winter at sea. **The young** migrate south as far as W. Africa. **Gannets** feed on fish by plunge-diving from 25m, and *nest* in large, noisy colonies. The *nest* is a pile of seaweed. A *single egg* is *incubated* for 44 days. **The young bird** is fed by **both parents** and flies after 90 days. | 'bird'-chain
Birds
Gannets
They
The young
Gannets
The young bird
both parents

move away from land
migrate south | 'breeding'-chain
breed
nesting
the young
nest
the nest
single egg
incubated
both parents

feed on fish
fed by | 'sea'-chain
open ocean
small islands
coast
from land
at sea
seaweed

NW coast of Europe
W. Africa |

Figure 8.1 A cohesion analysis of a text fragment

A VISUAL FRAMEWORK FOR COHESION

The basic idea

As we have seen, cohesion is an essentially *non-structural* resource for text construction. Performing a cohesion analysis on a text generally shows the text as a web of cohesive ties cross-cutting structural organisation both within and across sentences. This reliance on dependency in interpretation rather than structural configurations requiring particular types of grammatical elements has made it relatively natural to consider the possibility that similar relations might hold *even when the elements in a cohesive tie are not linguistic elements at all.*

Thus, we might have examples of cohesive 'repetition' or 'reference' whereby the phrase 'the dog' in some text is tied not to a pronoun or other linguistic element but to a corresponding picture of some dog in an accompanying image. In such cases, cohesion-based approaches generally consider the verbal and visual modes to be contributing more or less equally to a *jointly constructed multimodal communicative act.*

Note that this is not the only option that could be taken – if, for example, an image was considered as part of the 'context' of the textual information, then strictly speaking following the definition of verbal cohesion we would *not* have a case of cohesion. This would instead consider the use of, for example, a pronominal reference to an image from a text as more akin to saying 'here' or 'this one' while pointing in a face-to-face spoken situation. Several approaches consider text-image relations more from this 'pragmatic' perspective. The cohesion approach, in contrast, starts from the assumption that 'texts' can be constructed with verbal and visual parts which should be considered *together* as constituting the object of analysis. This is then compatible with many accounts that have their origins in, or are closely connected with, text linguistics – including, for example, those of Barthes, Spillner and so on that we saw in Unit 2.

When we treat text and image together as parts of a single 'textual' unit, many cases of text-image relationship are rendered compatible with the definition of cohesion. Considering, for example, a picture of a dog and the phrase 'the dog' as belonging to the same 'text' invites us to explore how such connections are similar or different to the single modality case of various phrases referring to the dog. When the picture of the dog is considered only really interpretable in the light of the information in the text – we know that the text pictured is just that dog that is talked of in the text – and both are *designed* to operate together, then we have a prototypical example of cohesion at work.

Furthermore, just as with the linguistic views of cohesion, such multimodal cohesive relations can hold across units independently of any 'structural' organisation that might be assumed to hold over the elements of the page. Thus, in these frameworks, it is usual to find individual phrases from a larger linguistic text being brought into connection with individual image elements somewhere else on the page. There are few limitations imposed on just where the contributing elements might appear.

We can illustrate this concretely by examining the text in Figure 8.1 placed back in its original context of use. An extract of this is shown in Figure 8.2. Here we see many links similar to those we previously saw *inside* the text now reaching out both to pictorial and diagrammatic material and to *other* (but nevertheless still co-present) texts. The lines in the diagram pick out some of these connections, although there are many more that could be isolated if we attempted to be exhaustive. We see, therefore, that 'coast' in the text links cohesively to the coastlines shown in the outline map lower left as well as to the photograph

Figure 8.2   A cohesion analysis of a text-image fragment taken from the GeM corpus of multimodal documents (cf. Bateman 2008)

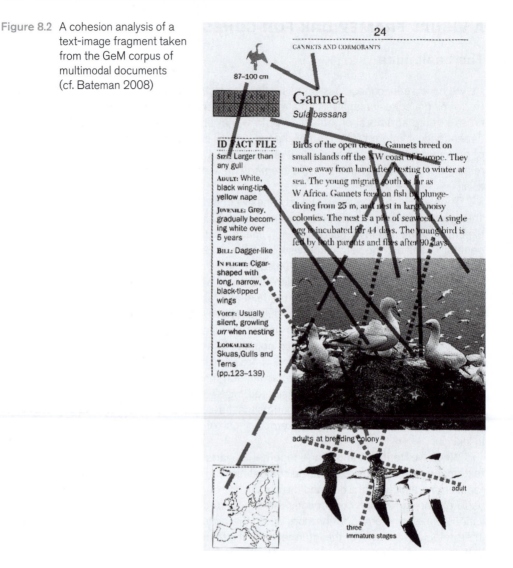

evidently showing a coast immediately below the main text block; similarly reference in the text to 'nesting' is linked cohesively to the nests shown in the photograph, while reference to the 'young bird' is picked up again in the labelled 'immature stages' in the drawings shown bottom centre.

As we shall see when we return to psychological models of text-image relationships in Unit 13, there is considerable evidence that such linkages are employed for understanding text and image together. The question for a multimodal cohesion framework is just what kind of links there are and whether there are good criteria for finding and distinguishing them.

Royce's model

When considering *which kinds* of cohesive ties might operate between elements in text-image combinations of the kind just seen, one plausible starting point is to hypothesise that relations will be found that are similar to those operative in verbal cohesion. However, until examined in detail with respect to actual data, this suggestion remains a hypothesis. In addition, there is the corresponding question of just what and how any such relations might contribute to the interpretation of the text-image combinations found. Both considerations taken together define an active area of research in text-image relationships.

The account that has taken the linguistic model of cohesion furthest in the service of such multimodal descriptions is Royce's model of **intermodal complementarity** (Royce 2002, 2007). Although actually rather broader in scope, Royce's account contains as one prominent part an extensive consideration of how cohesive ties can be used between text and images. The aim of drawing such ties between text, image, graphics and so on is to explain the construction of meanings additional to any brought about by the contributing semiotic modes alone. This then serves to provide 'texture' for multimodal artefacts just as verbal cohesive ties have been proposed to operate in verbal language. For current purposes, we will focus on just this aspect of Royce's framework because this is most relevant for text-image relationships; it is also the most distinctive feature of his account and so warrants discussion in its own right.

Analyses in Royce's framework rely on the assumption of a specific kind of prior organisation that allows the different modalities to be placed in a constructive inter-relationship. This is his solution to the basic 'multiplication problem' that we introduced right at the beginning of Unit 1. As a starting point, Royce proposes that **visual message elements** (or **VME**) should be identified for all of the non-verbal components of an artefact – that is, the pictures, diagrams, graphs, etc. It is then these VMEs that allow connections to be specified both with texts and with other images.

VMEs are defined by drawing on a visual re-working of a particular area of grammatical organisation: that of *clause transitivity*. In many functionally oriented accounts of grammar, and in Hallidayan-style systemic-functional grammar in particular, clause transitivity is described in terms of configurations of a *process*, typically expressed as a verbal group (i.e., the verbal elements in a clause) and a collection of participants that act within the process. Such participants can also be more finely distinguished in terms of whether they are necessary for an action to take place at all – called *participants* proper and expressed in English typically as nominal phrases – and more *circumstantial* information such as time, location and so on that may be given but is not necessarily present, typically expressed as prepositional phrases or adverbials (cf. Halliday and Matthiessen 2004: 175–178). An example of such a process configuration grammatical organisation is shown in Figure 8.3.

Kress and van Leeuwen (2006 [1996]: 74–75) take this basic model for 'organising experience' and apply it to *visual* depictions also. Grammatical descriptions need to be based on linguistic evidence concerning the distribution of particular word classes and other recognisable structural criteria and so it is interesting to consider how a proposal for such an organisation for visual information can be warranted. As we discussed in Unit 3 ('Static medium *vs.* dynamic interpretation', p. 57) in relation to visual narrative, Kress and van Leeuwen build here on visual *vectors*, that is, visible 'lines' of movement, action or gaze that can be identified within a visual depiction. The corresponding visual example for our sentence here was discussed in Figure 3.2 in Unit 3.

Royce's approach is to assume, first, that it is possible to identify *visual* processes and their *visual* participants in any visual part of a 'text' as Kress and van Leeuwen suggest and, second,

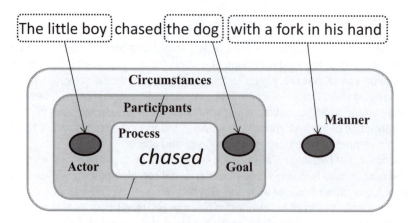

Figure 8.3 Grammatical configuration for the clause 'the little boy chased the dog with a fork in his hand'

that these elements may then be brought into relation with the *verbal* participants, processes and so on identified in any *linguistic* part of that 'text'. Then, since the kinds of organisation adopted in both visual and verbal transitivity are so similar, we have a natural basis for defining a level of abstract similarity between the textual and the visual representations. Royce argues that this is then appropriate for defining cohesive relations that operate *across* text and image.

To see this in operation, let us consider again the visual example that we saw in Figure 3.2 *and* the representation of the grammatical organisation shown in Figure 8.3. In the former case, we have an image; in the latter case, we have a linguistic clause. However, if we turn instead to the visual and verbal transitivity configurations we find very similar structures: both are assumed to have process, participants and circumstances – and, in this case, these are more or less the same. We can therefore speak of a connection, or *repetition*, between the visual process and the verbal process, between the visual participants and the verbal participants, between the visual circumstances and the verbal circumstances, or between the configurations as whole units. These kinds of connection are then precisely what Royce builds on for the purposes of defining intermodal cohesion. This intermodal relationship is summarised graphically in Figure 8.4.

Moreover, if there are processes and participants in both the image and the text, then the analyst can examine them independently in order to ask whether they are similar in some way or another, if they are different, unrelated, and so on. The ways in which they can be similar or different are considered analogous to the cohesive relations already identified for texts. Royce then takes the notion of 'intersemiotic complementarity' to apply whenever a correspondence can be drawn between the verbal and the visual units. As intermodal cohesive relations Royce proposes repetition, synonymy, antonymy, meronymy, hyponymy and collocation – all familiar from the introduction to verbal lexical cohesion above.

Let us take a further concrete illustration to show this at work. For this we refer to one of Royce's own principal examples, an intersemiotic cohesive analysis of a two-page article layout from a 1993 issue of *The Economist* magazine. A re-created version of this layout, plus some of the cohesive relations Royce identifies, is shown in Figure 8.5. The original page layout and contents are shown in miniature in the upper left-hand corner of the figure; in the centre are representatives of various cohesive chains that help bind the page together; just those of the first few sentences are shown here since these will already be sufficient to see the main operations at work.

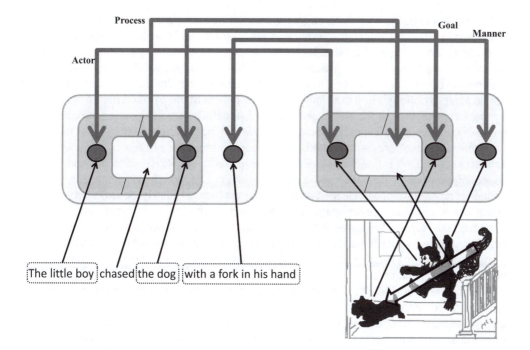

Figure 8.4 Graphical rendition of intermodal cohesion between a textual and a visual rendition of an episode

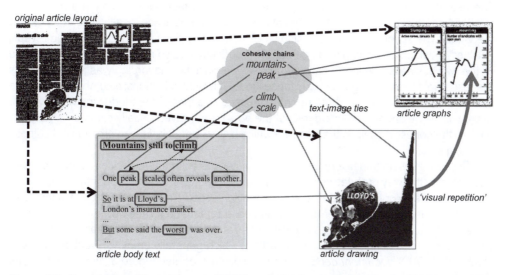

Figure 8.5 Graphical rendition of Royce's (2007) analysis of a page layout from a 1993 issue of *The Economist* magazine. The article drawing, retouched here for copyright reasons, shows two businessmen pushing a large boulder up a steep incline. Dashed arrows within the figure show traditional text-internal cohesive ties; grey arrows leading outside the text show text-image and image-image relations

Royce's analysis proceeds, as suggested above, by carrying out a grammatical analysis of the text in order to produce the verbal transitivity structures for all the clauses present. He then carries on and does the same for the *visual* material, identifying VMEs on the basis of Kress and van Leeuwen's classifications as described above. The 'visuals' to be classified are assumed to be fairly self-evident, which is largely the case here although in general this might not be at all so obvious. Here then, the visual components of the page consist of the cartoon on the first page, the graphs on the second page, and the intrusion of part of the cartoon on the text-justification for the main article copy down the right-hand side of the first page.

One might also consider the 'rhetorical cluster' contributions of titles, by-lines, and so on as discussed in Unit 6 ('Adding more structure', p. 133), but Royce does not address this aspect of the visual organisation particularly. In addition, although the visual transitivity of the cartoon is probably relatively clear – two business men (actors) push (process) a large boulder ('goal') on a mountain (circumstance) – the situation with the two graphs requires more attention than Royce undertakes in his description. In this case it would be beneficial to draw more on detailed visual semantic accounts of diagrammatic representations such as those pioneered by Bertin (1983) – particularly with relation to the *parts* of the graphs, the captions, titles, axis labels and so on.

Royce then considers how the various verbal transitivity frames and the VMEs might be related according to his classes of intermodal cohesive relations. In each case where there is a connection, Royce sees this as an instance of intersemiotic 'complementarity' since more meaning is being constructed than in each of the text and image when considered separately.

Taking the first case from the figure, then, we see that the verbal transitivity frame for the article title "Mountains still to climb" identifies both an action 'climbing' and what is being climbed, 'mountains'. This relates to the cartoon and its VME in that we see two individuals climbing a mountain. This is therefore a case of intersemiotic *repetition*. Moreover, Royce also sees here a relationship of repetition between 'mountains' and the lines shown in the graphs. The use of 'peaks' in the subsequent verbal unit he suggests as standing in a *meronymic* relation to both mountains and the lines shown in the graphs, since 'peak' picks out a part of the whole. The action of climbing is also picked out in the clause: "One peak scaled reveals another", in which 'scale' shows some sense of difficulty and so resonates with the struggle of the two businessmen in the cartoon: this Royce classifies accordingly as a *synonym*. As the text unfolds, continuing to employ these kinds of lexical selections, a combined message accumulates with meanings that are not expressed in either of the modes individually – for example, the weight and awkwardness of the boulder portrayed visually can then be applied back to the cohesive chain in the text with which it is linked: 'solutions to problems', 'business plan' and so on.

Royce argues that uncovering the diverse instances of intersemiotic complementarity for an artefact in this way provides convincing illustrations of just how well the contributing modes are orchestrated. For the article as a whole, cohesion appears to play a central role in this case – which is quite usual in this genre of multimodal artefact and for the newspaper medium in general. There is substantially less explicit cross-referencing of text and graphics than would be expected, for example, in a scientific article, which generally employs Paraboni and van Deemter's (2002) *document deixis*, using phrases such as 'see Figure 3' and so on (cf. Unit 5, 'Text-image relations in comics', p. 107).

In the present case, the cross-referencing across text and visual material is mostly left to the suitably literate reader, who is assumed to be able to make the necessary connections as suggested in the figure. In this sense, the working of the text and image in this kind of document shows suggestive similarities with the case of picturebooks discussed in Unit 4.

The texts and the images are intended to be interpreted together, but it is left to the reader to determine the actual connections that hold.

However, this indeterminacy also applies to the analyst unfortunately. Although the approach often makes visible just how many connections are being suggested in a complex text-image combination, there is rather little guidance offered for the analyst concerning just which may be necessary for an understanding of the meanings being created, which are intended and which perhaps accidental, and so on. As is the case with cohesion in general, whether or not cohesive ties are found does not lead straightforwardly to any predictions concerning the effectiveness or otherwise of the artefact under study. Indeed, sometimes reported results raise some intriguing difficulties – Corrigan and Surber (2009) ask why it is that children's picturebooks can be *less* cohesive than books for adults.

INTERSEMIOTIC TEXTURE

Three further approaches drawing explicitly on models of, or similar to, cohesion as a semiotic resource in the spirit of systemic-functional socio-semiotics are Martinec (1998), Baldry and Thibault (2006) and Liu and O'Halloran (2009).

We mention the first two only briefly here. Martinec's (1998) extension of linguistic cohesion across modes was originally aimed at language and action and not image-text relations; it does becomes relevant below, however, as it is also adopted within Martinec and Salway's (2005) detailed grammar-derived text-image classification. We will return to it accordingly in Unit 10. Baldry and Thibault (2006: 137) in turn draw on a related, more semantically oriented notion of cohesion proposed in Lemke's (1983) *intertextual thematic systems*, a framework designed for showing how knowledge content is constructed as a technical text develops. Baldry and Thibault extend this across the visual and verbal modes by positing general correspondences between the visual and verbal transitivity frames in a manner very similar to that used by Royce and as described above (Baldry and Thibault 2006: 122).

Liu and O'Halloran (2009) is a rather more substantial re-contextualisation and further development drawing both on Royce's account and O'Halloran's extensive work on intermodal semiosis in the context of the discourse of mathematics, an inherently multimodal form of communication combining interesting properties rather different to those of verbal language in general (cf. O'Halloran 2005). Liu and O'Halloran, however, focus specifically on the nature of 'texture' when seen from the perspective of multimodality and text-image relations. In particular, they consider just what the deployment of certain text-image complementarities *achieves for the meaning-making process*.

'Intersemiotic cohesion', as Royce and others use it, is then seen as just one way of realising, or expressing, the semantics of *intersemiotic texture*, in a manner entirely analogous to Hasan's (1985) model for verbal language. By these means Liu and O'Halloran aim to construct a model that can account for the *integration* of information from different modalities rather than simply documenting their 'linkages'. A number of extensions are then made to the account as described by Royce.

First, the catalogue of intersemiotic 'sense' relations is extended. One important additional category here is intersemiotic *polysemy*. We have seen the importance of polysemy and the role that text-image relations can play in exploiting ranges of potential meanings at various places so far, beginning of course with Barthes' notion of the role of anchorage in Unit 2 ('Getting the ball rolling: Roland Barthes', p. 31). Liu and O'Halloran (2009: 384) take this further and point out that linkage, and then integration, of meanings can pivot on polysemous linguistic terms whose distinct meanings can just as well be brought out by co-present visuals. Examples of this have also been discussed by Spillner (1982) as we saw in Unit 2.

The other important extension concerns the levels of abstraction at which intersemiotic connections can be drawn. We shall see in several subsequent units that much use is made of distinctions originally developed for the stratum of *grammar* within the linguistic system. However, although often discussed in connection with grammar, cohesion is primarily oriented towards discourse and text. It therefore forms part of the communicative resources provided by the more abstract *discourse* stratum of the linguistic system. Liu and O'Halloran then propose placing *intersemiotic cohesive devices* as just one of the kinds of such resources that are available for building multimodal texts and discourse. Alongside this they propose *intersemiotic logical relations* forming connections between messages and *intersemiotic parallelism*. As Liu and O'Halloran argue, there are several good reasons for focusing on the discourse-level of description when considering intersemiotic, or multimodal, relations – we also discussed some of these in 'What *are* text-image relationships?' in Unit 2 earlier.

Intersemiotic logical relations are similar to, and indeed build on, the proposals of several other discourse-oriented researchers in multimodality and we return to their detailed treatment in Unit 11. Intersemiotic parallelism, Liu and O'Halloran suggest, occurs when similar organisations of information are offered across distinct modes – such as, for example, when an entire transitivity frame of someone doing something and a visually expressed message are 'congruent' or parallel. This was the situation in our introductory comparison of the grammatical clause and the visual depiction of Max running down the stairs above (cf. Figure 8.4).

Cases of congruence such as this give rise to a notion of *co-contextualisation*, where the information expressed visually and verbally each provides a context of interpretation for the other and those contexts share points of contact supporting meaning extension. The mechanism and workings of such contextualisation are developed further in O'Halloran's proposals for *semiotic metaphor*, which we introduce and discuss in more detail in Unit 9.

PROBLEMS AND OPEN QUESTIONS

Decomposing visual elements to the extent required for fine-grained multimodal cohesion is in certain respects problematic. It is an essential property of images, such as photographs and other visual depictions, that they do *not* come ready labelled with their component elements exhaustively characterised. In a naturalistic picture of two people looking at one another, one can be relatively certain that it will be two people looking at one another that will be perceived by its viewers. How much *more* than this will be perceived will be highly variable, depending partly on the use of salient, 'pre-attentively' accessible characteristics of form, the interests of the viewer, and so on. This includes overall structural properties of the pictorial material, including balance and spatial 'masses', and so on.

This relates to the very general question of whether images have 'parts' at all. Consider, for example, the printed advertisement from the 1970s recreated and anonymised in Figure 8.6. What are its parts? Whereas some parts of the image will be readily picked up by virtue of naïve natural visual perception – we will always attend to and recognise human faces and postures for example – other 'parts' seem to arise in a manner which is far more bound to context and to the particular interpretative goals of a viewer.

The advertisement is one used by Gaede (1981: 10) as one of his many illustrations of visual rhetoric (cf. Unit 6). The particular rhetorical force of the advertisement is achieved both visually and verbally. The pictorial component is accompanied by the main slogan of the

Figure 8.6   Recreated and anonymised sketch of a cigarette advertisement taken from Gaede (1981: 10)

advertising campaign: "I'd walk for miles . . .". Only when we have this additional information are we required to identify that significant information is to be gleaned concerning the sole of the depicted figure's shoe. The shoe sole has a hole in it, thereby visually arguing and supporting the claim that the character has indeed done what the slogan suggests. Now, *without* this slogan, it would be far less compelling that we list the hole in the shoe as one of the VMEs that need to be considered when producing a cohesive analysis. Indeed, there are many very similar visual forms scattered around the image – for example in the knots in the wood making up the building the character is leaning against. It therefore seems more likely that it is the interaction of the image and the text that *brings the necessary VMEs into existence*. This is closely related to the issues of dynamic interpretation discussed earlier in 'What *are* text-image relationships?' in Unit 2.

This raises significant methodological issues for Royce's account. If we can only posit VMEs when we have done the cohesive analysis, we can scarcely set out the necessary VMEs *beforehand* in order to find the cohesive ties present. Thus, while the inter-semiotic relationship between text and image no doubt holds, it is less convincing that the visual contribution can be analysed independently of the verbal and then brought into relationship with it so as to show cohesive ties at work. Analyses in this style could always draw a wide variety of VMEs out of their pictures, but it is difficult to say in advance which of them are going to be relevant.

Searching for VMEs may nevertheless offer a method of focusing attention during analysis. Pictures, for example, can contain considerable information that may or may not be relevant for the text-image relationship. If one uses the interaction with textual information to guide recognition of elements within visual contributions, such as photographs, pictures, diagrams, and so on, then this begins to provide more analytic control of just what will be picked out of an image and what not. Thus, if information is *also* picked up cohesively with information in other modes, then this gives criteria for what should be attended to in analysis and what not.

CONCLUSIONS AND DISCUSSION

In general, the value of proposing particular classes of cohesive ties is that it begins to make more explicit just what kinds of semantic consequences follow from relating particular text-image elements. In contrast to Barthes' looser characterisation, the cataloguing of types of relations makes it possible to draw out notions of repetition, contrast, part–whole and many more in order to show meanings being constructed that would not have been made by either mode alone. Nevertheless, this raises many open questions concerning both the recognition and the effect of multimodal cohesive relations. Analyses are fairly straightforward to perform, but just what they are revealing may remain unclear. A closer link between assumed cohesive relations and the inferential and interpretative processes being pursued by a viewer/reader needs to be pursued since finding a profusion of cohesive links does not necessarily tell us very much concerning how a text is working.

This is exactly the situation that holds for purely linguistic texts also. One can find texts with extensive cohesion which are incoherent; and *vice versa* – that is, we can find verbal texts with very little explicit cohesion but which still function well. We need, therefore, to push the analysis further to show how cohesive links or similar relations can contribute to our under-standing of multimodal documents as, for example, attempted by Liu and O'Halloran. The simple occurrence of presumed links is not enough.

Using metaphor for text-image relations

A very common approach to the relationship between text and images in communicative artefacts is to appeal to some notion of *metaphor*. One reads quite often of some not quite straightforward visual message or combination of text and images, as in advertisements, that they are 'metaphorical'. In some cases, however, this means little more than there is something odd going on, some non-literal, figurative interpretation. And some researchers have explicitly taken 'metaphor' to be more or less equivalent to the notion of *trope* that we introduced in Unit 6 as one of the broadest classifications of types of rhetorical figures – this would then include all that we saw there for other types of rhetorical figures also.

It is worthwhile being much more restrictive with the term, however. There are particular properties that metaphors have, as well as some particular theoretical developments made concerning them, that lead to a quite different style of approach to text-image relations. These are sufficiently important in their own right that we will now examine them on their own.

The discussion proceeds from the traditional definition of metaphor, as one of the rhetorical figures and, as such, a primarily verbal affair, through to its current broad adoption as one of the fundamental mechanisms for thought and 'sense'-making. We will also track its extension along the way from verbal to visual realms. One of the main proponents for visual, or pictorial metaphor for many years has been Charles Forceville, and we will draw extensively on Forceville (1996), where he discusses various approaches to the definition of metaphor that have been taken and sets out his own account of visual metaphor in detail.

We will not engage with many of the fine points of the arguments raised concerning how metaphor should be described, but will instead focus on elements of the discussion that are relevant to text-image combinations. In some places, however, we will also 'push the envelope' of traditional accounts to draw out some beneficial distinctions and motivations that can be proposed when we take a visual perspective.

BEGINNINGS: VERBAL METAPHOR

The starting point for definitions of metaphor was naturally language, because metaphor was just one of the many distinct kinds of figures discussed in classical rhetoric and classical rhetoric was about language. Moreover, examples of metaphor abound not only in discussions of poetry and other types of text where figurative language is to be found, but also in varieties of language ranging from everyday talk to scientific discourse. It is then difficult to find language use that does *not* involve metaphor.

Straightforward cases of metaphor include examples such as:

(1) Man is a wolf.
(2) Life is a journey.
(3) Religion is the opiate of the masses.

The basic idea is clear: some properties of the latter term are somehow to be transferred so that they apply to what is picked out by the former term. The interesting questions begin when we consider in more detail just what is to be transferred where (and how). Although all commentators agree about there being some kind of transfer (which is what will make the notion useful for us later when we get back to text-image relations), the precise terms and mechanisms assumed show considerable variation.

We expand on this first staying within the linguistic system.

In much (linguistically) naïve discussion, it is rather common to focus exclusively on 'words' – words are, after all, one of the most immediately recognisable parts of language and people are generally aware of their and others' choices of words without special training. There are consequently suggestions for the workings of metaphor that focus on words. However, this raises many problems for an account because it should be evident that it is not really words that are at issue – something 'more' is being done than simply using a word in a figurative sense.

This leads to the position, probably now the most commonly accepted, that metaphor is actually a *structural* relation – that is, it works between structures rather than between words or between collections of words. Let us examine example (1) from this perspective more closely. First, 'man is a wolf' seems to suggest that certain features of what we know about wolves – perhaps being predatory – are to be applied to 'man'. Note also we might get rather different wolf-like properties being picked out depending on whether we take 'man' to be an old-fashioned attempt to refer to 'humans' or its current more gender-specific usage! This brings out an important point about metaphor in general: it is not possible simply to read off of the form what the intended transfer is. The transfer will depend on the particular senses that words are being used in *and* their contexts of use.

Forceville (1996: 16) provides the following compelling demonstration of this. Consider the contrasting 'mini-discourses':

(4) a. Roy managed to carry the refrigerator upstairs all on his own. Truly, the man is an elephant.
     b. Even thirty years later, Roy still remembered the names of all those present at the occasion. Truly, the man is an elephant.
     c. Roy had hardly sat down when the chair collapsed. Truly, the man is an elephant.
     d. Roy immediately after the funeral started urging remarriage on the widow. Truly, the man is an elephant.

In each case, the particular elephant properties picked out are quite distinct.

Black (1979) calls the structures that are being related in a metaphor **implication complexes** which contain all the general knowledge and assumptions that come along with the kind of entities mentioned. Wolves are cruel and predatory; elephants have long memories, are very strong, can be a bit clumsy (regardless of whether this is true or not), and so on. Some of this information is selected for transferral; some is not. For example, the fact that the wolf and the elephants are both four-legged seems to play no role in the interpretation processes here.

Since we are going to distinguish the two entities and their respective implication complexes from now on, we should give them appropriate labels – traditionally the first entity in metaphors expressed in the forms shown above is the *target* and the second is the *source*. The source acts as the source of properties that are to be transferred to the target. This means that we could view the situation graphically as suggested for the wolf example in Figure 9.1. On the target side some of the properties of wolves are picked out and transferred and some are not.

As Forceville emphasises, although it is often discussed in less detail it is important to see *both* the source and the target as implication complexes – the reason is straightforward: if we take properties from the source we cannot just throw them at the target and hope that they will stick. What actually appears to happen is that very specific properties of the target are addressed, either modifying existing categories or filling in possibilities so that specific values are imputed. The elephant examples make this particularly clear, so we show in Figure 9.2 two contrasting cases with the implication complexes filled in on both sides of the metaphor.

The account so far shows, then, that we are dealing with 'semantic' organisations rather than with combinations of words. Thus, even within the linguistic system, it would be necessary to consider metaphor more abstractly than just a lexical, or word-based operation.

This has several important consequences. First, we need not only concern ourselves with these very simple 'N is N' constructions. Whenever there is the possibility of setting up transference from one implication complex to another, we are dealing with a metaphor; examples are:

(5) His rusty joints ached.
(6) The office worker ploughed through the pile of orders.

As Forceville discusses, it may not always be immediately clear from such usages which is the source and which is the target, but the principles remain the same. The semantics of the

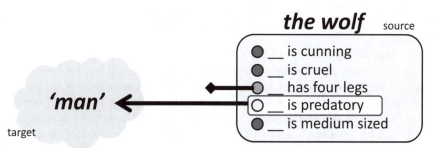

Figure 9.1 Graphical representation of the metaphor 'man is a wolf' from the perspective of the source

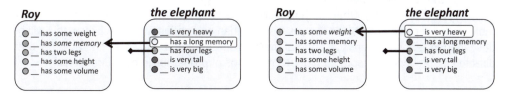

Figure 9.2 Graphical representation of two of the metaphors for Roy and elephants

sentences provide candidates that need to be related metaphorically; deciding on precisely which candidate gets to play which role may require more contextual interpretation. However, by moving from words to semantics, we also have a good basis for the further step to pictorial metaphor because it is not only language, of course, that can suggest entities to be related.

Second, we can also address a little more effectively a question that always arises when discussing metaphor – that is, are they reversible? Some researchers have suggested that they can be reversed, others have argued that this is not how they work. The motivation for seeing them as ordered rather than reversible is brought out very succinctly in the following contrast discussed by Forceville (1996: 12):

(7) a. Surgeons are butchers.
     b. Butchers are surgeons.

This example is particularly effective because changing the order reverses the meanings being exchanged to almost their diametric opposites. In (7a), we appear to have an extremely negative evaluation of surgeons, suggesting perhaps that they treat their patients as hunks of meat to be chopped up; in (7b), we have the quite different extremely positive appraisal of butchers, suggesting that they are workers of considerable precision and skill.

The allocation of target and source roles therefore appears to be very important. We can also pull this apart with a little more linguistic sophistication. The two examples here are different in at least two respects. First, one is a statement about surgeons and the other is a statement about butchers. This almost trivial observation is important because it changes the entire status of the entities that are being brought together. It is not the case that changing the order leaves the 'meaning' of the utterances unchanged. The structure of the clauses themselves therefore imposes particular *functional interpretations* on the entities mentioned. We need not go into detailed grammatical analysis here but, in short, the meaning of phrases such as this is that the first element, the grammatical subject, is being assigned a *value* in some respect – thus, the former entity serves a completely different function to the latter entity. This means that the two variants with their different orders also have very different meanings. Whether we assign some value to butchers or some value to surgeons are just very different statements.

This is also why we do not get the same properties being transferred in the two cases. When we are looking at the value participant in clauses such as this, we need to interpret whatever entity we are given *as a value* and not as a simple reference to some class of professions. If we then ask what *values* are conventionally associated with surgeons, then we end up in the area of skill and professionalism. But if we do the same for butchers, however unfair this may be, we arrive in a very different area of evaluation. Thus, although the *mechanism* of transferring properties remains the same, precisely which implication complex is given to provide those properties makes a big difference.

This will also help us with the pictorial case below since there we need to consider what happens when it is by no means so clear which parts play which roles. This is a general property of many visual depictions. Whereas language places clear hierarchies of interpretation on the table, visual depiction can often say yes to more than one option at a time. Below this will be described in terms of *blends*, a general mechanism that can be used to characterise both directed metaphors and more ambiguous mergings of properties in both directions.

CONCEPTUAL METAPHOR

It is often difficult to halt the move away from words to more abstract levels of description once begun. When metaphors are seen to relate complexes that involve more or less *knowledge* about the entities being discussed, then it is possible to ask whether in fact metaphor is a *cognitive* operation rather than one situated in the linguistic system. Many researchers in the area of *cognitive linguistics*, Forceville included, now accordingly consider metaphor as a conceptual phenomenon. On the one hand, this makes it amenable to psychological experimentation of various kinds; on the other, it also makes the move to pictorial metaphor more straightforward, since it need not be assumed that metaphor is inherently restricted to the linguistic system.

Probably the best-known and most far-reaching developments in this direction are the proposals of the linguist George Lakoff and the philosopher Mark Johnson popularised in Lakoff and Johnson (1980a). According to this framework, more or less conventionalised metaphors are seen to structure much of our cognitive apparatus, providing basic *building blocks* for making sense of the world. Examples of such metaphors visible in everyday phrases are 'argument is war', 'life is a journey', 'time is money', and so on.

Regardless of how such structuring is managed inside our heads, it certainly appears to play a significant role for extended language use. It is often the case, for example, that metaphors are not made once and then immediately forgotten but instead may serve to provide structure for an entire portion of a text. Different parts of the metaphor may be picked out and used to develop further components of the discussion. Thus, if 'argument is war', then an argument also has opposing sides, there may be attacks and counter-attacks, there may be defences, and so on.

Some researchers see such structures as evidence of the role that linguistic organisation plays for how we think; others see such structures as revealing cognitive organisation (Lakoff and Johnson 1980b) – regardless of which position one takes, however, there is clearly a significant textual phenomenon to be described and explained. And, as we shall see below, Forceville and others have now applied metaphor building blocks such as these to a host of visual materials also.

METAPHORS AND IMAGE SCHEMAS

One final development on the notion of metaphors needs to be mentioned before we proceed further. This has far broader significance than exploring pictorial metaphors alone and returns in many otherwise quite diverse approaches to the issues of combining semiotic systems or modalities. The addition draws on Johnson's concerns with the philosophy of mind and his commitment to the fundamental importance of *embodiment* (Lakoff and Johnson 1999). Drawing on this, many linguistic theories nowadays consider embodied experience as an essential component for how language works – and, indeed, brain scanning studies show many more connections between language use and situated physical movements and emotional responses than assumed in more traditional 'modular' theories of mind. Many challenges are raised here for linguistic positions anchored in the traditional Saussurean world of 'arbitrary' semiotics systems as well.

The specific connection to metaphor is as follows. If instead of both domains in a metaphor being symbolic and abstract (e.g., 'argument', 'life'), what if one of the domains is *embodied experience*? This suggests a possible path towards a solution to the age-old problem of relating mind and body: the mind may be the more symbolic, language-influenced half of the metaphor, and body the other half. The metaphorical process then offers a communication channel, or structuring mechanism, between them.

Image schemas are then examples of these basic embodied structures that can serve as the source for adding embodied experience to interpretations. Classic image schemas include:

■ Containment: where some entity is bound within the confines of some other,
■ Source-Path-Goal: where one moves from somewhere along a path to reach some destination,
■ Counterforce: where some movement is worked against by an opposing force,
■ Balance: where a system would seem to be in equilibrium.

There are many more of these image schemas; Johnson (1987: 126), for example, provides a quite comprehensive list. The essential component that is added in this approach for all such schema is the same, however: it should be possible to 'feel' their application – that is, we are all physically and experientially familiar with pushing against some obstacle, or in moving along some path, and so on. All of our bodily sensations and memories concerning such activities are, then, via the embedding of the corresponding image schema in a conceptual metaphor, made available for 'fleshing out' (pun intended) our intuitive dealings with more abstract configurations or meanings. Whereas some general notion of containment might be employed in the abstract, accessing the corresponding metaphor adds a very different intuitive grasp of just what it is like to 'be contained', 'to move', 'to face physical resistance', and so on to our understanding.

This allows interpretation chains to be built such as 'anger is a hot fluid being contained under pressure', 'illness, decay and death is down', 'happiness is up' and many others. Such patterns provide a physical grounding for the more abstract linguistic choices that might be used across a text. Different parts of a text may build on the same metaphor, thereby motivating certain patterns of 'cohesive' links rather than others. These then might also not only give rise to linguistic patterns of use and connections between words, but also may directly motivate certain conventions of pictorial depiction. Both Kennedy (1982) and Forceville (2005b) have discussed this particularly for some of the conventions used in comics, for example.

'Hybrid' models of this kind then support the argument that many human cognitive abilities build on metaphorical organisations of experience that provide embodied foundations for more abstract concepts (Lakoff and Johnson 1980b, Gibbs Jr. 1996). Since such constructs are available to both the linguistic and non-linguistic systems, it is considered plausible that metaphorical foundations can be found that are relevant in both domains. Thus identifying the metaphors that hold might also provide a clue to information integration.

PICTORIAL METAPHORS

The role of metaphors in relating distinct domains (e.g., in their transfer of properties from a source domain to a target domain) has also been suggested as a means of enabling information to flow across modalities (cf. Forceville 2002, 2005a, 2009). This builds naturally on the notion, popularised by Lakoff, that metaphor is about thinking and not about figures of speech – there is then, as Forceville argues, little reason to restrict discussion of metaphor to verbal metaphor.

Drawing also on earlier work on visual rhetoric – much of which we saw in Unit 6 above – Forceville considers a broad range of visual material and concludes that it is indeed beneficial to consider them as exhibiting metaphors. Several exploratory studies have now been performed where viewers of, for example, advertisements have been shown materials including pictorial metaphors of various kinds according to Forceville's definitions in order to see if (a) the metaphors are recognised (without needing to actually state that a metaphor is on hand), and (b) the interpretations given of the metaphors are consistent across viewers (Forceville 1996). It appears that both occur with considerable reliability, although the *range* of interpretations that viewers come up with is more variable – that is, some viewers would transfer a considerable amount of information from the source, others less. This depends on a variety of conditions specific to individuals.

As also remarked in Unit 7 earlier, Forceville pays particular attention to the criteria by which the presence of a metaphor in pictorial material can be recognised. This is very important given the usual surfeit of potential relationships and objects present in any complex pictorial representation and is, as we have seen, one of the principal sources of uncertainty in many forms of analysis. For this, Forceville takes his lead from the strong definition of metaphor of Black and others that we began this unit with above. For there to be a metaphor, it must be possible to identify two elements where one acts as the source and the other the target; furthermore, it must be the case that qualities of the source are transferred so as to hold for the target. If this is not possible, then we are not dealing with metaphor.

Somewhat similar in spirit to the classification suggested by Durand (1987) that we saw in Figure 6.2 in Unit 6 for rhetorical figures of 'similarity', Forceville classifies cases of visual metaphor according to the nature of the elements that are being brought together to build a metaphor. His classes are:

- MP1: where a metaphor obtains but with only one of the elements presented pictorially,
- MP2: where a metaphor obtains with both elements presented pictorially,
- VPM: where a metaphor obtains in which one element is presented verbally (V) and the other is presented pictorially (P).

Forceville also relates this to the cross-classification given by the Groupe Mu scheme that we showed in Table 6.4 in Unit 6. Making it explicit just what one should be looking for when checking the presence or not of a putative metaphor is clearly an important benefit.

Examples of the pictorial categories given by Forceville are shown in Figure 9.3 (Forceville 1996, 2005a); these then also relate to van Mulken *et al.*'s (2010) categories as remarked in Unit 7. The first is a case of MP2, because both elements, the 'car' and the 'dolphin' are present in the image: this may then also be seen as a 'simile' because the 'car is like a dolphin'

 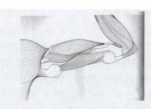 

Type a: Simile (Car is like a Dolphin)   Type b: Hybrid Metaphor (Car is a Muscle)   Type c: Contextual Metaphor (Car is a Shark)

Figure 9.3 Examples of Forceville's typology of pictorial metaphor

is expressed with both elements present in the pictorial material; the third is MP1 (van Mulken's 'contextual metaphor'), a message of the form 'the car is a shark' is expressed only by impli-cation: a shark fin is visible but no car, although the shark's fin is apparently moving along a road. The second example is more complex in that it combines the two elements of the metaphor into a single visual form: the form of the car has been merged with the form of the muscle in the arm. This is therefore still an example of MP2 but it differs substantially in complexity and effect, as van Mulken's experiments with advertisements that we discussed in Unit 7 showed.

Although all three of Forceville's types, MP1, MP2 and VPM, show a host of interesting phenomena, it is clearly the third type that is most relevant for our current concerns since this is inherently a text-image relationship. It is actually striking how this relationship is either missing from many other classifications or included at such a high level of generality (e.g., 'extension', 'addition', etc.) that its particular properties go unremarked. Multimodal cohesion can pick out a relationship of repetition of various components linked with source and target but the particular structural behaviour of metaphor is not typically made prominent.

Forceville argues that moving beyond purely verbal metaphors in this way raises new challenges that have not been in focus in, for example, conceptual metaphor theory so far (Forceville 2009: 29). In particular, he notes that it is relatively common – for example in comics, advertising, animation, and so on – to have metaphors that operate entirely within the 'concrete' domain. This sidesteps the essential idea of conceptual metaphor theory that a bridge be constructed from the concrete (and hence easier to understand) to the abstract. Combining visually, for example, a depiction of a cat and a depiction of an elephant brings about a transfer of properties from one to the other precisely as in other cases of metaphor, even though both source and target are concrete.

Other extensions involve the need to consider transferrals of properties beyond the actually involved entities – as in, for example, an advertisement that places a product together with a famous actor or other potential role model: the idea here is that certain positive connotations of the use of the product are to be transferred rather than simply the actor or product themselves. Particularly these latter type of transfers can be, and usually are, culturally specific and would vary depending on which particular groups an audience would belong to. They are then also some distance from the embodied image schemas that form the main core of conceptual metaphor theory.

MULTIMODALITY: METAPHORS AND BLENDS

Forceville (2009) sets out some of the issues that arise when metaphor is not only considered verbally or pictorially but also *multimodally* as given in his VPM class. Here recognition and processing of the metaphor necessarily draws on more than one mode of information expression in order to construct the source or target of a metaphor. Also, as remarked above, there appear to be cases where information from the verbal and visual modes is combined rather than being transferred. Some researchers suggest that this should also be seen as 'metaphor' (e.g., Carroll 2001), but here we will adopt a different take on this by introducing the notion of **blending**.

This related but rather different mechanism for transferring meaning allows us to continue distinguishing one particular type of semiotic device called a pictorial or verbo-pictorial metaphor from those cases that resemble combinations or 'hybrids'. Metaphors can then remain necessarily irreversible since their function is precisely to transfer information to a

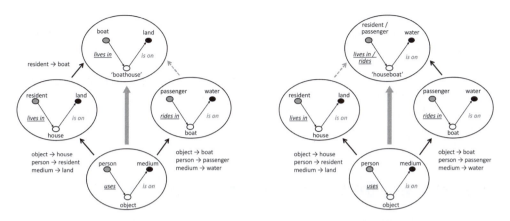

Figure 9.4 Two blending diagrams generating 'houseboat' and 'boathouse'

selected target. When we find a construction that appears reversible, then we can talk of blends and not metaphors. This will allow us to differentiate between the meaning-making strategies involved.

The notion of a blend comes from work in the cognitive linguistic tradition that has sought ways of characterising the conceptual integration of information of various kinds. Information integration appears to play a crucial role for intelligent behaviour and so is clearly a key issue. A common source of examples is word combinations where the meaning of the combination builds on aspects of all of the words combined.

A classic case is the distinction in meaning between 'houseboat' and 'boathouse' discussed at length in many approaches to cognitive blending and conceptual metaphor theory (cf. Fauconnier and Turner 2003). This pair of words is interesting in that their respective meanings can be generated from a systematic process of structural composition. This is suggested in the diagrams in Figure 9.4 adapted from Goguen and Harrell (2010) and earlier discussions.

Diagrams such as these show mechanisms analogous to those we have considered for metaphors up until now. We see in the circles in each blending diagram four 'spaces' that have structured mappings defined between them. These mappings preserve the overall structure within each space, while changing those entities that are placed within the structure. Following the arrows between the spaces is equivalent to making the changes indicated along those arrows. The 'top' space in each case is then the *blend* of the spaces below it. The 'bottom' space provides the *common ground* for comparing and relating the two spaces in the middle so that a blend can be generated. The two blends corresponding to 'houseboat' and 'boathouse' can then be seen to draw on different components of the spaces being blended as indicated in the diagram and the respective mappings performed when following the arrows.

Goguen and Harrell provide a formalisation of this process of blending that can be used to look for potential blends automatically. They report that in this particular case, their algorithm finds no fewer than 48 possible configurations obeying a variety of well-formedness constraints that they derive on both formal and semantic grounds, and a further 736 partial blends that are considered intuitively less plausible (Goguen and Harrell 2010: 304). Blends, especially when formalised in this way, offer a powerful way of generating new meanings and help us see further how the notion of metaphor might be extended and defined.

In contrast to metaphors, however, we can see that blends as illustrated are not directed and so are reversible. This can also happen in certain situations of *pictorial* mixing, where a pictured entity can take on properties of various source images. This is a very common technique in advertising and other designed images aimed at attracting attention, such as drawn magazine covers and caricatures; the blended car and muscle example from Forceville shown in Figure 9.3 is perhaps a good example, at least until it is embedded rhetorically within the context of being a car advertisement. This reversibility means that the relationship of blending to metaphor needs to be considered more carefully because the one is not simply a replacement for the other.

SEMIOTIC METAPHOR AND SEMIOTIC BLENDING

The relevance of metaphor as a means of transferring meanings and integrating different kinds of information has also been seen in work deriving from linguistic and semiotic traditions. This has taken a different path to the cognitively motivated development we have seen so far, although many of the resulting suggestions can be seen as similar. O'Halloran (1999), in particular, has developed an account of relationships across modalities that draws on such a notion of metaphor.

O'Halloran sees semiotic metaphor as a basic process for managing the integration of meanings across semiotic modes. She proposes the existence of both parallel and divergent semiotic metaphors. Both processes work on the principle that it is possible to have broadly compatible representations of visual and verbal information as we saw applied in Royce's approach to multimodal cohesion in Unit 8.

Parallel semiotic metaphor is then when both the verbal and visual representations are congruent, but extra information is passed over between the two modalities being related. O'Halloran offers as an example the case where verbal information may identify objects and some abstract relations, while the visual information provides additional relative spatial information. The two kinds of information are not in any kind of disagreement and their information mutually supports each other. This is then an extension rather than a blend, although most of the structural relationships are maintained as is generally the case with blends.

Divergent semiotic metaphor is when additional substantive information that is not present in one of the modes is added by the other. Here O'Halloran offers an example from the domain of physics where the visual modality adds information concerning a 'boundary' whose existence is simply not extractable or predictable from the verbal information. This is thus a far stronger relationship of intersemiotic combination. The transfer of the properties being unwieldy and difficult to manage from the visually depicted boulder to the verbally described bank problems discussed by Royce in Unit 8 ('Royce's model', p. 167) is a further example. It is somewhat unclear, however, in what way this is necessarily 'divergent'. The distinction may again perhaps be better drawn along the lines of elaboration *vs.* extension from grammar that we have mentioned before and will see in more detail in Unit 10: the information added does not need to be in 'conflict' across the two modes and so can be described in terms of various forms of information 'addition'.

The meaning that results from the operation of semiotic metaphor then 'contains' the results of combining the respective sources. Along the lines of the definitions introduced in this unit, therefore, it may also be better to consider the mechanism that O'Halloran describes as kinds of semiotic *blends* rather than metaphors, since it is quite possible for there to be no directed transfer from a source to a target but rather a *growth* of meaning drawing on both.

CONCLUSIONS AND DISCUSSION

We have seen that the proposal that metaphor may be applicable to pictorial materials and text-image combinations reoccurs across several distinct disciplines. This unit has introduced metaphor in general with illustrations from where it has been most commonly applied. Metaphor seems in many respects an obvious starting point for consideration of the visual and the verbal since it provides a well-established means of talking about relations of 'similarity' or 'transfer' of meanings across potentially very different domains.

Moreover, essential properties of metaphor, such as the transferral of meanings from a source to a target domain, can be directly compared to the idea of 'multiplying' meanings suggested by Lemke back in Unit 1 ('Multimodality and "meaning multiplication"', p. 5). This also brings semiotic metaphor together with the more general cognitive notion of 'blending' on the one hand, and more formal models intended to capture the meaning of this process on the other.

> Indeed, 'multiplying meanings' may itself be considered a more concrete metaphor for the rather more abstract notion of *semiotic* blending.

Making the definition of metaphor more precise helps clarify how meaning multiplication may work. Our illustrations of the use of metaphor taken from the work of Forceville have also suggested some of the steps that can be taken towards making application of the concept more reliable. This is then one concrete way of talking about the relationship between meanings expressed verbally and meanings expressed visually and their contribution to the construction of interpretations.

Modelling text-image relations on grammar

Unit 8 showed how certain elements and ideas from a specific part of the description of language – cohesion – have been applied to describing and systematising the relations between texts and images. In this unit we see how similar attempts have been made starting from the linguistic 'stratum' of *grammar*. We might well ask, before going into details, just why this might be thought to be a good idea. Language is very different from the semiotic modes that operate with images and certainly does not seem to have any 'grammar' in the superficial sense of being made up of grammatical structures, words, subjects and objects and the like. It might then seem unlikely that there would be much of use for building accounts of non-linguistic communication forms.

The motivation for this move can be broken down into two components.

First, many working in socio-functional systemic linguistics assume that a good functional description of language should in fact be sufficiently general as to suggest useful organisations for other modalities. This rests on the basic premise that resources that evolve to serve similar purposes become streamlined for those purposes. Thus, because of their use in similar or even the same social contexts, language, images and their combinations should all come to exhibit parallels in their organisation. As we have mentioned in several previous units, authors such as Theo van Leeuwen, Gunther Kress and Michael O'Toole have developed descriptions for images on precisely these grounds.

Second, a further assumption of socio-functional systemic linguistics is that the relationship between different levels of abstraction in the linguistic system is *not* an arbitrary one. This means that functional organisations in grammar, that is, in the forms of linguistic expressions, should parallel functional organisations in semantics, that is, in what those forms mean. Martin (1991, 1995) has described this in terms of a **solidary** relationship between the two levels of description and several rather diverse linguistic traditions now subscribe to some version of this assumption. Differences in grammatical behaviour are considered indicative of potential semantic distinctions – after all, that is why they are there! This means that distinctions developed on the basis of grammar may well provide good templates for distinctions to be considered for semantics and discourse as well.

So, whenever language and image occur together or apart, but for similar or conjoined communicative purposes, then similarities in their organisation will be expected. Moreover, some of the detailed descriptions of the functional organisation of grammar, worked out after long years of empirical probing of the distinctions, may then also serve as starting hypotheses for other levels of descriptions and for other modes. Even though there may well be differences between the areas considered, as a place to start the finely articulated linguistic accounts have many advantages over less well thought out or theoretically unreflected characterisations.

Two areas of grammatical description have been particularly influential for proposals for text-image relations. The first we have already seen at work in Unit 8: that of **clause transitivity**

(Halliday and Matthiessen 2004: 170–178). As noted, this is also the basis of Kress and van Leeuwen's description of images. We showed the correspondence between 'visual transitivity' and grammatical transitivity in Figure 8.4; we will see further examples of the application of this kind of description in this unit as well. The second influential area of grammar is that of **clause-combining relations** (Halliday and Matthiessen 2004: 373–378). This is the area of grammar that describes the various ways in which grammatical clauses can be combined into larger 'clause complexes'.

As we shall see, a very finely articulated set of distinctions for such combinations has been worked out and this offers a useful perspective on the problematic notion of 'adding' information. At various points in previous units we have encountered the basic classification problem when considering text and image of deciding in what ways information provided in text and in image may be considered to be 'complementing' or 'completing' one another. The clause-combining relations suggest a beneficial and rather general perspective on this issue.

Both clause transitivity and clause combining are drawn on in Martinec and Salway's (2005) approach to text-image relations. This is probably the account that stays closest to the organisational principles of systemic-functional grammar – so close, in fact, that some commentators mistake their approach for a grammatical account of text-image relationships. This is not the case, however. As explained above, instead the organisations imported from grammar are used as templates for exploration. There is no assumption that what is being described is 'grammatical' in the strict sense of conforming to a linguistic notion of grammar. Thus, although the categories employed are *drawn from* grammar, the account is *not then automatically a grammatical account.* We will get a better sense of what this means as we proceed.

Martinec and Salway's starting point is Barthes' characterisation of text-image relationships that we introduced in Unit 2 ('Getting the ball rolling: Roland Barthes', p. 31). They argue that Barthes' categories actually conflate distinct dimensions of organisation, while also leaving out some logical alternatives. This they characterise not as a question of lack of detail, since one can always make an account more detailed, but more as a concern with 'covering the space' of possibilities. If some basic *types* of image-text relationships are missing, then it does not help to make some of the *other* already existing types more specific.

To fill in this space, Martinec and Salway take a similar position to that of Royce discussed in Unit 8 – that is:

> This endeavour therefore presupposes descriptions of text and images, descriptions that must to a great extent be compatible. Systemic-functional linguistics and semiotics provide such a theoretical and descriptive framework and we therefore draw on them when building our system.
>
> (Martinec and Salway 2005: 338)

They then relate Barthes' statements concerning text-image relationships specifically to the kinds of relations developed for clause combining within systemic-functional grammar in order both to show the gaps and to determine possibilities for filling them. Their conclusion is that the gaps and imprecisions in Barthes' original proposals can indeed be removed by combining it with the notions of clause combining. This is then a direct example of using distinctions derived from grammar for non-grammatical purposes.

We will introduce Martinec and Salway's account in some detail – first, however, we need to introduce the grammatical framework they build on, showing its overall organisation and distinctions so that we can follow its application by Martinec and Salway to text-image relations. Following this, we will briefly consider some further developments of the account as well as some alternative proposals that have been made.

GRAMMATICAL ORIGINS

We focus here specifically on the area of functional grammar concerned with combining clauses into bigger, more complex clauses; this has been developed over a period of almost 50 years and on the basis of extensive text analyses and so is known to be very broad in its coverage of the linguistic phenomena considered.

The framework distinguishes two main areas of clause-combining relationships: relations of **projection** and relations of **expansion**.

Clause combining and projection

As mentioned in Unit 4 ('Conclusions and discussion', p. 86), projection is associated with events of saying, thinking, perceiving, and so on and refers to the relationship between those events and *what* is being said, thought, perceived and so on. In English and many other languages, there are very specific grammatical constructions that are used for expressing this kind of relationship – mostly made up of a *projecting* event and a *projected* element with some structural linking material between them. A simple example would be:

(1) Max said that he wouldn't stay.

The projecting clause is "Max said"; the projected element is "he wouldn't stay"; and the ". . . that . . ." construction binds them together. It is evident that projection also occurs readily as a text-image relation. It is the kind of relationship regularly found expressed in speech balloons and thought bubbles (cf. Halliday and Matthiessen 2004: 377, Figure 7.5) and is consequently considered relatively easy to locate. We discussed in Unit 5 ('Text-image relations in comics', p. 107), for example, some of the more detailed descriptions offered of the ways in which projection can appear in comics.

As we shall see, Martinec and Salway then also import projection into their account of text-image relations. In fact, they use this as a further argument of the benefit of looking to grammar for workable sets of distinctions. Since language has been driven to make distinctions that are fine enough for all speech situations that occur, it is likely that it is going to offer much of what is needed when looking at other forms of expression. Projection is, so to speak, already in the 'toolbox' and ready to be used.

Clause combining and expansion

The other area of clause combining, expansion, is rather more complex. Halliday's account posits three subtypes of the relationship, each picking out a rather different way of 'adding' information. These subtypes are: **elaboration, extension,** and **enhancement.** For understanding the general distinctions between these more easily, Kong (2006) offers the following helpful metaphor, also given in Reed (1997: 206):

The three types of expansion can be compared to elaborating an existing building, extending a building and enhancing the environment.

(Kong 2006: 211–212)

The three can thus be seen to be very different in their respective emphases and also show distinct patterns of grammatical realisation; this latter will not, however, be our focus here. We will work rather with some examples and then proceed to their use in the text-image context.

It may not always be possible from just a few examples to know where the boundaries of these categories are meant to be. The distinctions drawn can be subtle and require some practice when being used for analysis – nevertheless, the distinctions do appear to draw out some significantly different meanings that allow us to see rather more clearly the diverse ways in which 'adding' information can be performed. Simple illustrations of the three categories are then:

elaboration   The little boy chased the dog, which was a mean thing to do.
extension   The little boy chased the dog and the dog ran away very fast.
enhancement The little boy chased the dog after he had banged a nail into the wall.

Thus we can see that 'elaboration' here takes the existing statement – 'Max chasing the dog' – and tells us more about it; 'extension', in contrast, moves us on from the first statement so that we end up with a larger statement to consider; and finally, 'enhancement' takes the existing statement and tells us more about the circumstances, setting or environment, in which the situation described by that statement took place.

Note that all of these can be described as 'adding' information – which is the main problem with this loose characterisation when we turn to text-image relations and ask how text and image are combining. There is a relatively clear intuitive sense that the three distinct types of expansion are rather different with respect to the meanings they are making, but this is often difficult to put into words. The three-way alternation elaboration / extension / enhancement then gives us the necessary vocabulary to talk and reason about this.

It will be useful to maintain an overview of the three distinct kinds of relationships of 'adding information' as they reoccur in many of the approaches that we discuss. Those approaches either relate themselves explicitly back to grammar or implicitly draw on similar distinctions in the definition of their classifications. The different styles of adding information are summarised graphically in Figure 10.1. The overlapping or separate circles represent

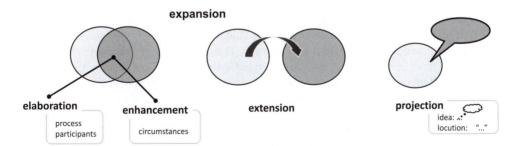

Figure 10.1 A graphical view of the different types of clause combinations proposed with systemic-functional grammar

particular areas of content being expressed. Both elaboration and enhancement can consequently be seen to be concerned with different aspects of adding information 'in place', while
extension is the form of expansion that 'moves on'. Projection is distinguished from all three
types of expansion since it performs a completely different kind of function as we have
described above.

MARTINEC AND SALWAY'S FRAMEWORK

Martinec and Salway's goal is to construct a single classification system for text-image
relations that holds for all cases where text and image occur together. As evidence for coverage of their account they present examples drawn from entries in electronic encyclopaedias,
print advertisements, news websites, online gallery sites, anatomy and marketing textbooks
among others. Martinec and Salway then ask for all the examples they consider how each
identified combination of text and image can be located within their classification system. The
aim is that all such combinations find a clear place in the system and so, as a consequence,
the intended meaning or interpretation of the text-image combination becomes clear.

An additional goal that underlies their work is then to achieve 'empirical adequacy' – that
is, Martinec and Salway want to make their account specific and well-defined enough so that
analysis becomes more reliable than has generally been the case in studies of text-image
relations hitherto. This can also be seen as a beneficial *methodological* import from grammar:
when working with grammar, it is an obvious requirement that structural predictions should
result concerning just which configurations can appear and which cannot. Most prior approaches
to text-image relations have not had this goal firmly in mind and so recognition, identification
and discrimination criteria tend not to be addressed with sufficient rigour. This means that:

> it is not sufficient simply to classify potential relationships between text and image, it
> must also be possible to recognise reliably when relations of particular kinds hold and
> when not – that is, how can the analyst ascertain whether some particular relation obtains
> rather than another?

Lack of attention to these issues creates situations where different analysts come up with
different descriptions of the same objects of analysis. By and large, such variability is *not* due
to multimodal artefacts exhibiting a rich array of meanings to be drawn out. Instead such
variability simply documents the fact that the descriptive apparatus is not yet sufficiently well
developed. This means that improving the descriptive apparatus is an essential step towards
being able to see more of the actual richness of meaning that might be involved. To meet this
goal, Martinec and Salway attempt to set out criteria by which an analyst can know whether
each of their categories applies or not. Although Martinec and Salway might not achieve this
in all the cases they discuss, they certainly present a finer set of recognition criteria than most.

The first point of departure is then to return to Barthes' original set of distinctions and to
consider whether it is always clear just which of the possibilities he sets out holds. As we noted
in Unit 2 ('What *are* text-image relationships?', p. 44) and the discussion of Kloepfer, Nöth
and others, this seems not to be the case – it is relatively easy to find gaps and potentially
ambiguous classification situations. The different ways of 'adding' information that Barthes
sets out do not appear to constrain interpretations finely enough. This intuition can then be
made more precise by explicitly relating Barthes' relations to the clause-combining relationships imported from grammar.

Thus, Barthes' anchorage, where the language takes on the function of elucidating or fixing the meaning of the image, seems to be compatible with the clause-combining relationship of *elaboration*. Anchorage serves to just fix what is already on offer and so, like elaboration, stays very much with what is already 'there'. However, it might also be the case that 'enhancement' might anchor what is being depicted as well – the selection of anchorage therefore seems to underconstrain just what kind of relationship is being exhibited. Similarly, relay, where both text and image make their own contributions to the combination, Martinec and Salway see as corresponding to 'extension' but "perhaps also enhancement" (Martinec and Salway 2005: 342) – in both cases, new material is brought to bear. Again the classification seems underspecified.

Some of the problems in selecting classifications faced when carrying out an analysis following Barthes are then inherent in Barthes' account. Indeed, as Martinec and Salway explain at several points, Barthes' description seems more concerned with what they characterise as the 'relative status' of the text or the image in the communication. The issue here is then which, the text or the image, is being taken as the main contributor to which the other stands in some supportive relationship. There are obviously three possibilities: either the text is more important, or the image is more important, or they are equal in importance. Putting these alternatives together with the different kinds of relations correlating with anchorage and relay then already gives several options which Barthes did not explicitly address.

To deal with this, Martinec and Salway suggest that the distinctions for clause combining offered by a functionally motivated grammar and as summarised in Figure 10.1 already separate out more cleanly the possibilities that Barthes was working towards. Thus, pursuing this more systematically may well offer a more exhaustive account of text-image relations in the spirit of Barthes, but with greater empirical adequacy and coverage.

Martinec and Salway consequently decide to build their classification system around two of the main dimensions already developed for finer classification of the grammatical clause-combinations: *status*, indicating relative importance, and *logicosemantic* relations, characterising the distinct types of relations that apply in terms of expansion and projection that we have just introduced. Thus, here again we can see that the grammatical description already has distinctions available that seem relevant and useful for the new task of characterising text-image relations. We will now run through each of these dimensions in turn, discussing a selection of Martinec and Salway's examples.

Status

The status dimension is relatively straightforward. Relations between texts and images are considered to assign their elements either *equal* or *unequal* status. When they are unequal, there must be a decision about which is more important, the text or the image.

Martinec and Salway consider the equal status relationship the appropriate place to cover Barthes' notion of 'relay' and so introduce two further subtypes: *independent* and *complementary*. Relay is then the 'complementary' case, both text and image are equally important and both contribute to a combined complex meaning. This means that, following Barthes, the text and image are both considered to contribute to a single complete unit, or 'syntagm'. It is also possible, however, for text and image to occur together *without* being complementary: in this case image and text do not combine and exist as parallel, distinct contributions – this Martinec and Salway describe as an equal, 'independent' relationship.

As noted above, in order to draw this distinction reliably, it is important to give recognition criteria – that is, Martinec and Salway have to state explicitly just when two elements are to be considered independent or not. Making such judgements on intuitive grounds is renowned for its unreliability. For this, Martinec and Salway therefore draw explicitly on their assumption that the text and the image can receive independent descriptions and that those descriptions are compatible. This is based on the functional interpretation of visual process configurations proposed by Kress and van Leeuwen (2006 [1996]), which, as we saw in Unit 8 ('Royce's model', p. 167), operates by identifying visual 'Gestalts' in terms of processes, participants and circumstances depending on the presence or absence of visual 'vectors'. Thus independence in Martinec and Salway's sense means that there *is no connection* between the 'process' of the image and the 'process' of the clause.

This will be clearer with an example. Figure 10.2 shows a map of the world, a particular shaded region and a legend below. The legend of the map is made up of a small square of the same colour as the shaded region of the map and the text fragment "Region: shallow tropical and subtropical seas". The original example discussed by Martinec and Salway was taken from an online encyclopaedia describing the moray eel – the function of the map for the entry was then to indicate where the moray eel lives. Martinec and Salway argue that the appropriate analysis of the text-image relationship holding here according to the status dimension of their framework is *equal* and *independent*. Let us see how they come to this conclusion.

First, we must provide *transitivity analyses*, that is, analyses in terms of process config-urations involving processes, participants and circumstances, of both the image and the text. The analysis of the text is then drawn with respect to grammatical transitivity; the analysis of the image with respect to visual transitivity. The corresponding analyses for the text-image relations for the map as a whole are summarised in Figure 10.3 to help follow the discussion; as we can see, these are very similar to the grammatical and VME analyses assumed in Royce's cohesion analysis (cf. Unit 8).

Beginning with the visual component: if we take the image to be the map as depicted, then there are clearly no vectors of movement to be found in it. Kress and van Leeuwen's categorisation for this case is a 'conceptual' process where some 'carrier' of properties is assigned an 'attribute'. Further, applying some Gestalt principles of foreground-background to the image, we can assume that the background is the outline of the countries and oceans, while the foreground is the shaded band. The visual process configuration that is being characterised then consists of the 'world' (shown in outline) as the **carrier** and the sub-area

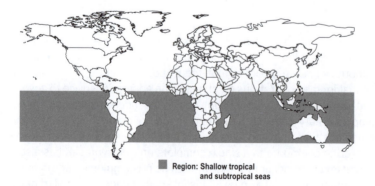

■ Region: Shallow tropical
   and subtropical seas

Figure 10.2 A map created along the lines of an example from Martinec and Salway (2005: 344)

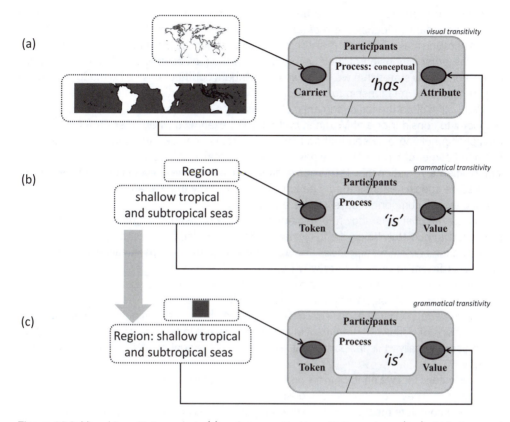

Figure 10.3 Visual transitivity analysis (a) and grammatical transitivity analyses (b, c) of Martinec and Salway's map example

of the world indicated by shading as **attribute.** We might paraphrase this linguistically as 'the world has this indicated subregion' as indicated in Figure 10.3(a).

Turning to the textual part of the text-image combination, Martinec and Salway argue that it is made up of two 'clauses' in the legend – although it must be said that much of these clauses is left implicit. One clause then identifies a 'region' (the token-participant) as being 'shallow tropical and subtropical seas' (the value-participant), where the colon takes the place of the verb 'to be' (Figure 10.3(b)). The other is also an 'identifying clause' – this time made up of, on the one hand, the small shaded box and, on the other, the previous clause (Figure 10.3(c)). Thus, the first transitivity configuration identifies the 'region' by means of its value of being 'shallow tropical and subtropical seas'; the second identifies the square icon of the key by means of the previous configuration.

The analysis of text and image in terms of grammatical and visual transitivity summarised graphically in Figure 10.3 shows that the process configurations derived from the text and those derived from the map *have no relation to one another* – in no case does one of the process configurations need to 'include' input from both the visual and the textual components. Martinec and Salway can therefore assert that the case at hand is an *independent* text-image relationship in the sense they define.

This may at first glance appear a strange conclusion since the last thing one would probably expect between the legend of a map and the map itself is that they are to be considered independent of one another. To understand what Martinec and Salway mean by this it is important to focus on the *different kinds* of contributions that their two dimensions of classification make. The necessary dependency between legend and map is actually picked up by the *other* dimension of their account, that of the logicosemantic relations. The status dimension simply states that we have two independent contributions being made that do not require their inter-relationship to be considered when constructing their interpretations.

We will explore the logicosemantic classifications in a moment but, before we do, it will be useful to consider one of Martinec and Salway's examples where there *is* a dependency relationship holding between text and image so that we can see the contrast. In the upper left-hand corner of Figure 10.4 we have an example that Martinec and Salway describe as a 'complementary' relationship. This is again taken from the wildlife encyclopaedia and expresses what some species eats as food. The knife and fork show that we are talking about eating and the textual component says what is eaten.

This relationship is shown in the figure by the corresponding process configuration presented immediately below the text-image combination itself. The central, darker part is the configuration containing a process and a particular kind of participant, called a 'goal'. This is already sufficient to demonstrate why Martinec and Salway consider this as a dependent, complementary text-image relationship – one *single* process configuration – that is, one single configuration of process, participants and (optionally) circumstances – is being carried by *the text and image in combination*. This means that they belong to a single 'syntagm' and the contributions of visual and grammatical transitivity are not independent: the process 'eating' is expressed visually while the participant in the process, the goal, or what is eaten, is expressed verbally.

This means that we need *both* the visual and the textual material to create a *single* process configuration. They are then also obviously of 'equal' status, since we can't leave one out and still have a complete message – re-expressing this just using language, leaving the process out would give us 'fish and small prey' but not tell us what to do with these; leaving the participant out would leave us just with 'eat', which also fails to be a complete message. For Martinec and Salway, therefore, modes may combine in the service of single transitivity configurations and, when this occurs, neither mode can stand on its own. A combination is necessary for a complete message to be formed even though it is not the case that any one mode is considered subordinate to the other.

The right-hand example in the figure is a further contrasting case that does *not* exhibit complementarity. The description of the process configurations below the example shows that

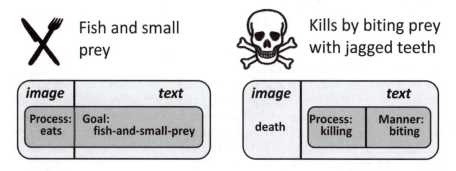

Figure 10.4 Two contrasting cases of text-image combinations adapted from Martinec and Salway (2005, Figures 9 and 22)

the skull and crossbones, presumably standing as a warning or symbol of death or danger, does not participate in the information expressed textually. The process configuration corresponding to the text is (relatively) complete on its own – it has its own process and (here) circumstance and does not need to be completed by information from the visuals. In this case, then, the text-image relationship is again one of independence since the 'entire' image relates to the 'entire' text – each has its own complete 'process configuration' description.

Thus, although the two examples in Figure 10.4 superficially look similar in that we appear to have a quite common combination of icons and text, the actual relationships holding between the visual and the textual information are rather different. Moreover, the analyst is guided to this interpretation by the need to set out appropriately the process configurations being expressed.

When instead *unequal* relationships are involved, there is a dependency in interpretation either from text to image or from image to text. The subordinated element cannot stand alone without losing its intended interpretation or reference. Possible identification criteria are then that equal status applies when an 'entire text' is related to an 'entire image', while unequal status applies when *part of* a text or image relates to the image or text respectively (Martinec and Salway 2005: 343). Moreover, texts can exhibit dependency on images in various ways. One possibility is by explicit deixis – such as "this picture" – or, as Martinec and Salway (2005: 348) suggest, by a present tense description of some action or behaviour (as common in newspaper images). Conversely, visuals are considered to depend on text when only parts of the text are 'picked out' by the image. Martinec and Salway summarise this as follows:

> Image subordination is realized by the image relating to part of the text; text subordination is realized by deixis from text to image, either by reference items or present tense combined with material or behavioural processes.
>
> (Martinec and Salway 2005: 348).

Again, the appeal here to particular grammatical features of the texts involved is made whenever possible in order to improve the reliability of application of the proposed categories.

We can see, then, that to carry out analyses reliably according to this framework, we have to be *very careful and specific* about *precisely which* grammatical and visual processes we are combining. The decisions to be made here are not always obvious. But only when we have done this, can we make a motivated decision about which of the text-image relations is to be taken as applying. This is one reason that differences in opinions can arise during analysis – different processes have been singled out for comparison.

Logicosemantic relations

Turning then to the second dimension of classification, the logicosemantic relations, this dimension captures the specific logical relationships taken to hold between text and image *regardless* of their relative status. Following the overall organisation shown in Figure 10.1, projection is considered relatively unproblematic and the main work of description is taken on by applying the categories under expansion.

Specifically Martinec and Salway propose the following re-workings of the grammatical categories to apply to text-image combinations:

- Elaboration restates, adds further information at the same level of generality, or exemplifies, in which case either the text is more 'general' than the image or *vice versa*. An example of 'image more general than text' is the skull and crossbones combination in Figure 10.4 above because the skull and crossbones just refers to danger in general and might not specifically be connected to death by biting.
- Extension adds further, semantically *intrinsically* unrelated information. The connection between the knife and fork and the verbal information in Figure 10.4 offers an example. This is extension because the verbal and visual information each make their own semantically unrelated contributions – that is, other things might have been eaten and other activities might have been carried out on the fish and small prey. There is no *intrinsic,* inalienable connection between eating and fish.
- Finally, enhancement offers qualifying information specifically to do with time, place, manner, reason, purpose and other generally 'circumstantial' restrictions. Examples of enhancement include cases where the text identifies some action or relation and the visual identifies the location where the action or relation occurs, the time of occurrence, a result of the action, and so on.

These more fine-grained categories therefore offer a further restriction on the kind of 'connections' between text and images going beyond that found, for example, within cohesion.

Martinec and Salway's classification as a whole is set out in Figure 10.5. The explicit cataloguing and organisation of relations into a hierarchical set of contrasts provided by application of the principles derived from, but not limited to, grammar makes it clearer, on the one hand, just what options are available while, on the other, also suggesting more of the semantic connections created when text and images are combined. This then makes a direct

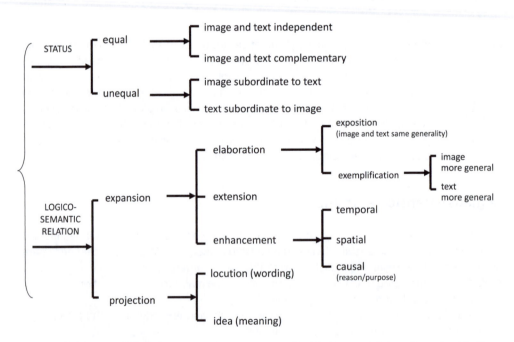

Figure 10.5 The network of image-text relations proposed by Martinec and Salway (based on Martinec and Salway 2005: 358)

contribution to multimodal coherence and supports a closer exploration of the semantic relationships holding between texts and images. Setting the possibilities out within a classification network provides a good sense of the overall potential – of what kinds of options need to be considered and weighed against each other during analysis. As is often the case in such *paradigmatic* analysis, knowing what something is *not* is an important step towards knowing what it *is* (or might be).

This is then a significant step towards a more complete set of text-image relations. It advances beyond the lists of possible rhetorical relationships given within applications of traditional rhetoric to visual relationships and their, generally rather more shallow, classifications by virtue of its explicit aims of both 'covering' the semantic space *and* providing strong criteria for deciding between the possibilities that apply.

The system is also 'closed' in the sense that there can be no further type that is introduced alongside the others. Growth of the framework can only be in terms of introducing finer categories: this is an explicit descriptive and methodological restriction so as to avoid simple open-ended lists as far as possible. Forcing classification choices into particular well-organised classes and subclasses is a more effective way of driving empirically motivated development of the analytic framework further. It forces the system to be able to 'break' rather than always bending to accommodate cases that might not fit. Also, the *separation* of the status and the type of the relations provides a more effective account compared to many working more directly from Barthes' original distinctions, where these distinctions still tend to be conflated.

DISCUSSION AND FURTHER ISSUES

Although Martinec and Salway's description in many places provides strong guidelines for identifying text-image relations, there remain some difficult issues and challenges. We briefly mention some of these here before proceeding to the other approaches to be discussed.

Identifying units and layout

One difficult issue concerns, again, the units selected for analysis. Discussion here recurs throughout Martinec and Salway's description but it is often difficult without close reading to know precisely which bits of text are being related to which bits of image and on what basis this decision is made – the reader has to assume that it is, on the one hand, 'the' text and, on the other, 'the' image – even when there may be several distinct textual elements and several distinct image elements. The decomposition of each entire example then proceeds according to cohesively motivated decomposition, but does not reflect the visual decomposition at hand. Segmentations are introduced as necessary for the discussion.

Martinec and Salway seem to assume this is obvious but, even for relatively straightforward examples, analytic decisions may need to be made more carefully. This kind of detail is one of the main contributions that an appropriate characterisation of *layout* provides, even though Martinec and Salway explicitly decide to rule out the contribution of 'layout' to their model (Martinec and Salway 2005: 338). They suggest instead that the main work is done by the realisations of text and image *within* some layout, which is certainly one contribution but only operates within the overall composition of a page or other 'canvas' where the verbal and visual information is being presented.

One of the typical problems that arise for analysis when unclear specifications of units are given can be seen even with the simple map example used above. Just *why* is the square icon grouped separately from the text fragment rather than with the word "region" before the colon? This appears equally likely – at least without more context and information about the genre decisions taken in this publication. And, in other examples, Martinec and Salway are happy to consider quite distinct headings and text bodies as 'the text' despite their being clearly separated visually – even though in one case (p. 356) they are forced by their cohesive analysis to suggest that a heading is in fact a separate unit after all. Mutually inconsistent choices of this kind are good indications that their consideration of units may require further specification.

Without an explicit account of layout it quickly becomes difficult to say just which elements are to be related with which others – this is also the problem that we saw with simple cohesion approaches in Unit 8: can any element be cohesively connected with any other? Layout provides structure for the units to be considered and omitting this can readily lead to increased indeterminacy in analysis. A more explicit consideration of layout can constrain just which features of the images and texts are going to be significant and lead to particular kinds of relations rather than others.

Images come in several flavours

Although Martinec and Salway aim for their account to be applicable to all cases of text-image relations, there are many different kinds of images as we have seen throughout this book and it is not immediately obvious that these will all operate in the same way. This becomes perhaps most clear in Martinec and Salway's discussion when they address examples which are *diagrammatic* rather than pictorial.

In one example, an abstract diagram is presented consisting of particular spatial regions, each identified by printed textual labels placed within the regions concerned. This is a very common form of visual representation but differs from straightforward pictorial representations in many respects. Martinec and Salway attempt to extend their framework to apply to this class of artefacts by extending the notion of 'projection' (Martinec and Salway 2005: 354). They argue that projection should include not only the original relationship that we have seen above between a process of, for example, saying and that which is said, but also take in the 'translation' relationship between, for example, a text and a diagrammatic summary of the text (Martinec and Salway 2005: 349).

This turns projection into a much more powerful relation in Martinec and Salway's account than might have been presumed. It would then cover cases of cross-semiotic 'translations' or representations (such as a diagram representing the content of some text). It is rather unclear, however, whether such a dramatic extension is warranted. There is virtually no sense in which the text 'says' the diagram – someone, a designer or other document producer, uses the text and the diagram to perhaps say the same thing, but this is a very different kind of relationship.

As a consequence, this seems more to indicate a gap in the framework as presented, which again would need further study and, ideally, consideration of other approaches where the modalities involved in diagrammatic representations have received more systematic investigation (cf., e.g., Bertin 1983, Tufte 1997, Tversky *et al.* 2000, Kostelnick and Hassett 2003). As we shall note again in both the next section and the unit following, however, projection and the kinds of relationships concerned with labelling and directly 'bridging' visual and verbal information reoccur as areas of concern for many accounts. There is clearly more to do here.

EXTENSIONS: UNSWORTH'S APPROACH TO EDUCATIONAL MATERIALS

Several researchers have built on Martinec and Salway's studies, suggesting refinements and alternatives based on the analysis of further data. Others have started in parallel to Martinec and Salway, also drawing on the distinctions drawn in grammar and applying these to combinations of image and texts (e.g., Unsworth 2007, Matthiessen 2007).

Particularly detailed analyses have been pursued by Len Unsworth and colleagues in the area of school textbooks and other educational materials. Unsworth (2007) presents numerous such examples and argues for the value of an overall classification of the kind developed by Martinec and Salway for analysing how texts and images are being used together. A particular concern of Unsworth and colleagues is to reveal where assumptions are being made in the text-image combinations that are either incompatible with the communicative purposes of the artefacts or which present comprehensibility challenges for younger learners.

On the basis of the data examined, they propose the refined classification network shown in Figure 10.6; changes with respect to Martinec and Salway's network are shown underlined. Some of these differences are due to simply filling in more detail which would in any case be predicted from the grammatical model. The finer division under projection is of this kind; several distinct subtypes of projection are grammaticised differently in language and this has simply been added to the network.

The task that goes with this, however, is that we find recognisable *visual* or *text-image* differences that would similarly motivate the inclusion of this distinction in the classification network here. Simply 'copying over' distinctions found for language to a classification involving visual information is insufficient. Possible examples of such distinctions might again be found in the use of visual vectors of various kinds – for example, perception may draw on gaze vectors of seeing and similar, whereas cognition would involve more 'inward' directed signs of attention. This can again draw on functional interpretations developed by Kress and van

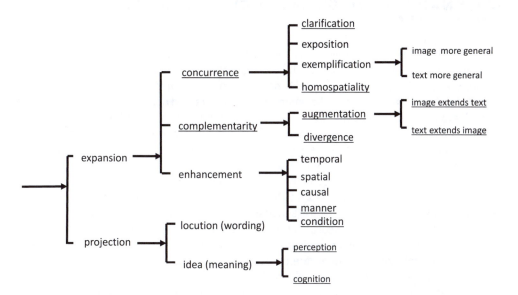

Figure 10.6 Text-image logicosemantic classification network adapted from Unsworth (2007: 1175)

Leeuwen. Unsworth explicitly notes, however, that the case of projection requires more research – the detailed account offered by Cohn (2013a) as discussed in Unit 5 ('Text-image relations in comics', p. 107) may usefully be considered here as well. Unsworth and Cléirigh (2009: 155), in a similar vein, draw on a different area of grammar and talk instead of **intermodal identification**.

Other extensions that Unsworth and colleagues develop also provide useful new additions. The area of 'elaboration' is refined under the guise of the new label 'concurrence', which includes both the previous exposition and exemplification and two new categories. *Homospatiality*, a term used by Noël Carroll in his discussions of visual metaphor (e.g., Carroll 2001), is used here to refer to the case where text and image are combined in such a way that the *visual* aspects of the text, that is, its typographical form, are taken up in the image and used for visual effect. The example that Unsworth offers for this is where a picture of a fire has the word 'HOT' written above it as if made out of steam or 'heat'; the other category, *clarification*, is a particular kind of 'restatement' in which relevant additional details are provided. Unsworth suggests a natural language gloss of the form 'that is, to be precise' and so on. Extension is also expanded in the form of 'complementarity' so as to capture explicitly both the directionality of the extension and the possibility of *divergence*. Although not in Martinec and Salway's account, as Unsworth notes and we saw in some detail in Unit 4, there are some genres and media where divergence plays an important and not at all uncommon role.

This kind of extension of options can be seen as a useful way of exploring text-image relations further. One takes the classifications that have been proposed and examines (a) whether the classifications can be readily applied to some new body of data and (b) whether finer distinctions or rearrangements of distinctions can improve on this. Unsworth's general approach has now also been taken further in a number of empirical studies, investigating the differential use and understanding of text-image relationships particularly in educational contexts (cf., e.g., Chan and Unsworth 2011).

ALTERNATIVES: KONG'S MULTILEVEL DESCRIPTIVE FRAMEWORK

Appearing at the same time as Martinec and Salway's proposal but developed independently, Kenneth Kong's framework (Kong 2006) for characterising relationships between text and images draws both on the systemic-functional grammar notion of logicosemantic relationships that we have seen above and on other, more discourse-oriented descriptions overlapping with those that we introduce in Unit 11. The account therefore stands as a bridge between this unit and the next, again showing that the accounts proposed for text-image relations all need to be seen as working as 'discourse'-level descriptions no matter whether their sources of inspiration are drawn from grammar or elsewhere.

Kong builds on a broader range of such sources, many of which we have seen in previous units, and proposes what he terms a 'multi-layered' framework that considers the relations between text and images from several simultaneous perspectives. His principal aim with the account is also to support empirical analysis – that is, he offers the framework as a multi-layer annotation scheme which can be applied to collections of naturally occurring data in order to search for patterns and regularities; the corpus-based method is described in more detail in Unit 13 ('Corpus-based approaches', p. 248).

The first layer of Kong's description is then the logicosemantic relationships derived from functional grammar. This approach, like the grammatically based account of Martinec and

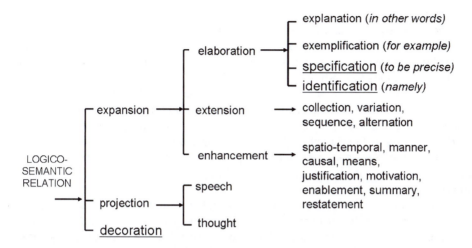

Figure 10.7 The network of image-text relations according to Kong (2006: 213)

Salway, consequently adopts the three-way elaboration/extension/enhancement split, modified and extended slightly for the kinds of relationships found in text-image combinations. This gives the classification shown in Figure 10.7; the figure is again adapted slightly to resemble more the systemic networks that we have used in other parts of this book and also by omitting some of the more standard sub-categories that we have already seen in other approaches. Additional relations not found, for example, in Martinec and Salway's proposal are again shown underlined.

At the top-level, Kong adds a general 'decoration' relation (taken over from Marsh and White's (2003) category A1: cf. Figure 6.3) – where some image is provided for essentially evaluative or aesthetic reasons; this would presumably be an independent relation in Martinec and Salway's classification. There are also some additional relations under 'enhancement' – for example, justification, restatement – which would be considered either 'interpersonal' or 'textual' meanings in grammatical or rhetorical accounts. Here they are grouped in with other logicosemantic relations.

Moreover, two new categories are included under 'elaboration': *specification* and *iden-tification*. These are interesting in that they coincide precisely with the cases that present the most problems in Martinec and Salway's approach and which, as we discussed above, led to a considerable extension in the meanings attributed to 'projection'. Kong addresses the same problem by adding new relationships, which is also similar to the approach taken in some of the other discourse-derived accounts that we will see in Unit 11.

Some of the most significant extensions included by Kong are to be found in the other layers of his account, however. Here Kong looks both 'downwards' in abstraction towards the documents being analysed and their compositional form and 'upwards' in abstraction to explicitly discourse-derived descriptions. The former addresses precisely the problem we noted above with Martinec and Salway's account that it did not offer a way of folding the influence of *layout* into their classifications. Kong, in contrast, begins with some of Kress and van Leeuwen's (2006 [1996]) proposals for treating entire pages, particularly their division of pages according to *framing* and *information value*. Kress and van Leeuwen consider vertical and horizontal dimensions of a two-dimensional canvas to carry specific communicative functions and so pick out this aspect of composition particularly in their descriptions.

Kong also adds both an *evaluative* component to his classification as well as several other descriptive categories, such as metaphor (cf. Unit 9) and 'textual importance'. The latter is similar to the 'status' area of Martinec and Salway but draws not on the logicosemantic area of grammar but from discourse-derived accounts, in particular from the notion of symmetric and asymmetric relations from Rhetorical Structure Theory that we will introduce in Unit 11 ('Rhetorical Structure Theory', p. 213). This sets out the three possible attributions of relative communicative importance between text and image as usual (equal, text more important, visual more important) but adds in additional commitments *concerning their relative spatial positioning on the 'page'*. Finally, although Rhetorical Structure Theory proposes its own set of 'rhetorical relations' for relating elements, Kong instead applies his extended classification of logicosemantic relationships as shown in Figure 10.7, thus providing a hybrid between the two forms of description.

One result of this is to bring in a finer view of layout and composition, as we suggested would be beneficial above, by encouraging that attention be paid to the *interaction* between layout and text-image relationship classifications. For example, Kong addresses several cases from instruction manuals where use is made of 'identifying' labels. The positioning of these labels with respect to what they are labelling is analysed to reflect both Kress and van Leeuwen's information value – in that what is placed on the left may be seen as *given*, while that on the right is seen as *new* – and the Rhetorical Structure Theory notion of relative com-municative importance – in that what is 'given' is the **nucleus** (most important) and what is 'new' is ancillary information (called 'satellites') (Kong 2006: 207). The Rhetorical Structure Theory part of the account consequently offers a structural unit within which the allocation of meanings to relative positions according to Kress and van Leeuwen's proposals can operate. Kress and van Leeuwen's original account says little about potential structural units smaller than the page and so is often difficult to apply in practice (for discussion, cf. Machin 2007: Chapter 8, 159–188).

Kong's linking of these principles can then make predictions concerning how information will be placed on the page and also supports critique if information is positioned in ways that do not match with the communicative intention of a particular combination of text and image. As he notes, however, there is still a considerable need for further empirical studies to flesh out the details of how such combinations are actually employed in varying genres of documents employing text and image together. As we shall see in the next unit, however, as soon as we have stronger principles for segmenting a page or other 'canvas' under analysis, it becomes much easier to pursue focused empirical work. Kong, for example, has himself now conducted some extensive empirical analyses of text-image combinations employing his method.

Some of the results of this study are presented in Kong (2013). Here Kong contrasts the use of text-image relationships across cultures by addressing a corpus of 55 pairs of articles from Chinese-language and English-language newspapers. Each article is analysed according to his scheme, focusing specifically on the status, or relative 'nuclearity', organisation of the text and images in each article. He also provides detailed realisational information concerning the types of images (diagrams, photographs, icons, etc.), layout elements (headings, titles, captions, etc.) and typographic information. This provides considerable information about the details of each article and offers many grounds for comparison. We focus for current purposes just on the structures capturing the overall text-image organisation. Figure 10.8 shows two contrasting structures produced for one of the article pairs.

Kong finds several interesting differences and it would be worthwhile going through his article in detail; Kong also offers a good overview of previous literature both on cultural comparison and on the particular study of contrasting text-image and visual practices across

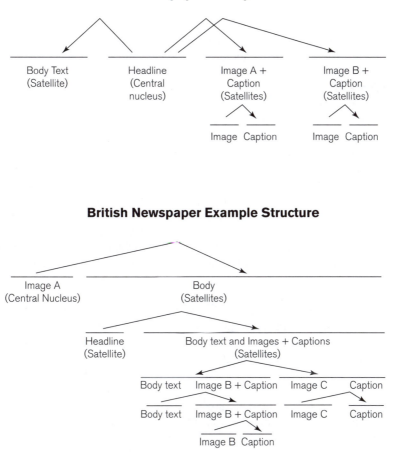

Figure 10.8 Two contrasting text-image structures for English- and Chinese-language newspapers extracted from Kong (2013: 190; Figure 11); used by kind permission of the author

cultures. One of his results is that, even though both classes of newspapers make extensive use of visual material, what is *done with* that material is very different. This is already suggested in the structures shown in Figure 10.8. The Chinese newspapers appear to prefer a "more 'fragmented' atomization approach" to their presentation of news items, whereas the British newspapers favour a "'top-down' graphic composite approach" (Kong 2013: 192). Such results partly support earlier studies of differences between the two cultures concerning their respective preferences in forms of representations and depictions, but also suggest new insights. The results also underscore how shallower analyses, such as might be delivered by simply counting the proportions of text and image employed for example, would not have shown deeper differences in design decisions and news presentation practices. This is certainly an area, therefore, where there is a considerable amount still to be discovered.

CONCLUSIONS AND SUMMARY

The approaches we have seen in this unit typically adopt extensions of the so-called 'logical' dependency relationships developed within grammar by Halliday, and so draw on the relations characterised as 'expansion' (i.e., elaboration, extension and enhancement). The other area commonly taken over from grammar is the organisation of events into processes, participants and circumstances set out in most detail in Kress and van Leeuwen's account of visual transitivity. This has also been shown to be beneficial not only for describing visual depictions but also for forming criteria for assigning text-image relations more reliably. Martinec and Salway, Unsworth and Kong all adopt various aspects of these grammatically inspired classifications, showing how they are equally applicable to the non-grammatical area of text-image relations.

The common aims of discourse-derived and grammar-derived approaches are sometimes obscured by the fact that systemic-functional linguistics posits a 'solidary' relationship between grammar and semantics (Martin 1991, 1995); this means that grammar is often 'taken as a model' for constructing semantics and so similar terms and distinctions may appear across different linguistic strata. Indeed, some relationships of this kind, particularly those described as logicosemantic, are now taken to be sufficiently abstract that they can be seen at work at many different levels and scales: including grammar, semantics and mixed-mode contributions as we have now discussed.

When moving away from grammar, however, the question of the nature and identification of units of analysis becomes more complex. Martinec and Salway attempt to address this question explicitly and their account makes some progress by decomposing the verbal side into clauses with well-established relationships known from grammar (such as independent, hypotactic dependent and subordinating) and the image side according to elements picked out by visual prominence or by cohesive relationships formed with the accompanying textual material. As we began to see with the account of Kong, however, there are also approaches to text-image relations that draw more directly on *discourse* levels of representation rather than importing notions from grammar. This is the topic of the next unit.

Modelling text-image relations as discourse

Just as appropriately abstract accounts from grammar can be considered for their potential relevance for text-image relations, linguistic accounts couched more at the stratum of *discourse* can be considered too. Two models of discourse developed within linguistics have been particularly influential for discussion in this regard: James R. Martin's *Conjunctive Relations* (Martin 1992) and William C. Mann and Sandra Thompson's *Rhetorical Structure Theory* (RST) (Mann and Thompson 1988). These have both been applied extensively, although largely independently, to the text-image question. The use of these frameworks for capturing text-image relations emerged in the early 1990s at around the same time that interest in multimodal documents and presentations began to grow more generally. In this unit we provide simple sketches of both conjunctive relations and Rhetorical Structure Theory and show them in operation with respect to text-image relations.

The basic idea underlying the adoption of linguistic theories of discourse to text-image relations is similar in both cases. Regardless of framework, discourse is generally considered to be made up of 'discourse moves' of various kinds that serve to advance the communicative goals pursued by a speaker or writer. Since communicative goals are rather abstract, it is then natural to think of whether *linguistic* expressions are the only ways of achieving them. For example, it is perfectly possible to answer a question with a nod, or to answer some verbal request by performing a relevant action, such as passing the salt. Multimodal accounts of discourse consider whether particular proposals for discourse organisation can be extended with *images* taking on some of the roles of discourse moves.

A very similar idea is found in accounts drawing on broadly 'pragmatic' approaches to communication, including text linguistics, Gricean theories of communication, activity models and other notions that have been invoked for text interpretation; some of these will be seen in Unit 12. The main difference between approaches of this kind and the accounts we see in this unit is how much they rely on mechanisms and classifications that have been explicitly elaborated for *discourse organisation*. More 'pragmatics'-based approaches tend to see language use, and particularly discourse, as just one example of intelligent, goal-oriented behaviour, applying general 'problem-solving' techniques and building on a close relationship to other kinds of cognitive processing. In contrast, discourse description frameworks are defined in terms of structural configurations of particular forms of verbal expressions and images that are quite specific to discourse.

Both types of approach have their beneficial aspects and corresponding drawbacks. For example, discourse-based approaches tend to offer more constraints for performing analysis and so guide analysts to produce more reliable and comparable descriptions. Pragmatic approaches are, conversely, targeted more towards very flexible interpretations of text-image combinations where substantial context-dependent reasoning is necessary to work out what is intended.

Both types of account no doubt have a role to play in any complete picture that may emerge. Discourse cannot be understood without paying attention to the inferences that readers, hearers and viewers must perform; but these inferences may well also need to draw on more discourse-specific kinds of organisation that need description in their own right.

IMAGE-TEXT RELATIONS AS DISCURSIVE CONJUNCTIVE RELATIONS

Within the systemic-functional tradition to language there are several accounts focusing on discourse semantics rather than grammar. Particularly central here has been the account of *conjunctive relations* set out by Martin (cf. Martin 1983, Martin 1992: 179, Martin and Rose 2003: 119). This provides extensive classification systems of the relations responsible for 'building discourse', considering discourse as a dynamic unfolding of successively related messages. Just as was shown to be the case with grammar in the previous unit, several researchers – most prominently Theo van Leeuwen and Kay O'Halloran (van Leeuwen 1991, 2005b, Liu and O'Halloran 2009) – have now explored the application of these classifications to mixed media artefacts and behaviours as well.

Approaches that construct analyses using discourse semantic conjunctive relations adopt more or less fine subclassifications drawn from the categories that Martin originally identified for language. Many other frameworks for discussing text-image relations can be usefully related to these. Language as a semiotic resource has expended considerable 'effort' evolutionarily to articulate a generic and very fine network of discriminations for linking messages. This is what Martin's analysis draws out. As a consequence, the framework provides a broadly applicable 'template' for considering such relations whenever and in whatever semiotic mode they appear. It then remains a challenging and exciting research question to find out more precisely just whether there are further relations that are supported in other semiotic modes and to determine which particular subsets of the linguistic conjunctive relations may be employed and which not.

The conjunctive relation framework

Martin's treatment of conjunctive relations in language is anchored in the concrete step-by-step interpretation of linguistic units as they contribute to an unfolding discourse. This focus on the *dynamics* of discourse development and discourse connectives is an essential component of the theory that opens up new possibilities for incorporating the role of the viewer/reader in their interaction with multimodal artefacts. As we have seen at many points up to now, this is an important factor to consider for all multimodal artefacts.

Martin's original motivation for providing a classification specifically of discourse connectives was to capture linguistic generalisations that went beyond those that could sensibly be described within grammar (cf. Martin 1992: 168). It appeared to be the case that certain semantic regularities could be found operating across *very diverse grammatical realisations*. This can be seen by comparing the following examples:

(1) a. We walk the ring with our dogs. **Afterwards** we just wait.
    b. We walk the ring with our dogs **and then** we just wait.
    c. **After** we walk the ring with our dogs we just wait.

    d. **After** our walk with the dogs, we just wait.
    e. Our tour of the ring **precedes** our wait.
    f. . . . our tour of the ring **prior** to our wait . . .

Each of these is a possible, but very different, grammatical realisation of *one particular discourse semantic relation*, that of 'temporal succession' (Martin 1992: 168–169). All the examples state that one event occurs after a preceding event. However, it would be very awkward indeed to try and place this variety underneath any single grammatical category. We have instead realisations scattered over the entire grammatical system – from clause combinations to relations within clauses, prepositional phrases, right down to relations within noun phrases and selections of particular verbs. Moving to the discourse semantic level provides a more usable, and also more appropriate, level of abstraction to express what all the examples *have in common*, namely their linking of messages with a temporal relation.

    The framework continues in this spirit exploring just which kinds of connecting relationships between messages are distinguished linguistically. It defines four main classes of semantic relation: *additive*, concerned with adding meanings together, *comparison*, for making comparisons, *time*, for expressing temporal sequence and other temporal relationships, and *consequential/causal*, for explaining reasons, causes, conditions and so on. Each of these is divided into further subcategories, leading eventually to features that are specific enough for particular conjunctions, prepositions and other lexicogrammatical categories and constructions along the lines of the examples in (1) to be identified that signal their use.

    A graphical depiction of the main distinctions available for connecting discourse messages is given on the left-hand side of Figure 11.1; this is intended as the corresponding discourse version of the diagram that we showed for grammar in Figure 10.1 in the previous unit. Several of the options given there for grammar are here no longer present – projection, for example, is not listed. This is because of the difference between grammatical and discourse descriptions: in English and many other languages, projection is *grammaticised* as we saw in Unit 10

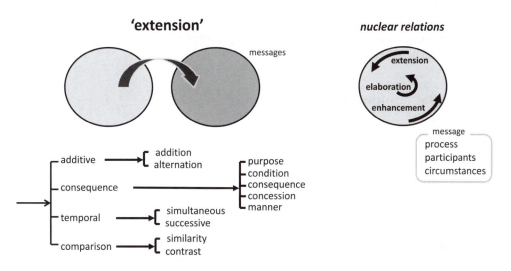

Figure 11.1 A graphical view of the different types of message connections proposed by systemic-functional discourse semantics – NB: the two uses of 'extension' on the left and right of the figure are independent of one another and do *not* refer to the same relation!

('Grammatical origins', p. 188), that is, there is a special grammatical form that expresses the relationship. In contrast, there is no dedicated *discourse construction* for expressing this way of combining messages and so it is not listed at the discourse level.

This simple fact opens up considerable potential for confusion when reading accounts of text-image relations since, as we have seen, projection *is* an important text-image relation. Including projection in an account therefore does *not* mean that we are suddenly dealing with grammar rather than discourse. Whereas English as a language might not have specific discourse mechanisms for expressing projection, many visual modes certainly do – as we saw in Unit 5, for example, projection and its explicit expression as a text-image relation is one of the primary distinguishing features of comics.

Martin also develops a discourse perspective view on what is happening *within* grammatical clauses. This is what is shown on the right-hand side of Figure 11.1 under **nuclear relations**. Here we find the three-way extension, elaboration, enhancement division that we set out in detail in the previous unit. Martin sees these here not in terms of their grammatical properties but instead as particular ways of *building a discourse semantic message*. To take an example, a simple sentence such as:

(2) Max chased the dog with a fork

can be described both in terms of its grammatical construction and in terms of its semantic contribution. The former is the task of the linguistic stratum of grammar, the latter is the task of the linguistic stratum of (discourse) semantics. Grammatically, the 'with a fork' is a circumstance of manner expressed as a prepositional phrase – this says something about how the clause is being constructed. Semantically, the meaning of the phrase 'with a fork' is used in the construction of the semantic message expressed by the clause as a whole by 'enhancing' the nuclear meaning 'chasing the dog'.

In this case, the grammatical and the semantic descriptions are very close – they are **congruent**; in other cases they can be broadly divergent. This is why one needs both levels of description in order to always be able to capture relevant generalisations. As we saw in the previous unit, Martinec and Salway (2005) use such 'nuclear' relations extensively for text-image relations also. Martin's description makes it explicit that this can also be seen as a *discourse* description rather than a grammatical one.

Multimodal conjunctive relations

The multimodal development of the conjunctive relation framework then takes the diversification of potential realisations illustrated by the examples under (1) a step further so as to allow *non-linguistic* realisations also. This extension was first pursued in detail for multimodal artefacts and text-image relations in the work of van Leeuwen (1991); a good overview of the relations adopted as well as some connections with other related notions in the literature at large is given in van Leeuwen (2005b: 219–247, Chapter 11). Table 11.1 collects together this description of image-text connections, showing just those relations and subtypes that van Leeuwen argues to be relevant for this combination of modes.

Van Leeuwen's account bridges between the abstract possibilities for linking messages provided by the conjunctive relation system on the one hand, and Barthes' original text-image relations that we have seen at many points above (cf. Unit 2, 'Getting the ball rolling: Roland Barthes', p. 31) on the other. The correspondence between Barthes' categories and van

Table 11.1 Overview of the possible linking relations between visual and verbal elements compiled from van Leeuwen (2005b: 230, Figure 11.4)

Image-text relations

Elaboration	Specification	The image makes the text more specific	*illustration*
		The text makes the image more specific	*anchorage*
	Explanation	The text paraphrases the image (or vice versa)	
Extension	Similarity	The content of the text is similar to that of the image	
	Contrast	The content of the text contrasts with that of the image	
	Complement	The content of the text adds further information to that of the text, and *vice versa*	*relay*

Leeuwen's conjunctive relations is given in the last column of the table. This is the connection that Martinec and Salway (2005) also draw on in their account as described in Unit 10 ('Grammatical origins', p. 188).

Although both Martin and van Leeuwen are working within a conjunctive relation framework, we can note that the classifications offered in fact look rather different. Similar terms appear throughout but their precise organisation and placement within their respective classification systems differ. Even at the more general level, whether any particular account adopts the two-way elaboration/extension split derived from discourse or the three-way elaboration/enhancement/extension division derived from grammar is at present largely a matter of individual style. Van Leeuwen (2005b) adopts a discourse-oriented approach and uses the classifications described above; Martinec and Salway (2005), as we saw in the previous unit, adopt the three-way distinction from grammar; Liu and O'Halloran (2009: 384) preserve Martin's four discourse categories at the top level and diverge only below this; and Martin and Rose (2008) fall between these – after carefully explaining that their approach is to be considered an account of discourse throughout, their classification of image-text connections then stays very close to grammar and adopts the grammatically derived three-way split and its many subcategories.

This vacillation across classifications is partly due to the programmatic nature of most analyses that have been offered to date. Examples are given of how one *could* do some analysis rather than extended research on larger bodies of data. Making more principled decisions amongst the various possibilities and, indeed, perhaps proposing new organisations, requires empirical work that goes beyond a few illustrative examples. Research in this area in the future must engage, therefore, with far more extensive collections of data. This also means that these approaches will need to confront the issues of reliable analysis and accurate coding. It is not known at present, for example, if the various schemes proposed differ in how reliably analysts can use them. For this, 'inter-coder reliability' studies as standard in many areas of corpus-related research (cf. Unit 13) will need to be carried out. And for this, the criteria for the applicability of one category rather than another will need to be given more clearly and consistently than is currently the case.

Proponents of these frameworks may argue that the selection of one coding scheme rather than another will generally depend on the purpose for which an analysis is being conducted. Thus, when exploring some particular discourse it can be beneficial to see the relations between text and image as very similar to those operating within the verbal component. This then orients to the *situated discourse interpretation* offered for a text-image combination – that is, if, after careful consideration, we believe that a piece of text is, for example, 'explaining' an image, then that is the relation we choose regardless of whether this is signalled or cued in the material under observation or not. This appears to be the motivation in, for example, Martin and Rose's (2008) account, from which we will see an example below. When exploring the process of meaning construction and meaning multiplication across modalities, however, we need also to be able to 'break into' the interpretation process at earlier stages prior to 'final' situated interpretations in order to see just how those final interpretations are reached.

This means quite concretely that it may be problematic to adopt a text-image relationship, for example, of 'temporal simultaneity' because this is not something that can be *directly* expressed simply by putting text and image together. It can be 'suggested' by a variety of means, but not expressed. Van Leeuwen's description above is thus more conservative in the sense that it stays closer to just what can be expressed in the text-image combination itself. This is then similar to the distinction remarked upon in Unit 6 ('Characterising rhetorical figures on the basis of their form', p. 133) concerning sources of motivations for text-image relation classifications. Focusing on what can be achieved within single modalities or combinations of modalities in this way may then be beneficial for building more reliable classification schemes.

In fact, van Leeuwen's description is one of the few to explicitly raise the possibility that different modalities might have different sets of relations. His account thus offers different catalogues for verbal conjunctive relations, which largely follow those of Martin, for *image-image* discourse relations, which van Leeuwen relates more specifically to montage and editing in film, and for his *image-text* relations that we have seen above. Although all conform broadly to the conjunctive relation scheme, the particular relations found and their inter-relationships vary.

Figure 11.2 shows his classifications for the image-image and image-text relationships reworked for purposes of comparison as systemic classification networks. The image-image classification might then be contrasted with other accounts we have seen in this area, such as McCloud's inter-panel transitions in comics discussed in Unit 5 ('Frames, panels and gutters', p. 96), as well as with the far more diversified characterisation of such sequences in picturebooks explored by Claire Painter and colleagues (cf. Painter 2007; Painter, Martin and Unsworth 2013), in which a socio-semiotic perspective is combined with standard narratological concerns such as narrative time and pace, focalisation, and characterisation (cf. Unit 3, 'Narratives and narratology', p. 63).

Both the image-image and the image-text relation sets are very much reduced when compared to the extensive set of relations that Martin proposes for language. We have now seen one of the reasons for this. Whereas language has a finely articulated system of relating messages – consider, for example, the differences in meaning between the temporal conjunctive relations corresponding to 'before' and 'after' or between the causal relations 'because' and 'therefore' – the distinctions that can be carried *purely* by the juxtaposition of visual and verbal elements are very much more restricted. Indeed, it is often difficult to find 'formal' – that is, different technical signals, cues, words, shapes, and so on – points of discrimination at all. Liu and O'Halloran (2009: 378) then use this "paucity of conjunctive expressions between linguistic and visual modes" as a further argument for preferring a discourse-based account.

Nevertheless, as van Leeuwen notes, the range of relations available should also be related to 'need' – a semiotic mode can always develop further, more discriminating resources *if its community of users finds this necessary.* The combination of text and image may well, however, already be sufficiently powerful as to make this development less likely – only time will tell.

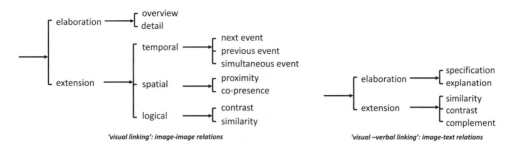

Figure 11.2 Classification network of discourse conjunctive relations for image-image and text-image relations drawn from van Leeuwen (2005b)

An example of analysis

Despite the apparent complexity of these classification schemes, the form of analyses that follow in this type of framework are in fact relatively simple. Particular elements are selected from a multimodal artefact and relations are asserted to hold between them. This is similar to the method illustrated in the account of Marsh and White (2003) in Unit 6 ('Expanding the categories while still recognising them', p. 129), but claims the additional advantage that the distinctions drawn are more theoretically motivated and, therefore, more homogeneous — this should improve coding accuracy but, as remarked above, this remains to be tested. It would therefore be interesting to compare the two forms of analysis in order to explore further their similarities and differences. In both cases, however, and just as we also criticised for cohesion in Unit 8 and for Martinec and Salway's approach in Unit 10, the precise criteria for establishing the units to be related are rarely spelled out with any precision.

Nevertheless, as an example of analysis, we can consider one particular treatment offered by Martin and Rose (2008: 179) of a doublepage spread from a school Geography textbook (Scott and Robinson's *Australian Journey: environments and communities* from 1993, pp. 21–22). The spread discusses the mulga tree, a small tree widespread across Australia that is capable of surviving long droughts. The main communicative purpose of the page is to explain the tree's survival mechanisms. This is done with a mixture of text, photographs, maps, drawings and diagrammatic representations. The layout of the spread consists of a large diagrammatic representation in the centre with a text with subheadings and paragraphs and other visual material running down one side and across the bottom of the page, and some further material and text on the extreme right.

Although Martin and Rose's main purpose is to discuss issues of genre rather than multimodality as such, the inclusion of examples such as this usefully shows how genre also needs to be considered from a multimodal perspective. The page presented is analysed as an instance of the genre of *reports and explanations*, and therefore possesses identifiable features common to an entire family of texts sharing this sociocultural purpose (cf. Figure 3.4 in Unit 3 for the family of 'recounts' as a similar example in a different area). The additional recognition of visual features and particular patterns of relations between texts and images may well support even finer genre discrimination for a broader range of multimodal artefacts, while the placement against possible genres provides useful information concerning the intended *socio-cultural function* of the elements deployed. This can also be related to Bucher's view of communicative action that we will see in Unit 12 ('Theories of action and images', p. 234).

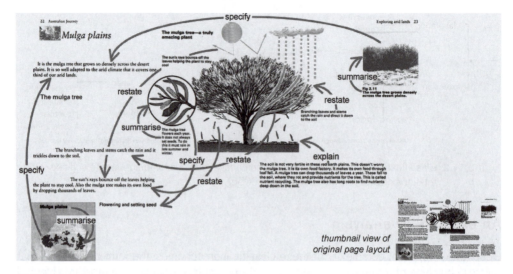

Figure 11.3 An analysis of a Geography textbook doublepage spread (shown lower right) taken from Martin and Rose (2008: 179, Figure 4.31)

The result of Martin and Rose's analysis is shown in Figure 11.3 along with a small 'thumbnail' sketch of the original textbook layout in the lower right. The approach combines several components of cohesion and conjunctive relations, drawing all the while on a semantic or discourse perspective. The method of analysis is to segment the information on the page and suggest discourse connective relationships holding between the various units identified. The main units Martin and Rose select are the verbal main body text, captions to images, images and *parts* of images, such as arrows.

These elements can be distributed anywhere on the page and, as is typical in designs of this kind, text fragments in fact reoccur in various locations – for example, material can be repeated in the main text body and in captions or 'call-outs' in the diagrams – as well as in very similar information expressed in different modalities – for example, the text states "the sun's rays bounce off the leaves", while the reader is also presented with iconic (actually diagrammatic) pictorial representations of sun and tree with an arrow between them abstractly depicting the 'sun's rays'. The analysis consequently includes both conjunctive relation-like connections (e.g., 'explain', 'summarise', 'specify') and links resembling cohesion (e.g., 'restate'). Thus captions tend to *summarise* their images, and the map, showing geographic distribution of the plant, further *specifies* the text fragment:

> It is the mulga tree that grows so densely across the desert plains. It is so well adapted to the arid climate that it covers one third of our arid lands.

Both 'summarise' and 'specify' are subtypes of 'elaboration'. The selection of one kind of relation rather than another is consequently relatively intuitive, but in general has the same kind of difficulties discussed for cohesion. An explicit application of Martinec and Salway's (2005) criteria for determining visual processes would aid the analysis, making it clearer just what information is being used to motivate notions of restatement, explanation and so on.

Until this part of a framework is filled in, analyses will continue to show minor differences with respect to both the particular relations selected and the classification of those relations relative to others. It is then unclear whether such differences are important or simply variations with little import. Again, taking up these tasks as parts of broader programmes of empirical research will be useful both for developing the framework further and for making it more reliable and consistently applicable.

Analyses of this kind do, however, already clearly support paying more explicit attention to the relations that need to be drawn between parts of a complex multimodal artefact. Encouraging this activity is certainly beneficial for educational purposes and can be expected to develop multimodal literacy, which is one of Martin and Rose's goals.

In other respects, there is still much to do. Quite analogously to the critique raised by Cohn with respect to McCloud that we discussed in Unit 5 ('Comics and visual narrative: Neil Cohn', p. 100) concerning treatments of relations between panels in comics, it is difficult here to derive from Martin and Rose's analysis any *constraints* concerning how information on the page will be organised. The account does make some predictions related to genre and the communicative purposes that a genre pursues – which is a definite advance over the account of Marsh and White – but how these are played out in actual design decisions is not addressed. The page analysed in fact exhibits a range of less than optimal design decisions, but the analysis does not reveal these.

RHETORICAL STRUCTURE THEORY

We saw in Unit 6 that several approaches have attempted to approach text-image description by applying categories and techniques developed within both traditional and more contemporary approaches to rhetoric. We saw in Unit 7 that particularly for the study of advertisements, where the persuasive aspect of meaning is unavoidable, studies of the rhetorical combination of visual and textual material are long established. There is consequently widespread acceptance that some kind of rhetorical analysis can make an important contribution to our understanding of how multimodal documents function, although there is less agreement concerning the frameworks that might be most appropriate for this.

One very different account of 'rhetorical' organisation is provided by *Rhetorical Structure Theory* (RST) (Mann and Thompson 1988), an approach to text developed within linguistics and discourse studies. RST is now widely used in text research and has also been applied extensively for multimodal analysis. Many descriptions of the RST framework are available – for example, Taboada and Mann (2006a, 2006b) as well as in a very abbreviated form in Bateman and Delin (2006) – and so our introduction here can be quite brief. We then move directly to examples and discussion of the application of RST to artefacts containing both text and images.

The basic framework

RST was developed originally for text linguistic purposes and is less concerned with an analysis of *persuasion* than with an analysis of communicative 'effectiveness' as such. In contrast to the conjunctive relations, the treatment of text in RST is less anchored in the concrete step-by-step interpretation of linguistic units and is instead more concerned with intentions and the knowledge and beliefs of speakers and hearers. It is therefore more 'abstract' – that is, further away from details of form (cf. Bateman and Rondhuis 1997).

In RST, the analysis of text proceeds by constructing a 'rhetorical structure' drawing on a repertoire of defined 'rhetorical relations'. Each rhetorical relation comes with a definition that concerns what is said and what the effect of successfully applying the given relation is for the speaker and hearer's beliefs and intentions. The aim of analysis is to construct a single overarching hierarchical analysis that (a) covers all the text and (b) respects all the definitions. The resulting hierarchical structure then shows precisely how the components of the text and their combinations contribute to achieving the goals of the text as a whole. If it is *not* possible to construct a single such structure for a text without breaking the constraints imposed by the definitions, then *the text is assumed to be defective in some respect and so is less than optimally effective.*

'Classical' RST defines around 25 rhetorical relations, including relations such as elaboration, justification, motivation, enablement, circumstance, and more. These relations come in two flavours: symmetric and asymmetric. An asymmetric relation singles out one of its text components, called **text spans**, as being of central importance for the communicative effect that the relation is responsible for achieving. That is, if that element is removed, the entire sense of that part of the text collapses.

An example is the following showing the rhetorical relationship of enablement:

(3) Open the door. You must grasp the handle firmly.

The two sentences make up two text spans standing in an enablement relationship because the second gives information about how the action in the first is to be performed if it is to be performed successfully. Enablement thus divides up its own text span into two smaller text spans distinguished according to whether they are the action being enabled or the information that enables. The first is the part which is most important for the text; the latter is less so. The most important part is called the **nucleus**, the less important part, or parts as there may be several of them, are called **satellites**.

We can see this to be the case for example (3) by removing one or the other text span and seeing how the resulting 'text' works (or fails to work). First, we remove the nucleus, then the satellite – imagine each of the following sentences occurring on their own:

(4) You must grasp the door handle firmly.
(5) Open the door.

If the purpose of the text is to get you to open the door, then (4) is rather oblique – it is unclear whether the door is to be opened, whether this is general advice, or instructions in case of an earthquake. In (5), the purpose is clearly stated and this sentence by itself would still have the overall effect of performing an instruction to open the door. Thus satellites are 'less important' in that they do not carry the main weight of the message of the text, even though they may also have a significant influence on whether the effect is in fact achieved in any particular case.

Example (3) also shows that, in distinction to the less abstract accounts of discourse and grammar described so far, it is often necessary to find rhetorical relationships even when there is no explicit linguistic 'marker' that some kind of conjunction or conjoining is taking place. One sentence (or larger block of text) is simply placed next to another one. This lack of explicit signals notwithstanding, if we do not recognise the rhetorical relationship, we have not understood what has been said. One of the main developers of RST, William Mann, referred to this crucial property of discourse as the use of 'implicit assertions'. If we do not understand, for example, that the second sentence in (3) is in fact a satellite in an enablement relationship, we would be left wondering what the information is for. Therefore, the fact of it being an enablement is *implicitly asserted* when the rhetorical relation is recognised.

Multimodal RST

In the early 1990s, Elisabeth André extended the RST form of analysis to cover text structures that combined textual and visual elements (Wahlster *et al.* 1993, André 1995). The under-lying intuition in the use of this approach for multimodal representations is the following: if segments of a text contribute to that text's coherence in systematic and specifiable ways, then segments of a *multimodal* document, involving pictures, diagrams and texts, may con-tribute similarly. With RST, then, just as it would be possible in a text to offer a textual element standing in an enablement or elaboration rhetorical relationship, in André's and subsequent multimodal RST accounts the additional elements may just as well be pictorial.

We illustrate this with the simple example shown in Figure 11.4, drawn from a constructed set of instructions for how to leave a train in an emergency. On the left-hand side of the figure we have a portion of the instructions as they occur; on the right-hand side the corresponding multimodal analysis. This also shows us the typical graphical form used for RST analyses. The horizontal lines represents text 'spans', that is, the units of the artefact receiving analyses, the labelled arc indicates the rhetorical relation holding between those spans, and the vertical lines show which of the spans is selected for 'nuclearity', the relatively most important unit for the communicative function being achieved by the immediately 'dominating' (i.e., higher) span. The lowest level spans are the elements that actually occur in the text being analysed.

Whereas a traditional RST analysis would only include text elements in these positions as spans, here we see that a segment from the pictorial material is also included. We see, then, that in the present case the combination of text and image on the left is analysed as giving the second part of a *sequence* of emergency instructions; this particular part then requests that the reader/viewer break the window (the nucleus), while the image presents supporting information (the satellite) about how this is to be done. Various treatments can be taken for the number '2' – it might be considered a label as described below or be motivated instead as a *navigational* element realising the structural configuration of the *sequence* relationship.

The kind of extension seen with this multimodal version of RST is, in essence, similar to many of the extensions for descriptions from text to image that we have seen so far. Whenever a description is looking at *how* a text is working, then it becomes reasonable to consider other forms of achieving the same effects – this was the case for the traditional and more recent rhetorical approaches we have seen, as well as for the functional linguistic accounts in the previous units.

In André's case, the main motivation for the extension was the construction of com-putational systems that were capable of taking information from knowledge bases and

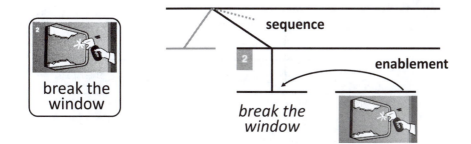

Figure 11.4 A multimodal RST structure for enabling the reader/viewer to carry out an emergency instruction

automatically producing documents that sensibly combined text and images. Concrete examples are instructional texts, which typically include both texts and images. RST had already
been used successfully for producing verbal texts (i.e., without visual materials) automatically
and so it was a natural extension to consider their use for the automatic generation of
multimodal documents as well. The motivation for such research in general is that more
complex pieces of equipment might require substantial technical manuals. Keeping manuals
synchronised with the technical specifications is then a major task in its own right and is
generally extremely error prone. Automating the process would be one way of ensuring that
the technical documents always reflect the current state of the device described. Research
in this area continues and there are many unsolved problems.

One of André's test domains included technical instructions for using and maintaining
coffee machines. Such instructions need to inform their users what actions are to be performed, with which parts of the coffee machine, and where those parts are. A slightly modified
form of one of the first 'multimodal' analyses proposed by André in this domain is given in Figure
11.5, which shows then a more complex case in which we can see the hierarchical text
organisation suggested by RST. Each textspan may itself be decomposed further by the
application of rhetorical relations until the smallest units of analysis are reached. The resulting
illustration that the RST description would generate is depicted upper left in the figure.

The RST tree as a whole gives information about how to remove some cap on the coffee
machine in order to add water. The basic instruction, that is, the nucleus of the entire span
under consideration, is to 'turn the cap'; the rest of the tree then stands in an enablement
relationship – that is, it provides information that will enable the reader/viewer of the
instructions to perform this action. This includes giving further 'background' information
about where the relevant parts of the machine are located, as well as particular dials that
must be turned and directions in which parts must be moved. Many of these are represented
purely visually – sometimes as small versions of parts of the machine as line drawings,
sometimes as visual depictions of actions (and their directions) expressed by arrows. Thus
we can see that the overall RST organisation suggests very precisely just how the visual
and verbal parts of the entire text-image combination function together for the purposes of
the text.

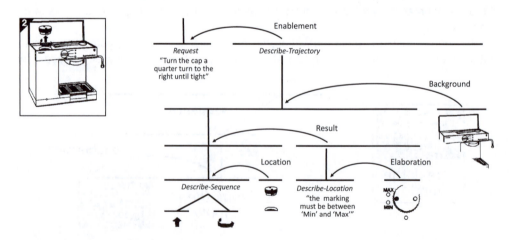

Figure 11.5 A multimodal RST structure for instructions for a coffee maker adapted from André (1995:
54, Figure 3.7)

This approach has since been extended and adapted in many multimodal frameworks. On the one hand, further computational systems have been constructed that automatically produce combinations of text and graphics that are coherent by virtue of their placement within an overarching rhetorical structure following the extended definitions of RST (cf., e.g., Bateman *et al.* 2001, Hartmann 2002). On the other, empirical and corpus-based studies of documents containing text-image relationships have also been pursued (cf. Bateman 2008, Taboada and Habel 2013).

It is interesting to compare the kinds of analyses produced by a multimodal RST account with others. For example, Schriver's notion of rhetorical clusters that we saw in Unit 6 ('Adding more structure', p. 133) includes very many fewer rhetorical 'relations' and so here, as with conjunctive relations, it is again an open question whether the full set of RST relations is required for multimodal relationships or whether a subset, or even different, relations are required – we return to this again in a moment. RST is also different from many of the accounts that we have seen in that it *does* place constraints on what is considered an acceptable organisation and what not. While these constraints appear to work well for verbal texts, using RST to derive design constraints is in its early stages. Proposals for this are made in, for example, Delin and Bateman (2002) and Bateman (2008: 166–174); these rely on the assumption that layout decisions should, if they are to be effective, largely coincide with rhetorical structure. Work on this issue continues (cf. Hiippala 2012).

The connection between layout and rhetorical organisation also suggests how it might be possible to offer further constraints concerning just what elements may be related to others when performing an analysis. As an example of this, we provide one last RST analysis, a re-working of the Geography textbook page considered by Martin and Rose above. A corresponding RST analysis for just the central diagrammatic component of the page is given in Figure 11.6.

The analysis represents a reading of this diagram in which a claim is made, that is, that the tree is "amazing", which then requires *justification*. The analysis then sets out how each of the diagrammatic components together with textual elaborations or background information contribute to providing that justification. Such analyses then help articulate the precise functions of the individual elements in a two-dimensional informational depiction in exactly

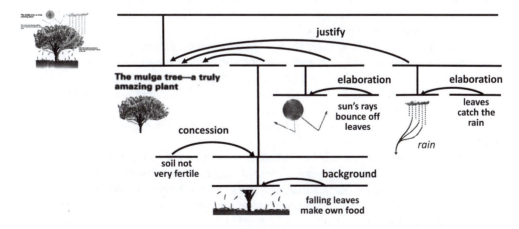

Figure 11.6 Multimodal RST analysis of the central diagram element (shown upper left) from the Geography textbook doublepage spread

the same way that they have been argued to do for monomodal texts. Moreover, they can be used to argue that it is not appropriate to draw discourse inter-relationships across *any* elements on the page – as we shall see below notions of spatial proximity and visual connection need to be respected as well.

ISSUES IN THE MULTIMODAL APPLICATION OF RST

Several issues arise that need to be addressed more carefully when considering the extension of RST-style analyses to multimodal artefacts. RST was not originally designed for mixed-mode 'texts' and so it is natural that certain decisions made in its design might not always be appropriate when the nature of the objects to which it is applied changes. A central research question of this kind is the extent to which the catalogue of rhetorical relations developed for natural language texts is necessary and sufficient for combined text-image representations.

This of course leads to the question of whether it makes sense to apply RST, an analysis tool developed solely for linear semiotic modes such as texts, to non-linear and spatial semiotic modes at all. There has consequently been considerable discussion of how models inherited from linguistics such as RST, which are essentially linear, may be maintained in the face of spatially-organised media – not just for rhetorical structure, but for all such applications.

The issue of linear order

The first difficulty lies then in basic properties of the modes being combined. Although there is broad consensus that visual materials are essentially spatially organised and verbal language is either temporal or 'spatial' in one-dimension (cf. the discussion at the beginning of Unit 3), the definitions of RST rely crucially on the *linear* nature of what they are describing. Relations are only possible (with some minor exceptions) between *connected* segments/spans. This is RST's strong **sequentiality assumption**.

With multimodal documents, the mutual spatial relations between segments change from relations in a string-like object to relations over regions. Segments can have not only a left and a right, but also an upper and a lower neighbour segment. In fact, in general one can imagine neighbouring segments in any direction, not only these four, and there can even be more than one neighbour in each direction.

The simplest solution is to maintain RST's sequentiality assumption by adopting some other basis for a strict ordering. For example, one can introduce a *reading order* on the segments of the document, which is then used as the sequence for building an RST structure. This is similar in many respects to the position adopted by Stöckl that we will see in detail in Unit 12. One must be careful with such assumptions, however; as we mentioned in Unit 3 ('Dynamic perception of static visuals', p. 60), our assumptions can easily fail to reflect actual reading behaviour.

A rather different solution could be to further generalise the sequentiality assumption so that RST relations are restricted to pairs (sets) of document parts (segments/spans) which are *adjacent in any direction* (Bateman 2008: 158); this is the strategy adopted in our mulga tree analysis. The extent to which this could solve the problems of 'spatial RST' in general is, however, still a matter of research.

The issue of minimal RST units: what is an RST segment?

The model of rhetorical organisation provided by RST requires that a description only be followed as far as individual 'messages'. For verbal language, these messages are generally clause-sized chunks, similar to the transitivity configurations we have seen in both the cohesion-based and grammar-derived models above. For this reason, the *grammatical clause* (cf., e.g., Figure 8.3 in Unit 8) usually serves as the minimal unit in traditional RST. This makes sense from the perspective of communicative acts because the semantic message corresponding to a clause is the smallest unit that can serve as a proposition, that is, something that can be *argued*, receiving elaborations, examples, concessions and so on.

With text-image combinations, however, it is quite common to have text-image relations between even smaller elements. We saw this in the RST analyses used as illustrations above. In the example from André, for example, there is the specification of where a particular cap is located: this is given by relating the 'cap' and an image of its position. Thus, rather than relating entire 'visual messages', as postulated in cohesion-based and discourse-based accounts, individual phrases and elements in visual messages can be picked out and used as a component in a multimodal RST relation. Another common occurrence is one between a picture of an object and its label or title in text form.

These cases require an addition beyond 'classical' RST as well. Since the rhetorical intention of such combinations appears to be either (1) to tell the reader how some pictured object is named, or (2) to show the reader how a certain object looks or where it is, it appears reasonable to consider these also as 'rhetorical' relations in the sense of other relations in the framework. Thibault (2001: 307) has suggested that the function of a 'linking' element standing between label and labelled, typically a vector shown as a line or arrow, should be considered analogous to a grammatical clause involving the copula 'be'. Bateman (2008: 160–163) consequently builds on this proposal by adding particular forms of 'identifying' and 'classifying' relationships to the library of rhetorical relations available for carrying out multimodal RST analysis. Relations can be drawn here with Unsworth and Cléirigh's (2009: 155) proposals for **intermodal identification** as well.

It is again interesting to consider how different treatments of text-image relations have approached this particular problem. The labelling of visual depictions with textual information, or *vice versa*, is one case where accounts originating in single modalities always need extension. This was, for example, approached by Martinec and Salway (2005) by extending the notion of projection as we saw in Unit 10 ('Images come in several flavours', p. 198), while Cohn (2013a) applies his emergent text-image interface to such relations as we saw in Unit 5 ('Emergent text-image relations as interfaced modalities', p. 109). This is an area evidently deserving closer attention.

Multiple simultaneous discourse relations

Finally, it has also been noted in several approaches extending the notion of rhetorical structure to multimodality that 'illustrations' can serve *multiple purposes* with respect to some text. This is definitely the case in instruction manuals where, for example, one and the same illustration can simultaneously serve (a) to identify a certain part of an object and (b) to show a certain action to be performed, or – another example – serve to identify several parts of one object. Although this is quite common in the examples discussed by André (e.g., André 1995: 49), how precisely this is to be reconciled with the definitions of rhetorical relations is, again, an open question – if not an entire can of worms in its own right! Multiple rhetorical relations are not possible with traditional text-based RST analyses because the hierarchical structures constructed during analysis are strict trees, in the formal sense of disallowing multiple 'higher level' dominating nodes: each span can have at most one 'parent' higher in the tree.

Proposals here vary from relaxing the tree-constraint, which brings with it the problem that it is unclear how much of the theory of RST remains when one of its major premises is removed, to suggesting that multiple connections are instead indicative of the fact that different *components* of an image are being identified and picked out to carry the different relations. The latter approach is argued for in Bateman (2008: 159) and is, again, used in our mulga tree analysis. More study is needed to see just what kinds of discourse structures might be appropriate in the multimodal case in general.

CONCLUSIONS AND DISCUSSION

We have seen in this unit how two approaches to discourse coherence have been extended and applied to communicative artefacts containing both texts and images working together. Using such schemes is beneficial for understanding more just what connections have to be drawn between elements by readers/viewers when faced with text-image relations at work. Performing such analyses can therefore be valuable for improving multimodal literacy and our understanding of the diversity of the possible relations between text and image.

We also saw a variety of problems and challenges, however.

For conjunctive relations, the precise organisation of the relations that are applied is still subject to some variation across authors and it is not yet clear to what extent they can be applied reliably for larger scale empirical analyses. There is also a lack of the predictive power that would be required to use the analyses for detecting potential communicative problems or for performing other kinds of critique. Taking this development further will require both empirical work and the accompanying improvement in definitions and recognition criteria that goes along with this. Here Liu and O'Halloran's (2009: 379) observation that particular text-image linkages will co-occur with *other* kinds of text-image relations, such as diverse forms of 'intersemiotic cohesion' (cf. Unit 8), may offer a way forward – clearly, for example, a discourse conjunctive relation of comparison will only be inferable if there are also sufficient points of cohesive similarity between text and image.

In the case of RST there is more experience in using *monomodal* RST analyses of verbal texts for empirical research and some substantial annotated corpora are available. This has permitted a range of empirical explorations of, for example, the relation between RST rhetorical relations and their linguistic expression as conjunctions and other grammatical forms. As noted in Unit 10, the kind of structural organisations provided by RST are well suited to such empirical studies; this also supported the *multimodal* empirical work of Kong (2013) described at the end of that unit.

The use of full RST as described in this unit has now also been followed up for multimodal documents in a recent study by Taboada and Habel (2013). This is probably the most extensive study of mixed mode documents currently available. Taboada and Habel examine no fewer than 1500 pages of material from three genres – two technical journals and the *New York Times* – including 600 figures, tables, maps and graphs. All of the material is annotated with respect to its rhetorical organisation drawing on a relatively standard version of RST. Taboada and Habel also calculated inter-coder agreement scores – using Cohen's kappa statistic (cf. Landis and Koch 1977, Carletta 1996) – and so can be reasonably confident that the analyses conducted are reliable.

The results are interesting in several respects. First, the number of rhetorical relations occurring supports the comments made above concerning the very reduced range of relations that appear in text-image combinations. Second, the precise distribution varied across the three genres examined and there would no doubt be other results for other genres – for example, the enablement relation we have illustrated above from instructional texts hardly occurred at all in Taboada and Habel's sample. Overall there were 61 per cent elaborations, 27 per cent evidence relations, about equal numbers of motivation and preparation relations at around 4 per cent, followed by circumstance, summary and restatement before reaching single occurrences. Third, there was also a clear difference between the rhetorical functions taken up by figures and graphs, tables and maps: as Taboada and Habel report, figures tended to elaborate on the text, tables offered evidence, and pictures supplied background and motivations for reading (Taboada and Habel 2013: 78).

Several questions are raised by the investigation. The preponderance of elaboration is also often remarked on in monomodal analyses; some have even proposed that it should not, therefore, be considered a true rhetorical relationship at all and may skew results (Knott *et al.* 2001). The nature of the genres selected for analysis also strongly disposes analysts to place the text in central (nuclear) position and the images then play only supporting roles. This may change dramatically in genres where there is a more equal balance in communicative loads. Taboada and Habel note also that there was some disagreement concerning the function of certain *types* of elements: for example, in scientific texts are tables providing evidence or elaborating information? Although coders made consistent choices *individually*, there was less agreement across coders. This might be indicative of a need to have a better understanding of the relationships between these kinds of information offerings in general so that the 'forced' choice in terms of rhetorical relationships might either be improved or replaced by the provision of other kinds of text-image relations. And, finally, there was no attention to issues of layout and composition – which might also feed into decisions concerning text-image relations.

Nevertheless, the study as a whole shows clearly how important and valuable it is to move towards larger-scale empirical analyses if we are to make progress in characterising how text-image relations are being employed. Discourse analyses of this kind appear to be one way in which this can be pursued and taken further.

MODULE V

Frameworks Relating to Context of Use

Text-image relations from the perspectives of text linguistics, pragmatics and action

One of the main challenges in approaching issues of visual representation in general, and text-image relations in particular, from the perspective of language is that of the apparent lack of clearly analysable units comparable to those of syntax, phonology and phonetics in the linguistic system. As we saw in Unit 2 ('What *are* text-image relationships?', p. 44) and again in Unit 8 ('Problems and open questions', p. 172), this fundamental difference between language and visual materials presents significant problems whenever analytic methods from linguistics are considered. In particular, it is very difficult, and in the general case probably impossible, to identify abstract and decontextualised properties of *form* that can be used to derive the visual information being communicated.

This has motivated orientations to visual communication that focus more on *what is being done* with the images rather than their form. Couched in terms of the well-known 'syntax-semantic-pragmatics' distinction from Morris (1938) as traditionally imported into linguistics, this directs attention towards **pragmatics** – the *use that speakers and hearers make of signs in context.* Since approaches that address the pragmatics of communication are already some distance in abstraction away from the details of verbal utterances, their extension to consider 'mixed-mode' communicative acts is often relatively straightforward, at least *in principle*!

The difficulties that arise in analysis are then often similar to those that arise when addressing purely verbal descriptions: that is, a lack of specificity can leave the analyst with insufficient constraints for detailed explanations and for making predictions concerning the artefacts they are analysing. For example, just how *do* we get from 'it's getting pretty cold in here' to a pragmatic interpretation of the utterance as a *request* to close a window? There is clearly much going on behind the scenes and the phenomenon itself does not directly show how it is to be analysed – this is by no means straightforward.

This issue of orienting towards pragmatics has not been so visible in the accounts we have discussed so far which drew on the systemic-functional socio-semiotic tradition precisely because that tradition does *not* build on Morris' three-way distinction. *All* of the socio-semiotic linguistic accounts see themselves as addressing the 'use' of language – that use simply involves descriptions at different levels of abstraction: these are the so-called 'linguistic strata' mentioned at many points in preceding units. But for linguistic accounts that do move with respect to the syntax, semantic and pragmatics distinction, the shift to include images within their remit remains a problem at all levels *apart* from the 'pragmatic'.

This has led to several approaches to text-image relations that adopt an explicitly pragmatic orientation, drawing on linguistic theories of pragmatics as well as more general, that is, not linguistically motivated, theories of action. Relations here are also commonly made with cognitive theories of verbal and non-verbal behaviour and reasoning, again as a way at getting at the *use* of visual and textual material rather than the form.

The starting point of 'use' does not of itself, however, provide particularly strong guidance concerning how to describe what is being used. For this reason, there is often a degree of heterogeneity to be observed in the approaches working in this way. Some of the descriptive apparatus employed is similar to approaches we have seen in previous units, other aspects are developed specifically within the individual accounts developed and for the tasks those accounts face.

This unit will briefly discuss two frameworks illustrative of such 'broadly pragmatic' accounts.

The first shows text-image relations from a perspective originating in what can be loosely characterised as 'text linguistics'. These are approaches most directly related to developments made in the early 1980s as the interest of many linguists turned to the phenomenon of 'text' as a linguistically respectable unit of analysis. A common starting point for such work is the definition of text offered by de Beaugrande and Dressler (1981). This approach, which has been followed particularly in Germany but also elsewhere, lies on a different branch of the overall family tree of linguistic approaches to text than those pursued in the Hallidayan socio-semiotic approaches that we have seen in several guises in earlier units. The orientation towards pragmatics and language as communicative action is consequently somewhat different (for further discussion, cf. Spitzmüller and Warnke 2011).

The second style of approach owes its origins both to work outside of linguistics and to the speech act theories of the philosophers John Austin and John Searle. Here the main focus of attention is on images as components of communicative acts. In many ways, it has been natural to consider an extension from actions restricted to verbal utterances to complex 'utterances' that might include a variety of contributing modalities. This is already necessary when discussing spoken face-to-face verbal interaction, for example, since gaze and gesture are inalienable parts of the whole (cf., e.g., Fricke 2012, 2013). There is also now the suggestion that this should apply to all communication, including printed or online combinations of text and image material.

TEXT LINGUISTICS AND IMAGES

The original proposals for a kind of 'text linguistics' made by the linguists Wolfgang Dressler and Robert de Beaugrande (de Beaugrande 1980, de Beaugrande and Dressler 1981) identified several basic conditions that need to be met if we are to consider a text to be present. In particular, they suggest seven criteria of 'textuality', briefly summarised as follows and dividing into text-oriented criteria (the first two) and text producer or consumer-oriented criteria (the remainder):

1 a text must exhibit *cohesion* (cf. Unit 8);
2 a text must exhibit *coherence* – this refers to a text 'making sense' in terms of the meanings communicated, which can be related to the notions of discourse semantics and rhetoric (cf. Units 6 and 11);
3 a text must be produced *intentionally*: that is, the text is a communicative product that is created with the explicit intention of a producer or set of producers, using the resources of language in order to make it likely that the intended effects will be recognised – this relates to our basic starting premise that our text and image combinations must be placed together with the *intention* of triggering their mutual interpretation (cf. Unit 1);
4 a text must conform to the notions of *acceptability* for its intended consumer(s), relating to issues of convention and communities of users;

5   a text must be *informative* for the intended consumer(s) in that it presents information
     with appropriate statuses as known, expected, and so on and should contain sufficient
     'new' material to warrant its production;
6   a text must be *situationally* relevant and appropriate – this relates to questions of style
     and register, as the kind of language to be used depends crucially on the intended
     reception situation: newspaper headlines are different to traffic notices are different to
     love poems, and so on;
7   a text may also rely on *intertextual* connections in that it might be a response to another
     text, an answer to a question raised there or a further development of an idea and so on
     – the text may then presuppose that its consumers are familiar with the necessary 'inter-
     texts'.

Any communicative occurrence meeting these conditions is then considered by Dressler and
de Beaugrande to be a text. Several of these aspects can be related more or less directly to
other approaches or assumptions currently made about text, although we will not take this
further here.

    What we do see, however, is that many of these considerations can also clearly be applied
to non-textual or mixed verbal-visual communicative occurrences. Particularly the criteria
oriented towards the consumer-producer of the 'text' have a less strong language-specific
bias. The extent to which coherence and cohesion apply in this case depends on the framework that is employed. Some of those we have seen so far, such as for example rhetorical
approaches, would certainly suggest that a visual or verbo-visual communicative artefact can
be considered with respect to its coherence. It was precisely the role of visual and verbo-
visual rhetorical analysis that we discussed in Unit 11 ('Rhetorical Structure Theory', p. 213)
to show how that coherence might be captured. Similarly, within the frameworks proposing
multimodal cohesion, the notion of text cohesion adopted is naturally extended to non-verbal
material. Thus, from this rather general perspective, 'text' might still be said to apply.

    One extensively developed position arguing that it is appropriate to consider images and
texts as similar is that of Hartmut Stöckl. Stöckl has been exploring a text linguistic approach
to artefacts combining text and pictures since the early 1990s, building on several of the perspectives we have seen in previous units both for examining texts within a text linguistic
perspective and applying this to image-text combinations; we will return to his account in
detail in a moment. Concerning texts and image, he notes: not only do images generally give
rise to a whole set of 'propositions' or statements, and so are analogous to texts with respect
to the 'quantity' of information given, but also, and more importantly, the way in which an image
can be flexibly employed in context, taking on particular communicative functions within the
communicative situation as a whole, also appears to be very similar to the range of options
available for texts (e.g., Stöckl 2004a: 96).

    This flexibility in use is a fundamental property of texts, rather than sentences. Sentences
remain abstract and have to be instantiated within texts so that their contextualised meanings
can be recovered. And this, as we have seen at several points, is rather similar to the situation
for images. The combination of 'visual text' and 'verbal text' is then considered to take place
within a larger scale 'whole text' (e.g., *Gesamttext*: Doelker 1997) or 'supertext' (Fix 1996: 116),
and so on.

    Although these pragmatic arguments for some kind of equivalence between images and
'texts' are certainly strong, none of the three logical alternatives that might relate units of the
language system and images – that is, image-as-word, image-as-sentence and image-as-text
– can be completely disregarded. We again need to be able to distinguish more finely between

Figure 12.1 Text, image, sentence, word?

different kinds of images and different kinds of usages of images – it is, as we have empha-sised at many points, insufficient to simply talk of 'image' as an undifferentiated category.

Consider the heart symbol in Figure 12.1, for example. This can scarcely be productively called a 'text' – and so this particular kind of usage of image-like material would need to be explicitly stated as an 'exception' were we to assume across the board equivalence of image and text. Moreover, on a broader scale, the sense in which one still has independent 'texts' when considering only the visual component of comics is, as we have discussed in detail in Unit 5, extremely debatable. In fact, it is equally debatable for the *verbal* component of such 'supertexts' or 'imagetexts'. Both of the 'text parts' of comics – that is, the verbal and visual components – considered isolated from the rest of the material on offer will in many cases have difficulty meeting even Dressler and de Beaugrande's criteria for textuality. Thus, to talk of 'text parts' in such contexts leaves open just how much of the properties attributable in general to texts remain.

There are, therefore, evidently going to be a range of distinct usages that can be made of visual materials when placed together with language and we need to tease these apart before making general proclamations. We should, accordingly, not assume any ready-made set of equivalences between text and image but let points of comparison emerge out of our analyses.

STÖCKL'S PRAGMATIC ACCOUNT OF MULTIMODAL DOCUMENTS

As we have seen from many perspectives up until now, however, much can be gained by treating combinations of text and images as composite 'texts' of some kind – most of the criteria and properties applying to texts without images appear to apply to texts with images equally well. What must then be specified in addition is the particular ways in which such combinations also exhibit cohesion, coherence and so on. This has been approached in considerable detail and in relation to a broad body of text-image combinations by the German multimodality researcher Hartmut Stöckl.

Stöckl's work began with a close consideration of analyses of advertisements (Stöckl 1997), drawing on rhetorical notions as introduced in Unit 7 and articulated in considerable detail in work such as that of Gaede (1981). In more recent studies, Stöckl has extended this to other text-image artefacts so as to consider a broader range of text types (Stöckl 2004a), including narratives (Stöckl 2002) and TV advertisements (Stöckl 2003, 2011). Much of the more detailed description of this work is only available in German – for a brief review in English of the approach more broadly, however, see van Leeuwen (2005a). Here we will be concerned specifically with the treatment of the text-image phenomena. Let us look at a few cases of analyses within the earlier framework in order to see how the various components combine.

The style of analysis defined and illustrated in Stöckl (1997) builds on facets of visual and textual analysis that we have seen above, as well as adding some further new proposals for description, in order to build a fine-grained analytic instrument for exploring how artefacts containing text-image combinations operate. The goal is first and foremost to reveal patterns of distributions of textual and visual material and to relate these patterns to particular effects that the communicative artefacts may have on their readers/viewers. In the study of advertisements, as we have seen, it is considered particularly important to understand how an advertisement goes about persuading its audience. Stöckl accordingly builds on a developed notion of rhetorical figures related to a detailed view of text structure in order to bring out those properties of an artefact responsible for its working in one particular way rather than another.

Stöckl's advertisement analyses approach the task of multimodal description by viewing each advertisement from three perspectives and drawing statements from each of these concerning the likely rhetorical effect achieved. The three perspectives are (1) a text structural analysis of the verbal components of an advertisement, (2) a rhetorical analysis of the verbal effects employed in those verbal components, and (3) a characterisation of the text-image relationship according to a multidimensional classification scheme. Since each of these perspectives can bring with it rhetorical or persuasive effects, it becomes possible to suggest something of the *combined* effect of the text-image artefact as a whole.

We will look at each of the three perspectives briefly in turn, drawing on examples to illustrate the process.

In the 1970s and 1980s, several frameworks began to be developed for describing 'text structure'. We saw some reference to these with respect to narratives in Unit 3. As noted there, from the *linguistic* perspective it is usual to consider narratives as just one kind of textual organisation within a much broader range of text types, each of which may have its own significant structuring principles. Thus linguistic text structures attempt to provide frameworks for texts in general rather than being focused on narrative. It is therefore possible to apply these frameworks to a broad range of text types, advertisements included.

The text linguistic structure adopted in Stöckl (1997) draws on one of these early text structure approaches, that of Graustein and Thiele (1987), originally developed for scientific texts. Common to most of these earlier text linguistic approaches was the need to address the hierarchical organisation of texts and to show the relation of that hierarchical organisation to text functions – typically, but not only, argumentative functions as proposed even earlier in classic frameworks such as Toulmin (1959). The general idea is that particular combinations of argumentative functions work together structurally to build up a coherent textual unit. Particular kinds of relations are then defined to 'hold together' the individual text elements, and each text element can be broken down into finer and finer elements of structure. Mann and Thompson's (1988) Rhetorical Structure Theory (RST), which we introduced in Unit 11 ('Rhetorical Structure Theory', p. 213), is one of the more recent and well-established outgrowths of this earlier tradition.

An example of this analysis from Stöckl's (1997) corpus is shown in Figure 12.2. The figure shows a small fragment from a tourist advertisement for Spain and its hierarchical decomposition. On the left-hand side of the figure, we see an extract from the original verbal component of the advertisement; on the right of the figure, the corresponding extract from the hierarchical text structure. This follows the text organisation in a fairly intuitive fashion. The representation used here is changed slightly from that given by Stöckl in order to make comparison with other approaches to discourse organisation easier. It would be interesting to compare this style of analysis with other kinds of analysis, for example those that would result by applying RST – RST now has an extensive body of research behind it that has refined

Of course, should you tire of soaking up the sun lying down, you can always soak up the sea in a variety of other positions. For the energetic, most Spanish resorts offer every water sport under the sun (and several under the sea). And for the less energetic, a cooling glass of sangria (there's that letter again) is normally within easy reach.

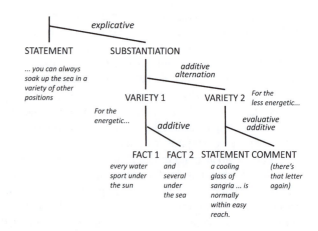

Figure 12.2 Adapted extract from the hierarchical text structure proposed for analysis by Stöckl (1997: 394–395; example *Spain 6*)

and strengthened the reliability of its analyses and there are many points of similarity (as well as some differences) with the structures that Stöckl's analysis produces.

Whereas RST places most of its descriptive work in the relations and their definitions, Stöckl's account operates in terms of rhetorical building blocks and argumentative patterns. Stöckl (1997: 145–197) presents a detailed overview of these patterns and their particular distribution and use within the advertisements covered. Examples of these patterns include:

- 'VARIETY1 – *alternative* – VARIETY2' or 'STATEMENT1 – *adversative* – STATEMENT2', where two facts are shown either as simple alternatives or as competing alternatives (similar to RST CONTRAST)
- 'STATEMENT – *evaluative* – EVALUATION', where an evaluation is supplied for a statement (similar to RST EVALUATION)
- 'PROBLEM – *consecutive* – SOLUTION', presenting a solution to a problem (similar to RST SOLUTIONHOOD)
- 'STATEMENT – *causal* – AUTHORITY', presenting evidence that a statement is reliable by virtue of the authority of the information's source (perhaps similar to RST JUSTIFY)

There are many more, classified into broad functional areas such as analogy patterns, narrative patterns, problem and method patterns, concession patterns as well as patterns supportive of perception (such as providing headings or other visual indications of organisation). **Design patterns** as such are used in various disciplines.

Stöckl relates these patterns further both to some cues in linguistic form and to particular kinds of communicative functions and 'persuasive effects'. The persuasive functions in Stöckl's model are attracting attention, being memorable, inspiring imagination, improving understanding, distracting, pleasing and 'yield', where the advertisement seeks to gain the acceptance of the viewer/reader. All of these functions are defined in terms of the effects that are assumed to hold for the viewer/reader and are developed on the basis of a general rhetorical view of communication, although this does not appear to have been verified empirically as, for example, the approaches to advertisements in Unit 7 have tried to do.

Each of Stöckl's proposed levels of analysis are placed in relation to this common set of persuasive effects. And it is this that then allows the account to suggest how disparate

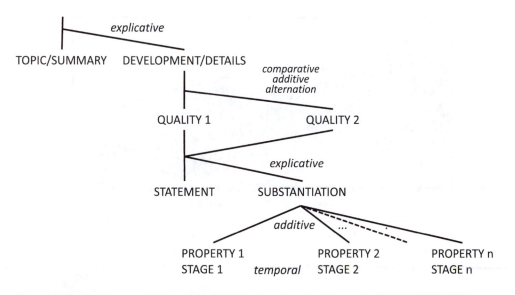

Figure 12.3 Stöckl's generic hierarchical text structure for advertisements (Stöckl 1997: 153)

resources may *work together* within a complex multimodal artefact in order to achieve intended communicative results.

On the basis of his corpus analysis, Stöckl proposes a general text organisation for advertisements that regularly appears, albeit with variation and extensions as each individual case calls for. This hierarchical text structure of the 'generic' advertisement is shown graphically in Figure 12.3, again adapted slightly in its representational form.

One further example will allow us to focus on the relation drawn between image and text. Figure 12.4 is a recreated sketch summarising an advertisement for Mazda cars from Stöckl's corpus (Stöckl 1997: 332–333; *Mazda 3*). It depicts a ballerina's slightly stretched-out lower leg, foot and ballet shoe, resting on the wooden floor of, presumably, a practice room. This image is accompanied by the text as shown in the figure. Stöckl separates out the visual component from the verbal component and analyses each with respect to its respective properties. For the verbal component, Stöckl offers analyses in terms of both its hierarchical structure, as described above, and its linear structure.

For the linear structure, Stöckl adds an analysis in terms of the individual rhetorical figures that are taken to apply in the text. Two examples of this linear analysis, somewhat simplified, are shown in Table 12.1. Stöckl provides such entries for every grammatical unit distinguished in the advertisement, such as clauses, visually isolated single phrases, and so on.

The 'functional parts' that are recognised, such as body copy, slogan, signature, and so on, provide motivated labels for the identifiable parts of the advertisements analysed; these are similar to the named parts of rhetorical clusters as defined by Schriver (1997) in Unit 6. The 'linguistic structure' refers to the communicative work that the linguistic unit is performing in the linear unfolding of the text, while the 'text configuration' picks out the particular labels given in the hierarchical text structure that we saw above. The final column identifies the rhetorical figures holding; these we have seen in previous units, particularly in Unit 6. These are then linked to the communicative functions and 'persuasive effects' identified above. As an illustration, those rhetorical figures present in the extract in Table 12.1 are identified as supporting the following effects:

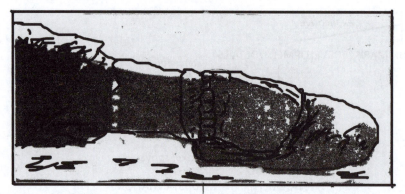

A dancer expresses herself with her body. As she moves and turns, she forgets everything - we feel what she feels as she creates a new reality with each step. Just as movement is the reflection of a dancer's dream, so an engine is the reflection of an engineer's. Since 1967, the power and smoothness of a car with a rotary engine has been one expression of Mazda's new way of thinking - its realisation, the result of many years' hard work, the conquest of many difficulties. It is a thing of beauty to be experienced only through Mazda.

On the road to civilization. MAZDA

Figure 12.4 Re-sketched rendering of Stöckl's corpus example: *Mazda 3*, depicting a ballerina's stretched-out lower leg and foot (Stöckl 1997: 332–333)

Table 12.1 Extract from the rhetorical analysis of the *Mazda 3* car example from Stöckl (1997: 403)

Functional part	Linguistic structure	Text configuration	Text	Rhetorical figures
Body copy	ARGUMENT	QUALITY	*Just as movement is the reflection of a dancer's dream, so an engine is the reflection of an engineer's*	similitude, parison, alliteration
Slogan	CONCLUSION	EVALUATION	*On the road to civilisation*	ellipsis

- similitude supports *comprehension*,
- parison supports *comprehension* and *memory*,
- alliteration supports *comprehension* and *memory*,
- ellipsis supports *attention* (Stöckl 1997: 211).

Stöckl (1997: 242–243) sets out this linking of rhetorical figures and effects in tabular form for all the rhetorical figures recognised.

Subsequently, the final component of the analysis is the characterisation of the relationship between the verbal component and the pictorial material. For this, Stöckl draws on most of the traditional rhetorical figures combining visual and verbal components proposed by Gaede (Unit 6, 'From verbal to visual rhetoric', p. 127), as well as approaches to style within

German text linguistics, and Barthes' visual semiotics (Unit 2, 'Getting the ball rolling: Roland Barthes', p. 31). Particularly useful here (for German speakers) is Stöckl's summary of previous approaches to text-image relations, again mostly drawing on results obtained within German text linguistics in work such as Kloepfer (1977) and Spillner (1982) that we discussed generally in Unit 2.

One of the main results of this work is Stöckl's proposal of a complex **picture relation type** (PRT) classification that offers a multifaceted description of the relations constructed in an artefact across the verbal and visual modes. PRT is divided into several major components. Its basic divisions are the following (Stöckl 1997: 140–144):

- The position of the picture with respect to the text: preceding *vs.* following, and whether the picture is subject to *visual emphasis* by virtue of being near the optical centre or on the main scanning diagonal (top-left to bottom-right); that is, an aspect of the relationship that follows simply from the structural arrangement interpreted according to the principles of perception (cf. Unit 3).
- The relationship between picture and text according to Barthes' categories of *anchorage* and *relay* (cf. Unit 2).
- The semiotic nature of the image itself, according to which of the categories of icon, index and symbol (taken from the semiotician Peirce) that it reflects, its colour, saturation, degree of reality (cf. Unit 6).
- A characterisation of the 'content' of the image material according to whether it works with 'positive' or 'negative' associations.
- The full range of visualisation methods activated within an image-text combination, following Gaede (1981) that we introduced in Unit 6.
- The particular aspects of Stöckl's model of persuasive communication – for example, attention, comprehension, acceptance, attraction, distraction, memorability, and so on (cf. Stöckl 1997: 71 ff.) – that are activated or supported by each visualisation method deployed in an image-text combination.
- The 'degree of verbalisation' in an image-text combination: that is, the extent to which lexical choices, phrases, etc. in the verbal text pick-up particular aspects present in the image. Analysis here provides a list of such verbal phrases and their "organisation in lexical nets" – this can be related usefully to Lemke's (1983) notion of *intertextual thematic systems* as well as multimodal cohesion in general (Unit 8).

Stöckl analyses all of the advertisements in his corpus of advertisements along these dimensions in order to make both general and particular statements about the multimodal genre of advertisements. The result of applying this classification to the Mazda advertisement with the ballerina is summarised in Table 12.2.

Stöckl's multilayer analysis for an entire corpus of advertisements represents one of the earliest and most detailed extensive empirical explorations of a selected corpus of multimodal artefacts. The result is a dense characterisation of certain aspects of the 'text type' of advertisements, including the relation between rhetorical effect and visualisation methods, between image placement and persuasion, and the distribution of rhetorical effects over the space of the advertisement. Although it can be questioned whether all of the categories can be applied with equal reliability, this kind of overview of a corpus of materials is an important step towards empirically motivated theory building. This is taken up further in Stöckl (2004a), where an equally detailed and empirically grounded framework is developed for describing the relations between text and image in 'mass media' texts such as magazines, newspapers and, again, advertisements.

Table 12.2   Stöckl's picture-relation type classification of the Mazda advertisement (Stöckl 1997: 411–412)

Category	Analysis
Position of the image with respect to the text:	preceding
Visual emphasis:	+
Embedding of the image in the entire artefact:	anchorage
Semiotic properties of the image:	iconic (naturalistic, resemblance)
Technical characteristics of image:	static, colour, natural, selective enlargement of reality
Global affective semantics of the image:	positive
Function of the image in relation to the text (visualisation methods):	synecdoche (foot for dancer), similarity (analogies drawn), repetition, determination (making precise)
Communicative effect of image-text combination:	comprehension, yield, pleasing
Use of image for motivating verbalisations:	dancer, body, step, a thing of beauty, moves, turns, movement

It is unfortunate, therefore, that exposure to Stöckl's results and approach has been limited by the fact that is has only appeared in German – many analyses that have appeared since would have learnt much from the methodological and practical concerns addressed by Stöckl, as well as from the theoretical and descriptive results achieved. Relating these results in detail to genre would be very worthwhile, but is unfortunately beyond the scope of what we can pursue here; certainly there is much to do to relate the specifics of the detailed analysis with generic statements for the genre. Similarly interesting questions apply for the hierarchical rhetorical structures proposed and their relationships both to the image material and to other accounts of text such as RST.

THEORIES OF ACTION AND IMAGES

The most abstract source of evidence concerning text-image relationships that we will consider in this book draws on accounts of communication as a kind of action. This follows in the tradition of the 'pragmatic turn' seen in many areas of linguistics, in which linguistic units are treated as communicative acts used by concrete speakers and hearers in particular contexts to achieve particular goals.

The earlier philosophical positions on which these approaches are based involve proposals such as those of the philosopher H. Paul Grice (Grice 1969) and his account of cooperative action. These positions actually made few assumptions that would restrict their application to verbal acts and so the extension nowadays to consider all kinds of acts as potentially communicative in this sense is natural (cf. Sachs-Hombach 2001, Sachs-Hombach and Schirra 2006). Positions here vary according to the theories of action that they build upon. Approaches ranging from Muckenhaupt's (1986) treatment of advertisements through to Knieja's (2013) approach to comics – and innumerable others in between – have adopted fairly direct interpretations of speech act theory and its views of intentional action and relation to text structure, whereas Kress (2010) sees action very much as a reflection of ideology and social relations as common in systemic-functional approaches. Hans-Jürgen Bucher (2007, 2011b), on the other hand, focuses more on *concretely situated action* for achieving immediately relevant communicative goals. Bucher's account in particular offers a significant advance on previous models of this kind by making more explicit the necessarily 'dialogic' interaction holding between material and interpretation; we will discuss this in more detail therefore.

Bucher sees interpretation as anchored within particular purposive activity patterns or schemata. The material that is being interpreted is then considered in the light of these patterns in a process of mutual constraint – that is, the activities provide the contextualisation necessary for interpretation to proceed. This view has several benefits: it is, for example, straightforward to extend treatments beyond the narrow confines of text-image relations since, in principle, any kind of cue that is presented for interpretation may exert an influence.

This is important even for adequate treatments of text-image combinations since certain properties of both text and image – for example, the layout and typography of the text or particular pictorial features of the image – are often not considered sufficiently within text-image relation accounts even though they also clearly have consequences for interpretation. What remains less clear at this stage is how precise analyses of particular cases would appear. There is still considerable empirical work to be undertaken before the complexities of the interpretative processes can be unravelled. Moreover, since these mechanisms are placed against the background of cognitive processing in general, a specific analytic framework is still some way off.

The most detailed presentation of Bucher's position on multimodal interpretation is that given in Bucher (2011b); this also contains a review of many approaches that have been taken to multimodal and text-image analyses. Empirical analyses building on his general framework are also being conducted (cf. Bucher and Schumacher 2011, Bucher and Niemann 2012), while several more important studies are, again, currently available only in German. Bucher's starting point is to take seriously the task of analysing the reception of multimodal artefacts by their consumers; this then places the entire enterprise on the 'pragmatic' level noted above and is, moreover, developed largely independently of particular modalities. As Bucher emphasises, text-image relations are to be seen as just one special case among the much broader range of multimodal communication in general.

Given this, it can be questioned just how far linguistically oriented approaches can provide the tools necessary to do the job. Bucher underscores this concern directly with a detailed critique of previous accounts. Many similar points of criticism have been raised in previous units, but it is also valuable to bundle them here again as Bucher does so that it is easier for the necessary lessons to be drawn.

Bucher first discusses some important distinctions to be made when discussing multimodality and its use in communication. Here he introduces and refines the notion of **non-linearity** familiar from accounts of hypertext and new media. Bucher goes further and argues that:

> multimodality as a phenomenon cannot be studied sensibly without incorporating a solid approach to non-linearity.

This is because the bare co-presence of information offerings in differing modalities raises a fundamental reception question concerning their order of processing. Non-linearity here refers to the fact that readers/viewers that are confronted with the task of using a multimodal document *must themselves make decisions* concerning which portions of that document they are going to access and bring into relation with other components for the purpose of meaning-making.

Thus non-linearity becomes an intrinsic part of any medium employing multimodal resources and is a far broader notion than that of non-linearity generally adopted for hypertext. The non-linearity of multimodal artefacts involves all levels of their reception, starting with perception processes directed by interest and salience, all the way up to more conscious interpretation. The real-time operation of such decisions can be seen very well in empirical investigations of natural visual perception using eye-tracking methods as we shall see more in Unit 13.

With this foundation, Bucher considers several of the approaches that have been taken to multimodal artefacts, particularly those involving text-image combinations. These he divides into grammatically inflected approaches, social semiotic approaches and 'dynamic-pragmatic' approaches – thus partially paralleling our own division of labour in Unit 10 and Unit 11.

Problematic with grammatically inflected approaches is their apparent reliance on a separate level of interpretation for the 'parts' to be combined. We raised this issue in particular with respect to cohesion above (Unit 8). If an analyst has first to provide semantic or formal interpretations of images and text and only then is allowed to look for correspondences, then this presupposes the meanings to be sufficiently independent of one another as to be sensibly isolated. As remarked at various points, and as Bucher provides several more examples of, this is a questionable premise.

The problem of knowing just which of the relationships theoretically accessible in an artefact are actually going to be necessary, or even useful, for analysis is also raised. Approaches such as cohesion and many grammar-derived accounts remain silent on this issue. Moreover, when examining the particular effects that text-image relations based on grammar are supposed to produce, the level of description appears to be far closer to an account of communicative action in any case rather than reflecting grammatical concerns. In part this shows the different orientation of systemic-functional grammatical approaches mentioned above, in which Morris' distinctions are simply not followed. Even basic logicosemantic relations from grammar such as 'elaboration' are described in terms of 'adding additional information', which is something that a *recipient does* with information during interpretation rather than an abstract relation. This, Bucher suggests, is a clear indication that communicative action is going to be a more appropriate level of description to pursue – systemic-functional approaches, on the other hand, would say that one needs both but, in fact, have traditionally paid very little attention to the interpretation process.

Among the socio-semiotic approaches, Bucher includes particularly that of Kress and van Leeuwen that we have mentioned at several points in previous units (cf. Kress and van Leeuwen 2006 [1996], 2001). Here Bucher criticises some of the more direct connections that have been drawn in this model between aspects of composition and ideological, social interpretations; we have not discussed these issues in this book, although further critique can be found in, for example, Machin (2007) and Bateman (2008). Bucher points out that the proposals made in these approaches are in need of considerably more empirical investigation and, in some cases, already seem to have been shown to be inaccurate or inapplicable. Here again the general point is made that it is the reader/viewers, and their reception processes, that pursue interpretation on the basis of the information presented in some artefact. It cannot be that the compositional forms themselves lead directly to one ideological interpretation rather than another.

Lastly, Bucher's dynamic-pragmatic approaches cover a rather disparate collection of accounts, including both theories based on multimodal 'transcription' (of various kinds: Jäger 2004, Holly 2009) and proposals that multimodal meanings must be derived from the interaction of the modalities involved. Although the adoption of more dynamic aspects is positive, Bucher sees the majority of these approaches as still being too restricted in terms of the flexibility and mutual *co-determination* of the elements being related. This can also be related to problems that have been raised with theories that rely on the recognition of non-conventional or unexpected usages for triggering inferences (cf. Unit 6).

As solutions to these difficulties, Bucher proposes that 'interaction' in the internal reception process should be adopted as a foundational property. This means that interpretations of multimodal combinations are not achieved 'all at once' in a manner that would allow them to be described in terms of relations holding between more or less fixed elements but, on the contrary, must be derived in *an active process of interpretation*. This leads very naturally to *empirical* and *experimental* investigations of what is occurring during the reception process. Examples of such investigations can be seen in the eye-tracking experiments described in the next unit as well as in some of Bucher's own studies (cf. Bucher 2011a).

Interaction-based models of multimodal reception must concern themselves with rather different problems than the more descriptive analytic frameworks seen previously. Reception involves different stages of processing which are necessary for interpretation to proceed. For example, to begin, a reader/viewer must first *select* what is going to be related in subsequent interpretation. This is the question of determining the units of analysis mentioned in previous units, but here re-stated not as a task for the analyst but as part of the non-linear reception process. Bucher lists a range of interpretative tasks that must be performed, including:

- identifying the type of multimodal artefact being interpreted drawing on information such as logos, titles, brand colours;
- identifying at what point in an entire communicative process the artefact is occurring by drawing on information such as tables of contents, page numbers, colour-coding, graphical separation lines;
- identifying the hierarchical relations that might obtain between different elements of the communicative process by drawing on typography, placement of text and use of white-space;
- identifying how to move from element to element drawing on navigational elements such as cross-references, hyperlinks, tables of contents;
- identifying what belongs with what by drawing on framing, titles and headers;
- identifying sequences and other ordering principles drawing on text-type specific conventions and graphical indications.

This relates the properties of any multimodal artefact to cues that can be employed for solving the interpretation problem that that artefact sets. These processes lead to many hypotheses that can be directly explored in empirical studies. Essentially what is then investigated is the complex interrelationships holding between the stimulus (what is available in the visual-field), perception of that stimulus, selection and comprehension.

Interpretation as such is then seen as an interactive process that builds on the available information in order to construct a coherent view of the communicative actions that are being performed. The occurrence, form *and* interpretation of elements mobilised in this process are all subordinated to the overall action hypothesised as being performed. This then gives an action-based foundation for exploring text-image relationships. An example of how Bucher

Table 12.3 Bucher's (2011) example of a communicative action structure expressed in a multimodal artefact

A informs B about X *in that:*	A *reports* that X has occurred	text
	A *shows* where and how X happened	photograph, graphic, film extract
	A *indicates* the value that the report about X has	design
	A *indicates* what belongs to the report about X	design

sees this functioning in order to provide an interpretative framework is shown in Table 12.3, translated from his article and slightly simplified. Any individual elements that may be selected for interpretation are then to be considered *in terms of their contribution to the communicative action under way*, thus suggesting far more situation-specific and problem-oriented paths of inference.

CONCLUSIONS

The inclusion of reception studies and close attention to the interpretative challenges that multimodal artefacts raise suggests an important additional perspective on how text-image relationships should be seen. In Bucher's view, much of the *meaning multiplication* effect is achieved by virtue of embedding information with different kinds of communicative possibilities within single, coherent courses of communicative action as suggested in Table 12.3.

This will clearly need to be taken further in subsequent research and all approaches to text-image relations need to be aware of these reception-oriented considerations. However, although valuable, Bucher's critique of other approaches nevertheless assumes that those approaches are inherently static and so cannot consider reception processes as required. This may not be equally true in all cases. Indeed, in certain respects this view of text is still articulated in a form that echoes the early text linguistics from the early 1980s introduced at the beginning of this unit. Following a host of developments in the early 1990s, however, linguistic approaches to discourse have now *also* moved to a far more dynamic view in which the material of the text and the receiver of a text enter into an interaction.

Making this fundamental aspect of linguistic approaches to discourse clear would both support a sharper characterisation of the kinds of meanings that are made visually and jointly by verbal and visual material and pave the way for a closer connection between descriptions of the text-image relations possible and their potential take-up during processing. This is an important clarification that needs to be made in order to underscore the fact that many uses of terms like 'visual grammar' and 'visual syntax' actually have little to do with grammar or syntax, but are *already essentially discoursal* as we suggested in Unit 2 ('What *are* text-image relationships?', p. 44). And discourse, as many now accept and regardless of its modalities, is an essentially dynamic phenomenon.

Text-image relations and empirical methods

At many points in the preceding units it has been stressed that we have now reached a point where it is necessary to engage in research on a larger scale. There are many different frameworks for describing text-image relations – but which ones work? for what purposes? and for what kinds of text-image relation uses? In several areas there are different kinds of classifications available, so how can we decide whether these classifications are sufficient? It is also unclear to what extent the theoretical underpinnings of these approaches are sound and how much they overlap.

There is little doubt that substantial further developments are going to be necessary. For these reasons, text-image relations research itself needs to engage far more with *empirical methods* so that real uses of text-image relations can be studied. There are several fields and approaches where such work is already underway. Some of these will be briefly introduced in the present unit. In principle, any of the approaches discussed up to now would benefit from application of some, or all, of the methods set out here, and some already are.

This also makes closer contact with the general field of recipient studies, where the effects and consequences of media on their consumers are explored. Such approaches typically employ empirical methods from the social sciences but are also, nowadays, increasingly turning to direct data collection involving eye-tracking and other physical measurements. All of these approaches are now being employed to explore the text-image situation and its reception as well.

TEXT-IMAGE RELATIONS IN COMPREHENSION

There is a long research tradition of investigating how people go about making sense of what they are *reading* by applying methods from psychology and cognitive science. Studies have explored how readers extract information from a text and what means they have for putting that information together into a coherent whole. While reading studies examine how properties of written and printed texts, such as line length, spacing between lines, typographical choices, contrast between print and background and so on, might affect reading speed and comprehension, now we turn to the broader question of whether we can learn about text-image combinations by applying similar experimental methods to more complex multimodal artefacts of the kind we have been examining throughout the book.

Situation models and scaffolding text comprehension

Psychological work on understanding discourse has been prominent since the beginnings of text linguistics. Classical approaches, such as that of Graesser, Singer and Trabasso (1994), involve having experimental participants read stories and other texts and then probing their understanding with targeted banks of questions or other kinds of problems. One essential idea behind these experiments is that people construct an internal representation in terms of a *situation model* (van Dijk and Kintsch 1983) or *mental model* (e.g., Johnson-Laird 1983). That is, as readers read a text, they are assumed to progressively construct a corresponding model capturing the relations, activities, attributes and so on described in the text. A further refinement of this idea is that readers only pursue such activities to the extent they need to in order to resolve problems in their model construction and to resolve issues of local and global coherence. It is this process of resolution that drives the particular inferences that readers carry out. Various aspects of this model have now been corroborated empirically and research continues; the corresponding body of literature is substantial.

Relevant for us here is the extension of such research to involve not just textual but also visual and combined text-image materials. Similar questions can then be raised concerning the construction of situation models, the level of detail of such models, and the kinds of inferences that are followed to populate them with information. It has, in fact, long been known that the provision of information about a text by means of visual or pictorial information can significantly improve our ability to understand that text. A classic psychological experiment demonstrating this was reported by Bransford and Johnson (1972). In this study experimental participants were asked to read a somewhat obscure description of an even more obscure situation in which a loudspeaker for a guitar is to be raised by means of balloons so that the music being played by a singer and guitar player can be heard high up in a building. In other words, a singer–guitar player is seeking to serenade someone on the top floor of a high-rise building.

Participants then had to answer comprehension questions concerning what they had read. Experimental conditions were varied according to whether the text was accompanied by a drawing depicting the state of affairs or not. The result was that those experimental participants who did not see the picture had little idea of what was going on in the text, whereas those who did see the picture had no problem. This is then clear experimental evidence of 'anchorage' going in the opposite direction to that proposed by Barthes – that is, the text on its own remained underspecified and difficult to pin down, but accompanied by the picture the problems disappear.

Bransford and Johnson go into considerably more detail concerning combinations of text and other sources of information, such as short verbal topic descriptions and so on, since their main concern was on text comprehension rather than text-image relations *per se*. However, variations of this experiment naturally suggest themselves for further empirical investigation of particular combinations and distributions of information across modes.

Since then, a range of studies have explored the potential role of image-based information as a facilitator for text comprehension in diverse types of documents. Glenberg and Langston (1992), for example, report on experiments where different representations of *procedures* were presented with and without appropriate pictorial support and with the layout position of that support varying with respect to the text. Interesting here was the result that when participants were presented with appropriate pictures, they mentally represented the procedure being communicated; in contrast, without the pictures, their representations stayed far closer to the text – which caused problems when the text presented information in orders that did not closely follow the temporal relations required to carry out the procedure described.

Studies of this nature continue up until the present time, exploring the interactions of positioning of text and image, of different kinds of pictures and other visual representations, and distinct types of texts and related tasks. The general result remains, however: presentation of visual material is beneficial. Eitel *et al.* (2013), for example, present results from an experiment in which information concerning quite complex configurations of systems of pulleys was presented visually and textually and for varying lengths of time. Results here showed that experimental participants were able to extract useful information about the configuration from the visual depiction extremely quickly; this then improved their understanding of the text description. The idea here is then that the visual information provides a powerful mental **scaffold** for extracting information from text.

The significance of this has also been discussed for the theory and practice of multimedia and multimodal learning. As Carney and Levin (2002) set out, in many areas a good understanding of just when pictorial information can be beneficial and for whom has been achieved. Carney and Levin are consequently able to offer several practical guidelines for teachers when preparing mixed media information drawing on solid empirical results. Clear differences in the uses made of pictorial material in textbooks have been found that correspond to that material's function; this therefore needs to be respected in design. Text-image functional relationships such as decoration, representation, organisation, interpretation and transformation, for example, are each shown to interact in different ways with comprehension. Carney and Levin present useful examples of each kind, as well as a useful review of the relevant literature.

There are, however, many open issues and challenges. Accounts of visual and verbal perception have suggested that image and text are processed in very different ways, resulting in different internal forms of representations (cf. Paivio 1986), and the information in these representations then has to be integrated for comprehension of text-image combinations to result. Many factors appear to have an influence on the effectiveness of this integration, however – which leads directly to issues of particular relevance to education. How do children *learn* to perform this integration? Or, taking up again some of the debate mentioned right at the outset in Unit 1 ('Literacy', p. 22), do they have to learn it at all?

Recent studies, for example those of Hochpöchler *et al.* (2012), raise a number of issues showing that the questions here are far from answered and that education should be doing more about them. In a series of studies examining the use of text and images across ages and aptitude-related types of school in Germany, Hochpöchler *et al.* demonstrate that the two modalities have very different 'patterns of usage' when combined. On the basis of previous work (e.g., Schnotz 2002), they hypothesised that the usage of text should follow what can be described as a *global coherence strategy*, while the use of images would be more in line with a *task-specific information selection strategy*, whereby viewers consult the visual material for local, or small-scale, information 'on demand'. Their results supported the first hypothesis but showed a considerably more complex state of affairs with respect to the second.

When processing images, the school students appeared *first* to employ a global coherence strategy, using their overall impression of the visually depicted material to construct a scaffold for interpretation as suggested above. Following this, what happened depended on the aptitude level of the school:

> Students with higher learning prerequisites (i.e., students from higher track schools) seem to adapt their processing to the difficulty of the task at hand, as they invest more time into graphics processing when items become more difficult. . . . [S]tudents with lower learning prerequisites . . . do not use graphics more intensively when items become more difficult.
> (Hochpöchler *et al.* 2012: 15)

There could be many factors contributing to this differential use of the information presented visually. Hochpöchler *et al.* refer to differences in the forms of representation themselves. However, also possible would be cultural conditions where children are progressively taught (often by omission) to downplay the importance of visual information in the learning situation. This would conform to the general distrust of the visual that we have noted at several places in previous units, but is particularly ironic (and harmful) in today's multimodal world. As in many areas, not explicitly teaching how to use certain forms of material tends to be far more damaging for lower aptitude students than higher-aptitude students who can, at least partially, make up for the deficits in education themselves.

Discourse relations as psychological entities

A further body of psychological research has focused more on the nature of discourse relations, or 'coherence relations' as they are often called, as such. Psycholinguistic accounts of discourse comprehension explore how successive utterances or sentences can be related to one another during reception by finding appropriate discourse relations. On the basis of such empirical studies, several 'core' relations have been found that, on the one hand, appear to be used for combining messages during text comprehension and, on the other hand, also appear to correspond with basic cognitive mechanisms.

These relations are as a consequence intended to offer a more plausible set of mechanisms for cognitive processing during text understanding than the rather more discriminating sets of relations found in, for example, Rhetorical Structure Theory or Conjunctive Relations (cf. Unit 11). The idea is that whereas it is unlikely that language users instantly recognise such complex relations as 'evidence' or 'solutionhood', they may well recognise more basic relationships from which composite coherence relations can be derived. Ted Sanders, Wilbert Spooren and Leo Noordman have carried out extensive experiments probing these core relations (Sanders *et al.* 1992, Sanders, Spooren and Noordman 1993) and propose four fundamental relation categories that appear both sufficient for deriving more complex meanings and psychologically plausible in that experimental participants reliably recognise the distinctions drawn.

These categories are summarised in systemic network notation in Figure 13.1. The first captures whether or not a causal connection is assumed to be holding between the content of two messages, the basic/non-basic distinction refers to the order in which cause and caused are presented; positive *vs.* negative is whether the specific coherence relation is asserted as holding or as not holding; and semantic *vs.* pragmatic indicates whether the relation holds of the semantic *content* of the messages or of the messages themselves.

This last distinction in meaning is illustrated in the alternation: 'He is not coming to the party because he is sick' *vs.* 'He is not coming to the party because I just saw him in the pub' – the former refers to external states of affairs, the latter introduces an implicit 'I say that' before the first message; that is, seeing him in the pub is the reason *that I say that* he is not coming. Another term for this distinction introduced by Martin (1992) is **external** *vs.* **internal**, referring to the sources of motivation for the assertions made – that is, either that motivation is in the 'external' world (corresponding to the 'semantic' alternative) or 'in the text' or interaction (corresponding to the 'pragmatic' alternative).

It is interesting to consider whether similar core relations might operate between text and images. Since their operation is taken to be primarily concerned with the information content of the elements being related rather than their form, it would be natural to posit overlapping

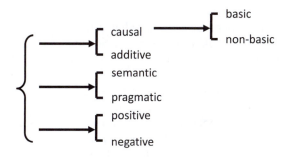

Figure 13.1 Hierarchy of core coherence relations according to Sanders *et al.* (1992) and expressed as a systemic classification network

cognitive mechanisms for their operation and so to pursue their use in mixed-mode artefacts as well. Some studies of this kind can be found in van Hooijdonk *et al.* (2006) and Maes and Schilperoord (2009). Predictions can then also be applied to combinations of texts and image in order to see whether evidence for similar, or other, relations can be found. Further research is required, however.

EYE-TRACKING METHODS

One of the methods sometimes used in the above fields of research, but which is now being employed for a much broader range of research questions, is **eye-tracking**. Eye-tracking techniques provide a means for recording precisely where, and for how long, people are looking at any moment. This is considered useful for empirical investigation of the reception process because where and how the eyes move appears to correlate closely with the *allocation of attention* (cf. Just and Carpenter 1980). Thus, eye movements can give important clues concerning just what is being attended to during the reception of more or less complex artefacts.

At least two kinds of visual processing are involved when 'taking in' the visual field. One kind gives a general impression of the whole, of patterns of light and shade, of balance and composition, of forms. The other uses that general information to pick out particular and very small regions of the image-field in order to construct an interpretation of the whole. It is this latter component of perception that eye-tracking addresses, relying on the physiological fact that the eyes move very rapidly between points of 'fixation' in order to gather information from the visual field for further processing. In fact, information is only gathered when the eye is not moving: during the rapid movements of the eye from fixation point to fixation point – paths called **saccades** – perception is, at it were, 'turned off'. No information is passed on during saccades, which is just as well because the eyes are moving so fast that there would be little more than a blur to recover in any case.

Current research has revealed much about how the visual system and attention work together and eye-tracking devices themselves are becoming cheap enough to be employed quite broadly. Many earlier proposals of where people are looking at images or other artefacts have been shown to be wildly inaccurate and so claims made without checking with real eye-tracking experiments should nowadays be considered very cautiously. We are just not conscious of what our eyes are doing at this kind of fine-grained level and so impressionistic or intuitive hypotheses may miss the mark.

Many of these eye movements and the points they single out for attention can be explained on evolutionary grounds. Eye-tracking studies have shown, for example, that if there are any eyes or faces in the visual field, these will almost always be attended to because humans are essentially a social species. The perceptual system always considers it relevant to look at other people and where *they* are looking. However, there is far more going on than a simple response to externally given sources of visual salience.

Other results from eye-tracking research have demonstrated that visual attention is, in fact, extremely selective. We do not look at everything, just those aspects of an image which the perceptual system identifies *as being potentially useful*. Moreover, what it is useful to attend to when, for example, confronting some visual depiction is by no means an automatic feature in response to the visual field alone. It instead depends in addition on a broad range of influences – *including the goals, interests and needs of the perceiver* (cf. Itti and Koch 2001, Schill *et al.* 2001). This makes eye-tracking an extremely sensitive and powerful tool for exploring the processes of interpretation as they happen.

One of the first uses of eye-tracking relevant for our current discussion was also in reading studies. Researchers were concerned with how readers were gathering information from written text and so carried out eye-tracking studies. This revealed many fine details of the comprehension process, showing where pauses and backtracking to collect information from the text occur. As a consequence we now know that even the perception of linear text is far from a straightforward linear perceptual process following letters one-by-one along a line of print.

It was then natural to extend this direction of research to combinations of text and other visual material. One such study carried out by Jana Holsanova and colleagues explored some predictions derived from socio-semiotic theory concerning reading paths and attention with

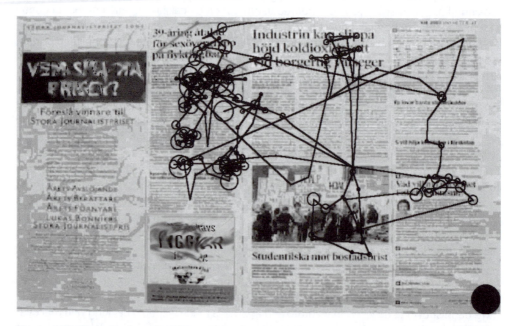

Figure 13.2 Example of eye-tracking results with respect to a newspaper spread reported by Holsanova *et al.* (2006) – the newspaper has been blurred here for copyright reasons; the figure itself is used by kind permission of the authors

respect to the behaviour of experimental participants while reading normal newspaper pages (Holsanova, Rahm and Holmqvist 2006). The results are interesting in many respects, demonstrating that, although some of the predictions made on socio-semiotic grounds could be corroborated, many were not.

Moreover, the importance of taking into consideration readers' familiarity with particular text types was made particularly clear in these studies. Consider the experimental results shown in Figure 13.2, for example. This shows a typical result of an eye-tracking experiment. The lines zigzagging over the page are the saccades and the circles at the end of the lines indicate where the eyes have fixated. The size of the circles indicates the length of time that the eyes remain at one point, which usually involves small fractions of a second.

We can see from this that there is little evidence of the often claimed top-left to bottom-right reading path mentioned in Unit 3 ('Dynamic perception of static visuals', p. 60). Some images are scanned, others are jumped over; some articles appear to be read in depth, others not. It does seem to be the case that the headlines of the articles that are subsequently read are at least briefly examined – although certainly not read in depth. There is also a preference for the top half of the page. What is very interesting, however, is the way the large adver-tisement on the lefthand side of the spread is completely ignored, despite its strong visual salience (in the original it is even in colour). This shows just how strong 'top-down' influences are during perception. If the task or interest is to read news, then the advertisement might not even be registered as existing at all!

This also corroborates Bucher's claims that we discussed in Unit 12 ('Theories of action and images', p. 234) concerning the problem-solving, goal-oriented nature of multimodal interpretation. The interaction of top-down, task-related decisions and bottom-up, visual feature-related decisions was first shown empirically by Yarbus (1967) and has now been demonstrated to apply to the perception of visual communicative artefacts in general. Results are available for a range of media, all raising interesting issues for further research (cf. Nielsen 2006, Bucher and Schumacher 2011).

One focused investigation of text-image relationships and the effect of design is reported in Holsanova and Nord (2010). In this experiment, various versions of a newspaper article giving health information about catching colds were produced. These were varied so that the influence of layout on reception behaviour and the construction of text-image relations could be systematically explored. The experiment was designed to test various design principles discussed in multimedia research. However, one aspect of the results is particularly relevant here.

It is increasingly often emphasised in general discussions of media reception that readers and viewers interact with communicative artefacts dynamically in order to extract information according to their requirements. This is then carried over to design, suggesting that designs should support such radical non-determinacy rather than enforcing particular reading strate-gies. To test how such designs are actually received by reader/viewers, two alternative designs were created for the experiment: one of these was *serial-based* and the other *radially based*. Both involved tightly connected text and graphics. On the one hand, the radial design in the experiment conformed to the non-determinate, multiple entry-point philosophy; the serial design, on the other hand, offered a more regimented tour through the material. Despite their differences, both designs contained the same information. Experimental subjects were then asked to read and understand the articles while being eye-tracked.

Some results of running the experiment are shown in Figure 13.3. These show that the radial design (top) failed dramatically to engage the attention of its readers. The serial design (bottom) not only was read more completely but also triggered many more so-called *integrative saccades*. These show where readers are explicitly bringing information expressed verbally

Figure 13.3 Eye-tracks for contrasting radial and serial designs of an information article taken from Holsanova and Nord (2010: 97) and used with kind permission of the authors and the designer, Jens Tarning

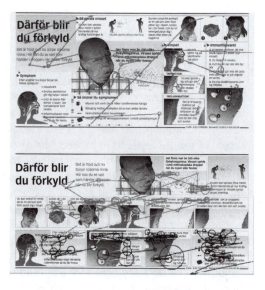

and information expressed visually together. Thus the multimodal design of the articles was crucial for their uptake – 'leaving it to the reader' was not at all an effective strategy. As Holsanova and Nord conclude:

> producers of media messages cannot neglect the role of visual design and multimodality. The same holds even for media and communication research – if we want to understand the structure and reception of modern media messages, we must take the multimodal approach seriously.
>
> (Holsanova and Nord 2010: 100)

Finally, eye-tracking research of this kind is now also providing insight into the question of just what *units* are going to be necessary when describing images and text-image relationships. It is not the case that this is a static, once-and-for-all analytic exercise as approaches drawing on linguistic frameworks would often suggest. Even the kinds of entities discovered in images may need to be described in terms of dynamic attention-based models.

As demonstration of this, Boeriis and Holsanova (2012) combine eye-tracking and verbal reports to determine both where individuals are paying attention while interpreting pictorial information and, consequently, what kinds of units they are constructing. These studies showed unit construction to be driven by a range of perceptual and other concerns, which means that the kinds of units that are actually used for meaning construction may well need to be re-considered. This is suggested in the extract from Boeriis and Holsanova's results presented in Figure 13.4. We see here on the left-hand side eye-tracking results with respect to a single page from one of the well-known *Pettson and Findus* picturebooks by Sven Nordqvist. Since the actual pictures are not the main point here, the figure as shown uses a sketch instead. Readers are recommended to refer to the original.

The interesting aspect of this page for our current question is that its interpretation is far from straightforward. The image is in fact a **Simultanbild**, that is, an image depicting several distinct moments in time in one pictorial representation. This is cued to the reader/viewer by showing recognisable individuals more than once, engaged in different (but related) activities. The research question is then how reader/viewers find the intended interpretation. The figure

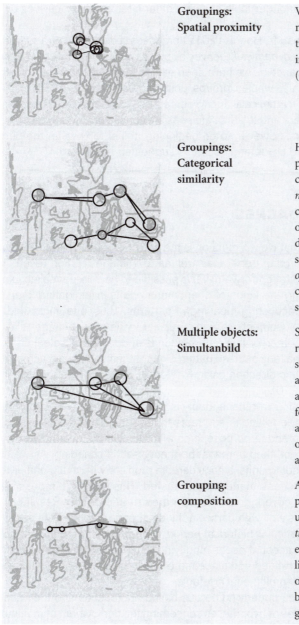

	Groupings: Spatial proximity	Viewers often inspect and mention groups of objects that are based on the image-inherent spatial proximity (*there are three birds*).
	Groupings: Categorical similarity	However, viewers also perceive and describe clusters of objects that are *not* spatially close. These clusters consist of groupings of multiple similar objects distributed over the whole scene (*four cats, four versions of Pettson*). This type of cluster is based on categorical similarity.
	Multiple objects: Simultanbild	Some viewers notice repetitive figures in the scene and describe them as four varieties of Pettson and Findus, whereas others focus on the event instead and describe one person and one cat involved in various activities.
	Grouping: composition	Another type of cluster perceived as a meaningful unit in the scene is *hills on the horizon*. The viewer's eyes follow the horizontal line, filling in links between objects. This cluster seems to be a compositionally guided grouping.

Figure 13.4 Extract from the eye-tracking results with respect to a *Simultanbild* extracted from Boeriis and Holsanova (2012: 274, Figure 7); used by permission of the authors

shows that reception of the page goes through distinct stages. First, it appears that groups of similar objects in spatial proximity are identified; then groups based more on *categorial similarity* (in this case, instances of Pettson and Findus) are identified even though they are not near one another; then multiple objects are identified as perhaps being indicative of a 'non-standard' pictorial representation (i.e., one involving time); and so on. The part of the table shown is in fact just one part of a longer table showing other interpretative activities of the viewers/readers as well.

As a consequence of such results, Boeriis (2012) proposes a descriptive framework in which the elements of analysis are *dynamically derived* by perceptual interpretative processes rather than being assumed in advance as we have seen earlier approaches to do. Units then operate at different scales – such as **wholes**, **groups**, **units** and **components** (cf. Boeriis and Holsanova 2012: 262) – derived dynamically during perception. Far more work is necessary to uncover just what is involved here and to articulate possible consequences for accounts of text-image relations. We do seem, however, to be beginning at last to take up the pursuit of dynamic processes of meaning co-determination as suggested by Kloepfer (1977) and others in Unit 2.

CORPUS-BASED APPROACHES

'A final area of empirical studies that we will mention is the use of *corpora*. This is of growing importance for multimodal research in general as well as text-image relation research in particular. The idea behind this is straightforward: if it is possible to have larger collections of naturally occurring data containing the kinds of phenomena one is investigating, then this gives a more reliable basis for uncovering meaningful patterns. Thus, one might find, for example, that particular kinds of documents rely on particular kinds of text-image relations for some purposes rather than another; or that different kinds of documents select different kinds of text-image relations; or that any of these patterns might themselves vary across time or audience. We saw a move in this direction using Rhetorical Structure Theory in Unit 11 ('Conclusions and discussion', p. 220).

Corpora are also ideal for testing whether a theory is making accurate predictions. If, for example, an account of text-image relations suggests that certain correlations are to be expected between relation and intended purpose, then a corpus can be used to verify that this is actually the case – if it is not, then perhaps the theory needs changing. As we have explained at many points in preceding units, a considerable problem with much earlier text-image research is that the predictions made are not tested. This makes it impossible to ascertain how well the theory is 'covering' its intended area of application. Results might indicate that some proposal works well with particular kinds of page layouts, or in particular genres, or in artefacts from a particular historical period, or in particular media, but not in others. Or one might find that the account needs modifying to be reliably applicable at all. In each case, the account has been refined and made more powerful with respect to its ability to inform us about the workings of multimodal artefacts.

This is the essence of the idea underlying corpus-based approaches and their use for empirical research. Similar examples of hypotheses concerning the deployment of multimodal resources can be made in almost all areas where multimodality is being explored. Such hypotheses can be more or less complex in their own right – with the current state of the art in multimodality research there are far more questions than answers and so there is much to be explored, even with relatively simple hypotheses. At the same time, the sheer quantity of multimodal data available is exploding, with online media such as news reports, image banks, online communications and so on playing a major role. It is therefore easier than ever before to explore theoretical hypotheses concerning multimodality with respect to data.

Carrying out corpus-based research on multimodality is, then, highly desirable at this time but does raise some challenges of its own. Once some target data have been fixed, they must first be *prepared* for corpus use. Bare data are generally insufficient for effective empirical research because it is difficult, or even impossible, to *interact* with the data in ways that are appropriate for framing and exploring research questions. For this, the overriding requirement is that it is possible to search the data for patterns relevant for some research question. And to support this, it is usual that the data in a corpus be *annotated* with additional information that can then be used for more effective searches and pattern recognition. More information and further pointers concerning annotation in multimodal contexts and its use in corpus-based research can be found in, for example, Bezemer and Mavers (2011), Hiippala (2011, 2012) and Bateman (2013).

Once a corpus has been annotated with reference to appropriate coding schemes, empirical research proceeds by examining the corpus for patterns of various kinds and checking whether expected correlations actually occur. As an example, we might consider a possible verification of the text-image classification developed by Martinec and Salway (2005) that we introduced in Unit 10 ('Martinec and Salway's framework', p. 190). As we saw there, this system takes the logicosemantic system of connections worked out for relating clauses in English grammar (Halliday and Matthiessen 2004) and suggests that this should also work to relate text and images. Now, this is an intriguing proposal full of analytic possibilities – but are the claims made correct?

In order to address such questions on the basis of corpus data, a representative sample of examples should first be annotated according to Martinec and Salway's scheme. Such annotation would usually be done by several independent analysts, or 'coders', so that the degree of agreement across coders – the *inter-coder reliability* – can be calculated (cf. Landis and Koch 1977, Carletta 1996). If the agreement is good, then we know that the proposed classification can at least be applied reliably. The provision of corpora involving such a level of annotation would represent a valuable resource in its own right, supporting a variety of further empirical studies.

For example, the annotation of two elements as linked according to Martinec and Salway's classification might also be considered to predict that readers/viewers attend to the related pieces of information together. We might then combine this with eye-tracking data and explore whether any regular correlation can be found in the annotated corpus between the existence of presumed text-image relations and attention allocation. This might reveal that there are further constraints that should be applied – for example depending on layout decisions or distance. Or, we might be able to verify or refine some of the recognition criteria that Martinec and Salway propose by showing correlations between other properties of form and their text-image categories. Until we have closed the empirical loop between interpretation and data in this way, subjective interpretation will often not be sufficiently constrained.

CONCLUSIONS

This unit has sketched some of the empirical methods that have been applied to investigate comprehension and the reception process with textual and visual materials. All of these approaches are now also being employed to explore the text-image situation, examining for example just when readers look at what on a page in their attempts to extract meaning, or what range of relationships can be expected in different kinds of documents, and so on. We have seen the basis of these methodologies and also some of the empirical results that are beginning to emerge. The time is certainly ripe for taking such explorations further.

UNIT 14

The continuing research agenda: topics for further work

This then brings us to the end of our whirlwind tour of approaches to the text-image question. We have seen many frameworks developed in diverse disciplines in order to address a variety of different kinds of verbo-visual artefacts. Our constant refrain has been just how much there is left to do. The problems started even with identifying how to distinguish between 'text' – in the sense of something exhibiting organisation that is similar to natural spoken languages – and 'images' – in the sense of visual material that is *not* similar to spoken languages – reliably at all. As depicted graphically in the comics panels from Scott McCloud (McCloud 1994: 43) (Figure 14.1), we appear to be dealing with a variety of continua. Text and image must then be placed at *different places* along these continua as we address different aspects of what they are and how they work.

Figure 14.1 Panels from Scott McCloud © 1994 (*Understanding Comics*, 1994, p. 49); reproduced by permission of HarperCollins Publishers

McCloud suggests that images can be 'received' without prior training and knowledge, thereby relating to a widespread assumption of images as natural resemblances, while written text needs to be 'perceived' in the sense of being interpreted, or 'read'. Although McCloud's uses of 'reception' and 'perception' here differ from those generally adopted in, for example, psychology, the intention should be clear. But we have also seen at many points how this needs to be taken much further – *some* aspects of *some* kinds of visual materials may be 'received' in this way, but many are not. And, moreover, as soon as we have text and image *working together*, the cards have been shuffled again and it is by no means always clear just what is being done with the resulting combinations.

Note, for example, how McCloud's panels work with text and image in various ways – even the visual *layout* of the three panels and their contents is meaningful as it resonates with his basic point, made verbally, concerning a *contrast* between text and image. There is, then, much more to images than pictures – as we have emphasised at many points throughout the book.

There are now several directions that could be taken to develop the ideas presented here further and to increase our understanding of just how text and image work together and what it is they are doing when this happens. Most straightforwardly, there are many points of connection and overlap to be explored *across* the different perspectives we have now introduced. This is necessary to counteract the tendency to only work within single disciplines or concerning single kinds of material. When extensions are made, then these tend to be from those perspectives – which may then need tempering with broader views. For example, both Cohn and Martinec and Salway work their way towards *diagrams*, although starting from very different perspectives – comics and grammar respectively. As remarked in the corresponding units above, though, it is not entirely clear that either of these extensions is justified or appropriate. Extending approaches developed with respect to one set of materials so as to apply to others always needs to consider carefully whether different principles may be at work. This is another reason why we have attempted here to take a rather broad view of just what approaches are 'out there'.

There are also further areas that we have not been able to discuss in this book at all but which could equally well have been addressed. Examples include more detailed investigations of the relations between captions and *press photographs* and how these have changed over time, explorations of text-image relations on the *web* and in *hypermedia*, the use of text-image combinations in *scientific articles* and *visualisations*, and many more. And, in all of these areas as well as in those we have discussed, the additional possibilities that we now have for empirical research, including corpus-based studies and eye-tracking methods, will need to be given far more attention than has traditionally been the case.

We can also consider exploring uses of textual and visual materials beyond the confines that we imposed on ourselves here. Despite our focus on static, page-based text-image relations, at several points we have also suggested that this restriction is artificial. The very nature of a focus on the text-image relation can therefore be problematised. Analyses of highly multimodal artefacts, such as the moving audio-visual image, make it increasingly clear that the basic phenomenon at issue is *multimodal* interpretation and discourse in general, and not just relations between text and image. The methods and frameworks we have seen here will help us with the questions that will arise, but we will also no doubt need extensions and changes.

Taking research of this kind further will in turn require building new frameworks on and around those we have seen in this book in order to address new and old areas where text and image work together. For example: *spoken language and gesture, spoken language and visual presentations* (using, for example, tools such as PowerPoint, Keynote, Prezi to accompany speech), *moving images and written language, animated text and visual presentations*, and many more are all combinations of modalities either already under investigation in particular research communities or are waiting for systematic study. In all cases, the importance of a dynamic approach to discourse organisation, including multimodal discourse organisation, must be stressed – it is this that will provide crucial ground rules for how to proceed. And this will also need to be done making use of *empirical methods* so that we can evaluate whether our proposals are successful or are in need of refinement or replacement.

The challenges arising will in many cases show similarities with those we have discussed. This will increasingly require us to cut across both disciplines and application areas. The similarities that occur are in all likelihood indicative of more fundamental issues concerning how the text-image relationship and other cases of meaning-multiplication across semiotic modes operate. And this means that there may well also need to be more effective ways of *sharing the work of analysis* – after all, is it really the case that work on picturebooks has to rediscover on its own all that is known in psychology about human colour perception? Or that work on narrative has to develop its own versions of fine-grained linguistic syntactic and semantic analyses? Or work in multimodal semiotics has to re-express categories and constructs long practised in art history?

Considerations such as these underscore the importance of a far more open attitude towards inter- and transdisciplinary work. The phenomena we have to deal with are now sufficiently complex that it is unreasonable to expect them all to be covered within the confines of single disciplines. Improved models of interaction between and across disciplines, both theoretically and institutionally, are therefore already essential and will only become more important in the future.

References

Abbott, L. L. (1986), 'Comic art: characteristics and potentialities of a narrative medium', *Journal of Popular Culture* **19**(4), 155–176.

Agosto, D. E. (1999), 'One and inseparable: interdependent storytelling in picture storybooks', *Children's Literature in Education* **30**(4), 267–280.

Aichele, K. P. and Citroen, K. (2007), 'Correspondence art history, or writing the end of Paul Klee's *Anfang eines Gedichtes*', *Word & Image: A journal of verbal/visual enquiry* **23**(3), 315–326.

Altmann, G. T. (1997), *The Ascent of Babel: an exploration of language, mind, and understanding*, Oxford University Press, Oxford and New York.

André, E. (1995), *Ein planbasierter Ansatz zur Generierung multimedialer Präsentationen*, Vol. 108, Infix, St. Augustin.

Anstey, M. and Bull, G. (2006), *Teaching and Learning Multiliteracies: changing times, changing literacies*, International Reading Association.

Arnheim, R. (1974), *Art and Visual Perception: a psychology of the creative eye*, University of California Press.

Arnheim, R. (1982), *The Power of the Center*, University of California Press, Berkeley, CA.

Austin, J. L. (1962), *How to Do Things with Words*, Oxford University Press, Oxford and New York. From lectures held in 1955, edited by J. O. Urmson.

Bader, B. (1976), *American Picturebooks from Noah's Ark to the Beast Within*, Macmillan, New York.

Bal, M. (2009 [1985]), *Narratology. Introduction to the theory of narrative*, 3rd edn, University of Toronto Press, Toronto, Buffalo and London.

Baldry, A. and Thibault, P. J. (2006), *Multimodal Transcription and Text Analysis: a multimedia toolkit and coursebook with associated on-line course*, Textbooks and Surveys in Linguistics, Equinox, London and New York.

Bardin, L. (1975), 'Le texte et l'image', *Communication et langages* **26**, 98–112.

Barthes, R. (1977 [1964]), 'The rhetoric of the image', in *Image–Music–Text*, Fontana, London, pp. 32–51.

Barthes, R. (1977 [1966]), 'Introduction to the structural analysis of narratives', in *Image–Music–Text*, Fontana, London, pp. 79–124. Originally published in French in *Communications*, **8**.

Bateman, J. A. (2008), *Multimodality and Genre: a foundation for the systematic analysis of multimodal documents*, Palgrave Macmillan, London.

Bateman, J. A. (2011), 'The decomposability of semiotic modes', in K. L. O'Halloran and B. A. Smith, eds, *Multimodal Studies: multiple approaches and domains*, Routledge Studies in Multimodality, Routledge, London, pp. 17–38.

Bateman, J. A. (2013), 'Using multimodal corpora for empirical research', in C. Jewitt, ed., *The Routledge Handbook of Multimodal Analysis*, 2nd edn, Routledge, London, pp. 238–252.

Bateman, J. A. (2014), 'Genre in the age of multimodality: some conceptual refinements for practical analysis', in P. Evangelisti, V. Bhatia and J. Bateman, eds, *Evolution in Genre: emergence, variation, multimodality*, Linguistic Insights, Peter Lang, Frankfurt am Main.

Bateman, J. A. and Delin, J. L. (2006), 'Rhetorical Structure Theory', *in* K. Brown, ed., *The Encyclopedia of Language and Linguistics*, 2nd edn, Vol. 10, Elsevier, Amsterdam, pp. 588–596.

Bateman, J. A. and Rondhuis, K. J. (1997), '"Coherence relations": towards a general specification', *Discourse Processes* **24**, 3–49.

Bateman, J. A., Kamps, T., Kleinz, J. and Reichenberger, K. (2001), 'Constructive text, diagram and layout generation for information presentation: the DArt$_{bio}$ system', *Computational Linguistics* **27**(3), 409–449.

Benveniste, E. (1986), 'The semiology of language', *in* R. E. Innis, ed., *Semiotics: an introductory reader*, Indiana University Press, Bloomington, IN, pp. 226–246.

Berger, A. A. (1997), *Narratives in Popular Culture, Media, and Everyday Life*, Sage, Thousand Oaks, CA.

Berger, P. and Luckmann, T. (1967), *The Social Construction of Reality: a treatise in the sociology of knowledge*, Allen Lane (Penguin), London.

Bernhardt, S. A. (1985), 'Text structure and graphic design: the visible design', *in* J. D. Benson and W. S. Greaves, eds, *Systemic Perspectives on Discourse, Volume 1*, Ablex, Norwood, New Jersey, pp. 18–38.

Bernhardt, S. A. (1986), 'Seeing the text', *College Composition and Communication* **37**(1), 66–78.

Bernhardt, S. A. (1996), 'Visual rhetoric', *in* T. Enos, ed., *Encyclopedia of Rhetoric and Composition: communication from ancient times to the information age*, Garland, New York, pp. 746–748.

Berninger, M., Ecke, J. and Haberkorn, G. (2010), *Comics as a Nexus of Cultures. Essays on the interplay of media, disciplines and international perspectives*, Critical Explorations in Science Fiction and Fantasy, 22, McFarland & Co.

Bertin, J. (1983), *Semiology of Graphics*, University of Wisconsin Press, Madison, Wisconsin. Translated *Sémiologie graphique* (1967) by William J. Berg.

Bezemer, J. and Mavers, D. (2011), 'Multimodal transcription as academic practice: a social semiotic perspective', *International Journal of Social Research Methodology* **14**(3), 191–206.

Biber, D. and Finegan, E., eds (1993), *Perspectives on Register: situating register variation within sociolinguistics*, Oxford University Press.

Black, M. (1979), 'More about metaphor', *in* A. Ortony, ed., *Metaphor and Thought*, Cambridge University Press, Cambridge, pp. 19–43.

Boeriis, M. (2012), 'Tekstzoom – om en dynamisk funktionel rangstruktur i visuelle tekster', *in* T. Andersen and M. Boeriis, eds, *Nordisk Socialsemiotik – multimodale, pædagogiske og sprogvidenskabelige landvindinger*, University Press of Southern Denmark, Odense, pp. 131–153.

Boeriis, M. and Holsanova, J. (2012), 'Tracking visual segmentation: connecting semiotic and cognitive perspectives', *Visual Communication* **11**(3), 259–281.

Bongco, M. (2000), *Reading Comics: language, culture, and the concept of the superhero in comic books*, Garland Publishing, New York.

Bonsiepe, G. (2008 [1965]), 'Visual/verbal rhetoric (1965, 2007)', *in* G. Joost and A. Scheuermann, eds, *Design als Rhetorik: Grundlagen, Positionen, Fallstudien*, Birkhäuser, Basel, pp. 27–44.

Bransford, J. D. and Johnson, M. K. (1972), 'Contextual prerequisites for understanding: Some investigations of comprehension and recall', *Journal of Verbal Learning and Verbal Behavior* **11**(6), 717–726.

Brill, J., Kim, D. and Branch, R. (2007), 'Visual literacy defined – the results of a Delphi study', *Journal of Visual Literacy* **27**, 47–60.

Bron, C. (1964), 'Preface', *in* J. Dubois and R. Dubois, eds, *La Presse enfantine française*, Editions H. Meseiller, Neuchâtel, Switzerland, pp. i–ii.

Bucher, H.-J. (2007), 'Textdesign und Multimodalität. Zur Semantik und Pragmatik medialer Gestaltungsformen', *in* S. Roth and J. Spitzmüller, eds, *Textdesign und Textwirkung in der massenmedialen Kommunikation*, UVK, Konstanz, pp. 49–76.

Bucher, H.-J. (2011a), '"Man sieht, was man hört" oder: Multimodales Verstehen als interaktionale Aneignung. Eine Blickaufzeichnungsstudie zur audiovisuellen Rezeption', *in* J. G. Schneider and H. Stöckl, eds, *Medientheorien und Multimodalität. Ein TV-Werbespot – Sieben methodische Beschreibungsansätze*, Herbert von Halem Verlag, Köln, pp. 109–150.

Bucher, H.-J. (2011b), 'Multimodales Verstehen oder Rezeption als Interaktion. Theoretische und empirische Grundlagen einer systematischen Analyse der Multimodalität', *in* H.-J. Diekmannshenke, M. Klemm and H. Stöckl, eds, *Bildlinguistik. Theorien – Methoden – Fallbeispiele*, Erich Schmidt, Berlin, pp. 123–156.

Bucher, H.-J. and Niemann, P. (2012), 'Visualizing science: the reception of PowerPoint presentations', *Visual Communication* **11**(3), 283–306.

Bucher, H.-J. and Schumacher, P. (2011), 'The relevance of attention for selecting new content: an eye-tracking study on attention patterns in the reception of print- and online media', *Communications. The European Journal of Communications Research* **31**(3), 347–368.

Burke, K. (1945), *A Grammar of Motives*, Prentice Hall, Inc., London.

Carletta, J. C. (1996), 'Assessing agreement on classification tasks: the kappa statistic', *Computational Linguistics* **22**(2), 249–254.

Carney, R. and Levin, J. (2002), 'Pictorial illustrations *still* improve students' learning from text', *Educational Psychology Review* **14**(1), 5–26.

Carrier, D. (2000), *The Aesthetics of Comics*, The Pennsylvania State University, University Park, PA.

Carroll, N. (2001), *Beyond Aesthetics: philosophical essays*, Cambridge University Press, New York, chapter 'Visual Metaphor', pp. 347–367.

Carroll, N. (2007), 'Narrative closure', *Philosophical Studies* **135**, 1–15.

Chan, E. and Unsworth, L. (2011), 'Image-language interaction in online reading environments: challenges for students' reading comprehension', *Australian Educational Researcher* **38**(2), 181–202.

Chandler, D. (2002), *Semiotics: the basics*, Routledge, London and New York.

Chatman, S. (1978), *Story and Discourse: narrative structure in fiction and film*, Cornell University Press, Ithaca and London.

Coffin, C. (2006), *Historical Discourse: the language of time, cause and evaluation*, Continuum, London.

Cohn, N. (2007), 'A visual lexicon', *Public Journal of Semiotics* **1**(1), 35–56.

Cohn, N. (2010), 'The limits of time and transitions: challenges to theories of sequential image comprehension', *Studies in Comics* **1**(1), 127–147.

Cohn, N. (2013a), 'Beyond speech balloons and thought bubbles: the integration of text and image', *Semiotica* **197**, 35–63.

Cohn, N. (2013b), 'Navigating comics: an empirical and theoretical approach to strategies of reading comic page layouts', *Frontiers in Psychology* **4**(186).

Cohn, N. (2013c), 'Visual narrative structure', *Cognitive Science* **37**(3), 413–452.

Cohn, N. (2014), *The Visual Language of Comics: introduction to the structure and cognition of sequential images*, Bloomsbury, London.

Cohn, N., Paczynski, M., Jackendoff, R., Holcomb, P. J. and Kuperberg, G. R. (2012), '(Pea)nuts and bolts of visual narrative: structure and meaning in sequential image comprehension', *Cognitive Psychology* **65**(1), 1–38.

Cook, G. (2001), *The Discourse of Advertising*, 2nd edn, Routledge, London.

Corbett, E. P. and Connors, R. J. (1998), *Classical Rhetoric for the Modern Student*, 4th edn, Oxford University Press, Oxford and New York.

Corrigan, R. and Surber, J. R. (2009), 'The reading level paradox: why children's picture books are less cohesive than adult books', *Discourse Processes* **47**(1), 32–54.

Cutting, J. E. (2002), 'Representing motion in a static image: constraints and parallels in art, science, and popular culture', *Perception* **31**(10), 1165–1193.

Czarniawska, B. (2004), *Narratives in Social Science Research*, Introducing Qualitative Methods, Sage Publications, London / Thousand Oaks / New Delhi.

de Beaugrande, R. (1980), *Text, Discourse, and Process: toward a multidisciplinary science of texts*, Vol. IV of *Advances in Discourse Processes*, Ablex Publishing Corp., Norwood, New Jersey.

de Beaugrande, R. and Dressler, W. U. (1981), *Introduction to Text Linguistics*, Longman, London.

Delin, J. L. and Bateman, J. A. (2002), 'Describing and critiquing multimodal documents', *Document Design* **3**(2), 140–155.

Ditschke, S., Kroucheva, K. and Stein, D., eds (2009), *Comics. Zur Geschichte und Theorie eines populärkulturellen Mediums*, transcript Verlag, Bielefeld.

Dittmer, J. (2012), *Captain America and the Nationalist Superhero: metaphors, narratives, and geopolitics*, Temple University Press, Philadelphia.

Doelker, C. (1997), *Ein Bild ist mehr als ein Bild: Visuelle Kompetenz in der Multimedia-Gesellschaft*, Klett-Cotta, Stuttgart.

Dubois, J. and Dubois, R., eds (1964), *La Presse enfantine française*, Editions H. Meseiller, Neuchâtel, Switzerland.

Duncan, R. and Smith, M. J. (2009), *The Power of Comics: history, form and culture*, Continuum, New York and London.

Durand, J. (1987), 'Rhetorical figures in the advertising image', *in* J. Umiker-Sebeok, ed., *Marketing and Semiotics: new directions in the study of signs for sale*, Mouton de Gruyter, Berlin / New York / Amsterdam, pp. 295–318.

Dyer, G. (1982), *Advertising as Communication*, Methuen, London.

Eco, U. (1990), *The Limits of Interpretation*, Indiana University Press, Bloomington.

Eisenstein, S. (1977), *A Dialectic Approach to Film Form*, Harcourt Brace and Company, San Diego, pp. 45–63.

Eisner, W. (1992), *Comics and Sequential Art*, Kitchen Sink Press Inc., Princeton, WI.

Eitel, A., Scheiter, K., Schüler, A., Nyström, M. and Holmqvist, K. (2013), 'How a picture facilitates the process of learning from text: evidence for scaffolding', *Learning and Instruction* **28**, 48–63.

Elleström, L. (2010), 'The modalities of media: a model for understanding intermedial relations', *in* L. Elleström, ed., *Media Borders, Multimodality and Intermediality*, Palgrave Macmillan, Basingstoke, pp. 11–50.

Fang, Z. (1996), 'Illustrations, text, and the child reader: what are pictures in children's storybooks for?', *Reading Horizons* **37**(2), 130–142.

Fauconnier, G. and Turner, M. (2003), *The Way We Think: conceptual blending and the mind's hidden complexities*, Basic Books, New York.

Fisher, W. R. (1987), *Human Communication as Narration: towards a philosophy of reason, value, and action*, University of South Carolina Press, Columbia, SC.

Fix, U. (1996), 'Textstile und KonTextstile. Stil in der Kommunikation als umfassende Semiose von Sprachlichem, Parasprachlichem und Außersprachlichem', *in* U. Fix and G. Lerchner, eds, *Stil und Stilwandeln*, Lang, Frankfurt am Main, pp. 111–132.

Fludernik, M. (2009), *Introduction to Narratology*, Routledge, London.

Forceville, C. J. (1996), *Pictorial Metaphor in Advertising*, Routledge, London.

Forceville, C. J. (2002), 'The identification of target and source in pictorial metaphors', *Journal of Pragmatics* **34**(1), 1–14.

Forceville, C. J. (2005a), 'Cognitive linguistics and multimodal metaphor', *in* K. Sachs-Hombach, ed., *Bildwissenschaft zwischen Reflexion und Anwendung*, Herbert von Halem Verlag, pp. 264–284.

Forceville, C. J. (2005b), 'Visual representations of the idealized cognitive model of *anger* in the Asterix album *La Zizanie*', *Journal of Pragmatics* **37**(1), 69–88.

Forceville, C. J. (2009), 'Non-verbal and multimodal metaphor as a cognitivist framework: agendas for research', *in* C. J. Forceville and E. Urios-Aparisi, eds, *Multimodal Metaphor*, Mouton de Gruyter, Berlin/New York, pp. 19–42.

Forceville, C. J. (2010), 'Balloonics: the visuals of balloons in comics', *in* J. Goggin and D. Hassler-Forest, eds, *The Rise and Reason of Comics and Graphic Literature: critical essays on the form*, McFarland & Co., Jefferson, NC and London, pp. 56–73.

Forceville, C. J. (2011), 'Pictorial runes in *Tintin and the Picaros*', *Journal of Pragmatics* **43**, 875–890.

Forster, E. (2005 [1927]), *Aspects of the Novel*, Penguin, London.

Foss, S. K. (1994), 'A rhetorical schema for the evaluation of visual imagery', *Communication Studies* **45**(3–4), 213–224.

Foss, S. K. (2005), 'Theory of visual rhetoric', *in* K. Smith, S. Moriarty, G. Barbatsis and K. Kenney, eds, *Handbook of Visual Communication: theory, methods, and media*, Lawrence Erlbaum Associates, Mahwah, NJ, pp. 141–152.

Foucault, M. (1969), *The Archaeology of Knowledge*, Routledge, London.

Freedman, A. and Medway, P., eds (1994), *Genre and the New Rhetoric*, Taylor and Francis, London.

Fricke, E. (2007), *Origo, Geste und Raum: Lokaldeixis im Deutschen*, de Gruyter, Berlin.

Fricke, E. (2012), *Grammatik multimodal: Wie Wörter und Gesten zusammenwirken*, Mouton de Gruyter, Berlin and New York.

Fricke, E. (2013), 'Towards a unified grammar of gesture and speech: a multimodal approach', *in* C. Müller, A. Cienki, E. Fricke, S. Ladewig, D. McNeill and S. Tessendorf, eds, *Body – Language – Communication / Körper – Sprache – Kommunikation*, number 38/1 *in* Handbücher zur Sprach- und Kommunikationswissenschaft / Handbooks of Linguistics and Communication Science (HSK), Mouton de Gruyter, Berlin and New York, pp. 733–754.

Frohlich, D. (1986), 'On the organisation of form-filling behaviour', *Information Design Journal* **5**, 43–59.

Fuhrman, O. and Boroditsky, L. (2010), 'Cross-cultural differences in mental representations of time: Evidence from an implicit nonlinguistic task', *Cognitive Science* **34**, 1430–1451.

Gaede, W. (1981), *Vom Wort zum Bild: Kreativ-Methoden der Visualisierung*, Langen-Müller/Herbig, Munich. 2nd edn, 1992.

Galfano, G., Dalmaso, M., Marzoli, D., Pavan, G., Coricelli, C. and Castelli, L. (2012), 'Eye gaze cannot be ignored (but neither can arrows)', *Quarterly Journal of Experimental Psychology* **65**(10), 1895–1910.

Gardner, R. (2008), 'Conversation analysis', *in* A. Davies and C. Elder, eds, *The Handbook of Applied Linguistics*, Blackwell Publishing, pp. 262–284.

Genette, G. (1980), *Narrative Discourse*, Cornell University Press, Ithaca, NY. Translated by Jane E. Lewin.

Genette, G. (1988), *Narrative Discourse Revisited*, Cornell University Press, Ithaca, NY. Translated by Jane E. Lewin.

Gibbs Jr., R. W. (1996), 'Why many concepts are metaphorical', *Cognition* **61**, 195–324.

Glenberg, A. M. and Langston, W. E. (1992), 'Comprehension of illustrated text: pictures help to build mental models', *Journal of Memory and Language* **31**, 129–151.

Glenberg, A. M., Wilkinson, A. C. and Epstein, W. (1982), 'The illusion of knowing: failure in the self-assessment of comprehension', *Memory and Cognition* **10**(6), 597–602.

Goggin, J. and Hassler-Forest, D., eds (2010), *The Rise and Reason of Comics and Graphic Literature: critical essays on the form*, McFarland & Co., Jefferson, NC and London.

Goguen, J. A. and Harrell, D. F. (2010), 'Style: a computational and conceptual blending-based approach', *in* S. Argamon, K. Burns and S. Dubnov, eds, *The Structure of Style: algorithmic approaches to understanding manner and meaning*, Springer-Verlag, Berlin and Heidelberg, pp. 291–316.

Gombrich, E. (1959), *Art and Illusion: a study in the psychology of pictorial representation*, Phaidon Press, Oxford.

Gombrich, E. (1982), *The Image and the Eye: further studies in the psychology of pictorial representation*, Phaidon, Oxford, chapter 'Moment and movement in art', pp. 40–62.

Gooding, D. (2004), 'Visualisation, inference and explanation in the sciences', *in* G. Malcolm, ed., *Multidisciplinary Approaches to Visual Representations and Interpretations*, Vol. 2 of *Studies in Multidisciplinarity*, Elsevier, Amsterdam, pp. 1–25.

Goodman, N. (1969), *Languages of Art. An approach to a theory of symbols*, Oxford University Press, London.

Graesser, A., Singer, M. and Trabasso, T. (1994), 'Constructing inferences during narrative text comprehension', *Psychological Review* **101**, 371–395.

Graustein, G. and Thiele, W. (1987), *Properties of English Texts*, VEB Verlag Enzyklopädie, Leipzig.

Greenberg, C. (1940), 'Towards a newer Laocoön', *Partisan Review* **7**. Reprinted in: *Clement Greenberg: the collected essays and criticism* (1986), edited by John O'Brian, Chicago University Press.

Gregory, M. and Carrol, S. (1978), *Language and Situation: language varieties and their social contexts*, Routledge and Kegan Paul, London.

Greimas, A.-J. (1983 [1966]), *Structural Semantics: an attempt at a method*, University of Nebraska Press, Lincoln and London. Originally published as *Sémantique structurale: Recherche de mèthode* (Librarie Larousse, 1966); translated by Daniele McDowell, Ronald Schleifer and Alan Velie.

Grice, H. P. (1969), 'Utterer's meaning and intentions', *Philosophical Review* **68**(2), 147–177.

Groensteen, T. (2007 [1999]), *The System of Comics*, Studies in Popular Culture, University Press of Mississippi, Jackson, Miss. Translated by Bart Beaty and Nick Nguyen, from the original French *Système de la bande desinée* (1999).

Groensteen, T. (2013 [2011]), *Comics and Narration*, University Press of Mississippi, Jackson, Miss. Translated by Ann Miller, from the original French *Bande desinée et narration: Système de la bande desinée 2* (2011).

Gross, A. G., Harmon, J. E. and Reidy, M. (2002), *Communicating Science: the scientific article from the 17th century to the present*, Oxford University Press, Oxford and New York.

Groupe μ (1992), *Traité du signe visuel: pour une rhétorique de l'image*, Editions du Seuil, Paris.

Hallberg, K. (1982), 'Litteraturwetenskapen och bilderboksforskningen', *Tidskrift för litteraturwetenskap* **3–4**, 163–168.

Halliday, M. A. K. (1971), 'Linguistic function and literary style: an enquiry into the language of William Golding's "The Inheritors"', *in* S. Chatman, ed., *Literary Style: a symposium*, Oxford University Press, London, pp. 362–400.

Halliday, M. A. K. and Hasan, R. (1976), *Cohesion in English*, Longman, London.

Halliday, M. A. K. and Matthiessen, C. M. I. M. (2004), *An Introduction to Functional Grammar*, 3rd edn, Edward Arnold, London.

Hartmann, K. (2002), *Text-Bild-Beziehungen in multimedialen Dokumenten: Eine Analyse aus Sicht von Wissenrepräsentation, Textstruktur und Visualisierung*, Shaker Verlag, Aachen.

Harvey, R. C. (1996), *The Art of the Comic Book: an aesthetic history*, University Press of Mississippi, Jackon, Miss.

Hasan, R. (1973), 'Code, register and social dialect', *in* B. Bernstein, ed., *Class, Codes and Control: applied studies towards a sociology of language*, Routledge and Kegan Paul, London, pp. 253–292.

Hasan, R. (1985), 'The texture of a text', *in* M. A. K. Halliday and R. Hasan, eds, *Language, Context and Text: a social semiotic perspective*, Deakin University Press, Geelong, Victoria, pp. 70–96. (Language and Learning Series). Also published by Oxford University Press, London, 1989.

Hatfield, C. and Svonkin, C. (2012), 'Why comics are and are not picture books: introduction', *Children's Literature Association Quarterly* **37**(4), 429–435.

Heffernan, J. A. (2006), *Cultivating Picturacy: visual art and verbal interventions*, Baylor University Press, Waco, Texas.

Heritage, J. and Atkinson, M., eds (1984), *Structures of Social Action: studies in conversation analysis*, Cambridge University Press, Cambridge.

Herman, D. (2009), *Basic Elements of Narrative*, Wiley-Blackwell, Chichester.

Hiippala, T. (2011), 'The localisation of advertising print media as a multimodal process', *in* W. L. Bowcher, ed., *Multimodal Texts from Around the World: linguistic and cultural insights*, Palgrave Macmillan, Basingstoke, pp. 97–122.

Hiippala, T. (2012), 'The interface between rhetoric and layout in multimodal artefacts', *Literary and linguistic computing* **28**(3), 461–471.

Hill, C. A. and Helmers, M., eds (2004), *Defining Visual Rhetorics*, Erlbaum, Mahwah, N.J.

Hochpöchler, U., Schnotz, W., Rasch, T., Ullrich, M., Horz, H., McElvany, N. and Baumert, J. (2012), 'Dynamics of mental model construction from text and graphics', *European Journal of Psychology of Education* **27**(3), 1–22.

Holly, W. (2009), 'Der Wort-Bild-Reißverschluss. Über die performative Dynamik der audiovisuellen Transkriptivität', *in* H. Feilke and A. Linke, eds, *Oberfläche und Performanz*, Niemeyer, Tübingen, pp. 93–110.

Holsanova, J. and Nord, A. (2010), 'Multimedia design: media structures, media principles and users' meaning-making in newspapers and net papers', *in* H.-J. Bucher, T. Gloning and K. Lehnen, eds, *Neue Medien – neue Formate. Ausdifferenzierung und Konvergenz in der Medienkommunikation*, number 10 *in Interaktiva. Schriftenreihe des Zentrums für Medien und Interaktivität (ZMI), Gießen*, Campus Verlag, Frankfurt / New York, pp. 81–103.

Holsanova, J., Rahm, H. and Holmqvist, K. (2006), 'Entry points and reading paths on newspaper spreads: comparing a semiotic analysis with eye-tracking measurements', *Visual Communication* **5**(1), 65–93.

Iedema, R. (2007), 'On the multi-modality, materiality and contingency of organizational discourse', *Organization Studies* **28**(06), 931–946.

Iser, W. (1978), *The Act of Reading: a theory of aesthetic response*, Johns Hopkins University Press, Baltimore.

Itti, L. and Koch, C. (2001), 'Computational modelling of visual attention', *Nature Reviews: Neuroscience*, **2**(3), 194–203.

Jäger, L. (2004), 'Die Verfahren der Medien: Transkribieren – Adressieren – Lokalisieren', *in* J. Forhmann and E. Schüttpelz, eds, *Die Kommunikation der Medien*, Niemeyer, Tübingen, pp. 69–79.

Jahn, M. (2005), 'Focalization', *in* D. Herman, M. Jahn and M.-L. Ryan, eds, *Routledge Encyclopedia of Narrative Theory*, Routledge, London, pp. 173–177.

Jansen, C. J. and Steehouder, M. F. (1992), 'Forms as a source of communication problems', *Journal of Technical Writing and Communication* **22**, 179–194.

Jewitt, C. and Kress, G. (2003), *Multimodal Literacy*, number 4 *in* New Literacies and Digital Epistemologies', Peter Lang, Frankfurt a.M. / New York.

Johnson, M. (1987), *The Body in the Mind*, University of Chicago Press, Chicago, Il.

Johnson-Cartee, K. S. (2005), *News Narratives and News Framing: constructing political reality*, Rowman & Littlefield Publishers, Inc., Lanham.

Johnson-Laird, P. (1983), *Mental Models: towards a cognitive science of language, inference, and conciousness*, Cambrige University Press, Cambridge.

Just, M. A. and Carpenter, P. A. (1980), 'A theory of reading: from eye fixations to comprehension', *Psychological Review* **87**(4), 329–354.

Kennedy, J. M. (1982), 'Metaphor in pictures', *Perception* **11**(5), 589–605.

Klock, G. (2002), *How to Read Superhero Comics and Why*, Continuum, New York.

Kloepfer, R. (1977), 'Komplementarität von Sprache und Bild. Am Beispiel von Comic, Karikatur und Reklame', *in* R. Posner and H.-P. Reinecke, eds, *Zeichenprozesse. Semiotische Forschung in den Einzelwissenschaften*, Athenäum, Wiesbaden, pp. 129–145.

Knieja, J. (2013), 'Die Cluster-Struktur des Comics: ein Weg zur Bestimmung des Textmusters', *in* O. Brunken and F. Giesa, eds, *Erzählen in Comic: Beiträge zur Comicforschung*, Christian A. Bachmann Verlag, Essen, pp. 131–144.

Knott, A., Oberlander, J., O'Donnell, M. and Mellish, C. (2001), 'Beyond elaboration: the interaction of relations and focus in coherent text', *in* T. Sanders, J. Schilperoord and W. Spooren, eds, *Text Representation: linguistic and psycholinguistic aspects*, Benjamins, Amsterdam, pp. 181–196.

Kong, K. C. (2006), 'A taxonomy of the discourse relations between words and visuals', *Information Design Journal* **14**(3), 207–230.

Kong, K. C. (2013), 'A corpus-based study in comparing the multimodality of Chinese- and English-language newspapers', *Visual Communication* **12**(2), 173–196.

Koop, A. (2012), *Die Macht der Schrift – Eine angewandte Designforschung*, Niggli Verlag, Sulgen, Zürich.

Kostelnick, C. (1989), 'Visual rhetoric: a reader-oriented approach to graphics and designs', *Technical Writing Teacher* **16**, 77–88.

Kostelnick, C. (1996), 'Supra-textual design: the visual rhetoric of whole documents', *Technical Communication Quarterly* **5**(1), 9–33.

Kostelnick, C. and Hassett, M. (2003), *Shaping Information: the rhetoric of visual conventions*, Southern Illinois University Press.

Kress, G. (1993), 'Genre as social process', *in* B. Cope and M. Kalantzis, eds, *The Powers of Literacy: a genre approach to writing*, University of Pittsburgh Press, Pittsburgh, pp. 22–37.

Kress, G. (2003), *Literacy in the New Media Age*, Routledge, London.

Kress, G. (2010), *Multimodality: a social semiotic approach to contemporary communication*, Routledge, London.

Kress, G., Jewitt, C., Ogborn, J. and Tsatsarelis, C. (2000), *Multimodal Teaching and Learning*, Continuum, London.

Kress, G. and van Leeuwen, T. (2001), *Multimodal Discourse: the modes and media of contemporary communication*, Arnold, London.

Kress, G. and van Leeuwen, T. (2006 [1996]), *Reading Images: the grammar of visual design*, Routledge, London and New York.

Kunzle, D. (1973), *The Early Comic Strip: narrative strips and picture stories in the European broadsheet from c. 1450 to 1825*, University of California Press, Berkeley, Los Angeles and London.

Labov, W. and Waletzky, J. (1978), 'Narrative analysis', *in* J. Helm, ed., *Essays on the Verbal and Visual Arts*, University of Washington Press, Seattle, pp. 12–44. (Proceedings of the 1966 Spring Meeting of the American Ethnological Society.)

Lagerwerf, L., van Hooijdonk, C. M. and Korenberg, A. (2012), 'Processing visual rhetoric in advertisements: intepretations determined by verbal anchoring and visual structure', *Journal of Pragmatics* **44**, 1836–1852.

Lakoff, G. and Johnson, M. (1980a), *Metaphors We Live By*, Chicago University Press, Chicago, Il.

Lakoff, G. and Johnson, M. (1980b), 'The metaphorical structure of the human conceptual system', *Cognitive Science* **4**(2), 195–208.

Lakoff, G. and Johnson, M. (1999), *Philosophy in the Flesh: the embodied mind and its challenge to Western thought*, Basic Books, New York.

Landis, J. R. and Koch, G. G. (1977), 'The measurement of observer agreement for categorial data', *Biometrics* **33**(1), 159–174.

Lee, D. Y. (2001), 'Genres, registers, text types, domains, and styles: clarifying the concepts and navigating a path through the BNC jungle', *Language Learning and Technology* **5**(3), 37–72. http://llt.msu.edu/vol5num3/lee.

Lemke, J. L. (1983), 'Thematic analysis: systems, structures, and strategies', *Semiotic Inquiry* **3**(2), 159–187.

Lemke, J. L. (1998), 'Multiplying meaning: visual and verbal semiotics in scientific text', *in* J. Martin and R. Veel, eds, *Reading Science: critical and functional perspectives on discourses of science*, Routledge, London, pp. 87–113.

Lessing, G. E. (1853 [1766]), *Laocoon: an essay on the limits of painting and poetry*, Longman, Brown, Green, and Longmans and others, London. Translated by E.C. Beasley.

Lewis, D. (2001), *Reading Contemporary Picturebooks: picturing text*, Routledge, London.

Lim, V. F. (2004), 'Developing an integrative multi-semiotic model', *in* K. L. O'Halloran, ed., *Multimodal Discourse Analysis: systemic functional perspectives*, Open Linguistics Series, Continuum, London, pp. 220–246.

Liu, Y. and O'Halloran, K. L. (2009), 'Intersemiotic texture: analyzing cohesive devices between language and images', *Social Semiotics* **19**(4), 367–388.

Lopes, D. (1996), *Understanding Pictures*, Oxford Philosophical Monographs, Oxford University Press, Oxford, UK.

Lowie, W. and Seton, B. (2013), *Essential Statistics for Applied Linguistics*, Palgrave Macmillan, Basingstoke.

Lyons, J. (1977), *Semantics*, Cambridge University Press, Cambridge. In two volumes.

Machin, D. (2007), *Introduction to Multimodal Analysis*, Hodder Arnold, London.

Maes, A. and Schilperoord, J. (2007), 'Classifying visual rhetoric: conceptual and structural heuristics', *in* E. F. McQuarrie and B. J. Phillips, eds, *Go Figure! New directions in advertising rhetoric*, M. E. Sharpe Inc., Armonk, NY and London, pp. 67–78.

Maes, A. and Schilperoord, J. (2009), 'Schemes and tropes in visual communication: the case of object grouping in advertisements', *in* J. Renkema, ed., *Discourse, of course: an overview of research in discourse studies*, John Benjamins, Amsterdam / Philadelphia, pp. 67–78.

Magnussen, A. and Christiansen, H.-C., eds (2000), *Comics & Culture: analytical and theoretical approaches to comics*, Museum Tusculanum Press University of Copenhagen, Copenhagen, Denmark.

Mann, W. C. and Thompson, S. A. (1988), 'Rhetorical Structure Theory: toward a functional theory of text organization', *Text* **8**(3), 243–281.

Marsh, E. E. and White, M. D. (2003), 'A taxonomy of relationships between images and text', *Journal of Documentation* **59**(6), 647–672.

Martin, J. R. (1983), 'Conjunction: the logic of English text', *in* J. S. Petöfi and E. Sözer, eds, *Micro and Macro Connexity of Discourse*, number 45 *in* Papers in Textlinguistics, Helmut Buske Verlag, Hamburg, pp. 1–72.

Martin, J. R. (1991), 'Intrinsic functionality: implications for contextual theory', *Social Semiotics* **1**(1), 99–162.

Martin, J. R. (1992), *English Text: systems and structure*, Benjamins, Amsterdam.

Martin, J. R. (1995), 'Text and clause: fractal resonance', *Text* **15**(1), 5–42.

Martin, J. R. and Plum, G. (1997), 'Construing experience: some story genres', *Journal of Narrative and Life History* **7**(1–4), 299–308. (Special Issue: Oral Versions of Personal Experience: three decades of narrative analysis; M. Bamberg Guest Editor).

Martin, J. R. and Rose, D. (2003), *Working with Discourse: meaning beyond the clause*, Continuum, London and New York.

Martin, J. R. and Rose, D. (2008), *Genre Relations: mapping culture*, Equinox, London and New York.

Martinec, R. (1998), 'Cohesion in action', *Semiotica* **120**(1–2), 161–180.

Martinec, R. (2004), 'Gestures which co-occur with speech as a systematic resource: the realization of experiential meanings in indexes', *Social Semiotics* **14**(2), 193–213.

Martinec, R. and Salway, A. (2005), 'A system for image-text relations in new (and old) media', *Visual Communication* **4**(3), 337–371.

Matthiessen, C. M. (2007), 'The multimodal page: a systemic functional exploration', *in* T. D. Royce and W. L. Bowcher, eds, *New Directions in the Analysis of Multimodal Discourse*, Lawrence Erlbaum Associates, pp. 1–62.

Mayer, R. E. (2001), *Multimedia Learning*, Cambridge University Press, Cambridge.

Mayer, R. E. (2009), *Multimedia Learning*, 2nd edn, Cambridge University Press, Cambridge.

McAllister, M. P., Sewell, Jr., E. H. and Gordon, I., eds (2001), *Comics & Ideology*, Peter Lang Publishing, New York, New York.

McCloud, S. (1994), *Understanding Comics: the invisible art*, HarperPerennial, New York.

McKenna, S. (1999), 'Advertising as epideictic rhetoric', *in* C. J. Swearingen and D. Pruett, eds, *Rhetoric, the Polis, and the Global Village*, Lawrence Erlbaum Associates, Mahwah, NJ and London, pp. 103–109. Selected Papers from the 1998 Thirtieth Anniversary Rhetoric Society of America Conference.

McQuarrie, E. F. (1989), 'Advertising resonance: a semiological perspective', *in* E. C. Hirschman, ed., *SV – Interpretive Consumer Research*, Association for Consumer Research, Provo, UT, pp. 97–114.

McQuarrie, E. F. and Mick, D. G. (1996), 'Figures of rhetoric in advertising language', *Journal of Consumer Research* **22**(4), 424–438.

McQuarrie, E. F. and Mick, D. G. (1999), 'Visual rhetoric in advertising: text-interpretive, experimental, and reader-response analyses', *Journal of Consumer Research* **26**(1), 37–54.

McQuarrie, E. F. and Mick, D. G. (2003), 'Visual and verbal rhetorical figures under directed processing versus incidental exposure to advertising', *Journal of Consumer Research* **29**(4), 579–587.

Meskin, A. (2007), 'Defining comics?', *Journal of Aesthetics and Art Criticism* **65**(4), 369–379.

Meskin, A. and Cook, R. T., eds (2012), *The Art of Comics: a philosophical approach*, Blackwell Publishing, Malden, MA and Chichester.

Messaris, P. (1997), *Visual Persuasion: the role of images in advertising*, Sage, Thousand Oaks, CA.

Meyer, B. J. (1975), *The Organization of Prose and its Effects on Memory*, North-Holland, Amsterdam.

Miller, C. R. (1984), 'Genre as social action', *Quarterly Journal of Speech* **70**, 151–167.

Miller, T. (1998), 'Visual persuasion: a comparison of visuals in academic press and the popular press', *English for Specific Purposes* **17**(1), 29–46.

Miodrag, H. (2013), *Comics and Language: reimagining critical discourse on the form*, University Press of Mississippi, Jackson, Miss.

Mirzoeff, N. (1999), *An Introduction to Visual Culture*, Routledge, London and New York.

Mitchell, W. (1986), *Iconology: images, text, ideology*, Chicago University Press, Chicago.

Mitchell, W. (1994), *Picture Theory: essays on verbal and visual representation*, University of Chicago Press, Chicago.

Moles, A. A. (1978), 'L'image et le texte', *Communication et langages* **38**, 17–29.

Morris, C. W. (1938), *Foundations of the Theory of Signs*, University of Chicago Press, Chicago.

Muckenhaupt, M. (1986), *Text und Bild. Grundfragen der Beschreibung von Text-Bild-Kommunikation aus sprachwissenschaftlicher Sicht*, Tübinger Beiträge zur Linguistik, Narr, Tübingen.

Müller, C. and Cienki, A. (2009), 'Words, gestures, and beyond: forms of multimodal metaphor in the use of spoken language', *in* C. J. Forceville and E. Urios-Aparisi, eds, *Multimodal Metaphor*, Mouton de Gruyter, Berlin / New York, pp. 297–328.

Müller, M. G. (2007), 'What is visual communication? Past and future of an emerging field of communication research', *Studies in Communication Sciences* **7**(2), 7–34.

Nel, P. (2012), 'Same genus, different species?: Comics and picture books', *Children's Literature Association Quarterly* **37**(4), 445–453.

Nielsen, J. (2006), 'F-shaped pattern for reading web content', *Jakob Nielsen's Alertbox*, http://www.useit.com/alertbox/reading_pattern.html.

Nikolajeva, M. and Scott, C. (2001), *How Picturebooks Work*, Routledge, London.

Nodelman, P. (1988), *Words about Pictures: the narrative art of children's picture books*, University of Georgia Press, Athens, Georgia.

Nodelman, P. (2012), 'Picture book guy looks at comics: structural differences in two kinds of visual narrative', *Children's Literature Association Quarterly* **37**(4), 436–444.

Norris, S. (2004), *Analyzing Multimodal Interaction: a methodological framework*, Routledge, London and New York.

Nöth, W. (1995), *Handbook of Semiotics*, Indiana University Press, Bloomington.

Nöth, W. (2004), 'Zur Komplementarität von Sprache und Bild aus semiotischer Sicht', *Mitteilungen des Deutschen Germanistenverbandes* (1), 9–22. Sprache und Bild I.

O'Halloran, K. L. (1999), 'Interdependence, interaction and metaphor in multisemiotic texts', *Social Semiotics* **9**(3), 317–354.

O'Halloran, K. L. (2005), *Mathematical Discourse: language, symbolism and visual images*, Continuum, London and New York.

Oomen, U. (1975), 'Word-Bild-Nachricht: Semiotische Aspekte des Comic Strip "Peanuts"', *Linguistik und Didaktik* **6**, 247–259.

op de Beeck, N. (2012), 'On comics-style picture books and picture-bookish comics', *Children's Literature Association Quarterly* **37**(4), 468–476.

O'Toole, M. (2011 [1994]), *The Language of Displayed Art*, Routledge, Abingdon, Oxon.

Painter, C. (2007), 'Children's picture book narratives: reading sequences of images', *in* A. McCabe, M. O'Donnell and R. Whittaker, eds, *Advances in Language and Education*, Continuum, London and New York, pp. 40–59.

Painter, C., Martin, J. R. and Unsworth, L., eds (2013), *Reading Visual Narratives: image analysis of children's picture books*, Equinox, London.

Paivio, A. (1986), *Mental Representations: a dual coding approach*, Oxford University Press, London and New York.

Paraboni, I. and van Deemter, K. (2002), 'Towards the generation of document-deictic references', *in* K. van Deemter and R. Kibble, eds, *Information Sharing: reference and presupposition in language generation and interpretation*, CSLI Publications, pp. 333–358.

Pegg, B. (2002), 'Two dimensional features in the history of text format: how print technology has preserved linearity', *in* N. Allen, ed., *Working with Words and Images: new steps in an Old dance*, Ablex, Westport, CT, pp. 164–179.

Phillips, B. J. and McQuarrie, E. F. (2004), 'Beyond visual metaphor: a new typology of visual rhetoric in advertising', *Marketing Theory* **4**(1/2), 113–136.

Posner, R. (1969), 'Zur strukturalistischen Interpretation von Gedichten: Darstellung einer Methoden-Kontroverse am Beispiel von Baudelaires Gedicht "Les chats". "Les chats" von Charles Baudelaire', *in* W. Höllerer, ed., *Sprache im technischen Zeitalter*, Vol. 29, W. Kohlhamme, Stuttgart, pp. 27–58.

Prince, G. (1982), *Narratology: the form and function of narrative*, Mouton, The Hague.

Propp, V. (1968), *The Morphology of the Folktale*, University of Texas Press, Austin, Texas. Originally published in Russian in 1928.

Reed, J. T. (1997), 'Discourse analysis', *in* S. E. Porter, ed., *A Handbook of the Exegesis of the New Testament*, Koninklijke Brill NV, Leiden, The Netherlands, pp. 189–218.

Rorty, R., ed. (1967), *The Linguistic Turn, Essays in Philosophical Method*, University of Chicago Press, Chicago.

Roth, W., Pozzer-Ardhengi, L. and Han, J. (2005), *Critical Graphicacy: understanding visual representation practices in school science*, Springer, Dordrecht.

Royce, T. D. (1998), 'Synergy on the page: exploring *intersemiotic complementarity* in page-based multimodal text', *Japan Association for Systemic Functional Linguistics Occasional Papers* 1(1), 25–49.

Royce, T. D. (2002), 'Multimodality in the TESOL classroom: exploring visual-verbal synergy', *TESOL Quarterly* 36(2), 191–205.

Royce, T. D. (2007), 'Intersemiotic complementarity: a framework for multimodal discourse analysis', *in* T. D. Royce and W. L. Bowcher, eds, *New Directions in the Analysis of Multimodal Discourse*, Lawrence Erlbaum Associates, Mahwah, NJ and London pp. 63–110.

Ryan, M.-L., ed. (2004), *Narrative across Media: the languages of storytelling*, University of Nebraska Press, Lincoln.

Sachs-Hombach, K., ed. (2001), *Bildhandeln: interdisziplinäre Forschungen zur Pragmatik bildhafter Darstellungsformen*, number 3 *in* Reihe Bildwissenschaft, Scriptum-Verlag, Magdeburg.

Sachs-Hombach, K. and Schirra, J. R. (2006), 'Bildstil als rhetorische Kategorie', *Image – Zeitschrift für interdisziplinäre Bildwissenschaft* 3, 175–191.

Saint-Martin, F. (1990), *Semiotics of Visual Language*, Bloomington University Press, Bloomington, IN.

Salisbury, M. and Styles, M. (2012), *Children's Picturebooks: the art of visual storytelling*, Lawrence King Publishing, London.

Sanders, T. J. M., Spooren, W. P. M. and Noordman, L. G. M. (1992), 'Towards a taxonomy of coherence relations', *Discourse Processes* 15(1), 1–36.

Sanders, T. J. M., Spooren, W. P. M. and Noordman, L. G. M. (1993), 'Coherence relations in a cognitive theory of discourse representations', *Cognitive Linguistics* 4(2), 93–133.

Sandig, B. (1972), 'Zur Differenzierung gebrauchssprachlicher Textsorten im Deutschen', *in* E. Gülich and W. Raible, eds, *Textsorten. Differenzierungskriterien aus linguistischer Sicht*, Athenäum, Frankfurt am Main, pp. 113–124.

Saussure, F. de (1959 [1915]), *Course in General Linguistics*, Peter Owen, London. Edited by Charles Bally and Albert Sechehaye; translated by Wade Baskin.

Schapiro, M. (2006), *Words, Script, and Pictures: semiotics of visual language*, George Braziller Inc, New York.

Schill, K., Umkehrer, E., Beinich, S., Krieger, G. and Zetzsche, C. (2001), 'Scene analysis with saccadic eye movements: top-down and bottom-up modeling', *Journal of Electronic Imaging* 10(1), 152–160.

Schirato, T. and Webb, J. (2004), *Understanding the Visual*, Sage Publications, Los Angeles, London, New Delhi, Singapore.

Schnotz, W. (2002), 'Towards an integrated view of learning from text and visual displays', *Educational Psychology Review* 14(1), 101–120.

Schriver, K. A. (1997), *Dynamics in Document Design: creating texts for readers*, John Wiley and Sons, New York.

Schüwer, M. (2002), 'Erzählen in Comics: Bausteine einer Plurimedialen Erzähltheorie', *in Erzähltheorie transgenerisch, intermedial, interdisziplinär*, WVT, Trier, pp. 185–216.

Schwarcz, J. H. (1982), *Ways of the Illustrator: visual communication in children's literature*, American Library Association, Chicago.

Scott, L. M. (1994), 'Images in advertising: the need for a theory of visual rhetoric', *Journal of Consumer Research* 21(2), 252–273.

Seldes, G. V. (1924), *The Seven Lively Arts: the classic appraisal of the popular arts*, Harper and brothers, New York.

Sendak, M. (1963), *Where the Wild Things Are*, Harper and Row, New York.

Sipe, L. R. (1998), 'How picture books work: a semiotically framed theory of text-picture relations', *Children's Literature in Education* **29**(2), 97–108.

Sirapik, V. (2009), 'Picture, text and imagetext: textual polylogy', *Semiotica* **174**(1/4), 277–308.

Sowa, T. and Wachsmuth, I. (2009), 'A computational model for the representation and processing of shape in coverbal iconic gestures', *in* K. Coventry, T. Tenbrink and J. Bateman, eds, *Spatial Language and Dialogue*, Oxford University Press, chapter 10, pp. 132–146.

Sperber, D. and Wilson, D. (1995 [1986]), *Relevance: communication and cognition*, 2nd edn, Blackwell, Oxford.

Spillner, B. (1980), 'Über die Schwierigkeit semiotischer Textanalyse', *Die Neueren Sprachen* **79**(6), 619–630.

Spillner, B. (1982), 'Stilanalyse semiotisch komplexer Texte. Zum Verhältnis von sprachlicher und bildlicher Information in Werbeanzeigen', *Kodikas/Code. Ars Semeiotica* **4/5**(1), 91–106.

Spitzmüller, J. and Warnke, I. H. (2011), 'Discourse as a "linguistic object": methodical and methodological delimitations', *Critical Discourse Studies* **8**(2), 75–94.

Stein, D. and Thon, J.-N. (2013), *From Comic Strips to Graphic Novels. Contributions to the theory and history of graphic narrative*, de Gruyter.

Stöckl, H. (1997), *Textstil und Semiotik englischsprachiger Anzeigenwerbung*, Peter Lang, Frankfurt am Main.

Stöckl, H. (2002), 'From space to time into narration – cognitive and semiotic perspectives on the narrative potential of visually structured text', *in* C. Todenhagen and W. Thiele, eds, *Investigations into Narrative Structures*, Peter Lang, Frankfurt am Main, pp. 73–98.

Stöckl, H. (2003), '"Imagine": Stilanalyse multimodal. – am Beispiel des TV-Werbespots', *in* I. Barz, G. Lerchner and M. Schröder, eds, *Sprachstil. Zugänge und Anwendungen. Ulla Fix zum 60. Geburtstag*, Winter, Heidelberg, pp. 305–323.

Stöckl, H. (2004a), *Die Sprache im Bild – Das Bild in der Sprache: Zur Verknüpfung von Sprache und Bild im massenmedialen Text. Konzepte – Theorien – Analysemethoden*, Walter de Gruyter, Berlin.

Stöckl, H. (2004b), 'In between modes: language and image in printed media', *in* E. Ventola, C. Charles and M. Kaltenbacher, eds, *Perspectives on Multimodality*, John Benjamins, Amsterdam, pp. 9–30.

Stöckl, H. (2011), 'Sprache-Bild-Texte lesen. Bausteine zur Methodik einer Grundkompetenz', *in* H.-J. Diekmannshenke, M. Klemm and H. Stöckl, eds, *Bildlinguistik. Theorien – Methoden – Fallbeispiele*, Erich Schmidt, Berlin, pp. 43–70.

Stroupe, C. (2000), 'Visualizing English: recognizing the hybrid literacy of visual and verbal authorship on the web', *College English* **62**(5), 607–632.

Swales, J. M. (1990), *Genre Analysis: English in academic and research settings*, Cambridge University Press, Cambridge.

Taboada, M. and Habel, C. (2013), 'Rhetorical relations in multimodal documents', *Discourse Studies* **15**(1), 65–89.

Taboada, M. T. and Mann, W. C. (2006a), 'Applications of Rhetorical Structure Theory', *Discourse Studies* **8**(4), 567–588.

Taboada, M. T. and Mann, W. C. (2006b), 'Rhetorical Structure Theory: looking back and moving ahead', *Discourse Studies* **8**(3), 423–459.

Thibault, P. J. (2001), 'Multimodality and the school science textbook', *in* C. T. Torsello-Taylor, G. Brunetti and N. Penello, eds, *Corpora Testuali per Ricerca, Traduzione e Apprendimento Linguistico*, Unipress, Padua, pp. 293–335.

Toulmin, S. (1959), *The Uses of Argument*, Cambridge University Press, Cambridge.

Trifonas, P. (1998), 'Cross-mediality and narrative textual form: a semiotic analysis of the lexical and visual signs and codes in the picture book', *Semiotica* **118**(1/2), 1–71.

Tufte, E. R. (1983), *The Visual Display of Quantitative Information*, Graphics Press, Cheshire, Connecticut.

Tufte, E. R. (1997), *Visual Explanations: images and quantities, evidence and narrative*, Graphics Press, Cheshire, Connecticut.

Tversky, B., Zacks, J., Lee, P. and Heiser, J. (2000), 'Lines, blobs, crosses, and arrows: diagrammatic communication with schematic figures', *in* M. Anderson, P. Cheng and V. Haarslev, eds, *Theory and Application of Diagrams*, Springer, Berlin, pp. 221–230.

Unsworth, L. (2001), *Teaching Multiliteracies across the Curriculum: changing contexts of text and image in classroom practice*, Open University Press.

Unsworth, L. (2006), 'Towards a metalanguage for multiliteracies education: describing the meaning-making resources of language-image interaction', *English Teaching: Practice and Critique* **5**(1), 55–76.

Unsworth, L. (2007), 'Image/text relations and intersemiosis: towards multimodal text description for multiliteracies education', *in* L. Barbara and T. B. Sardinha, eds, *Proceedings of the 33rd International Systemic Functional Congress (33rd ISFC)*, Pontifícia Universidade Católica De Sao Paulo (PUCSP), Sao Paulo, Brazil, pp. 1165–1205. Online publication at: http://www.pucsp.br/isfc/proceedings/Artigos%20pdf/59pl_unsworth_1165a1205.pdf

Unsworth, L. and Cléirigh, C. (2009), 'Multimodality and reading: the construction of meaning through image-text interaction', *in* C. Jewitt, ed., *The Routledge Handbook of Multimodal Analysis*, Routledge, London, pp. 151–164.

van Dijk, T. A. and Kintsch, W. (1983), *Strategies of Discourse Comprehension*, Academic Press, New York.

van Enschot, R., Hoeken, H. and van Mulken, M. (2008), 'Rhetoric in advertising: attitudes towards verbo-pictorial rhetorical figures', *Information Design Journal* **16**(1), 35–45.

van Hooijdonk, C., Krahmer, E., Maes, A., Theune, M. and Bosma, W. (2006), 'Towards automatic generation of multimodal answers to medical questions: a cognitive engineering approach', *in* I. van der Sluis, M. Theune, E. Reiter and E. Krahmer, eds, *Proceedings of the Workshop on Multimodal Output Generation MOG 2007*, Centre for Telematics and Information Technology (CTIT), University of Twente, pp. 93–104.

van Leeuwen, T. (1991), 'Conjunctive structure in documentary film and television', *Continuum: journal of media and cultural studies* **5**(1), 76–114.

van Leeuwen, T. (2005a), 'Book review: *Die Sprache im Bild — Das Bild in der Sprache — Zur Verknüpfung von Sprache und Bild im massenmedialen Text*', *Visual Communication* **4**, 375–378.

van Leeuwen, T. (2005b), *Introducing Social Semiotics*, Routledge, London.

van Mulken, M. (2003), 'Analyzing rhetorical devices in print advertisements', *Document Design* **4**(2), 114–128.

van Mulken, M., le Pair, R. and Forceville, C. (2010), 'The impact of perceived complexity, deviation and comprehension on the appreciation of visual metaphor in advertising across three European countries', *Journal of Pragmatics* **42**, 3418–3430.

Vogler, C. (1998), *The Writer's Journey: mythic structure for writers*, Michael Wiese Productions, Studio City, CA.

Wahlster, W., André, E., Finkler, W., Profitlich, H.-J. and Rist, T. (1993), 'Plan-based integration of natural language and graphics generation', *Artificial Intelligence* **63**(1–2), 387–427.

Walker, S. (1982), 'Describing graphic language: practicalities and implications', *Information Design Journal* **3**(2), 102–109.

Walker, S. (2001), *Typography and Language in Everyday Life: prescriptions and practices*, Longman, London.

Waller, R. (1980), 'Graphic aspects of complex texts: typography as macro-punctuation', *in* P. A. Kolers, M. E. Wrolstad and H. Bouma, eds, *Processing of Visible Language*, Vol. 2, Plenum, New York and London, pp. 241–253.

Waller, R. (1987), 'Using typography to structure arguments: a critical analysis of some examples', *in* D. Jonassen, ed., *The Technology of Text*, Vol. 2, Educational Technology Publications, Englewood Cliffs, NJ, pp. 105–125.

Waller, R. (2012), 'Graphic literacies for a digital age: the survival of layout', *The Information Society: an international journal* **28**(4), 236–252.

Waller, R. H. (1979), 'Typographic access structures for educational texts', *in* P. A. Kolers, M. E. Wrolstad and H. Bouma, eds, *Processing of Visible Language*, Vol. 1, Plenum, New York and London, pp. 175–187.

Wartenberg, T. E. (2012), 'Wordy pictures: theorizing the relationship between image and text in comics', *in* A. Meskin and R. T. Cook, eds, *The Art of Comics: a philosophical approach*, Blackwell Publishing, Malden, MA and Chichester, pp. 87–104.

Willems, P. (2008), 'Form(ul)ation of a novel narrative form: nineteenth-century pedagogues and the comics', *Word & Image: a journal of verbal/visual enquiry* **24**(1), 1–14.

Wolk, D. (2007), *Reading Comics. How graphic novels work and what they mean*, Da Capo Press, Philadelphia.

Wright, P. and Barnard, P. (1978), 'Asking multiple questions about several items: the design of matrix structures on application forms', *Applied Ergonomics* **9**, 7–14.

Wright, T. (2011), 'Press photography and visual rhetoric', *in* E. Margolis and L. Pauwels, eds, *The SAGE Handbook of Visual Research Methods*, Sage, London, pp. 317–336.

Wurman, R. S. (1996), *Information Architects*, Watson-Guptill Publications, New York, NY.

Yarbus, A. L. (1967), *Eye Movements and Vision*, Plenum Press, New York, NY.

Zettl, H. (2005), 'Aesthetics theory', *in* K. Smith, S. Moriarty, G. Barbatsis and K. Kenney, eds, *Handbook of Visual Communication: theory, methods, and media*, Lawrence Erlbaum Associates, Mahwah, NJ, pp. 365–384.

Index